Kenneth Burke
in Greenwich Village

The Wisconsin Project on American Writers

Frank Lentricchia, General Editor

Kenneth Burke in Greenwich Village

Conversing with the Moderns 1915–1931

Jack Selzer

The University of Wisconsin Press

The University of Wisconsin Press
114 North Murray Street
Madison, Wisconsin 53715

3 Henrietta Street
London WC2E 8LU, England

Library of Congress Cataloging-in-Publication Data
Selzer, Jack.
Kenneth Burke in Greenwich Village: conversing with the moderns,
1915–1931 / Jack Selzer.
304 p.   cm.
(The Wisconsin project on American writers)
Includes bibliographical references and index.
ISBN 0-299-15180-8 (cloth: alk. paper).
ISBN 0-299-15184-0 (pbk.: alk. paper).
1. Burke, Kenneth, 1897–1993—Homes and haunts—New York (State)—
New York.   2. American literature—New York (State)—New York—
History and criticism.   3. American literature—20th century—
History and criticism—Theory, etc.   4. Greenwich Village (New
York, N.Y.)—Intellectual life—20th century.   5. Modernism
(Literature)—New York (State)—New York.   6. Criticism—United
States—History—20th century.   7. Modernism (Literature)—United
States.   I. Title.
PS3503.U6134Z87   1997
818'.5209—dc20
[B]   96-18441

In honor of my father and in memory of my mother

The artist does not run counter to his age; rather, he refines the propensities of his age, formulating their aesthetic equivalent.

Kenneth Burke, "Dada, Dead or Alive," 1925

A man is necessarily talking in error unless his words can claim membership in a collective body of thought.

Kenneth Burke, *Attitudes toward History*

The Flower and the Leaf

All of an age, all heretics,
all rich in promise, but poor in rupees,
I knew them all at twenty six,
when to a sound of scraping shovels,
emerging from whatever dream,
by night they left their separate hovels
as if with an exultant scream,
stamped off the snow and gathered round
a table at John Squarcialupi's,
happy as jaybirds, loud as puppies.

They were an omnicolored crew,
Midwesterner and Southerner,
New Yorker and New Englander,
immigrant, Brahman, Irish, Jew,
all innocent in their pride because
not one of them had grown a paunch
or lost faith in himself, or was
deformed by any strict belief.
I saw the flower and the leaf,
the fruit, or none, and the bare branch.

This man strains forward in his chair
to argue for his principles,
then stops to wipe his spectacles,
blink like a daylight owl, and shake
his janitor's mop of blue-black hair.
He can outquibble and outcavil,
laugh at himself, then speak once more
with wild illogic for the sake
of logic pure and medieval;
but all that night he will lie awake
to argue with his personal devil.

This man is studiously polite.
Good manners are an armor which
preserves for him an inner hush,
also, I think, a harbor light
that steers young ladies to his bed.
There was no hush that winter night
when flown with Squarcialupi's wine,
he made a funnel, then adopted
the look of a greedy child and said
in a five-beat iambic line,
having flung back his enormous head,
"All contributions gratefully accepted."

And this man, who has spent his day
wrestling with words, to make them mean
impossibly more than words convey,
now pours them out like a machine
for coining metaphors. He stalks
between the tables. His brown eyes
gleam like a leopard's as he talks
with effortless brilliance, then grow smaller
and veiled, the eyes of a caged fox.
Our money counted, dollar by dollar,
we taxi to Small's Paradise,
but Hart storms out to roam the docks
in search of some compliant sailor.

I think of the tangled reasons why
this man should flourish, this one die
obscurely of some minor hurt;
why this one sought his death by sea,
and this one drank himself to death,
and this one, not of our company,
but born on the same day as Hart,
should harvest all the world can give,
then put a gun between his teeth;
or why, among the friends who live,
this one misled by his good heart,
and this forsaken by a wench,
should each crawl off to nurse his grief.
I saw the flower and the leaf,
the fruit, or none, and the bare branch.

The famous and the forgotten dead,
the living, still without a wound,
I see them now at a sudden glance,
the possibly great, the grandly failed,
the doomed to modest eminence,
gathered once more, but not around
that table stained with dago red.
For some inconsequential reason,
I see them now in a hilltop field
on the first day of hunting season
and wonder if, on such a day
of misty, mild October weather,
they would be friend and equal still.
A sound of guns drifts up the hill,
a wind drives off the mist, and they,
brothers again, break bread together,
empty a pocket flask together.

                              Malcolm Cowley

Contents

Illustrations

Preface

A BOOK ABOUT Kenneth Burke in the 1920s should probably be written in the form of a collage rather than as a formal academic essay. Not only would collage as form be appropriate to a discussion that centers around the concept of literary modernism, but an effective collage would suggest something of the complexity of Burke's personal and professional story, the complexity of a compelling personality and mind caught in a web of conflicting and cooperating personalities and ideas.

Collage being beyond my abilities, however, readers will I hope be satisfied with more-or-less-linear narrative about Kenneth Burke's activities in the period from 1915 (when, fresh from high school, he arrived in the New York City area) to 1931, when he placed for publication his critical and theoretical book *Counter-Statement* and his experimental novel *Towards a Better Life*, and when the economic crisis of the Depression and a confluence of related intellectual developments shifted Burke's concerns fundamentally and finally away from narrowly aesthetic concerns. A key figure in the articulation of modernist ideology, Burke in his poetry, in his short fiction (*The White Oxen, and Other Stories*), in the critical essays he wrote for *The Dial*, and in *Counter-Statement* and *Towards a Better Life* was contributing to the discussion about the nature of modernism that was being conducted in New York during those years. This book is an effort to understand how Burke's earliest work emerged through a dialogue with the other shapers of modernism who congregated with him in Greenwich Village before and after the Great War. These others included people like the leftists of *The Masses*, Eugene O'Neill and the other members of The Provincetown Players who were inventing a new American drama, the artists and writers associated with Alfred Stieglitz's art gallery "291," the poets known as the "Others," the literary nationalists of the political left, right, and center, and the leaders of the variety of literary magazines that made modernism such a various and contested term—most notably

The Dial, *Secession*, and *Broom*, but also *Others*, *The Little Review*, *Contact*, *Smart Set*, *The New Republic*, and any number of others. The only trace of a collage to be found will be in the related materials—Burke letters, unpublished poetry, essays on this or that development, a map of Greenwich Village, photographs—that appear from time to time within most of the chapters.

This book will interest two overlapping groups of readers. As a rhetorician by profession, I am writing to my colleagues in English, Rhetoric, Speech Communication, Communications, and related areas who have for many years found Burke's insights into rhetoric and critical theory compelling and captivating. In addition, as a contributor here to the vigorous current scholarship now going on in modernist studies, I am attempting to recover in the person of Burke some of the full variety that existed within the modernist moment. I hope that both groups of readers will be understanding if one or the other find themselves reading background explanations, particularly in chapter 1, that seem to them unnecessary but that seem to me required if I am to find a broad readership.

For their indispensable assistance with this project I am indebted to a great many people knowledgeable and gracious and patient. Foremost have been Charlie Mann and Sandy Stelts and the other staff members associated with the Rare Books Room and the Kenneth Burke Papers at Pattee Library at Penn State; many, many thanks to them for teaching me so much and for making it so comfortable for me to work on this project. Evelyn Feldman and her staff at the Rosenbach Museum in Philadelphia and Patricia Willis and her colleagues at the Beinecke Rare Book and Manuscript Library at Yale made working in their wonderful facilities both productive and pleasurable. Librarians at Princeton University, the University of Pennsylvania, Brown University, the Newberry Library in Chicago, the Cincinnati Public Library, and the Lilly Library at Indiana University (in particular Rebecca Campbell Cape) made my work much easier as well. H. Lewis Ulman (Ohio State) and Kathryn Flannery (Indiana) graciously helped me to secure copies of relevant materials, and John Logie saved me a trip to Chicago by checking out some matters there for me. Bertha Ihnet of the Ohio State University Archives graciously helped me locate information about Burke's Columbus connections.

Many of my colleagues at Penn State have gratified me by taking pleasure in my work and assisting me along the way. Early in my research Sanford Schwartz and Jeff Walker cheerfully offered formative lessons on modernism to a relative novice. My colleagues in the rhetoric group at Penn State invigorate my thinking on a daily basis. Members of a graduate seminar on Burke—Ted Armstrong, Alan Bilansky, Rosa Eberly, Ann George, and Janet Zepernick—materially advanced this project as they pursued their own studies of Burke, and members of my undergraduate course on Greenwich Village in the 1920s kept their enthusiasm while I was trying out my ideas on them. Brett Bowles gave me the benefit of a long conversation on Symbolist poetry, and Anne Borelli helped me to obtain a copy of a needed manuscript. My department head, Robert Secor, arranged my teaching assignments to facilitate my research and showed every confidence in and support for my work. The Institute for the Arts and Humanistic Studies and the College of Liberal Arts at Penn State both provided me with funds to permit me to visit collections of Burke papers. Charlie Mann, Andrew Stephenson, Sanford Schwartz, Ann George, and Linda Selzer read portions of the manuscript and made valuable suggestions. Linda Selzer also offered me the benefit of many productive conversations on the project—and much more.

Colleagues elsewhere also helped my work; so many people helped, in fact, that I've probably forgotten the kind intercessions of some of them. I do remember that Tillie Warnock (University of Arizona) and Paul Jay (Loyola University of Chicago) both offered warm support and suggestions at a time when I needed both, and that Greg Clark (Brigham Young University) and Cary Nelson (University of Illinois), reviewers of the manuscript for the University of Wisconsin Press, made constructive criticisms that improved the final product. Faculty and graduate students at Arizona, Brigham Young, and Ohio State made useful and encouraging responses to earlier versions of the manuscript, as did those who listened to my presentations at meetings of the Conference on College Composition and Communication, the Eastern Communication Association, and the Rhetoric Society of America. Allen Fitchen at the University of Wisconsin Press encouraged the project from its early stages, and members of the staff who worked on production of the book—notably Raphael Kadushin, Carol Olsen, and Sylvan Esh—were unfailingly professional and accommodating. I also offer special thanks to Kenneth Burke for welcoming a stranger into his home in his ninety-sixth year and for being the fascinating and compelling character who has made the research for this book the most enjoyable scholarly experience of my career.

Finally, I wish to thank and acknowledge the following for their generous permission to reprint photographs and to quote from books, articles, and correspondence: The University of California Press, for permission to quote from Burke's *Collected Poems, 1915–1967, Counter-Statement,* and *The Complete White Oxen, and Other Stories*; Michael Burke, Trustee of the Kenneth Burke Literary Trust, for permission to use photographs of Kenneth Burke, and to quote from *Towards a Better Life: Being a Series of Epistles, or Declamations,* and from Kenneth Burke's correspondence at Pennsylvania State University, the Newberry Library, the Rosenbach Museum, The University of Pennsylvania, Indiana University, Brown University, and Yale University; Elspeth Burke Hart, for photographs of Kenneth Burke and his family; Charles Mann, for permission to quote documents and letters in the Kenneth Burke Collection in Pattee Library, Pennsylvania State University; Robert Cowley, for permission to include "The Flower and the Leaf," and to quote from the letters of Malcolm Cowley to Kenneth Burke and to Harold Loeb; and the Newberry Library, for permission to quote from the Malcolm Cowley Papers; the trustees of the University of Pennsylvania, for permission to quote from the Van Wyck Brooks Collections, and the Waldo Frank Papers; Carl Josephson, for permission to quote from letters by Matthew Josephson to Kenneth Burke and to Harold Loeb; Marianne Craig Moore, Literary Executor for the Estate of Marianne Moore, for permission to quote from four of Marianne Moore's unpublished letters (all rights reserved), and Evelyn Feldman, Keeper of the Marianne Moore Archive at the Rosenbach Museum and Library, for permission to quote from several letters by and to Kenneth Burke and Marianne Moore at the Rosenbach Museum and Library; Mrs. Elizabeth Munson, for permission to quote letters by Gorham Munson; Nancy Tate Wood, for permission to quote from the letters and papers of Allen Tate at Princeton University; Helen Tate, for permission to quote from the letters of Allen Tate at Princeton University and Pennsylvania State University; Princeton University Libraries, for permission to quote from items in the Manuscripts Division, Department of Rare Books and Special Collections—namely, from the Harold Loeb Papers (box 1), from letters in the Broom Collection (box 1), and from the Allen Tate Papers (box 13 and box 3, folder 3); Mark Brown, Curator of Manuscripts at Brown University, for permission to quote from the correspondence of John Brooks Wheelwright; Patricia Willis, Curator of American Literature at the Beinecke Rare Book and Manuscript Library at Yale University, for permission to quote excerpts from the Kenneth Burke correspondence in the Hart Crane Collection, Matthew Josephson Papers, Jean Toomer Papers, and *Dial*/Thayer Papers in the Yale Collection of American Literature; Paul H. Williams and the Estate of William Eric Williams and New Directions Publishing Corporation, agents, for permission to quote excerpts from the letters of William Carlos Williams to Kenneth Burke.

Kenneth Burke
in Greenwich Village

1

Introduction

As Marjorie Perloff has recently noted, "Surely no literary term has raised more controversy and misunderstanding than the modest little word *modernism*" (154). Perloff's comment was directed to literary scholars and critics, especially to those who have been studying modernism in the past quarter-century, but her words describe just as fittingly the attitudes of the moderns themselves, in particular those moderns who lived, wrote, painted, acted, designed, and performed during the first two decades of this century—those decades when several, conflicting versions of what people today refer to as modernism in art were vying for ascendancy among the artists of Paris and Berlin, Vienna and Moscow, Chicago and New York. Indeed, while it was once conventional to describe modernism as a fairly coherent, even monolithic movement associated especially with the artistic theory and practice of Pound and Eliot in poetry, Joyce and Woolf in fiction, Wright and Gropius in architecture, Picasso and Braque in painting, Rodin and Brancusi in sculpture, Strindberg and Pirandello in theatre, Stieglitz and Steichen in photography, Cocteau and Eisenstein in film, Webern and Stravinsky in music, Duncan and St. Denis in dance, Nietzsche and Bergson in philosophy, and so forth, it now seems more fitting to think not so much of Modernism but of modernisms—of a cultural development diverse and vital enough, even before 1930, to accommodate all sorts of difference.[1]

In poetry, for instance, both Eliot and William Carlos Williams are quintessentially modern, even though Williams composed the stunning lyrics of *Spring and All* (1923) at least in part in order to counter the "classroom poetry" that he found in "The Waste Land" (1922). As Williams recorded in his *Autobiography*, Eliot's poetry seemed so different from his own—and so successful—that it "wiped out [my] world as if an atomic bomb had been dropped on it. . . . Critically Eliot returned us to the classroom just at the moment when I felt we were on the point of an escape to matters much closer to the essence of a new art form" (174). Other

3

modern poets such as Pound (mentor to both Eliot and Williams), Hart Crane, Mina Loy, Countee Cullen, Marianne Moore, and Carl Sandberg devised lyrics before 1930 that are as dissimilar as they are alike, even if all of them could agree with Max Bodenheim, writing in *The Dial* in 1920, that there are no inherently poetic subjects, and that "the old emotional eloquence, dramatic ecstacies of phraseology, and suave oratory with which most poets have always addressed trees, birds, flowers, and the lives of men is disappearing" from poetry (97). In fiction, modernism before 1925 permitted the interior monologues of Woolf's *Mrs. Dalloway* and Joyce's *Ulysses*, but also Jean Toomer's lyrical collage *Cane* and the hard objectivism of *The Sun Also Rises*. The visual arts encouraged early movements and counter-movements as diverse as Post-Impressionism, Cubism, Vorticism, Futurism, Expressionism, Dadaism, and Surrealism, and new music developed out of Coleman Hawkins as much as it did from Stravinsky. Modernism accommodated, albeit uneasily, a range of attitudes about masculinity, femininity, and sexuality; it animated alike Europeans, European-Americans, and the African-Americans involved in the Harlem Renaissance; and it offered a forum for various opinions about every feature of contemporary life.[2] Politically the moderns ranged from the far-right proto-fascists associated with Futurism and D. W. Griffith's *Birth of a Nation*, and Pound and Wyndham Lewis (who is anatomized in Fredric Jameson's *Fables of Aggression*), to the hard conservatives of the southern Agrarian movement, to the liberals and leftists associated with the Provincetown Players and Charlie Chaplin (as well as others "recovered" in Cary Nelson's *Repression and Recovery*). As individuals, moderns fall variously on the political spectrum between the leftist socialist activism of John Reed and IWW leader Big Bill Haywood (who frequented Mabel Dodge's famous salon before 1916) and the aesthetic avoidance of politics (itself political, of course) of Joyce, Yeats, and Eliot.[3]

Modernism, then, seems less a coherent and linear movement today than it once did and more a controversy or conversation—more a series of semiotic responses and counter-responses to the aesthetic, economic, and social tensions of the first half of the twentieth century.[4] In the final decades of the nineteenth century and particularly in the first two decades of the twentieth, modernism amounted to a dialogue on how people might appropriately respond to the civic and artistic stresses created when various nineteenth-century certitudes about nature and human nature eroded or collapsed. Post-Emersonian confidence in a God-animated nature, in a predictable universe presided over by a benevolent diety, for example, deteriorated when Darwinians turned up evidence of a vicious and hostile environment indifferent to human endeavor: as Bertrand Russell put it, "brief and powerless is Man's life; on him and all his race the slow, sure doom falls pitiless and dark."[5] If many Victorians sought a stable, hierarchical civilization and fostered it, in Arnoldian fashion, though education, the arts, and religion, if they sought to tame the beastly side of human nature by repressing sex and the emotions, if they honored propriety and decorum, then the moderns who read Freud called attention instead to the primitive and subconscious drives that control people unawares. Victorian faith in progress was corrupted by Nietzsche's argument that increases in material productivity have nothing to do with moral development or social amelioration, and by Spengler's contention that human history is marked by recurrent cycles of growth and decay. Similarly, nineteenth-century absolutes about law, morality, conduct, and the workings of nature were rendered relative by post-Newtonian physicists and mathematicians and philosophers: In 1902 Poincaré, inventor of non-Euclidean geometry, wrote that "one geometry cannot be more true than another; it can only be more convenient"; and William James testified that "the notion that the truest formula may be a human device and not a literal transcript has dawned upon us."[6] Artists sensitive to the decisive rupture that seemed to separate their modern world from a decaying prior one determined to look at things from radically novel, radically shifting, perspectives.

The desire to distance themselves from the certitudes of the past and from the genteel society that perpetuated those certitudes accounts for much of what the moderns depicted in their art and for the relentlessly experimental manner in which they carried out their rebellion. Several of the moderns responded by creating (or retreating into) some kind of a "usable past" (in the words of Van Wyck Brooks)—by trading the unappetizing Victorian past for a more remote and congenial one.[7] Others turned Victorian platitudes around, making heroes of villains and dramatizing the damages wrought by virtue. Or, schooled by French Symbolists and by other art-for-art's-sake advocates at the end of the nineteenth century, and convinced that art should ideally be autonomous (i.e., freed from the social and moral requirements imposed on it by the genteel tradition), they retreated into an aesthetic world of art that offered its own kind of refuge—a "momentary stay against confusion," in Frost's famous phrase, a stay against the chaos and relentless philistinism that seemed to surround them. In sympathy with Eliot, who wrote in *The Dial* in 1922 that the role of the artist was "controlling, ordering, giving shape and significance to the immense panorama of futility and anarchy which is contemporary history,"[8] many embraced the brand of modernism emphasized in Edmund Wilson's *Axel's Castle* (1931), a book which places Joyce, Yeats, Valery, Eliot, Proust, and Stein in the tradition of aesthetes Baudelaire, Mallarmé, Pater, Huysmans, and Gourmont. Still others, by contrast—John Reed, for instance, or John Dos Passos or Langston Hughes—opposed the notion of "autonomous art" and resisted looking backwards for a usable past; they saw themselves as artists at the beginning of a new age, as activist forerunners responsible for leading society through art in more progressive directions.[9] Similarly, still others—the Futurists, the Dadas, and others associated with the avant-garde—sought not a usable past but, above all, novelty and experimentation in expression and subject matter.

So diverse were the versions of early modernism that a single issue of an experimental modernist magazine like *Broom* might in February 1922 include everything from a Paul Morand story (translated by Matthew Josephson) to Paul Claudel's satiric drama "Proteus"; from essays on Ishijima to one on contemporary Russian poetry; from cubist paintings by Josef Capek and a painting by Jan Zrzavy to a still life by Carlo Carra and a print by Jean de Bosschere (vol. 1, no. 4). An all-American issue of *Broom* published a year later (in January 1923, vol. 4, no. 2) featured things as various as Kenneth Burke's story "My Dear Mrs. Wurtelbach," Jean Toomer's collage "Karintha" from *Cane* ("to be read accompanied by the humming of a Negro folk song"), Marianne Moore's essay on H.D., photos of Mayan art accompanied by an explanatory article and by William Carlos Williams' essay "The Destruction of Tenochtitlan," a prose experiment entitled "Wear" by Gertrude Stein, and poetry by people as different as Kay Boyle, Hart Crane, Elsa von Freitag-Loringhoven, Charles Galwey, and Matthew Josephson. Almost simultaneously (in November 1922), *The Dial*, partly through the efforts of a twenty-five-year-old assistant editor named Kenneth Burke, could juxtapose Eliot's "The Waste Land" with a poem by Mina Loy, Yeats's play "The Player Queen" with fiction by Sherwood Anderson and Arthur Schnitzler, reviews by Malcolm Cowley and Bertrand Russell with a letter by Ezra Pound, and essays on the Dadas and censorship with reproductions of sculpture by Brancusi. Modernism, in short, was (and is) anything but a static and limited set of consistent, canonical tenets propounded by Ezra or Eliot, anything but a soliloquy or a unified chorus. Modernism is a dynamic polyphony, a protean heteroglot with many contending and cooperating programs and participants.

This is a book about Kenneth Burke's contribution to the modernist conversation. It is an effort to explain how Burke himself shaped and was shaped by modernist ideas during the first fifteen years of his career, from 1915 to about 1931, a time when he was steeped in the literary and political culture of Greenwich Village and when that narrow strain of modernism associated with Pound, Joyce, and Eliot (a strain characterized by a suspicion of the contemporary as well as of democracy and progress, and by an insistence on hierarchy and order) had not yet dominated and "repressed" (to adopt Cary Nelson's terminology) the more liberal, socially minded versions of modernism that were so important in the

United States in the years just before World War I and during the Great Depression—and that remained articulate, if muted, in the more socially and artistically conservative 1920s. Burke's works through 1931—not only his poetry and fiction but also his criticism—may be understood as responses and thrusts in this cultural conversation. For as a critic and artist Burke was certainly one of the more knowing and important voices in the New York City circle of modernists.

Of course there has always been more interest in the European, particularly Parisian versions of modernism than in the American ones that sustained Burke. Not only has Paris been understood by scholars as the central modernist site since at least the time of *Axel's Castle*, but for American letters, too, Paris has seemed the wellspring of modernist ideology. American modernists, so the story goes—Stein, Pound, H.D., Fitzgerald, Hemingway, E. E. Cummings, Kay Boyle, Djuana Barnes, John Dos Passos, Malcolm Cowley, and Allen Tate (to name only some of them)—had to leave the United States in order to flourish artistically, particularly when the climate for the American avant-garde deteriorated during the less tolerant, Prohibition-era days after the war. According to the accepted metanarrative, modernism was the product of European ideas—first Symbolism, then Vorticism, Cubism, Futurism, Dadaism, and Surrealism—which flowered in the work of the international set of artists who gathered in Paris before and after World War I. Pound had left the United States for London in 1907 and landed in Gertrude Stein's Paris, where he stayed from 1920 to 1924; this same Paris attracted and fostered a libertine avant-garde culture that nurtured Hemingway, Fitzgerald, Joyce, Picasso, Matisse, Brancusi, Tzara, Breton, Aragon, and any number of lesser others. While never exactly a "lost generation," the artists in Paris in the early 1920s shared liquor and ideas at the Dome and Rotonde and Deux Magots cafes, subsisted well enough on small incomes when European currencies lost ground against the American dollar, listened to new music by Erik Satie and patronized Cocteau burlesques, eavesdropped on surrealist seances, became characters in each other's fiction, observed an allegedly apolitical aestheticism, and in general slouched toward new if imprecisely defined values. When "The Waste Land" and *Ulysses* were published in 1922, when various Parisian sensations found themselves in the contemporary press, when movements "born" in Paris (Post-Impressionism, Dadaism, Cubism, Surrealism) were exported to other places, when Picasso, Cezanne, Stein, Matisse, Hemingway, Fitzgerald, Joyce, and others captured public fancy, and when the memoirs of participants from Cowley (*Exile's Return:* 1934) to Hemingway (*A Moveable Feast:* 1964) continued to feed public curiosity about the scene,[10] Paris was established, apparently forever, as "the hub of the modernist cultural wheel" (Perloff, "Modernist Studies" 158), "the international center of

7

Modernist activity" (Singal, "Towards a Definition" 8), and "that most concentrated awareness and expression of modernity" (Davies 146). Expatriate Paris still rightly fascinates scholars interested in understanding particular artists (e.g., Spanier's *Kay Boyle*) or in puzzling out the terrain of modernism in general (e.g., Benstock's *Women of the Left Bank*).

But modernism was not invented only in Paris, of course, nor was Paris the only important occasion for the modernist conversation. On the continent, Vienna and Berlin were as important or more important to early modernism as Paris was. As for the United States, though Benstock has called Greenwich Village in the mid-1920s "a moribund literary culture" (235), and though Daniel Bell has claimed that "while there were *modernists* in the United States, there was no *modernist culture* in content" there (163–64), the fact is that a truly remarkable circle of artists, writers, and thinkers converged in Greenwich Village in the decade before and the one after the end of World War I. While some American moderns undeniably took their lead from Paris and the Continent, others (including William Carlos Williams, Waldo Frank, Georgia O'Keeffe, Man Ray, Eugene O'Neill, and Hart Crane) promoted peculiarly American versions of modernism. Without contesting the importance of Paris as modernist incubator, I would note that a well-documented modernist community, one with similar but certainly not identical values to the ones current on the Continent and one with equally spectacular artistic and intellectual progeny, existed in New York City. That community drew from Paris and Berlin and London and Chicago, but it also itself contributed fundamentally to the development of modernist ideas on the Continent, even in Paris, whose artistic community confronted with varying degrees of enthusiasm more-or-less-American modernist developments such as the skyscraper, jazz, cinema, and photography.

Detailing the particulars of Greenwich Village culture from 1915 to 1930 is the task of my next chapter. Here, by way of introduction, it is worth noting that New York City as early as 1913 was already capable of sustaining two notable modernist events, the Armory Show of modern art and John Reed's dramatic pageant on behalf of the Patterson silk industry workers.[11] Alfred Stieglitz in 1908 had begun to display modern art by Cezanne, Rodin, Picasso, and Matisse, so the Armory Show was not entirely new in bringing to New York experimental works. But the size and reach of the Armory Show was spectacular: thirteen hundred items in all were displayed, including Fauvist canvases by Gauguin and Cezanne, Cubist paintings by Picasso and Braque, nudes by Matisse, and Marcel Duchamp's notorious "Nude Descending a Staircase"—not to mention other examples of Impressionism, Post-Impressionism, and Futurism. When John Reed concurrently mobilized one thousand striking workers into appearing at Madison Square Garden in his pageant reenacting the Patterson strike, modernist form was married to activist politics in a manner that would be missing in the moveable feast of Paris a decade later. Both the Armory Show and the Patterson pageant were supported by Mabel Dodge, who then sponsored a famous weekly salon for the purpose of encouraging innovative thought and action about art, politics, social *mores*, and their interconnection.[12] Just as European moderns were reacting to Victorianism, so Americans—perhaps most startlingly in the acerbic prose of H. L. Mencken—were reacting against the stable givens of the Gilded Age: the economic values of thrift, diligence, and materialism on display in the novels of Horatio Alger, and the cultural values articulated in *The Atlantic Monthly*, *Harper's*, and *The Saturday Evening Post*. In Greenwich Village, artists challenged the genteel notion that art should reflect the world, civilize the masses, and promote Christian virtue and civic order. William James offered an American analogue to the revisionist Continental philosophies of Bergson and Nietzsche. A Greenwich Village brand of Dadaism in 1915 anticipated the one that erupted in Zurich a few months later. New publishers (e.g., Knopf, Boni and Liveright) and new publications (e.g., *The Little Review*, *Others*, *The Dial*) appeared on the Greenwich Village scene. And in the years 1915 to 1931, so did a legion of experimental, anti-genteel writers and artists, including, all before 1918, Reed, Duchamp, Stieglitz, Ray, Marsden Hartley, Theodore Dreiser, Djuna Barnes, Wallace Stevens, Max Eastman, Floyd Dell, Francis Picabia, Alfred Kreymborg, and Eugene O'Neill; and, during the war or soon after, Allen Tate, Marianne Moore, Hart Crane, Jean Toomer, Willlam Carlos Williams, E. E. Cummings, Edmund Wilson, Malcolm Cowley, Georgia O'Keeffe, Charles Sheeler, Charles Demuth, Katherine Anne Porter, and many others. All of them either congregated in the area of Greenwich Village, lived in close proximity to it, and/or were frequent visitors. Many of them knew each other personally as friends or rivals or both. Even forgetting for a moment about the artists of Harlem—and the Greenwich Villagers at this time do seem to have quarantined themselves pretty completely from the artists of Black Manhattan, except for patrons of Toomer and jazz—it is clear that New York City in general and Greenwich Village in particular constituted a major scene for the enactment of modernist dialogue.[13]

It would be wrong to oppose New York City too strenuously to Paris. As I have been implying, the two sites share plenty of common ground, and there was a good deal of interchange between them. In 1924, 32,000 Americans lived permanently in Paris, many thousands of others visited, and American films, newspapers, cigarettes, and singers were everywhere in evidence (Douglas 108). Stein, Hemingway, Loeb, Crosby, and the others associated with "the lost generation" in Paris had many ties to Greenwich Village; Freud, Jung, Duchamp, Francis Picabia, and

Four generations of Burke's maternal family. Photograph courtesy of Elspeth Burke Hart.

any number of other Continental artists visited New York; and many of the artists and critics most identified with the American scene—Sherwood Anderson, Hart Crane, William Carlos Williams, E. E. Cummings, Djuana Barnes, Kay Boyle, Gorham Munson, Matthew Josephson, Margaret Anderson, Malcolm Cowley, Marsden Hartley, Charles Demuth, and Alfred Kreymborg—all spent time in Paris. Harold Stearns, having moved to Paris to handicap horses after putting together *Civilization in the United States* (1922), a savage critique of genteel America, reported that in Paris "you could have sworn you were only in a transplanted Greenwich Village . . . except for the fact [that] some people stubbornly persisted in talking French" (Douglas 109). Nevertheless, there was a distinct and vibrant American site for modernist intercourse in New York City, where more than one artist (but by no means every artist) sought cultural emancipation from Europe. And the influence was not all in one direction: people and ideas in both places mutually interanimated each other.

A pivotal figure among the Greenwich Village moderns was Kenneth Burke. Born in 1897 in Pittsburgh, Burke was among the first class of graduates at Peabody High School there. When his father took a job in the New York City area, Burke moved with his family in 1915 to an apartment on Boulevard East in Weehawken, New Jersey, just across the Hudson River from 42nd Street and near the mouth of the Lincoln Tunnel that was then under construction. Burke quickly became intimate with the literary

Photographs from the 1914 and 1915 Peabody High School yearbooks. *Clockwise from upper left:* Malcolm Cowley, Susan Jenkins, James Light, and Kenneth Burke.

and artistic scene in Greenwich Village. Though he studied at Ohio State during the spring semester of 1916 (with his thoroughly modernist friend James Light), and though he commuted from Weehawken to courses at Columbia University throughout 1917, Burke gradually determined to take his instruction from Greenwich Village, and, having insinuated himself into the literary and political scene, he moved to Greenwich Village early in 1918. There he met, associated with, befriended, and/or worked with a host of Village writers, artists, and critics, including (to mention only the ones that seem most prominent today) William Carlos Williams,

11

Map of Greenwich Village

12

Some of Kenneth Burke's Residences

1. 86 Greenwich Avenue ("Clemenceau Cottage"): 1918 (with Berenice Abbott, Djuna Barnes, Stuart Davis, Charles Ellis, Sue Jenkins, James Light, Norma Millay)
2. Patchin Place: late 1918 (also later the residence of E.E. Cummings, Djuna Barnes, Alyce Gregory, Gaston Lachaise)
3. 143 Waverly Place: January–May, 1920
4. 50 Charles Street: January–April, 1921; September 1921–January 1922
5. 45 Grove Street: December 1923–January 1924 (sublet from Hart Crane)
6. 40 Morton Street: March–December, 1925; parts of 1926 and 1927
7. 65 Bank Street: early 1929
8. 58 Perry Street: late 1930
9. 381 Bleecker Street: late 1931

Other Residences

10. Lily Batterham's residence before her marriage to Kenneth Burke (3 Bank Street)
11. Home of Randolph Bourne and Eugene O'Neill after 1921 (Milligan Place—courtyard off Sixth Avenue)
12. Willa Cather's residence (5 Bank Street)
13. Malcolm and Peggy Cowley's place, 1924–25 (33 Bank Street)
14. Theodore Dreiser's residence, 1915–18 (165 West 10th Street)
15. Bruno Guido's famous garret (58 Washington Place)
16. Sue Jenkins' residence, 1922–24; then Allen Tate and Caroline Gordon's residence (30 Jones Street)
17. Edna St. Vincent Millay's first NYC address (139 Waverly Place)
18. Marianne Moore's residence (14 St. Luke's Place)
19. John Reed's residence (42 Washington Square South)
20. Allen Tate and Caroline Gordon's residence, 1926 (27 Bank Street)
21. Scofield Thayer's apartment (80 Washington Square East)
22. Edmund Wilson's and John Dos Passos' residences (3 Washington Square North)

Other Landmarks

23. Alfred Stieglitz's Studio (291 Fifth Avenue)
24. Hotel Brevoort, and its sidewalk cafe (Fifth Avenue and 8th Street)
25. *Broom* American office, site of Lola Ridge's parties (3 East 9th Street)
26. *The Dial* offices, 1920–29 (152 West 13th Street)
27. Golden Swan Saloon, including Eugene O'Neill's "Hell Hole" room (Sixth Avenue at West 4th Street)
28. Liberal Club (above); Polly's Restaurant, later the Dutch Oven (below) (137 MacDougal)
29. New School for Social Research (66 West 12th Street)
30. Mabel Dodge's Salon (23 Fifth Avenue)
31. Provincetown Playhouse, after 1918 (133 MacDougal)
32. Washington Square Arch
33. First Provincetown Playhouse (above); Washington Square Bookstore (below)(139 MacDougal)

who maintained a vigorous correspondence with Burke from 1921 to 1963; Malcolm Cowley, Burke's lifelong friend, who spent the early 1920s amid the Dada crowd in Paris; Hart Crane, who once sublet his apartment to Burke; Marianne Moore, his boss at *The Dial* from 1925 to 1929; Eugene O'Neill, several of whose colleagues in the Provincetown Players lived in the same rooming house with Burke in 1918; and Alfred Stieglitz, Georgia O'Keeffe, Van Wyck Brooks, Edmund Wilson, Allen Tate, Jean Toomer, and Katherine Anne Porter. While spending much of his time after 1922 writing, reading, editing, and translating at his Andover, New Jersey, farm (where he died over seventy years later), Burke remained very much a physical and verbal presence in the Greenwich Village modernist scene. Though he immersed himself as early as high school in Continental modernist literatures and remained keenly interested in Continental developments in fiction, poetry, and criticism, and though he also sometimes wished for the opportunity to visit Paris, Burke continued to live and work productively in the Village through the 1920s, either commuting from his farm (after 1922) to his job at *The Dial* (the most prominent modernist magazine of the era) or maintaining a room in the Village and commuting on weekends while he worked at other jobs to help support his family in Andover. From Greenwich Village and Andover, Burke contributed poetry, fiction, criticism and translations to modernist magazines such as *Others*, *Smart Set*, *The Little Review*, *Contact*, *Broom*, *Secession*, *The Freeman*, and *The Dial*. Burke was on hand for the most experimental and successful period of the Provincetown Players. He set Eliot's "The Waste Land" into print for its *Dial* publication in 1922 and later provided editorial services on behalf of Crane, Pound, Thomas Mann, Arthur Schnitzler, Stevens, and Williams. And he maintained his social and artistic relations through extensive, occasionally spectacular correspondences with Williams, Crane, Cowley, Light, Moore, Tate, Stieglitz, Matthew Josephson, Gorham Munson, Waldo Frank, Margaret Anderson and Jane Heap, Harold Loeb, R. P. Blackmur, Austin Warren, Yvor Winters, and any number of others.

Burke as a writer did much more than keep up a vigorous correspondence. He published a number of poems in modernist magazines. He wrote and published a couple of dozen short stories, collecting most of them in *The White Oxen, and Other Stories* in 1924. He translated the Modern Library edition of *Death in Venice* still in print today. He published reviews, criticism, and essays on literary topics in *The Dial*, *Vanity Fair*, *Hound and Horn*, *The Bookman*, *The Freeman*, *1924*, *The Saturday Review*, *The Little Review*, *The New Republic*, and elsewhere, and in 1931 he collected a number of these articles into *Counter-Statement*, his first book of criticism and theory. So promising and influential was Burke's earliest writing that he was recognized as one of a half-dozen members of "that youngest generation" for whom Gorham Munson founded the experimental magazine *Secession* in 1922. He was also included in the circle of contributors to the international modernist magazine *Broom*, which was founded (and named) in order to help sweep the old literary order off the scene. Burke also published a modernist novel, *Towards a Better Life*, in 1931. For his contributions, Burke was awarded The Dial Award for 1928, an honor previously extended in the 1920s to Sherwood Anderson, T. S. Eliot, Van Wyck Brooks, Marianne Moore, E. E. Cummings, William Carlos Williams, and Ezra Pound.

One good way, then, to understand Kenneth Burke—at least the early work of Kenneth Burke—is against the backdrop of modernism in general and the culture of Greenwich Village, 1915–31, in particular. But, despite a notable exception here and there (e.g., Warren; Warnock), scholarship on Burke has mostly discounted the early, modernist Burke. That is neither surprising nor blameworthy: Burke's tremendous contributions to literary and rhetorical theory after 1930 have for good reason attracted tremendous interest to that part of his life and work, and so scholars have understandably attended mostly to the theoretical and critical works in Burke's canon, most of them published after 1931, rather than to the critical and literary works that Burke produced before that time. When W. H. Auden wrote that Burke is "unquestionably the most brilliant and suggestive critic now writing in America" (59), for example, he was reviewing *The Philosophy of Literary Form* (1941). When Wayne Booth agreed that Burke was "without question, the most important living critic" ("Kenneth Burke's Way" 1), or when Trevor Melia called him "the most significant contributor to rhetorical theory since Cicero,"[14] it was not on the basis of anything Burke wrote before 1940. When Geoffrey Hartman spoke admiringly of Burke's work in *Criticism in the Wilderness*, he was discussing Burke's criticism after 1930. When J. Hillis Miller recently remarked on Burke's "deep influence" on him, he was recalling not the Burke of *Counter-Statement* but Burke's dramatism and his efforts as "the wisest and most intelligent Freudian critic and Marxist critic of his time" (Olson 320). Even Paul Jay's essay on Burke's "consciously Modernist critical practice" concerns itself with Burke's work after 1932 ("Modernism" 345).

In addition, Burke has customarily been considered as an "individual,"[15] as a solitary genius and a gadfly, as someone apart from movements and schools. Because of the originality of his insights, Burke is often admired, with some justice, as an unaffiliated scholar and autodidact who was somewhat immune from social and intellectual movements, somehow free to pursue in his own strange way his own personal and idiosyncratic agenda—an unaffilated scholar and maverick genius (sometimes infuriatingly so) not only in the sense that he remained remote from and critical of intellectual fashions current on university campuses but in the sense that his ideas remained eccentric from and independent of other recognizable intellectual schools. One of the best recent overviews of Burke's criticism, for example, begins by stressing "his irregular career." "Without a college degree, with minimal formal training in literature, philosophy, psychology, or political science, with no permanent full-time academic appointment, and with no conventional area of specialization, Burke . . . has [produced] a body of work whose breadth, rigor, and theoretical grounding is unmatched by the work of any other American critic" (Paul Jay, "Kenneth Burke" 68).[16] Another notes "the free play of private idiosyncracies" in Burke's work (Jameson, "Symbolic Inference" 508). Throughout his long career Burke himself consistently insisted on his own independence. For example, he remained separate from doctrinaire communism in the 1930s even though he sympathized with the leftist program. "I am not a joiner of societies, I am a literary man," he said. "I can only welcome Communism by converting it into my own vocabulary. . . . My book [*Auscultation, Creation, and Revision*][17] will have the communist objectives, and the communist tenor, but the approach will be the one that seems significant to me" (Burke to Cowley, June 4, 1932). Later in his life, asked if he was a Marxist or Freudian, Burke characteristically replied, "Marxoid" and "Freudoid" to emphasize his independence (Tompkins 120). He also wrote very public rejoinders to Booth and Jameson when they wished to claim him as a critical pluralist and ideological critic ("Dancing," included in Booth's *Critical Understanding,* and the 1978 "Methodological Repression"). This book, too, while placing Burke in the broad context of modernism, will show that Burke from his earliest years as a writer and critic was intent on maintaining his independence.

If they have not stressed Burke's independence and his later work, then scholars have understood Burke in a variety of contexts rather different from literary modernism. Vincent Leitch, for instance, discusses Burke in relation to the New Critics, who were certainly modernist enough: "At the heart of Burke's project was a formalist exegetical method" (41). But Leitch also concludes, correctly, that Burke remained separate from the formalists because he fashioned his "complex machine for textual analysis" out of various other-than-formalist hermeutical approaches—biographical, psychological, sociological, philosophical, political, ethical, religious, and anthropological (41–43). Henry Bamford Parkes (209), Giles Gunn, and Paul Jay (*American Literary Criticism*), among others stressing Burke's emphasis on symbolic action, have noted Burke's relationship to the pragmatists. Fredric Jameson understands Burke not as a modernist but as a poststructuralist ideological critic ("Ideology" and "Symbolic Inference"). Cary Nelson similarly regards Burke as a poststructuralist (171), and Frank Lentricchia has lately studied Burke

16

as "a man of the 1930s" (56) in order to recapture both the political Burke (*Criticism and Social Change*) and the historical thinker ("Reading History with Kenneth Burke").[18] Other poststructuralist critics have understood Burke as a proto-deconstructionist (e.g., Harris, "Critics"; Lentricchia, "Reading History" 136).[19] And cultural studies critics of the past decade have embraced Burke as one of themselves (e.g., Eberly, George, Kennedy, and Byard; and Jay, in "Kenneth Burke" and "Kenneth Burke and the Motives of Rhetoric").[20]

Scholars in rhetoric, who also emphasize Burke's independence and mostly attend to his work after 1940, have also understood Burke apart from modernism. Burke's invention of "dramatism" and "identification" have of course captured particular attention since the publication of *A Grammar of Motives* in 1945 and *A Rhetoric of Motives* in 1950; the two notions, especially dramatism, have often been understood as forming the key to his interpretive system (e.g., Rueckert; *Drama*; Fogarty; Irmscher; Foss, Foss, and Trapp; Bizzell and Herzberg). Others associate Burke not with modernism but with one or another kind of neo-classicism. He has been interpreted as a neo-Aristotelian by Virginia Holland, for instance, and associated with neo-Aristotelians of the Chicago school by Booth (*Critical Understanding*) and Donald Jammerman, and Cynthia Sheard, Michael Hassett, and others have emphasized his ties to the sophists.[21] In the past decade, as rhetoricians have turned their attention to setting and context, Burke has been seen as a prescient social constructivist.[22]

It has always been difficult, then, to "place" Burke; he is famous for his independence and his uneasy relation to any number of schools and movements. Nor is it the aim of this study to "correct" these legitimate ways of understanding Burke or to "smooth out" Burke's thought or his prose, for it is largely his independence and iconoclasm that make him and his work intriguing and fascinating. Still, Burke's independence has been overstated, and it has been too easy to excuse him from membership in formative cultural groups that gave Burke his intellectual lifeblood—and that drew lifeblood from him.

This book will show, therefore, some of the values and tactics Burke gained from the conversation we call modernism and what he himself strove to contribute to that movement, particularly as modernism was being "invented" in the United States during the dozen or so years before the Great Depression. Though Burke's apprenticeship in the midst of modernism undoubtedly influenced his later work too, here it will be the details of that apprenticeship that are under scrutiny: this book is an effort to understand how Kenneth Burke's earliest work was developed through his dialogue with the shapers of modernism who congregated with him in Greenwich Village after World War I. As is already abundantly clear from my diction here and throughout this introduction, my key metaphor, one chosen for its appropriateness to Burke's own theory of discourse, is "conversation": my aim is to uncover some of what Burke picked up from modernist conversations and controversies and what he contributed to them; or, to adopt yet another Burkean metaphor, to identify what role(s) Burke played in the modernist drama during the fifteen years before the Great Depression, who the other players were—models and guides and adversaries—how they all interacted, and how the drama developed.[23] By looking at Burke's writing in the context of the little (and sometimes not-so-little) magazines that inspired and nurtured it, by observing Burke's place in the various and diverse modernist circles to which he belonged, by listening in on the memoirs of the period produced by some of his friends and associates, and by reading Burke's amazingly extensive correspondence with any number of modernist principals, I've sought to understand the web of associations that intersected so thoroughly with Burke during this period of his life, and I've tried to offer here as thick a description as possible of the social and intellectual forces that interanimated Burke's work through 1931.

My argument is that Burke was a key point of articulation for modernist ideology—that Burke defined himself and his work both with and against several key strains in the modernist conversation, strains that will be elaborated in the chapters to follow. During his formative years in the Village, Burke involved himself with a remarkable set of interconnected modernist groups and individuals that will be described in some detail in chapter 2: the socialists of *The Masses* and *Seven Arts* before and during the war; the crowd of poets, painters, and dramatists associated with *Others* magazine, with Alfred Stieglitz's gallery 291, and with The Provincetown Players; the iconoclasts of the older generation identified with H. L. Mencken and Theodore Dreiser, *Smart Set* and *The American Mercury*; the group of literary nationalists who invented *Contact* and *The New Republic*; the New Humanists; and the avant-garde writers, artists, and critics, most of them in close touch with Continental modernism, who produced *Broom*, *Secession*, and *The Dial*. This second chapter will also in passing provide something of a biographical sketch of Burke's life through 1931.

Then, in the chapters that follow, I will concentrate on some of the roles that Burke took on and then discarded—if not always completely—in the course of his professional and artistic growth. Chapter 3 will describe the aesthetic young "Flaubert" who wrote experimental, free-verse poetry after the fashion of the Symbolists and the members of the *Others* circle. Chapter 4 considers Burke's innovative short fiction in the context of the avant-garde, quasi-Dadaist magazines *Broom* and *Secession* that were edited by his expatriate friends Malcolm Cowley, Gorham Munson, and Matthew Josephson. Chapter 5 overviews Burke's early criticism and finds it thoroughly in keeping with the aesthete ethos of the stunning modernist periodical *The Dial*, where much of it was published. Chapter 6 argues that *Counter-Statement* (1931) can be seen as both a modernist and counter-modernist text, one that articulates Burke's inventive and dynamic solutions to modernist aesthetic problems—solutions that both constituted a distinctive contribution to modernist aesthetics and ironically contributed to his marginalization within so-called "high-modernist" circles. And in chapter 7, Burke's novel *Towards a Better Life* is read not as a sort of veiled autobiography but as a modernist experiment in narrative form that dramatizes some resolutely counter-modernist tenets. The book concludes with a frankly utilitarian gesture. In the absence of a biography of Burke—would-be biographers have no doubt been attracted by the interest value of Burke's life and the wealth of primary biographical materials that he left behind, but intimidated by the prospect of documenting seventy years of active professional work— the appendix provides an informal chronology of Burke's life from 1915 through 1931, one that might serve as a ready reference for readers of individual chapters.

In general, Burke's modernism can be seen as in keeping with the amazing creative voices that articulated the literary and critical substance of Greenwich Village in the decade and a half before 1931. Burke entered the 1920s as something of an aesthete, in the tradition of Flaubert, Remy de Gourmont, and the French Symbolists. His politics may have leaned toward the left in an increasingly conservative period, but as a writer and critic he pledged himself to the literary avant-garde, to the invention of novel aesthetic forms, and to an appreciation of form. As an influential member of the coterie inventing literary modernism in America, Burke as the 1920s wore on rethought his aestheticism. While many of the moderns took after the politically conservative example of Pound, Eliot, Stevens, Moore, or Williams, Burke was turning toward a more social criticism; against the tide of the 1920s in the United States and in Europe, he began to advocate—and thereafter never ceased advocating—an increasingly rhetorical and social criticism, one that acknowledged "readers" and "effects," "ideology" and "culture." Burke thus should be understood as a modernist writer and critic, but not narrowly so. His modernism, in keeping with current notions of modernism, is identifiable but shifting and eclectic—truly Burkean in its individuality, truly Burkean in its ultimate acknowledgment of the social and situated. Burke's voice in the modernist conversation was to an extent drowned out by the high modernist chorus that dominated literary studies through the 1960s, but in the past few decades his voice has been recovered, especially in those rhetorically self-conscious moments within modernism that have come to be associated with the political left and with postmodernism.

2

Overview: A Flaubert in
Greenwich Village

ON SEPTEMBER 17, 1917, James Light wrote a desperate letter from Columbus, Ohio, to his close friend Kenneth Burke in Weehawken, New Jersey. "We [Light and his companion Sue Jenkins] must get to New York, and you must make it possible," he wrote. "I beg you by everything that's between us to help me and help me quickly. . . . Send your answer by special delivery." There was plenty "between them." Light, who had met Burke in high school and then briefly studied architecture and painting at Carnegie Tech, had spent the previous two academic years at Ohio State, and during the spring semester of 1916 was Burke's roommate there. Indeed, it was Light who had persuaded Burke, suspicious about dress codes, chapel, and mandatory, uniformed drill (Light to Burke, January 22, 1916), to give Ohio State a try in the first place, and Light who persisted in encouraging Burke (albeit unsuccessfully) to return even after a semester of "clean, healthy liberal Protestant Philistinism . . . , clean, healthy living, 'extracurricular activities,' [and] provincially uncritical *mores*" (Warren 227).[1] With Burke's support Light had initiated an irreverent experimental literary magazine *Sansculotte* (its title, derived from a term for French Revolutionaries, was meant to imply the equivalent of "mooning" the genteel establishment), and he published some of Burke's earliest stories and poems in it in 1917. When Burke dropped out of Ohio State after the one semester and enrolled instead at Columbia early in 1917, Light continued to solicit Burke's further submissions to *Sansculotte* and to share news and reading lists: Light reported on Symons, Rimbaud, Baudelaire, and Nietzsche, and Burke offered descriptions of Floyd Dell and Polly Holliday's famous Greenwich Village restaurant.[2]

Now, having arrived in Columbus for his junior year, Light learned that his favorite professor, Ludwig Lewisohn, a German-born naturalized citizen and Columbia University Ph.D. who taught German and had mentored one of Burke's high school instructors,[3] had just been forced from his position on account of his heritage amid the hysteria surrounding American entry into World War I.[4] Lewisohn had introduced Light and Burke to Thomas Mann and other contemporary Continental writers, had contributed to *Sansculotte*, was himself soon to be recognized as a distinguished intellectual, artist, writer, and critic, and already had two books, a play, and several stories to his credit. Outraged, Light wrote Burke:

If you can possibly help me, do so now. I am here at Columbus, Sue and I, and have found on our arrival at the university that Lewisohn and Keidel[5] have been dismissed. All the hate of Columbus, all the disgust—all that wearying deadening killing disgust is upon us. We are in an impossible condition. The place is filled with soldiers, the damn few good course[s] are up the spout—Lewisohn's lyric course of course with the rest. Remember how you have raged here and help me get out. If you can invite me to your home for a few weeks I'll come to New York and enter Columbia. (September 17, 1917)

Burke apparently did encourage Light to come to New York, join him at Columbia, and find living quarters in Greenwich Village, for a week later he and Jenkins were living in New York.[6] Too late to enter Columbia for the fall term, however—he never did enroll—Light by chance fell in instead with a small group of people trying to establish an experimental theatre in the Village. Light, it seems, while looking for an apartment had run into Charles Ellis, an artist acquaintance from Ohio State who had also contributed to *Sansculotte*, and the two took shelter together above a small playhouse at 139 MacDougal Street, near the Village landmarks Polly's, The Liberal Club, and the Washington Square Bookstore. Ellis began to paint scenery for the group, which was beginning the process of moving to larger quarters at 133 MacDougal. For lack of anything better to do, Light began to offer his services as well, first as a general aide and then, later in the year, as an actor. Next Light, Jenkins, and Ellis— and, early in 1918, Kenneth Burke, who had by now resolved to drop out of Columbia himself—moved to a tenement building a short walk from the theatre, at 86 Greenwich Avenue. Frequent visitors were the leaders of the theatre group—George Cram "Jig" Cook, Susan Glaspell, and Eugene O'Neill.[7]

The theater company called themselves The Provincetown Players. Cook and Glaspell, midwesterners fresh from the Chicago modernist scene, had arrived in Greenwich Village and been married in 1913, about the time of the Patterson pageant. Socialists as well as writers, Cook and Glaspell were repelled by the commercialism of the prevailing Broadway theatre scene, then dominated by genteel musicals by Irving Berlin, sentimental comedies like *Peg O' My Heart*, and melodramas like *The*

21

Count of Monte Cristo (which starred O'Neill's father James), so they became active in the little theatre movement then taking shape in Greenwich Village. Taking part of their inspiration from the Abbey Players of Dublin, who visited New York in 1911, as well as from experimental theatres in Paris, Berlin, Chicago, and Moscow,[8] Villagers had patronized The Thimble Theatre presentations of Strindberg and Chekhov in 1911 as well as The Waverly Place Players (1911–12) and the Washington Square Players, who produced plays by Schnitzler, Maeterlinck, Ibsen, Shaw, Strindberg, and Chekhov, in addition to ones by Americans John Reed and Theodore Dreiser, at various Village locations after February 1915. The Washington Square Players even produced Glaspell's *Trifles*, but then refused to offer her spoof of Freudianism, *Suppressed Desires*. Consequently, while living at Provincetown, at the tip of Cape Cod, in the summer of 1915, Cook, Glaspell, and a few of their friends (Reed, Mabel Dodge, Hutchins Hapgood and his wife Neith Boyce, and the anarchist Hippolyte Havel) decided to present *Suppressed Desires* and a few other plays in a small, cooperative, non-commercial setting they called The Wharf Theatre. In the summer of 1916, the group (supplemented now by Reed's fiancée Louise Bryant, Max Eastman and his wife Ida Rauh, and the artists Charles Demuth and Marsden Hartley) experimented with additional plays, and when several of the plays seemed successful—particularly one called *Bound East for Cardiff* by the young man who joined them at Provincetown that summer, Eugene O'Neill—they all resolved to present their plays in Greenwich Village in the fall and winter of 1916–17. During that season the group presented not only *Trifles*, Bryant's *The Game*, and *Bound East for Cardiff*, but also Floyd Dell's *King Arthur's Socks* and Alfred Kreymborg's *Lima Beans*. In two poorly lit rooms of a house at 139 MacDougal, one room set up for the audience, the other for the performers, the Players featured impressionistic set designs by Robert Edmond Jones, a repertory of one-act plays novel in form and content, unpaid performers working at odds with the Broadway star system, cooperative decision-making, and, in the words of the Players' manifesto, "the writing of American plays of real artistic, literary, and dramatic—as opposed to Broadway—merit." In the summer of 1917, the group repaired once again to Provincetown, where O'Neill wrote four more plays, and planned their 1917–18 fall and winter season.

When Light arrived in the fall of 1917 and Burke in the first days of 1918, therefore, the Provincetown Players were in the midst of one of the most productive and vigorous enterprises in American theatre history. The group now included Light, Jenkins, Ellis, the Village sensation Edna St. Vincent Millay, and Millay's sister Norma (who, having arrived late in 1917 with her sister, soon moved into 86 Greenwich Avenue with Ellis, later her husband). Together, and in somewhat larger space at 133 MacDougal, they offered Glaspell's *Close the Book*, O'Neill's *In the Zone* and

The Long Voyage Home, James Oppenheim's *Night*, Max Bodenheim's *The Gentle Furniture Shop*, Cook's *The Athenian Woman*, and Dell's *Angel Intruders* and *Sweet and Twenty*. The creative vigor sustained itself. In the next two years the Players would produce, among other things, Edna St. Vincent Millay's *Aria da Capo*, Edna Ferber's *The Eldest*, Reed's *The Peace That Passeth Understanding*, Djuna Barnes's *Kurzy of the Sea* and *Three from the Earth*, and other plays by Schnitzler and Kreymborg (all of which Light appeared in and/or directed)—as well as their greatest success, O'Neill's expressionistic *The Emperor Jones*, which opened November 1, 1920, featuring the African-American actor Charles Gilpin in the title role. Maintaining their experimental momentum proved difficult for the Players: Cook and O'Neill had a falling out, other members left the group for one reason or another, Cook and Glaspell in March 1922 finally decided to leave New York and visit Greece, where Cook passed away two years later, and no plays at all were produced in the 1922–23 season.[9] But it is still easy to understand why Josephson could claim that during the time when Burke came to live "at 86 Greenwich Avenue the little theatre movement bloomed" (Josephson 42). And it is easy to understand why, recalling the period with pleasure late in his life, Burke could understate, "I got a good education in the drama that way [from the Provincetown Players]" (Rountree, *Conversations*). Though there is no evidence that Burke himself acted in any production, he established or deepened friendships with Players such as Foster Damon, Pierre Loving (whose *The Stick-Up* was produced by the Players in 1922), and Percy Winner (who acted in O'Neill's *Moon of the Caribbees* and other plays in 1918 before going to France and establishing an extensive correspondence with Burke). Burke also remained in contact with Light, who directed many later Provincetown Players productions, notably O'Neill's *The Hairy Ape* (March 1922) and *All God's Chillun Got Wings* (1924, featuring Paul Robeson), and Cummings' obscure, experimental, and sensational *Him* (1928). The Provincetown Players, therefore, might be considered the first group of moderns that Burke was affiliating with in New York.

BURKE AND *THE MASSES*

They were of course not the only moderns that Burke was meeting. Also living at 86 Greenwich Avenue, besides Light, Jenkins, Ellis, and Norma Millay, were Djuna Barnes, a painter, poet, essayist, and playwright who played an important role from 1919–31 among the Paris expatriates[10]; the painter Stuart Davis, who illustrated the cover of Williams' *Kora in Hell* and whose work would appear often in *The Dial* in the early 1920s; and the occasional Provincetown actress Berenice Abbott, who was painting and serving as an apprentice to the American modernist painter-photographer and proto-Dadaist Man Ray, and who was soon to become an eminent photographer herself. Among the other frequent visitors recalled by Burke, Jenkins, and Josephson were Edna St. Vincent Millay; Jim Butler, a young naturalist and painter who had learned about art back home in Giverny, France, from his step-grandfather Claude Monet; and the social activists Floyd Dell, Max Eastman, and Dorothy Day (a reporter for radical periodicals, a sometime companion of Eugene O'Neill, an actress in Provincetown productions, and later the first editor of *The Catholic Worker* and the founder of New York City mission houses).[11]

Day, Dell, Eastman, and Davis all were associated with *The Masses*, Day and Davis as frequent contributors, Day as an acting editor, Eastman (who had studied and taught under Dewey at Columbia) as editor, and Dell (who had known Cook and Glaspell back in Iowa and in Chicago) as associate editor. The famous leftist publication from the time Eastman took over as editor in 1912 until its final issue in December 1917 circulated 15,000 copies on the average each month, copies that cost its readers a dime for 24–30 pages of political commentary, literature, and art (cartoons, lithographs, drawings). Relentlessly socialist in perspective, the periodical can be understood as part of the early modernist revolt against genteel conventions in art, religion, politics, and social mores. Cooperatively owned by the artists, writers, and office workers who produced it, *The Masses* not only championed workers' cooperatives and strikes, but also called for and published working-class art and (countering modernist aesthetes) fostered the conviction that art could be a lever for social change. Eastman, Dell, Reed, John Sloan, Art Young, and the others associated with *The Masses* supported successful experiments in theatre, art, and poetry.[12] They consistently portrayed middle-class capitalists as grasping, hypocritical, and tasteless dupes of the rich, and they ridiculed conventional religion by depicting Christ as a longshoreman or fisherman sympathetic to unions, by encouraging a "new paganism" that looked backwards to a pre-Christian, pre-industrial Dionysian sensuality, and by depicting conventional Americans as overly sanctimonious and industrious rotarians of the sort soon to be satirized in Sinclair Lewis's *Main Street* (1920). *The Masses* circle also shocked the respectably genteel by taking very early to Freud and Freudian psychoanalysis (*The Interpretation of Dreams* was translated into English in 1913). Dell, Eastman, and Mabel Dodge all underwent analysis before 1913 in the belief that it could encourage social amelioration, and Dell even believed Freud to be more important to leftist politics than Marx. They also used Freud, somewhat questionably, to champion sexual liberation: sexual experimentation, respect for the libido, and the pursuit of the "instinctive" and "primitive" (both commonly associated, unfortunately, with African-Americans and immigrants) all were pervasive *Masses* themes.

Ever on the lookout for the new, *The Masses* editorialized on behalf of everything from progressive education, pacifism, and women's suffrage to Emma Goldman's workers' agenda and Margaret Sanger's program on birth control, which was presented as a means of furthering the class struggle. Refreshingly free of dogma, able to laugh even at itself— its masthead proclaimed *The Masses'* resolve "to do what pleases and conciliates nobody, not even its readers," and to help raise funds it sponsored wild entertainments that Dell dubbed "Pagan Routs"—*The Masses* was nevertheless revolutionary enough to become the target of systematic repression. First the keepers of conventional public morality, Anthony Comstock and his successor John Sumner of the New York Society for the Suppression of Vice, tried to get *The Masses* suppressed for corrupting public mores. Then librarians cancelled subscriptions. Finally, the government itself under the aegis of the Espionage Act put Eastman, Dell, Young, and later John Reed on trial in April 1918, and then again in October of that year, for conspiring to obstruct war recruitment and conscription.[13] Both trials blended farce with the spectacular and both ended in hung juries, but because the Postal Service wouldn't handle *The Masses* after August 1917, and because contributors were split over American entry into World War I, the publication ceased in December of that year, to be resurrected in somewhat tamer form as *The Liberator*, and still later as *The New Masses*.

Burke certainly came under the spell of *The Masses* and knew many of the people who produced it. As early as July 1915, Light had advised Burke to "look up *The Masses*" now that he had arrived in the New York City area, to go to the offices and meet Reed and other *Masses* writers.[14] Other letters reveal Burke's intimacy with "Max," with Dell, and with *Masses* articles.[15] And if Burke, who took up formal residence in Greenwich Village only after its final issue appeared, never wrote for *The Masses*, he did publish one of his first poems, a lyric complaint entitled "Spring Song," in a short-lived offshoot of *The Masses* known as *Slate*. A voice of the progressive movement in education as well as of the new literature and art, *Slate* was edited by Jess Perelman, a New York City elementary teacher. In 1917 it offered five issues worth of articles, poems, stories, and drawings by many of the same people who appeared in *The Masses*.[16] Sue Jenkins worked for a time on *Slate*, introduced Burke to "Jess," and solicited Burke's (and Cowley's) contributions; though "Spring Song" and the ironically titled "Hymn of Hope" both appeared in the journal, the equally ironic Burke poem "Revolt" was rejected.[17] All in all Burke was influenced enough by *The Masses* circle that in September 1917, while still studying at Columbia and while settling Light in Greenwich Village, Burke could report to Cowley that he and Josephson were "both socialists now more or less."[18]

Burke Meets Dreiser

November 6, 1915

Dear Malcolm,

Last night I had the fullest hours of my life; I was at Dreiser's. I am not going to write you about all I experienced. It would seem almost like sacrilege to me. You see, to me the evening was an epoch. For all the time I was making my debut, I was wondering if my debut was to be my end. Dreiser was so cold to me, so perfunctory, that I was frightened. It was not until late in the evening that he would even let me talk, to say nothing of paying attention to me. But happily, I was not in bad form, and once or twice I managed to say something noticeable even under these difficulties. One fellow, for example, said that when Mark Twain wanted to think he would lie with his head near the fire. I made the unfair but effective reply that often he did not get close enough. I made the horrible blunder of picking out what Dreiser evidently considers his best work technically as the illustration of a fault. I brought the house down, but I had the good sense to immediately acknowledge myself beaten, although I am still quite certain that I am right. As we neared the end of our stay I managed to worm my way shyly into conversation with Dreiser, but not until I had suffered the painful humiliation of finding myself addressing the air. As he talked I made a very gratifying discovery; you and I could give him kindergarten lessons in convolutions. He calls things subtle which are plainer as Hell—he talks about religion as though it were bread—he admits that the Easterners are in possession of greater brains, greater intellectual development, than the Westerners, and then adds that he cannot understand the more Eastern type, without seeming to be aware of the conclusion that was implied. He says he cannot explain the psychology of a weak temperament, a temperament which is not aggressive. . . .

I did obtain an offhand invitation to come again. From a very charming friend of his I received a cordial invitation to come again. Needless to say, I am brimming over with gratitude for her. She is perfectly able to set one at his ease. It was she, by the way, who read your poem to us—but more of that anon. One of the astounding paintings Dreiser has on his walls is of her. When I saw it I forthwith described her to Mrs. Wilkinson as a cash girl who had read Nietzsche. You can imagine how embarrassed and repentant I was when she made things so comfy for me. She is tall, and judging from the way her clothes hang on her, her body must be exquisite. She is exactly the type of woman Dreiser bestows on his most favored villains. . . .

Your poem was received as I had prophesied. It was neither enthused over, nor was it condemned. Dreiser, who is a great admirer of Masters, said it was the usual waves that one could expect to follow in his wake. But please don't think I am exulting over you. I was very pleased to find myself up in arms to defend you.

26

I am honestly sorry the poem did not make a stronger impression. As I was still being consistently ignored by Dreiser when the poem came up, I did not venture a long harangue in your favor, but we must take the will for the deed. I really think though, that the fault is where I pointed out—you are not dramatic. Before an audience which had no intention stirring itself you would have to be a little more exclamatory. As it was, Dreiser got the impression that you were doing nothing more than imitating Masters. It so happens, from the way you used to plague me with your discussions about trees and all that, that I was able to read you in the poem. But, you see, to them it looked perfunctory. . . .

I hope you can come here for a little while around Christmas. I have a very assertive little Bohemian restaurant to take you to, a couple, in fact. It is done in the futuristic way—its yellow, for instance, is as shameless as that on the seats of the El cars. After being there one must blush to think he was ever moved by the Gonfarone [Restaurant]. Then too, I am dying to show you the city just as a work of art. I cannot express it, it is too sweeping—and thus I want to purchase the consolation which comes of merely showing it to someone who can rhapsodize with me. To be out on the river by the Cortlandt Street Dock about a quarter to six is simply agonizing. Then there is the nocturne I was telling you about by the Latrine of Endymion. Oh, oh! if I ever can express those things with words I shall be proud and impregnable. And the skies—I often wonder if the skies are especially gorgeous here, or if I had not awakened to them in Pittsburgh. In one place Jennie Gerhardt cries because she cannot express such things. I hardly dare to be so confessedly sentimental as that, naturlich, but at times I permit myself to swear most abominably. But I am neglecting my studies.

Kenneth Burke

THE "OTHERS" AND STIEGLITZ'S "291" GALLEY

Of course, Burke wasn't *just* a socialist, for he had been accepted into other modernist circles as well. Leftists like Cook, Glaspell, Reed, Bryant, Dell, and Eastman were associated with the Provincetown Players, but so were moderns of more moderate political persuasion, including the artists associated with the poetry magazine *Others*. The *Others* group and its relation to Burke's poetry will be the subject of the next chapter, but it is worth introducing here the people who produced *Others* from July 1915, just as Burke was arriving in New York, to May 1919, when its final issue appeared, and who socialized together frequently through 1921, when the expatriate exodus distributed them in various places. Just as a flood of experimental verse was emerging from Americans in Britain at the time of the Great War—John Gould Fletcher published several books of poetry in 1913, H.D.'s original lyrics were pouring out at the same time, Pound's *Des Imagistes* appeared in 1914, and Robert Frost's poetry was first published in Britain in 1915—so too a new poetry began to appear in America itself: in Edna St. Vincent Millay's "Renascence" in 1912, in Amy Lowell's annual anthology of imagist poetry from 1915 to 1917, in Edgar Lee Masters' *Spoon River Anthology* in 1916, in Alfred Kreymborg's imagist *Mushrooms* in 1916, and in Carl Sandburg's Chicago poems, among others. Harriet Monroe's Chicago magazine *Poetry* was founded in 1912 to carry experimental verse. To encourage experimental writers in the New York area, Kreymborg in 1913, from an artists' colony in Grantwood, New Jersey, began publishing *Glebe*, a short-lived (ten-month) series of inexpensive editions of plays, fiction, and poetry by Joyce, Pound, H.D., Lowell, Williams, Hueffer, Aldington, and others.

Then in 1915 Kreymborg met a fellow poet, Walter Arensburg, and decided to produce *Others*, a magazine whose title and whose motto ("The old expressions are always with us, and then there are others") suggest their intention to offer an experimental alternative to the poetry of the genteel tradition. Kreymborg and Arensburg had also befriended a New York insurance executive named Wallace Stevens, and, especially because Arensburg was an avid patron of modern art, an informal circle of moderns soon grew up around the three of them that included Williams, Mina Loy, and Lola Ridge (all of whom placed poems in the first issue of *Others*[19]) as well as Man Ray, Marcel Duchamp, Francis Picabia, Charles Demuth, Marsden Hartley, and Joseph Stella. According to accounts by Kreymborg (*Troubadour*), Williams (*Autobiography*), and Munson (*Awakening*),[20] over the next few years "the Others" also included Hart Crane, Robert McAlmon, Malcolm Cowley, Peggy Johns (soon to become Cowley's first wife), Edna St. Vincent Millay, Kay Boyle, Max Bodenheim, Marianne Moore, and E. E. Cummings. "Miscellaneous members," claims Richard Whelan, included Isadora Duncan, Max Eastman, and the composer Edgard Varese (347). The group met informally but regularly for conversations at Mabel Dodge's salon or at Arensberg's home, for picnics at Grantwood, or for parties at Kreymborg's loft on East 14th Street. Not only did various members of the circle produce *Others* and participate in Provincetown Players productions, they also published anthologies (under the imprint of Alfred Knopf), developed an Others Lecture Bureau, and presented their own Others Players experiments in poetic drama. Williams, for instance, appeared in Kreymborg's 1916–17 Provincetown play *Lima Beans* and later wrote some plays for the *Others* set, Loy appeared in some of the plays, and Kreymborg and Millay wrote poetic dramas that were produced in 1918.[21]

Letters from Sue Jenkins and Louis Wilkinson establish that Burke was reading *Others* in 1915, and that Wilkinson was encouraging Burke to meet the members of the *Others* crowd late that same year.[22] Wilkinson reported to Burke on December 19, 1915, that Kreymborg had written, "I am keeping Kenneth Burke's 'Revolt.' It is excellent. . . . [I] should like to meet him one of these days"; and on December 31, 1915, Wilkinson reiterated that Kreymborg wished to meet Burke. Kreymborg never did in fact publish "Revolt"—he scheduled it for an *Others* anthology, but Alfred Knopf refused to permit it to be printed[23]—but he did publish "Adam's Song, and Mine" in *Others* in March 1916. It was Burke's first publication. Kreymborg (*Troubadour* 370), Munson (*Awakening* 36), Thirlwall (William Carlos Williams, *Selected Letters* 44), James Breslin (33), and Donald Hall (27) all place Burke in the *Others* circle. But it was probably on the fringes of that circle. Burke was just eighteen when *Others* began appearing, the members of the community were for the most part a generation older, and his interests after 1920 shifted somewhat away from writing poetry. However, through the *Others* set Burke did establish a number of long-term relationships: with Hart Crane, whose special intimacy with Burke is suggested by Burke's letters to and from Cowley in 1958 (Jay, *Selected Correspondence* 331–35); with Marianne Moore, who worked closely with Burke at *The Dial* and remained in touch after *The Dial* folded in 1929; and, of course, with William Carlos Williams, who exchanged hundreds and hundreds of letters with Burke from January 1921 until Williams' death in 1963.[24]

Several of "the Others," including Ray, Duchamp, Picabia, Williams, Kreymborg, Arensberg, Crane, Demuth, Stella, Cummings, and Sheeler, were also associated with Alfred Stieglitz's famous "291" art gallery, located at 291 Fifth Avenue. (A number of moderns worked in several artistic media: Cummings, for instance, wrote poetry, produced a play and the war memoir *The Enormous Room*, and painted; Williams wrote poetry and plays and fiction, and painted as well; Hartley painted and published poetry; Barnes painted and wrote poems and plays and fiction; Dos Passos published poetry as well as fiction, tried his hand at drama, and painted too; and Burke of course wrote poetry, fiction, and criticism.) Stieglitz himself was born in 1864 in Hoboken, so he was perhaps the oldest of the Village moderns. He was raised in New York and studied optics and photography while living as a bohemian in Germany and other parts of Europe from 1881 to 1890. Upon returning to New York, he helped form the New York Camera Club in 1897, as well as the world's foremost photography magazines, *Camera Notes* and, later, *Camera Work*. He began photographing scenes of New York City life that were increasingly abstract, nonrepresentational, and experimental. In his revolt against realism and in seeking to impose a personal vision on his subjects, Stieglitz was moved by a number of modernist influences: first the members of the late nineteenth-century German and Austrian avant-garde, some groups of which used the term "secessionist" to proclaim their positions vis-à-vis convention; then the Symbolists and their artistic rejection of bourgeois society and their pursuit of emotional states and forbidden topics; Bergson's emphasis on emotion and intuition; and, later, modernist vogues such as Italian Futurism (particularly its celebration of technology), primitivism, and Dadaism.[25] Stieglitz, in short, made photography an instrument of personal expression and experimentation, and he explored the implications of modern painting for photography, and of photography for modern painting.

But it was as a collector of art and as a patron of artists that Stieglitz left most of his mark on Burke and "the Others." He opened his small Village gallery in 1905 as a showplace for modern art—in photography, but also in painting and sculpture—and was soon displaying Rodin and Matisse (1908), Cezanne and Picasso (1910–11), Arthur Dove and John Marin, African "primitives" (1914), and Duchamp's infamous ready-made "Fountain" (a 1917 urinal inscribed pseudonymously "R. Mutt," the name of a local plumber). Just as important, Stieglitz's gallery, like the *Others* gatherings, offered an opportunity for writers, painters, and photographers to converse about their craft. Historians of 291[26] comment at length on Stieglitz's role as a promoter of modern art and on his ability to converse prophetically (and prodigiously) on the possibilities that modern art could realize.[27] Burke's friends Williams (*Autobiography* xii–xiii) and Munson (*Awakening* 47–50) recall 291 as a gathering place for conversation and Stieglitz as someone who would intone for hours on contemporary art. Particularly after Duchamp, Ray, and the Mexican-born caricaturist Marius de Zayas arrived in 1915, and particularly in the magazine *291* (which appeared in twelve issues from March 1915 to February 1916,[28] and which juxtaposed satires, manifestos, and stunning visual and verbal experiments), Stieglitz's circle percolated modernist theory and practice, European as well as American—just as Burke was establishing himself in New York and Greenwich Village.

After the 291 gallery closed in 1917, its pioneer work accomplished, and after *Camera Work* and *291* ceased publication, Stieglitz became involved with Georgia O'Keeffe, who came to New York permanently in 1918. The two married in 1924 and opened "The Intimate Gallery" (1925–29) in order to feature O'Keeffe, Demuth, Dove, Hartley, Marin, and Paul Strand, all of whom were working closely together in a non-commercial art community dedicated to furthering American art. Even before "The Intimate Gallery" opened, and certainly after that time, Burke had through *The Dial* (which employed Paul Rosenfeld as music critic), and perhaps through Williams and Crane, certainly established personal relations with Stieglitz, O'Keeffe, and their friends, and he also knew their work very well.[29] Through Stieglitz and his circle, Burke was immersed in the ferment in modern art that was taking place on the Continent and in America.

THE LITERARY NATIONALISTS

The artistic nationalists that Burke encountered in the Stieglitz circle were also affiliated in various ways with the literary nationalists who produced *Soil, Contact, Seven Arts, The New Republic,* and *Smart Set. Soil* was a nationalistic monthly which operated from December 1916 to July 1917. Founded and edited by Robert Coady, *Soil* aggressively promoted the "young, robust, energetic, immature, daring, and big spirited" aspects of American culture. It printed photographs of steam engines, bridges, and tall buildings, celebrated prizefighting, football, and baseball, defended ragtime, vaudeville, movies, and the dime novel, and published work by Gertrude Stein and Wallace Stevens.[30] In his Whitmanesque catalogues of ready-made American art, Coady "exhorted American artists to strip away every preconceived notion of art that might block the expression of American life" (Tashjian, *Skyscraper* 74).

Burke never published in *Soil,* and I have discovered only indirect references to it in his correspondence.[31] But he was very intimate with what might be called its "successor," *Contact,* the medium through which William Carlos Williams and his friend Robert McAlmon attempted to promulgate a distinctly American art. Williams had been enthusiastic about *Soil,* but he also expressed reservations about "Coady's preoccupation with the surface of American phenomena and came out in favor of exploring their psychological implications" (Tashjian, *Skyscraper* 72). Rather like the artists sponsored by Stieglitz whom he knew so well (as poems like "The Wildflower" and "The Great Figure" indicate, he was extremely close to O'Keeffe and Demuth and Hartley[32]), Williams was a committed artistic nationalist who sought the means to steer American art away from European traditions and conventions and subjects. He and McAlmon insisted on the American artists' need for "contact" with their cultural environment: "We, *Contact,* aim to emphasize the local phase of the game of writing," Williams wrote in an editorial Comment in the second number. "We want to give all our energy to the setting up of new vigors of artistic perception, invention, and expression in the United States." In opposition to Eliot, on the one hand, Williams wished to distance American writers from worn European traditions—from "the classroom" and "the library"—by rooting art "in the locality which should give it fruit" (*Autobiography* 174); in opposition to late nineteenth-century American writers, on the other hand, he stood for "direct, uncompromised writing" indigenous and primitive and new, intensely in contact with the objective, seeable, contemporary

American world (*Autobiography*, chapter 30).[33] From December 1920 to early 1921, Williams and McAlmon produced four issues of *Contact*, the first two mimeographed and stapled together, the last two somewhat more elaborately produced.[34] These issues included essays by Williams, McAlmon, and Marianne Moore, reviews by Pound and Moore, poetry by Williams, Bryher, Mina Loy, Hartley, Stevens, and Kay Boyle—and Burke's essay "The Armour of Jules Laforg[u]e" as well as his poem "Ver Renatus Orbis Est."

The genesis of Burke's friendship with Williams seems in fact to have coincided with the genesis of *Contact*. A November 1920 letter from Josephson to Burke mentions that Williams has "expressed a desire to meet you," and Josephson's *Life among the Surrealists* describes the ensuing introduction (72–75). Williams' first and second letters to Burke (January 12 and 26, 1921) and Burke's first letters to Williams (January 24 and 27, 1921) concern Burke's encouraging words about *Contact* and discuss the possibility of contributions by Burke and Cowley; the January 27 letter also indicates Burke's acquaintanceship with McAlmon and an upcoming meeting "on Friday" at McSorley's restaurant to discuss *Contact*.[35] Williams' letters in February and April also comment on Burke's prospective contributions to *Contact*. And for the next several years in the letters Williams comments now and again on Burke's submissions or on Williams' attempts to get Burke to submit to an international issue of *Contact* that McAlmon was putting together in London (apparently it never appeared).[36] The early correspondence is filled with indicators of Williams' passion for artistic nationalism. He accepted for *Contact* Burke's essay on the French Symbolist writer Laforgue, for example, but with nationalist reservations: "I suppose I am somewhat influenced in my shyness toward Laforg[u]e by a knowledge of what a too close study of his work has done to Eliot—and others, even Pound" (January 12, 1921). He noted as obvious Burke's designation of him as a "Whitmanite" ("Jezus Christus what lightening-like penetration!"—February 24, 1921). He also expressed his misgivings about Burke's respect for the writing of Remy de Gourmont (March 22, 1921), his own admiration for American painters, and his disdain for French literature in general (March 31, 1921): "The two most useful things I can think of right now would be to destroy Freud and the French by some capable Manifesto" (April 27, 1921). Williams furthered his nationalistic goals by writing *Spring and All* and *The Great American Novel* (1923), and in 1925 he brought out *In the American Grain*, a vision of the American past built around Williams' very personal histories of Eric the Red, Columbus, de Soto, Cortez, Daniel Boone, Sir Walter Raleigh, John Paul Jones, Benjamin Franklin, Aaron Burr and Alexander Hamilton, Lincoln, and others, all written in the style of each person as Williams imagined it. In reinventing the American past, in its ridicule of "puritans," and in its characterization of Franklin as grasping and avaristic, *In the American Grain* is in sympathy with the efforts to reinvigorate the American past that were called for by *Seven Arts*'s Van Wyck Brooks.

Seven Arts—another competitor and companion of *Soil*—was founded in November 1916 by socialists James Oppenheim, the editor, and his close associates Van Wyck Brooks, Waldo Frank, Paul Rosenfeld, and Randolph Bourne, the last being the spiritual center of the venture. Brooks as early as 1908 in *The Wine of the Puritans* had anatomized the Puritans as the prototype of the overly industrious, commercial, sanctimonious, conformist, anti-artistic, and anti-intellectual Americans of the late nineteenth century who were still (in Brooks's opinion) dominating American culture. He thereby established the term "puritan" for the moderns as an epithet of anti-genteel scorn. In 1915, in *America's Coming-of-Age*, Brooks continued the critique, blaming Jonathan Edwards, the Transcendentalists, and the Boston Brahmins for inhospitability towards art and for just about everything else wrong with American culture, and commending the simpler, more primitive past that existed in America before industrialization. Then in the April 11, 1918, issue of *The Dial*, Brooks published his famous modernist manifesto "On Creating a Usable Past." In it he attacked the professoriat for "disparag[ing] almost everything that comes out of the contemporary mind" and for "reaffirm[ing] the values established by the commercial tradition [in American literature] . . . that crowns everything that has passed the censorship of the commercial and moralistic mind." He called on Americans to create a new, anti-puritan orthodoxy after the example of writers such as Melville, Dreiser, Whitman, and London—to "invent a usable past" with "new ideals" and "finer attitudes" than those in "our existing travesty of a civilization." Along similar lines, Frank in 1919 published *Our America*, a book whose very title opposed it to the values of the genteel representatives of "their America." *Our America* was a nationalistic call to arms for a new generation of writers and artists—Brooks, Stieglitz, Sandburg, Amy Lowell, Rosenfeld, Charlie Chaplin, and others—who, Frank hoped, could together counter the problems tabulated by Brooks and who might continue the anti-puritan, anti-genteel sentiments Frank observed in Huck Finn, Abraham Lincoln, and H. D. Thoreau. Bourne, a charismatic "cultural radical who wanted to redesign society along socialist lines in order . . . to make it more responsive to the needs of the individual" (Abrahams 35), was disillusioned with European culture even before the Great War broke out. As a critic of culture he vigorously promoted progressive education, women's emancipation, and socialism through a series of books and essays that he published before he fell victim, at the age of 32, to the great flu epidemic of December 1918.

33

Seven Arts promoted economic equality and optimistically heralded the creation of an American cultural renaissance: "We are living in the first days of a renascent period," the first issue proclaimed. Bourne, Frank, Brooks, Rosenfeld, and the others felt they could encourage a new and indigenous American culture that would combine radical politics with artistic experiment. Accordingly, *Seven Arts* published poetry by Frost, Sandburg, Kreymborg, Amy Lowell, and Vachel Lindsay; fiction by Sherwood Anderson (including the first *Winesburg, Ohio* stories), Eugene O'Neill, and Frank; a play by Dreiser; and articles by Rosenfeld, Dell, Dreiser, Hartley, John Dos Passos, Mencken, Dewey, Bertrand Russell, Brooks, and Bourne. Wishing to sever nearly all cultural ties with Europe, *Seven Arts* vigorously opposed American involvement in the Great War; when the United States did join the Allies, in April of 1917, Bourne and Reed continued to publish anti-war articles like "This Unpopular War" (Reed) and "The Collapse of American Strategy" and "Twilight of Idols" (both by Bourne). These articles, however, succeeded only in undoing *Seven Arts*, for the magazine's patron was so incensed by them that she withdrew her financial support. *Seven Arts* passed away, but its principles and personnel, as we shall see, were passed on.[37]

The New Republic became a rival of *Seven Arts* even before America entered the war, for it took a distinctly liberal as opposed to radical approach to social amelioration. As early as 1914 the Villager Walter Lippmann renounced radical socialism and Mabel Dodge's salon in favor of political liberalism and *The New Republic*, whose first issue appeared in November. *The New Republic* remained closely associated with the radical left through 1917—Bourne published a great many essays in the weekly, for instance—but it finally parted ways with radicalism (and hence helped to inspire *Seven Arts*) when it adopted a progressive line, attacked John Reed and *The Masses* group for personal irresponsibility, and firmly supported American entry into the war, on the grounds that the war offered an opportunity for lasting social reform. Henceforth liberal rather than radical, produced in Chelsea rather than Greenwich Village, carrying Dewey rather than Bourne, supporting Wilson and not the Wobblies, *The New Republic* held that domestic tranquility was necessary for social progress. Lippmann, his co-editor Herbert Croly (whose nationalistic *Promise of American Life* had appeared in 1909), and the others associated with *The New Republic* were troubled by the increasing fragmentation of American life, particularly under the pressures of immigration, and by the appalling conditions they observed in the cities. To counter those conditions and to restore a cohesive American culture, they proposed not the solutions advocated by *The Masses* or *Seven Arts*—socialism mixed with personal freedoms, and social and artistic experimentation— but rationalist and scientific control of industrial capitalism and personal self-discipline.[38] A public affairs magazine more than a literary one, *The New Republic* nevertheless remained committed to establishing a vigorous and coherent and anti-genteel American culture, supported civil liberties and free speech during the increasingly repressive 1920s,[39] praised new literary heroes (e.g., Sandburg, Masters, Dreiser, Lewis, Cather), and published numerous articles on art and culture—many of them reinforcing Croly's program for American artistic nationalism (in December 1920, for example, D. H. Lawrence contributed an essay exhorting Americans to follow American, not European, traditions).

Smart Set was as committed to cultural nationalism as *Seven Arts* and *The New Republic*. Its famous editor, H. L. Mencken, came to the magazine in 1908, became co-editor with George Jean Nathan in 1914, and henceforth commuted to New York every third week until the end of 1923. Mencken joined the critics of *Seven Arts* in ridiculing genteel American culture and in promoting indigenous writers who promised to reinvent American life. Taking their cue from Nietzsche's disdain for "the herd," Mencken, Nathan, and the contributors that they permitted into *Smart Set* satirized "puritanism," the "booboisee," and their instruments and institutions: evangelical Christianity, "Comstockery," prohibition, women's clubs, the middle class, and the small town. No admirer of European culture (although he esteemed Shaw, Nietzsche, and many aspects of German culture), the Anglophobic Mencken praised Twain and other users of the American vernacular, published in 1919 his famous *The American Language* (an effort to distance American usages from English rule), and supported realists and naturalist like Norris, London, Stephen Crane, Sherwood Anderson, Ring Lardner, and particularly Dreiser. Dreiser, who may have first recommended Mencken to *Smart Set* and who lived for long periods in Greenwich Village, published his most famous work while closely associated with Mencken: *Sister Carrie* (reissued in 1907), *Jennie Gerhardt* (1911), *The Financier* (1912), *The Titan* (1914), *The "Genius"* (whose publication in 1916 was fought by Sumner's New York Society for the Suppression of Vice), and *An American Tragedy* (1925). Since Bourne, Brooks, and the others members of the Seven Arts group similarly touted Dreiser and other anti-puritan American writers, in one sense *Smart Set* and *Seven Arts* shared an agenda.

But unlike the radical and socialist *Seven Arts* and the liberal *New Republic*, *Smart Set* was more iconoclastic in its politics. For all his admiration for Nietzsche the arch-modernist, Mencken was far from a socialist and more of a politically conservative laissez-faire capitalist. He believed that only an intellectual and cultural elite could change American cultural tastes, and some of the owners of his magazine were members of the wealthy elite. Unlike the idealists of *Seven Arts*, who held that Americans were "living in the first days of a renascent period, a time which means for America the coming of the national self-consciousness which is the beginning of greatness,"[40] and unlike the social and cultural engineers who ran *The New Republic*, Mencken was a realist and pessimist who ultimately lacked confidence that mainstream American life could be fundamentally reformed. *Smart Set*, accordingly, took a somewhat more conservative approach to expressing opinions and publishing literary texts. It took fewer chances than its friskier competitors, maintained a lighter political tone (its subtitle was "A Magazine of Cleverness"), betrayed an ambivalence toward experimental verse (it lauded Pound but carried little free verse), and, more anxious for commercial success than willing to challenge too fervently the establishment, avoided the kinds of political controversy and forbidden subjects that could have aroused the ire of Sumner and his sympathizers. *Smart Set* retained a sharp satiric edge and offered little that could be seen by the genteel as morally uplifting, to be sure—it praised O'Neill and carried Fitzgerald, Lawrence, Joyce, and Cather—but neither did it publish anything sexually frank or politically heretical. Dreiser himself accused Mencken of making the magazine into "a light, non-disturbing periodical of persiflage and badinage, which now and then is amusing but which not even the preachers of Keokuk will resent seriously. It is as innocent as *The Ladies' Home Journal*."[41] The more established *Smart Set* became, the more it seemed to distance itself as much from the rebellious Villagers as from the sober Methodists that it baited so relentlessly. In the first days in 1924, Mencken and Nathan left *Smart Set* for their own new magazine, *The American Mercury*, a less literary and more cultural-political magazine (see the excursus below, "Aestheste, 1925") published by Alfred Knopf, which continued to trade on satiric irreverence toward genteel America for a mass audience well into the 1930s (Singleton).

Burke associated with and knew the work of just about all the literary nationalists, left, right, and center. I have already indicated his proximity to Williams and *Contact*, and there is ample reason to believe that he was well acquainted with *Seven Arts* as well. For example, sometime in January 1917 (precise date unknown), Cowley wrote to Burke about *Seven Arts* and mentioned that he had submitted something to it for publication—unsuccessfully as it turned out; on June 7, 1917, Cowley from France (where he was serving as an ambulance driver) asked Burke to send him issues of *Seven Arts*; Cowley again mentioned *Seven Arts* familiarly to Burke on May 25, 1918; Light refers to *Seven Arts* in a letter to Burke from Columbus (June 5, 1917); and Burke's friend and fellow contributor to *Sansculotte* Nan Apotheker published a poem in *Seven Arts* in 1917. After *Seven Arts* folded, Burke's relationships with the Seven Arts group grew personal. Burke worked more or less amicably with Rosenfeld at *The Dial*, where Rosenfeld was music critic during most of the 1920s,[42] and he corresponded with Van Wyck Brooks and Waldo Frank.[43] Burke in a January 23, 1923, letter to Cowley reports on dinner and socializing with Brooks, who has "been with [Burke] several times lately" and whom Burke calls "an awfully likable man." Burke's relationship with Frank grew close enough, especially under the sponsorship of Burke's close professional friend Gorham Munson, that the two socialized on occasion,[44] and Frank offered compliments and commentary on Burke's writing (some of it still in draft form), advice on finding a publisher for Burke's collection of short stories, and lengthy discussions of aesthetics and metaphysics.[45] Burke clearly was also familiar with the content of *The New Republic* because he spoke of it to Cowley (e.g., August 28, 1921; February 6, 1922; etc.), because Munson's exchanges with Burke mention it, and because Burke in 1930 and 1931 himself published a handful of articles and reviews there, as well as a rejoinder to a *New Republic* review of *Counter-Statement*, after the demise of *The Dial* (Burke's preferred venue) and after Cowley joined *The New Republic* at the invitation of Edmund Wilson in late October of 1929. As for Mencken and *Smart Set*, Burke was reading it even before arriving in New York City, for a Peabody High School teacher had introduced him to it back in Pittsburgh (Parker and Herenden 88). Louis Wilkinson occasionally exchanged observations with Burke about *Smart Set* before World War I, Burke published two of his first efforts in fiction there—"Idylls" (November 1918) and "A Man of Forethought" (May 1919)—and he and Cowley were rejected other times.[46] And the record of his celebrated meeting with Dreiser (see excursus, "Burke Meets Dreiser") suggests how much Burke respected Dreiser, Mencken, and that circle through the end of the war.

But by the early 1920s, Burke was keeping a respectful intellectual distance from the literary nationalists. I have already indicated that Burke's essay on the French writer Laforgue in *Contact* raised nationalist misgivings in Williams. Burke's own misgivings about Williams' nationalism come out in his humorous letter to Cowley of September 12, 1921, a letter concerning a Sunday conversation at Williams' place and some subsequent correspondence in which "Doc answered me in the capacity of a vigorous young American." In his exchanges with Williams, Burke tried to rescue Williams' aesthetics from a narrow nationalism:

For a whole summer, Malcolm, I patiently poured my most valuable discoveries into the sewer. Then recently I sent him some stories, and God bless me if he didn't begin at the beginning again, and complain that they were too cerebral. I was remarkably self-possessed, Malcolm. I counted ten, walked around the house, smoked a pipe, and then sent him a questionnaire. This questionnaire was introduced by rehearsing the above facts about a literary correspondence. Then I wrote down a list of topics to be answered by yes or no, so that in this way no one could accuse him of lacking opinions. Needless to say, the answer was rather sharp. I am now waiting for his issue of *Contact* to appear so that I can write and congratulate him that there is not a cerebral line in it. . . . I have just decided that: 1. His moi and my moi are irreconcilable. 2. Neither of us has gained by our contact, and certainly I have not gained by his *Contact*.

Over time Burke also became impatient with the *Smart Set* and *Seven Arts* groups. As early as March 26, 1916, Cowley could say, "I'll never be any good unless I quit reading Smart Set." By 1921, Burke could write that "you can hardly blame us for ignoring a rampant impressionist like H. L. Mencken.[47] By February 1924 Burke's friend Munson was referring to Mencken's latest venture as "the American Murkwry.[48] And by the end of 1924, of course, Burke himself would be ridiculing Mencken and his *American Mercury* as a co-conspirator in the *Aesthete, 1925* plot (see excursus, "Aesthete, 1925"). In his correspondence with Frank, Burke was respectful but also careful to keep his distance from Frank's aesthetic nationalism and from particular nationalists (in one exasperated moment on November 23, 1922, he called Rosenfeld "damned stupid"[49]). In a late 1922 *Vanity Fair* commentary on Brooks, Burke took issue with his elder's Freudian criticism,[50] and in a carefully crafted letter to Brooks a year earlier, he had already declared his independence—his broad "classicism" in opposition to American nationalism: "If we should rather linger with Matthew Arnold than H. L. Mencken, with Mallarmé rather than with [the American] Louis Untermeyer, that is simply our choice." He found the American artists trumpeted by Brooks to be aesthetically flawed: "We find in them no concern with conscious structure. . . . [Their works] are unripe . . . in matters of presentation, of organization. [They] are written without discipline." In a letter to Cowley (January 18, 1923), Burke restated his opposition to Brooks and Frank and their "skyscraper primitivism" in spite of their personal generosity to him:

Yes, you are right in looking to America as 'a land of promise, something barbaric, and rich.' But alas! I feel that in your admiration (theoretical, gained from Harold Stearns[51] and faugh! strengthened by Matthew Josephson) you have neglected to distinguish between a qualitative and a quantitative richness. Broadway is quantitatively rich; not a single light on it is worth a damn, but the aggregate of so many million lights demands attention. The same is true of our buildings downtown. It is the old fight against mass, a fight which you used to combat along with me: the fight for quality. . . . America is the purest concentration point for the vices and vulgarities of the world.[52]

These sentiments found their way into Burke's writings, perhaps most explicitly in a lead essay in *The Bookman* published in July, 1923 (but completed in the spring of 1921: see Burke to Cowley, May 10, 1921). Entitled "Chicago and Our National Gesture," the article is Burke's most measured commentary on the debate over literary nationalism. In it Burke inquired "whether there is anything exclusively American to represent, any American essence distinct from that of Europe." He concluded:

The characteristic fallacy which our nationalists have made is their confusion between the pioneer spirit and the promise of a distinct national entity. That is, they have taken the unmistakably un-European qualities of a passing phase of our national life as the evidence of a unique contribution which we shall offer as a completely ripe nation.

No such possibility for a distinct national culture exists, wrote Burke. America and Europe are inextricably bound together culturally; "the country itself is developing entirely in accordance with its own possibilities, and these possibilities are almost exclusively European":

The thing I cannot understand is why we should expect America to develop some distinctly un-European art expression. Fighting the same wars, selling the same goods, reading the same books, seeing the same plays, hearing the same music . . . it almost seems incredible that in the face of such normal interchange there are critics who can go on trumpeting the birth of a new culture. . . . Politically, economically, socially, racially, traditionally . . . in almost every consideration we are intimately linked up in the great thought currents of Europe.

The article goes on to explain why Whitman is not always an ideal literary model and to answer those who would blackball writers for not being sufficiently "American."[53]

THE NEW HUMANISTS

It was appropriate that Burke's critique of the nationalists appeared in *The Bookman*, for *The Bookman* was the magazine of the great rivals of the literary nationalists, the New Humanists. Led by Paul Elmer More, Irving Babbitt, and Norman Foerster, the New Humanists shared the modernists' negative assessment of contemporary American art and society and strove to reinvigorate American culture; they criticized the materialism, industrialism, and cultural philistinism that in their eyes dominated the American scene. Like the literary nationalists, they sought a "usable past" that would renew contemporary culture. But unlike the literary nationalists, whose usable past was in the American tradition and who sought to ameliorate American society through forward-looking artistic innovation, the New Humanists pursued the same goal as their sixteenth-century English namesakes: the recovery and rehabilitation of the "timeless" moral and aesthetic values present in classical texts and cultures. Rather like the southern Agrarians who were simultaneously producing *The Fugitive* and *I'll Take My Stand*,[54] the New Humanists opposed the moral and epistemological relativism of many of the moderns and cultivated instead a disciplined natural aristocracy, a cultural elite (Babbitt taught at Harvard, More at Princeton), who might return American culture to grounded aesthetic and moral standards rooted in tradition rather than leaving it to be invented by each new generation. More, Babbitt, and their admirers (one of whom was Babbitt's student T. S. Eliot, who accepted New Humanist essays for his *Criterion* and who once said that Babbitt and More "seem to me the wisest men that I have ever known"[55]) were the original conservative American culture warriors of the twentieth century. Suspicious of socialism, organized labor, artistic novelty, and most contemporary writing, they tried to recover instead pre-Romantic, classical texts and social mores. They even defended the Puritans of colonial America and attacked writers dear to the literary nationalists—Whitman, Dreiser, Sinclair Lewis. As a result, the New Humanists drew withering abuse from the literary nationalists within American modernism, particularly from Mencken in *The American Mercury*, who throughout the 1920s lumped More and Babbitt in with the contemporary "puritans" and scorned their pedantry, prudery, and resistance to the new.[56]

Burke flirted with aspects of the New Humanism in the first years of the 1920s. In the May 1922 issue of *The Dial*, he reviewed sympathetically More's *The Religion of Plato*, which traces Plato's influence on Christianity and combats the sophistic relativism of "man as the measure of all." Burke approved of More's "capacity to touch on permanent standards . . . when his facile contemporaries could see nothing but flux" and avowed "the existence of permanent principles of beauty."[57] Burke also argued New Humanist ideology with his friends—with Light (see Light to Burke, September 27, 1922), with Cowley (on February 5, 1924, Burke claimed to Cowley that More "is more our contemporary than, say, Mencken"), and with Frank:

You are perfectly right in saying that there is one part of me in rebellion against another part. For I have accepted that much of Paul Elmer More: I believe that we should operate in dualisms rather than monisms. The whole modern aesthetic is one of a single channel, of one-mindedness, rather than one of balance. . . . I am really being seduced by More's book [on Plato] after all these months—that there is another type of consistency, the consistency of blocking one weight with another. (Burke to Frank, October 7,1922)

The passage alludes to a central More dogma—the dual nature of the soul, one part fallen and evil, the other part potentially regenerative.[58]

The "rebellion" within Burke describes very well Burke's attitude towards More and the New Humanism. On the one hand, Burke appreciated More's dualism and was yearning for grounded assumptions and fixed standards. Even while his friends were experimenting with the Dada avant-garde (see chapter 5, below), Burke was experimenting with a "new classicism," in stories like "First Pastoral," for instance, that would be equally radical in its opposition to mainstream contemporary artistic practice. In their war with the genteel, Williams and most of the other nationalists rushed to embrace the new. Burke, while equally committed to seeking artistic novelty and while "wish[ing] to war against impressionism and subjectivism [in criticism], Contact, and emotion . . . [and] the lice of H. L. Mencken," turned "quite naturally . . . to the Golden Ages of European literature." "Philosophically," he said, "I turn to Spinoza; critically, to the dogmatism of Aristotle." One of Burke's tutors at the time was Richard McKeon, then a young graduate student working on a dissertation on Spinoza. McKeon had befriended Burke on their ferry rides from New Jersey to Columbia a half dozen years before and now was himself looking to philosophy to find "the scientific foundations of the aesthetic experience" (McKeon 6). Wrote Burke: "The one bright spot in my intellectual life is Richard McKeon, whom I see every couple of weeks, and who is a consolation to me because he *knows* things."[59]

On the other hand, Burke increased his distance from the rest of the New Humanist program even as the movement grew more popular in the increasingly conservative 1920s, particularly after 1928, when More published his *Demon of the Absolute*, Munson his essay on More in *Destinations*, and Foerster his *American Criticism*. Although Burke continued to publish on occasion in *The Bookman*—"A Decade of American Fiction" in August 1929, and "Thomas Mann and Andre Gide" in June 1930—he also remained very independent of the New Humanist program for reform. In the July 1923 issue of *The Dial*, Burke contributed an editorial Comment which praised classicism and predicted the advent of a new "classical era, a turn away from the recent religion of 'pure creation,'" but it wasn't exactly the classicism of the New Humanists: "Classical eras heretofore have always glorified the powers that be. Yet in these gnarled times, the classical spirit would be so inimical to the spirit of modern business that when all its ramifications have been followed through we learn that classicism would be nothing other than howling rebellion. [Classicism] would, in the present state of society, be much more radical than Bolshevism." He also mentioned being "a bit discomforted" by More in a letter to Cowley on February 5, 1924, and elsewhere claimed that "More had not worked out his aesthetic" (Munson, *Awakening* 171). And he contributed to *Aesthete, 1925* which took New Humanism as one of its targets (see excursus, "Aesthete, 1925"). Early in 1930 he was asked by Hartley Grattan to be one of the contributors to the *Critique of Humanism*,[60] a collection of thirteen essays that together exposed various shortcomings of the New Humanism. Burke's essay, "The Allies of Humanism Abroad," contended that "Mr. Paul Elmer More . . . is something to be wrathful about. . . . We should not be forced to conclude that an anti-Rousseau, anti-romantic, and anti-humanitarian policy is required for righting . . . the unsatisfactory elements in the life of today. . . . The loss of authoritarian principles, so decried by the Humanists, may be a healing process, a stage in readjustment, admittedly an impoverishment in itself, as with the razing of an old structure, but necessary to new building" (169, 189). In sum, Austin Warren's 1933 assessment seems accurate:

[His] philosophical turn of mind would seem to relate [Burke] to the New Humanists, who also refuse to report flux; and indeed Mr. Burke has been milder and more temperate in his dissent from the New Humanism [e.g., in *The Critique of Humanism*] than any other of its critics.[61] Like the Humanists, Burke holds that to exonerate art, as "unmoral," from relation to "life" or conduct, is, in reality, to doom it to weakness and futility, while he would dissent from their identification of the moral with the ethic of nineteenth-century liberal Protestantism. (Warren 7)

"THIS YOUNGEST GENERATION" OF MODERNS

An important motive for Burke's desire to remain independent of the literary nationalists and the New Humanists alike was that he felt himself to be part of another generation—the "Youngest Generation," to be precise. On October 15, 1921, Cowley contributed from Paris a lead essay, "This Youngest Generation," to *The Literary Review*, a weekly supplement to the *New York Evening Post*. Cowley's title and topic were meant to be incendiary. His title parodied a well-known essay by the late nationalist saint Randolph Bourne, "This Older Generation," which had defined a "younger generation" in "guerilla warfare" against a puritan, genteel, "older" one, and the article offered, in turn, yet another "youngest generation," an avant-garde setting themselves in opposition to Bourne's "younger" one.[62] Indeed, Cowley's essay is a sort of declaration of independence from the literary nationalists associated with Bourne, Brooks, and Mencken. It identifies "certain characteristics, held in common, [that] unify the work of the youngest writers, that generation which has just turned twenty"—the generation that included Cowley himself, Burke, Cummings, Dos Passos, Slater Brown, and Foster Damon.[63] One characteristic was that they were "not gathered in a solid phalanx behind H. L. Mencken." No puritans themselves, they were "willing to leave this battle [against puritanism] to their elder cousins and to occupy themselves elsewhere"—with "elsewhere" understood to be aesthetic territory rather than nationalist: "Form, simplification, strangeness, respect for literature as an art with traditions, abstractness—these are the catchwords that are repeated most often by the younger writers" (2), who are as likely to be inspired by French writers (like Flaubert or Gourmont) or Continentals (Slavs or Scandinavians) or classic English writers (e.g., Shakespeare, Jonson, Swift) as by American ones. Cowley's manifesto was noticed by

Brooks, who responded directly in his regular "Reviewer's Notebook" column in the issue of the radical weekly *The Freeman* dated November 9, 1921.[64] Brooks paternalistically dismissed "this youngest generation" as artistically naive ("they have no sense of proportion"), artistically ignorant ("present them with a truly magisterial American writer and I warrant they would refuse to look at the man twice"), conceptually preposterous ("from the standpoint of the youngest writers, Mr. Mencken is a back number, while Mr. Dreiser was a back number before the star of Mr. Mencken rose, [and] *Seven Arts* is enveloped in the haze of a middle distance; . . . thus we appear to have had four generations during a period when England, for example, has hardly exhausted one"), and faddishly superficial: "One draught from any spring is enough for them; their stomachs are not stout enough for prolonged potations. . . . It is an incorrigible infantile frivolity that possesses our writers; they digest nothing, they do not even swallow anything, they are like little boys who have eaten too many sweets."[65] Burke, declaring his allegiance to "this youngest generation," then immediately seconded Cowley's riposte in a personal letter to Brooks on November 5, 1921, that I have already quoted. The letter defended his generation's appreciation for the classics and for form: "It is precisely that condition of chaos you ascribe to present America [in *America's Coming-of-Age* and other works] which is leading us to renounce the contemporary gods," wrote Burke. "I can only stress that we are looking for some sound structure; and that we have omitted contemporary guidance simply because it has nothing of this nature to offer. . . . The [American] men we ignore are ignored not because of their popularity . . . [but because] we find in them no concern with conscious structure." Gorham Munson later used the generational analysis offered by Cowley and Burke as a means to organize his account of recent American literature in his 1928 book *Destinations*. The book divides contemporary writers into four groups—the Elder Generation (More and Babbitt), the Middle Generation (Dreiser, Edward Arlington Robinson, Vachel Lindsay), the In-Between Generation (Stevens, Moore, Williams), and the Younger Generation (Burke, Hart Crane, Jean Toomer)—and then discusses their work in generational terms that might today fit the term "the anxiety of influence."

THE LITTLE MAGAZINES: *SECESSION, BROOM, THE LITTLE REVIEW,* AND *THE DIAL*

Munson took up the banner of "the youngest generation" by founding a literary review early in 1922 that would feature their work.[66] Since *Secession*—and its better-known rival *Broom*—are such remarkable publications, and since they were so important to Burke, I have reserved a fuller account of them for chapter 4. But it is worth outlining here how

Secession was indeed invented as a vehicle for Burke and his "youngest" contemporaries, and how through it and through *Broom* Burke became identified and conversant with the modernist avant-garde in America, in France, and elsewhere on the Continent.

Munson, a year older than Burke, came to Greenwich Village after the Great War and befriended Hart Crane, Waldo Frank, and other literary nationalists. He too encountered the Others group, Stieglitz's circle, the little theatres, and the other sources of modernist ferment in New York, and he became acquainted with Burke's writing if not with Burke himself. In July of 1921, Munson went with other expatriates to Paris, where he became part of the Left Bank scene and met Burke's closest friends, Matthew Josephson and Malcolm Cowley.[67] When Munson mentioned his desire to found a literary journal, Cowley provided its concept: it would feature the "youngest generation" of American writers that Cowley had just identified. By the spring of 1922, the first issue of the quarterly *Secession* was in print, its name alluding to the Secession Art Gallery in Vienna, to the "sezession" group of German artists in Munich, to the Secession Club of London poets frequented for a time by Pound in 1909, and to Stieglitz's Photo-Secession in New York, all of these associated with the extreme advance guard in art.[68] That Munson had indeed determined to sponsor the "youngest" group is evident from the list of contributors: Burke, Cowley, Cummings, Brown, and Damon all showed up in one or more issues of the eight numbers that appeared before *Secession* ended in April 1924, and they were joined by close associates of the "youngest" crowd such as Josephson, Robert Coates, Hart Crane, Yvor Winters, John Brooks Wheelwright, Wallace Stevens, Marianne Moore, and William Carlos Williams. Allen Tate and Jean Toomer also submitted work, but were rejected.[69] Josephson quickly became officially attached to *Secession*, particularly to issues two, three, and four, and under his sponsorship French Dada writers Philippe Soupault, Louis Aragon, and Tristan Tzara also contributed experimental poetry. The magazine was produced in Vienna, in order to take advantage of the cheaper printing costs available there, and was distributed mostly in America.

Munson adopted a militant editorial tone in order to cast *Secession* as a prototypical avant-garde publication. In a letter to Burke (February 19, 1922), he wondered about Burke's suggested name for the review, "Massacre," and proclaimed a desire to make it in any case "a hard two fisted affair out for the massacre of imbecilities and any little slaughtering you wish to do will be very welcome at my desk." In the first issue he announced that "*Secession* exists for those writers who are preoccupied with researches for new forms," writers in the generation after Sherwood Anderson, Rosenfeld, Sinclair Lewis, and Untermeyer, and he mocked *The Dial* for being unfocused, old-fashioned, and unadventurous. In the second issue, he placed *Secession* between *The Little Review* and *Broom* on the list of publishers of experimental forms. In later issues he mocked Mencken, Brooks, and *Vanity Fair*. *Secession* was indeed "an organ for the youngest generation of American writers . . . [who] were defining a new position from which to assault the last decade and to launch the next" (Munson, "Fledgling" 31).[70]

Josephson was not the only one who helped Munson on an official basis. In late December 1921, Munson solicited from France Burke's artistic contributions to *Secession* and his "behind-the-scenes assistance" in attracting contributors.[71] Then on May 20, 1922, Munson arrived at Burke's Andover farm fresh off his steamer in order to offer Burke a place among the three "Directors" who together would select contents for the magazine. Among them, Munson, Burke, and Josephson chose nearly everything for issues three through six (the exceptions and the causes for those exceptions will be detailed in chapter 4, below), and Burke was actively involved in setting editorial direction and managing contents.[72] And of course Burke was contributing poetry ("Eroticon," to the third number), a review (to the fourth), and his fiction as well: "The Book of Yul" to the second issue, "First Pastoral" to the third, "In Quest of Olympus" to the fourth, "A Progression" to the seventh. Each issue of *Secession* was short—the longest was thirty-two pages—and its appearance was neat but unremarkable; only about five hundred copies of each number were printed, distributed, and sold. But *Secession* was extremely successful in putting compelling new work into print. In a post mortem Munson summarized its accomplishments:

The stories of Kenneth Burke in which an important theory of fiction is worked to unprecedented discoveries; several poems by Malcolm Cowley which are assured of preservation in anthologies; "Faustus and Helen" by Hart Crane; the verse doctrine of Yvor Winters; a manifesto by Waldo Frank . . . ; these are some of the claims of Secession to distinction. . . . Our clippings recall that in the Little Review jh [Jane Heap] attempted to wreck Secession; the Dial issued a brief evasion of our attack; Edith Sitwell wrote a long commentary in the New Age; Van Wyck Brooks published an editorial on Secession in The Freeman; Louis Untermeyer wrote tentatively and Amy Lowell fearsomely of us in the New Republic; the New York Times ran an idiotic column on its editorial page; S4N raised a racket, con and pro; the Criterion reviewed each number. There were boosts, hoots, or notes in the Double Dealer, American Mercury, Nation, London Mercury, Life and Letters, Playboy, Chicago Literary Times, etc. . . . [It was] the most remarkable stirring-up that any small magazine has achieved in America.[73]

Broom, more distinguished and more famous, was a few months senior to *Secession*. Founded in New York and in Europe during 1921 by Harold Loeb, a former New York bookshop owner with an inheritance that he was willing to put into a new literary venture (Loeb later served as the prototype of Hemingway's Robert Cohn in *The Sun Also Rises*), *Broom* was published in Rome, Berlin, and New York, monthly from November 1921 through November 1923, and then quarterly through January 1924, when it expired. *Broom* sought to publish the most interesting things being produced by the extreme avant-garde, whose members were determined, broom-like, to make a "clean sweep" of the past. It began as something of an American nationalist publication—indeed, its title seems to have derived from a passage in *Moby Dick*: "What of it, if an old sea captain orders me to get a broom and sweep down the decks!"[74]— because Loeb had secured as his associate editor the nationalist Alfred Kreymborg, who was then under the profound influence of Brooks and Rosenfeld and who "deplored the obeisance to Europe prevalent among Americans who aspired to culture" (Loeb, *Way* 7–8). The 1921 issues thus include Sherwood Anderson's "The Contract" and poetry by Amy Lowell, Conrad Aiken, Untermeyer, Lola Ridge, and Oppenheim. When Loeb reached Paris, however, the nationalist agenda was soon overwhelmed by the broader, eclectic versions of modernism in evidence there, particularly after Kreymborg left the magazine after a couple of issues and after Loeb early in 1922 secured as his associate editors the committed Dadaists Malcolm Cowley and Matthew Josephson. Especially during 1922, while Loeb's money supply lasted, and during most of 1923, when Cowley and Josephson had useful ties with the Dadaist and expatriate sets in Europe, *Broom* magnificently packaged some of the most arresting and experimental writing ever produced on the Continent and in the United States for a readership of over 4000 people. With reason, Cowley called it "probably the most interesting magazine which Americans ever produced" (Loeb, *Way* 156).[75]

From the first issues of 1922, *Broom* truly committed itself to excellence and innovation, and its contents included some of the most spectacular and innovative art works of the era: Gertrude Stein's prose experiment "If You Had Three Husbands" from *Tender Buttons*; Dos Passos's story "Two University Professors"; Man Ray's surreal para-photo "Seguidilla"; Picasso's drawings of Stravinsky and of dancers; Joseph Stella's "Brooklyn Bridge"; Fernand Leger's abstract cubist drawings of Chaplin; Virginia Woolf's story "In the Orchard"; Pirandello's *Six Characters in Search of an Author* (serialized over several issues in 1922); Dostoevsky's "Stravrogin's Confession" (a segment of *The Possessed*); Toomer's "Seventh Street" and "Kabnis" (from *Cane*); sculpture by Lipchitz; art by Gris, Gropper, Matisse, Sheeler, and Capek; poetry by Marianne Moore, Cummings, Cowley, Soupault, Crane, Stevens, Winters, and Williams; pictures of Gontcharova's costumes for Ravel's "Rhapsodie Espagnole"; essays on Mayan art, Russian poetry, Dada, and modern music; and a great deal more besides. Quintessentially modernist, ruthlessly avant-garde, *Broom*

Aesthete, 1925

The first issue of H. L. Mencken's much anticipated *American Mercury* appeared in the last days of 1923, breathing the same fiery invective that had made Mencken the most visible satirist of genteel American life in the country. The 128 pages offered no ads or photos, just words: some fiction, four poems by Dreiser, serious essays on Stephen Crane and the legend of Abraham Lincoln, and a series of features—e.g., essays, "Americana" (various bumpkinisms committed in publications from across the nation), and "Clinical Notes" by Mencken and his co-editor George Jean Nathan—that were all designed to poke fun at the Ku Klux Klan, the anti-saloon league, lodge-joiners, Methodists, the habits of university historians, and A. Mitchell Palmer and the Great Red Scare. The usual Mencken targets, left and right. In his first *Mercury* editorial, Mencken promised to "devote [himself] pleasantly to exposing the nonsensicality of all such hallucinations."

But the article in that first issue of *The American Mercury* that most interested Malcolm Cowley, Kenneth Burke, and their friends was Ernest Boyd's satire of a school of "Greenwich Village aesthetes," an extremist coterie, Mencken claimed in the same editorial, who together espoused "transcendental gibberishy theory" far from the artistic "middle ground . . . [where] good work is always done." Boyd, who had come to the United States from Ireland in 1914 and who had been contributing regularly to literary periodicals, including *The Dial*, picked up on Mencken's lead by composing a six-page satire called "Aesthete: Model 1924." The article was designed to ridicule its non-so-fictive subject, "a child of this Twentieth Century . . . [whose] thirtieth birthday is still on the horizon. His literary baggage is small, or non-existent—but he is already famous; at least, so it seems to him when he gazes upon his own reflection in the eyes of his friends, and fingers aggressively the luxurious pages of the magazine of which he is Editor-in-Chief, Editor, Managing Editor, Associate Editor, Contributing Editor, Bibliographical Editor, or Source Material Editor. He can now discourse with impunity about anything, and . . . he has evolved an ingenious style, florid, pedantic, technical, full of phrases so incomprehensible that they always persuade the reader that they must have a meaning."

It all seems harmless enough now. But when "Aesthete: Model 1924" appeared, Cowley was infuriated, sure that the character ridiculed in Boyd's broadside was based on himself (Munson to Burke, January 8, 1924). The character did indeed take after Cowley in certain respects. He "went to Harvard . . . and acquired New Englandism . . . and such other fleshly sins as that decayed city [i.e., Boston] might . . . offer. . . . From the pages of the *Masses* he gathered that the Social Revolution was imminent, . . . [but then] laid aside the adornments of life for the stern realities of a military training camp. . . . By luck or by cunning, he succeeded in getting out of the actual trenches, [and, after the war,] . . . was ready to participate in the joys of La Rotonde and Les Deux Magots . . . and breathe the same air as the Dadaists. . . . The now complete Aesthete returned to New York, and descended upon Greenwich Village, where he . . . under the propaganda and vaudeville department made his first contribution to literature, 'Young America and Yougo-Slavia.'" No one else seemed to identify Boyd's portrait with Cowley alone. Munson found it "entirely imaginary and related to no writer . . . that I could identify" (*Awakening* 186), and Boyd himself claimed he had never even heard of Cowley (Munson to Burke, January 8, 1924). Josephson considered it a composite portrait made of bits and pieces from Seldes, Cummings, Dos Passos, Loeb, Cowley, Frank, Crane, and himself (*Life* 268), and even Cowley in a calmer moment a few years later agreed that it was "based on the early careers of Gilbert Seldes, Kenneth Burke, Edmund Wilson, and Matthew Josephson, with touches . . . from John Dos Passos, E. E. Cummings, myself, Gorham Munson, and Waldo Frank" (*Exile* 198–99). But in December 1923 Cowley was certainly incensed by Boyd's portrait—if not for its all-too-personal references, then because the genre of the fictional portrait seemed to derive from Cowley's own "Young Man with Spectacles" (itself a composite portrait of Josephson, Burke, and Cowley himself) and/or because Boyd insinuated that the aesthetes were unmanly and/or because he seemed to reinforce threats directed at the makers of *Broom* (*Exile* 198; Josephson, *Life* 268) just at the point when they were under fire from the censors (see excursus, "A Great Date in History?" in chapter 4, below).

And so Cowley plotted revenge. At first he contemplated the direct approach: "We must do something. Perhaps someone ought to punch Boyd in the nose" (Josephson, *Life* 268). Next Cowley called Boyd and demanded a meeting so that things could be set straight; when Boyd refused, Cowley "swore a mighty oath and hung up" (Josephson, *Life* 269). A week or so later, Burke, Crane, and Cowley were at Josephson's place, and all took "turns at calling up Mr. Boyd and delivering our poor opinion of his composite portrait and his own character. . . . No one . . . actually threatened Boyd," recalled Josephson (*Life* 269), but Boyd felt threatened and told the world. At that point the affair spilled into the news. With perhaps just a bit of exaggeration, Burton Rascoe in the *New York Tribune* wrote that

East 19th Street swarmed with younger poets and when the venerable Boyd set out on his morning constitutional he was greeted with a fusillade of ripe tomatoes, eggs, sticks . . . and barely escaped with his life back to the house. There he was kept a prisoner for three days while the Dadaists pushed his doorbell, kept his telephone abuzz, scaled the walls to his apartment, and cast old cabbages and odor bombs through the windows, sent him denunciatory telegrams, and rigged up a radio receiving outfit with an amplifier through which they broadcast the information that he was a liar, sneak, thief, coward, and no gentleman. (Portions also quoted in Josephson, *Life*, 269, and in Tashjian, *Skyscraper*, 140; see also Cowley, *Exile*, 199.)

All the publicity was a great help to launching *The American Mercury*, whose sales soared, but nothing much else happened for a while. Cowley was working and trying to keep *Broom* afloat, Josephson was beginning a job on Wall Steet, and Burke went with his family to North Carolina, kept up his writing (among other things, he was completing "Psychology and Form" and "The Poetic Process"), returned in March to work for *The Dial*, and saw *The White Oxen* through the publishing process.

But at last Cowley and his circle of friends found a means to answer Boyd and Mencken. In the fall of 1924 they finally dreamed up the notion of defending their honor by satirizing the satirizers. Late in November 1924 they drafted a table of contents for what they decided to call *Aesthete, 1925*, a monograph which would contain a series of stories, poems, essays, and other contents—"as many amusing stunts as we can think of"—directed at every faction of the older generation, Mencken, Boyd, and Nathan, but also Paul Elmer More, Irving Babbitt, and fellow New Humanists Stuart Sherman and John Farrar; Paul Rosenfeld, Van Wyck Brooks, and Waldo Frank; and the first generation of modernist poets, Pound, Lowell, Masters, and Sandburg (see Cowley to Burke, November 11, 1924, and Cowley to Loeb, December 8, 1924). According to one of the participants in the caper, Allen Tate, "The entire issue was written over a Saturday night in January 1925 and through the following day in a room at the old Broadway Central Hotel in New York. . . . Also present were Slater Brown, Kenneth Burke, Malcolm Cowley, John Wheelwright, Hart Crane, Matthew Josephson, and perhaps one or two others. William Carlos Williams sent his statement by mail" (Tate document in Princeton University Library, January 28, 1942). Harold Loeb, Sue Jenkins Brown, and Hannah Josephson were also present (Loeb, *Way* 241–42), and Isidor Schneider and Peggy Cowley also contributed.[76]

When *Aesthete, 1925* appeared in bookstores in early February, readers got a thirty-two-page, 4-by-7, pamphlet-type publication with an avant-garde, black-and-white cityscape cover by Charles Sheeler. Inside they got an overview from one Walter S. Hankel, the fictitious editor, a retired St. Louis businessman just returned from Europe who put Mencken and Boyd in the same sentence with Calvin Coolidge, Billy Sunday, John Sumner, and Cecil B. DeMille. Hankel also offered a roster of the contributors and a guarantee that every article in the issue would be "in strictly bad taste." Then, in turn, came "Little Moments with Great Critics," in which Wheelwright quoted foolish or nearly foolish snippets from well-known critics and then rated them; "Homage to Walter S. Hankel" by Josephson, Williams, and Tate, with a picture of Hankel by Peggy Cowley and with allusions that devastated Mencken and Boyd; a piece of mock experimental fiction by Brown; "News Clips" (in the fashion of *American Mercury*'s "Americana") ridiculing Rosenfeld, Sherman, Mencken, Sherwood Anderson, and Boyd; Schneider's tally of silly lines of poetry by Untermeyer, Teasdale, Sandburg, Kreymborg, Masters, Lowell, and Robinson; Burke's "Dada, Dead or Alive"; poetry by "Walter S. Hankel"; a mock newspaper story and book review lampooning Boyd (by Josephson); and some bogus advertisements at the end, one of which offered a free issue of Boyd's *Success Talks* ("Be a Critic!") and another (by Burke)

49

Get Self Respect Like Taking a Pill

MENCKENIZE!

WE want smirks instead of piety.

We want to think it is intellectual to drink beer.

We want to laugh at our neighbours.

Who points out for us our national absurdities which are as glaring as electric signs?

Who consoles us if we prefer Stephen Benet to Plato?

Who has backed the rise of our national intelligence from that of a high school junior to that of a freshman co-ed?

It is said that Mencken is shaping public opinion. This is a DIRTY LIE. Mencken is *voicing* public opinion. Mencken's GROWING POWER is due to the fact that God sent him to express OUR AMERICA. That's why we want him.

We are for Mencken, editor and circulation-builder.

Mencken has been called a radical. This is a DIRTY LIE. Mencken is a conservative. Mencken expresses the conservatism of revolt.

Why Mencken is superior to Billy Sunday: Sunday wants us to go to church; Mencken makes it funny to stay away. Sunday wants us to avoid pretty girls; Mencken makes it charmingly naughty to look at the Follies. Sunday wants us to quit drinking; Mencken makes it intellectual to drink.

Up with MENCKEN—Down with BILLY SUNDAY

MENCKEN!

MENCKEN!

Can't you understand modern art?

Let Mencken show you the absurdity of the Ku Klux Klan.

Can't you follow modern philosophy?

Let Mencken snigger with you at William Jennings Bryan.

Did you flunk Trig?

Let Mencken ridicule professors for you.

MENCKEN!

will never betray you.

will never tax you.

will never talk above your heads.

gives you a standard product.

avoids all difficult thinking is for good sound common sense.

makes it clever to see the obvious.

says "damn" in public.

YOU CAN RELY ON MENCKEN

Since he has changed from *Smart Set* to *American Mercury* Mencken can be read without offence by women and children.

Would you like to be a snob without study? Look up Mencken.

Let Mencken cure your inferiority complex.

MENCKEN PROMOTION SOCIETY

"Menckenize," a mock advertisement in *Aesthete: 1925* by Kenneth Burke

that exhorted readers to "Menckenize!" by joining the Mencken Promotion Society. Altogether the magazine amounted to a sort of "Dada fling" (Tashjian, *Skyscraper* 142), an undergraduate (or graduate) student prank. Enough time had passed between the original pretext for the joke and the practical joke itself that the contributors could avoid real vituperation and rancor and concentrate on generating some laughs.

Burke was not eager to participate in the fun and took steps to ensure that it would be relatively harmless. In a letter to Cowley on November 25, 1924, Burke tried to dissuade Cowley from going through with his plans: "I share your hatred of Ernest Boyd, . . . [but] one can answer Boyd only by Boyd tactics," tactics that he did not wish to lower himself to, especially since Boyd had not (Burke felt) specifically attacked him. "I have been much more violently concerned with Benet's nasty remarks on me in *The Saturday Review*." A decade later he explained: "I do not believe Boyd wrote the article with any great degree of malice: he had a good idea for a barbeque. . . . As far as I was concerned, I was very busy when the [indecipherable] offense took place—and even fought [responding to Boyd]" (Burke to Harry Weymer, September 30, 1934; Burke's letter survives only in a draft scrawled on Weymer's letter of inquiry about the *Aesthete, 1925* incident). Burke was also in line for a full-time job at *The Dial* at the time and was therefore eager not to offend the older generation. Thus, "Dada, Dead or Alive" was the lengthiest and most serious item in the monograph. It scolded Waldo Frank for writing an essay (in the September issue of *1924*) critical of efforts to bring the spirit of Dada to the United States, defended "Dada aggrandized," and concluded with a serious (and somewhat aesthetic) statement of the aims and proper subjects of art: "The artist does not run counter to his age; rather, he refines the propensities of his age, formulating their aesthetic equivalent, translating them into terms of excellence. The artist, as artist, is not a prophet; he does not change the mould of our lives: his moral contribution consists in the element of grace which he adds to the conditions of life wherein he finds himself." The unsigned mock ad that Burke wrote to conclude *Aesthete, 1925*, touting in satiric terms the Mencken Promotion Society, urged Americans, after the fashion of *The American Mercury* and Boyd (who in 1925 published a laudatory biography of Mencken), to "Menckenize! Get Respect Like Taking a Pill!":

We want smirks instead of piety. We want to think it is intellectual to drink beer. We want to laugh at our neighbors. . . . Who consoles us if we prefer Stephen Benet to Plato? It is said that Mencken is shaping public opinion. This is a DIRTY LIE. Mencken is *voicing* public opinion. Mencken's GROWING POWER is due to the fact that God sent him to express OUR AMERICA. That's why we want him. We are for Mencken, editor and circulation builder. . . . Since he has changed from *Smart Set* to *American Mercury* Mencken can be read without offense by women and children. Would you like to be a snob without study? Look up Mencken. Let Mencken cure your inferiority complex.

The response to *Aesthete, 1925* was favorable enough that the group contemplated developing another, more serious follow-up. The six hundred copies that came off the presses early in February were celebrated at a party at Giovanni Squarcialupi's Italian restaurant (popular because it served wine with meals, Prohibition be damned), and disappeared quickly (Josephson to Burke, February 6,

1925). Perhaps two hundred copies were sent to old *Broom* subscribers who had never received full value for their subscriptions (Cowley to Wheelwright, February 18, 1925). Josephson then organized a meeting in March to arrange another issue, and Burke sent a statement (he couldn't attend personally) proposing that everyone produce a body of copy together and send it to Jane Heap at *The Little Review*; if she refused to publish everything, Burke offered, then the group could just go ahead on its own. But for whatever reason, the idea never materialized (Burke exchange with Josephson, March 14, 16, 20, 1925; Tate to Burke, March 21, 1925), and *Aesthete, 1925* died after just the one number. Walter Hankel lived on mostly only in the minds of "the aesthetes," his only subsequent appearances being in two other tongue-in-cheek ventures, *Whither, Whither, or After Sex, What? A Symposium to End Symposiums* (1930), and "New York: 1928" (Brown et al. 1928), with Burke contributing to both.[77]

The *Aesthete, 1925* story is an amusing one, but it's not *only* amusing. The tale also illustrates "the failure [of Americans] to engage an American Dada. Dada did not return to America during the 1920s as a movement quite possibly because it was never a movement in Europe. But far more decisive a factor in the failure of Josephson's program for contemporary American literature was the lack of agreement among friends. They were united solely by their commitment to literature, their animosity toward established critics, and a general interest in formal literary values" (Tashjian, *Skyscraper* 142). And the episode says something about Burke's personal and intellectual commitments at the time, particularly with respect to modernist ideologies. On the one hand, Burke generally agreed with the dismissive stance that his elders—both the New Humanists and the literary nationalists—took toward conventional society, and he shared their wish for a more vigorous American culture. But on the other, as a member of "the youngest generation" he also defined himself against his elders and in support of novelty, experimentation, innovation, and internationalism.

---

sought to ally itself with everything new—cinema, skyscrapers, jazz, advertisements. Even the covers contributed to the effect: designed by a variety of artists, they

> constitute an anthology of modernist styles . . . from the cool phenomenological intimacy of Alice Halicka's domestic scene to the warm tones of Edward Nagle's cubist collage . . . to the austere but playful abstraction of the three-dimensional numbers and letters arrayed in space in El Lissitsky's constructivist-influenced cover . . . [to] the most famous cover, [by Edward Gordon Craig, for the February 1922 issue, in which] a sexually ambiguous figure, stylistically evoking both contemporary taste and primitive myth, sits on its haunches and thumbs its nose at tradition and bourgeois values. (Nelson, *Repression* 923)

Magnificently produced on oversized, beautiful paper with wide margins, juxtaposing the already-nearly-canonical artist with the unknown, each issue of *Broom* was an art object itself—as arresting and unfixed and exploratory as modernism was itself in 1922.

Burke followed *Broom* closely from its inception. From the beginning he kept up a spirited correspondence with both Cowley and Josephson about the contents of the magazine.[78] He took up the invitation of his friends and contributed his work to *Broom*: "The Olympians" and "The Book of Yul" were rejected in September 1921 (*Broom* Files, Princeton; Cowley to Burke, September 28, 1921); "My Dear Mrs. Wurtelbach" was accepted in November 1922 for the January 1923 issue; and "Prince Llan" appeared in the final issue, in January 1924. (Indeed, a passage describing copulation in the most abstract terms and references to "breasts [that] stood out firm like pegs" and "sitters [that] undulated" in "Prince Llan" may have been the cause of *Broom*'s suppression by the United States Postal Service, a development that contributed to the final demise of the magazine.) Burke wrote to Loeb late in 1922 to congratulate him for Loeb's *Broom* essay "The Mysticism of Money," and the two then exchanged other letters on the contents of *Broom*; they probably also met in New York in January 1923 to discuss *Broom*'s future prospects (Cowley to Burke, January 6, 1923). Burke was cited by Loeb in his August 1923 history of *Broom* as among the new writers that *Broom*, like *Secession*, was then committed to championing (*Broom* 5.1: 55–58). Burke was also among those who frequented the American offices of *Broom*, staffed by Lola Ridge and her assistant, Kay Boyle: the two held open houses each Thursday afternoon and one evening a month at the *Broom* offices at 3 East 9th Street.[79] Burke was one of the contributors to *Aesthete, 1925*, which was conceived in part as a continuation of *Broom* (see excursus, "Aesthete, 1925"). And finally, when *Broom* was winding down, when Loeb, now broke, had in 1923 entrusted it to Josephson and Cowley to run as they saw fit and Josephson and Cowley had returned to America, Burke was among those who were included in the small group of people charged with keeping the magazine afloat. As I say, some of the details of these activities will be fleshed out in chapter 4; what is relevant here is that through *Broom* and *Secession* Burke became intimate with the theory and practice of modernism.

Through *Broom* and *Secession* and *The Dial*, that is. For even while he was closely involved with *Broom* and *Secession*, Burke was even more intimately involved with an even more important modernist magazine, *The Dial*, a connection I consider at length in chapter 5, below. During those marvelous years of 1922 and 1923, years when Burke was publishing his fiction and criticism everywhere and earning a reputation as "the most formidable of the younger Americans" writing then,[80] and for most of the remainder of the decade, Burke was affiliated in several ways with what he called at the time "the one magazine in America where the study of letters may occasionally be pursued in public" (Burke to Cowley, February 21, 1924), and what he later remembered as "a magic place, just wild, a transcendent place" (Rountree, *Conversations*): *The Dial*. Beginning in 1920 he placed several stories there, and in 1928 and 1929 he serialized a half-dozen sections of *Towards a Better Life* in *The Dial*. He also published much of his criticism there; Wasserstrom, in fact, calls Burke *The Dial*'s "representative critic" (115) on the basis of "Psychology and Form," his essays on Gourmont and Flaubert, and the score of reviews he published there. Burke also translated a great many things for publication in *The Dial*, including Mann's *Death in Venice* and other stories, a section of Spengler's *Decline of the West*, and works by Hugo von Hofmannsthal, Stefan Zweig, Arthur Schnitzler, and a number of others. And he worked on and off at *The Dial* in a number of production capacities—as an assistant editor from 1922 to 1925, as acting managing editor (in 1922 and 1923), and as acting editor (while editor Marianne Moore vacationed in 1925, 1926, and 1927). From the fall of 1927 until the demise of *The Dial* in July 1929, Burke served as its music critic, an office which gave him an opportunity to write about Stravinsky, Ravel, and Toscanini, Gershwin and Copland and The Hall Johnson Jubilee Singers, as well as new music from the continent. For his various contributions to literature, criticism, and the arts he was given the eighth Dial Award; previous winners had been Sherwood Anderson (1921), T. S. Eliot (1922), Van Wyck Brooks (1923), Marianne Moore (1924), E. E. Cummings (1925), William Carlos Williams (1926), and Ezra Pound (1927).

The Dial in the 1920s was in some ways a better heeled, more respectable relative of *Seven Arts* and *The Little Review*. Not that it was an absolutely brand new publication: *The Dial* had been published in Chicago from 1880 to 1918 as a weekly and fortnightly review of art, politics, and opinion. In 1916 its editor set it on a more liberal, even radical course in politics and the arts, presenting Randolph Bourne, John Dewey, Thorstein Veblen, and Charles Beard, spirited debates on *vers libre*, little theatres, the war, the League of Nations, and Erik Satie, and publicity for Reed's *Ten Days That Shook the World* and Trotsky's *The Bolsheviks and World Peace*. In mid-1918, in the aftermath of the demise of *Seven Arts*, new managers and financial backers brought the financially struggling journal to Greenwich Village. Two of those backers were Scofield Thayer and Sibley Watson, wealthy recent Harvard graduates who had been contributing to the magazine (despite some political misgivings) while it was still in Chicago. Thayer, whose uncle Ernest wrote "Casey at the Bat," was an enthusiast and patron of Joyce; Watson was a medical student with interests in avant-garde film and poetry. When financial exigencies at *The Dial* only intensified in New York, Thayer and Watson purchased the magazine late in 1919, determined to excise the politics from the magazine and to establish it as a leading modernist monthly magazine of the arts, no matter the cost.

At first *The Dial* drew on the *Seven Arts* tradition. Thayer and Watson apparently had hoped originally that they could save *Seven Arts* (which finally was officially absorbed by *The Dial* when it folded in 1917) or that Bourne might be the first editor of a new *Dial* (Joost, *Dial* 187), and their first issue of the new magazine in January 1920 opened with a tribute to Bourne and a story by him. Alyse Gregory, a close friend of Bourne's, was appointed assistant and later managing editor. The new owners also named Rosenfeld as music critic, published *Seven Arts*'s other leaders Brooks and Frank, and soon reviewed works by Brooks and Frank and Oppenheim.

The new *Dial* quickly outgrew *Seven Arts*, however. From its beginning it looked more like an elegant and less political *Little Review*, given its internationalism and its patronage of new poetry, experimental theatre, and modern art; and in fact the history of *The Dial* and *The Little Review* was intertwined until they both ceased publication in mid–1929. Margaret Anderson, the editor of *The Little Review*, learned her trade working for the old *Dial* in Chicago, and in 1914, supported by Frank Lloyd Wright, Emma Goldman, Floyd Dell, Ezra Pound, and other moderns, she founded her own quarterly in order to sponsor "the best conversation the world has to offer" (Anderson, *My Thirty Years' War* 35) on avant-garde works and causes—Futurism, anarchism, Bergsonism, imagism. In 1917 Pound officially became foreign editor, and Anderson and her associate Jane Heap moved to Greenwich Village, where they continued to publish— on a shoestring—criticism of books, music, art, and theatre, as well as poetry and some art and fiction, until they moved on to Paris at the end of 1921. During those years in New York *The Little Review* consistently printed Pound, Joyce, Wyndham Lewis, William Butler Yeats, and Eliot, and reproduced Brancusi's sculpture, among many significant other items. In 1918 Anderson and Heap began serializing Joyce's *Ulysses*, a move which got *The Little Review* into some celebrated trouble with New York censors. *The Little Review* also published Burke's stories "David Wasserman" (in the fall of 1921) and "The Death of Tragedy" (fall 1922), as well as two Burke translations in 1925 and 1926; and Burke was an interested follower of the magazine throughout its Chicago, New York, and Paris phases until it failed in May 1929.[81] After Thayer and Watson purchased *The Dial*, they published many of the same people appearing in *The Little Review*—Sherwood Anderson, William Carlos Williams, Djuna Barnes, Marianne Moore, Brancusi, Eliot, Pound, Ford Madox Hueffer, Wyndham Lewis, Burke, and Joyce had all appeared in both magazines by the end of 1921—but *The Dial* was far better financed and avoided the experimental literary oddities and the liberal politics of *The Little Review*.

By paying contributors handsomely and by sparing no expenses on production, Thayer and Watson succeeded in attracting wonderful contributions, particularly in the first half of the decade. (In 1925, when Watson went to Rochester and Thayer to Europe, its contents became markedly less exciting.) For the first four years of the decade, from January 1920 through to the end of 1924, *The Dial* offered its many readers unmatched excellence in about a hundred pages per issue: Eliot's "The Waste Land," Cummings' "Buffalo Bill's defunct" and "In just spring," several cantos by Pound and an excerpt from "Hugh Selwyn Mauberly," Sandburg's "Jazz Fantasia," Yeats's "Easter 1916" and "The Second Coming," Marianne Moore's "Picking and Choosing,"[82] Stevens' "The Emperor of Ice Cream," "Bantams in the Pinewoods," and "Hightoned Old Christian Woman," Rimbaud's *A Season in Hell* and *Illuminations*, and a great deal of other poetry, including works by Williams, H.D., and Kreymborg. Excerpts from autobiographies by Yeats and Anatole France appeared over several issues, alongside Pirandello's play "The Man with a Flower in His Mouth," Sherwood Anderson's "I'm a Fool," Mann's "Tristan" and *Death in Venice*, Lawrence's novella "The Fox," an excerpt from Woolf's *Mrs. Dalloway*, other work by Woolf, and more fiction by Dos Passos, Conrad, Valery, Gorki, Unamuno, Schnitzler, and any number of others. Also featured were art reproductions of Demuth, Van Gogh, Picasso, Marin, Wyndham Lewis, Matisse, Chagal, Cummings, O'Keeffe, Cezanne, Gauguin, and Lachaise; reviews of Bergson (by Slater Brown), Virginia Woolf (by Burke), *Ulysses* (by Eliot: "I hold this book to be the most important expression which the present age has found"), Moore (by Eliot), and Eliot (by Cummings and Moore), as well as of Cook's *The Provincetown Plays*, Chaplin, *The Cabinet of Dr. Caligari*, Al Jolson, Stein, Stokowski, Pirandello, Hemingway, and jazz; and essays such as Spengler's "Decline of the West" and Edmund Wilson's explication of "The Waste Land," others by Pound, Santayana, Hesse, Yeats, and Bertrand Russell, and still others on Dada, baseball, London (by Ford Madox Hueffer), and other subjects. Obviously its contents were diverse and eclectic; the magazine stood for no specific school, although the artists associated with Alfred Stieglitz were frequently reproduced and the poets Williams, Moore, Cummings, Eliot, Stevens, and Crane were frequently published. Just as obviously, *The Dial* concentrated on publishing relatively well-known and established writers and artists somewhat at the expense of turning up new talent, and it was clearly politically conservative during a conservative, censorious decade, despite its *Seven Arts* heritage and in contrast to the liberal *Little Review*.[83] Not only was political discussion missing from the pages of *The Dial*, but its criticism tended toward the aesthetic, emphasizing not the cultural contexts of a work but its aesthetic characteristics, especially "form"; not the social effects of literature but the aesthetic impact and significance of the isolated, autonomous art work as encountered by the isolated individual. In these senses some of the criticism of *The Dial* in *Secession* was justified.

But what *The Dial* was mostly was thrilling. Even now, seventy-five years later, the contents of each issue are exciting. Like *Broom*, *The Dial* was a work of modern art itself, particularly of what has come to be known as "high" modern art, art that is aesthetically self-conscious and formally sophisticated and innovative. Through *The Dial*, then, and through his other contacts—this is no exaggeration—Kenneth Burke became one of the best informed students and practitioners of modernist art in the world. Before the end of World War I Burke was already part of a web of interrelated groups that together through their written and oral, artistic and nonartistic, formal and informal exchanges composed the modernist conversation in Greenwich Village. Through periodicals like *The Masses*, *Slate*, *Seven Arts*, *291*, *Soil*, and *Smart Set*, through the plays of The Provincetown Players and other experimental theatre groups, through Stieglitz's art gallery and the Others group picnics, Burke and the other New York moderns discussed politics, poetry, sculpture, music, fiction, and their interrelationships.

CONVERSATIONS IN GREENWICH VILLAGE

Greenwich Village in 1918 already had a reputation as an intellectual haven and artistic bohemia, famous for Mabel Dodge's salon and for the political societies and meetings, bookstores and art galleries, teahouses and restaurants that all traded heavily on Villagers' needs for talk about politics and art. Burke patronized The Dutch Oven and Polly Holliday's restaurant and the cafe in the Brevoort Hotel, gathering places proximate to the Provincetown Playhouse and the Liberal Club and Washington Square Book Shop, places as celebrated and as important as the Dome and Rotonde were to expatriate Parisians. He no doubt frequented Arensberg's studio as well as Stieglitz's, and certainly he indulged in small talk at Masses parties and at O'Neill's hangout, the Hell Hole bar (Josephson, *Life* 64–65), and listened to lectures at the Liberal Club. Burke also watched as new publishers emerged to take advantage of the modernist ferment: Maxwell Perkins became an editor at Scribner's in 1914 (a position he held until 1947); Harcourt, Brace, founded about the same time, later brought out Burke's *Counter-Statement* and *Towards a Better Life*; Boni and Liveright (the Boni brothers owned the Washington Square Book Shop) published *The White Oxen, and Other Stories* and invented The Modern Library, which later included Burke's translation of

Death in Venice; and Alfred Knopf in 1915 began publishing a variety of
experimental moderns—O'Neill and other Provincetown Players, Pound,
Gibran, Eastman, Langston Hughes, James Weldon Johnson (Munson,
Awakening, chapter 10). In short, Greenwich Village before 1918 was
a residential island in New York of about 45,000 people (Ware 19),
an intellectual and artistic bohemia at once a part of the most vibrant
American city—two million of the five million residents of New York City
were immigrants, many of them constructing bridges and subways or the
Flatiron or the Woolworth or the Singer or some other skyscraper—and
yet separate enough from it (an improved Seventh Avenue and the West
Side Subway connected the Village with the rest of the city only after
1917) to permit its citizens to discuss openly and freely sexual *mores*,
women's rights, birth control, Freud, leftist politics, trade unionism, and
experimental art. Most people lived cheaply in small rooms or apartments
in tenements or converted houses on crooked, intimate old streets, all of
which encouraged people to congregate and converse together in parks
and bars and tearooms and other public spaces.[84]

After the Great War the talk continued, though not so frequently
about politics in a Village disillusioned by the war and its aftermath,
and by the turn to the right in national political affairs. In the leading
modernist magazines, *Broom* and *The Dial* and *The Little Review*, in
more mainstream publications like *The New Republic*, *Vanity Fair*, and
The American Mercury, and in more fleeting publications such as *Contact*,
Secession, *1924*, *S4N*, and *The Freeman*, versions of modern art were
presented, defended, and debated. When many of the moderns went off
to Paris and Berlin, they stayed in touch with people back in New York
through extensive correspondences. Prohibition seems to have been one
motive for the expatriate exodus, but in fact Prohibition seems to have
only driven the bars and restaurants of Greenwich Village underground;
speakeasies and Italian restaurants serving wine especially flourished after
the New York State Enforcement Act was repealed in 1923. "Talking
and tippling clubs" (as Burke called them) gave people an opportunity
to get together for literary and critical exchange; one that met weekly
in the winter of 1924–25 included Burke, Wilson, Toomer, Kreymborg,
Brooks, and Lewis Mumford (letter to Wheelwright, September 9, 1927),
and another the previous winter included Burke, Cowley, Brown, Crane,
Tate, Josephson, and Wheelwright (Josephson, *Life* 290; Bak 328–31).[85]
Occasions to organize more formally may have become less political, but
they were no less frequent—witness, for instance, the interest in G. I.
Gurdjieff's Institute for the Harmonious Development of Man, a mystical
group which interested Munson, Toomer, Crane, Frank, and Margaret
Anderson in the mid-1920s. Parties at Lola Ridge's place succeeded Mabel
Dodge's salon even before Ridge began working for *Broom* in 1922–23;

at one of them Thayer met Marianne Moore, and at another Williams and McAlmon hatched the idea for *Contact* (Williams, *Autobiography* 173). Alyce Gregory held many parties at her apartment on Patchin Place, too, and in December–April of 1923–24 and 1924–25 Thayer held a series of spectacular dinners to encourage discussion on the modernist cause.

Weekend parties at Burke's farm at Andover were opportunities to continue the talk. Burke bought the place as a way to avoid escalating prices in New York and to steer himself and his family clear of urban pollution. Early in the spring of 1922 he purchased about seventy acres of land with a dilapidated house for about $1500, which he gradually fixed up and paid off with royalties from his writing and with his salary from *The Dial*. The farm offered a lifestyle not unlike the ones Burke had enjoyed in 1919, when the newlywed and his wife spent the summer subsisting on the land near Candor, New York; or in 1920, when they spent the summer in rural North Carolina, with Lily's family; or in 1921, when the Burkes and Josephsons went to very rural Monson, Maine, for the summer rather than to Paris (Josephson, *Life* 67–72). For that matter, it was a life that Lily had come to appreciate in rural North Carolina, where her family gave her a love of the outdoors (Wheaton 166), and a life that Burke had enjoyed since his childhood, when he and Light and Cowley would retreat in the summer to the Cowley family farm in the village of Belsano, Pennsylvania, near Altoona (Cowley, *Exile*, chapter 1). Nor was the notion unique to Burke, for his friends were re-treating to Woodstock, New York, Sherman, Connecticut, Provincetown, Massachusetts, and Croton-on-Hudson, New York, all in an effort to correct the alienating aspects of urban life and to sustain creative vigor.[86] But Andover was no hermitage. Burke commuted a great many days to his various jobs in New York, either to *The Dial* or to the Laura Spelman Rockefeller Memorial Trust (where in 1926 and 1927 he did research on drug addiction and ghostwriting for Colonel Arthur Woods) or to the Bureau of Social Hygiene (where in 1928 and 1929 he did research for Woods on criminology). Often he maintained a room in New York City so that he could stay in the city for days, commuting back to Andover on weekends. And of course he was constantly inviting friends to join him and Lily at Andover. By the end of 1928 they had bought additional land, dammed a creek to create a lake deep enough for swimming and diving, built a tennis court, expanded the house, and added some outbuildings, to accommodate for the night or the weekend Williams, Brown, Cowley, Crane, Munson, Wheelwright, Josephson, Tate, or anyone else who might want to visit.[87] The "agro-bohemian Burkes" (as Burke customarily called them) would share with their guests the simple but bountiful provisions of their extensive garden, provide rice wine or other spirits, and for hours enjoy conversing with and about the moderns. "By owning a roof over his head and planting a kitchen garden, [Burke] the penurious man of letters could render his life both more salutary and more dignified; the severe economies of the rustic life would also enable him to gain more time for the serious pursuit of his art," wrote Matthew Josephson. "[Burke's] reports fairly glowed with the joy of life in that season of pioneering; soon his friends came for weekends to the green hills of New Jersey to inspect his gardens, the new-sown lawns, and the siding of fresh shingles he and his wife had provided for their old house. . . . Kenneth, moreover, hoped that in time several of his friends would help colonize his corner of rural New Jersey, for he could not live without conversation" (*Life* 301).

From the time that he took up residence in Greenwich Village, in the first days of 1918, until, a decade later, he was formally recognized by *The Dial* as one of the most important writers and critics of the time, Kenneth Burke was a full participant, a central participant, in the written and oral and artistic exchanges that comprised the modernist dialogue. He was widely, perhaps uniquely, attuned to a variety of schools of modernist ideology, from the political left, right, and center, from radical artistic experimentalists to those who wished to keep in touch with some literary past, from nationalists to internationalists, from artists to dramatists, musicians to poets, storytellers to critics. "From now on begins my academic career," he wrote to Cowley on January 6, 1918, in a letter announcing his withdrawal from Columbia. "The time has come for study." Burke was determined to educate himself through full immersion into the culture of modernism in Greenwich Village and then to write himself: "I shall get a room in New York and begin my existence as a Flaubert. . . . I don't want to be a virtuoso, I want to be a—a—oh hell, why not? I want to be a—yes—a genius. . . . I am in it for life and death this time. Words, words—mountains of words. If I can do that I am saved." Thirteen years later, as the next chapters will show, Burke had arranged those mountains into poetry, fiction, and criticism thoroughly animated and interanimated, in tenor and technique, by modernism.

3

Burke among Others:
The Early Poetry

Burke's letter to Cowley on January 6, 1918, was not the only place where he announced his intentions. Burke's mother was visiting relatives back in Pittsburgh at the time of his decision, and because she very much wanted her son to complete his college degree, Burke a day later felt compelled to explain himself to her as well:

Sorry, Ma, awfully sorry you know, but I must get out. It is time now for me to quit college and begin studying. For the fact is that the modern American college is hardly more than a distraction. I have learned that from going to the best one in America—and it is the one valuable thing which I have learned. My Latin, French, and German are all in good shape; I can do more in them by myself than with all the niggling and dallying that one goes through at a university. . . . God forgive us, but it is worth taking poison to get out of a mathematics course. . . .

No, it is time for me to start in a new direction. I want to get off by myself . . . and write like a demon. One must give all his energy, all his time, all his prayers, all his life-blood, to art if he is going to succeed at it. I am diffident, thoroughly distrustful of myself, but I am going to give it a trial. That is why I want to leave school.[1]

What Burke would "begin studying" in preparation for a writing career, of course, was what he had already been studying for several years: the modern writers and artists he had been reading and hearing about since high school in Pittsburgh and classes at Ohio State as well as at Columbia—particularly Continental writers like Mann and Flaubert, the French Symbolist poets, and the Anglo-American poets whose verse was patterned after the Symbolists. While still at Peabody High, Burke had already been part of a set that included Cowley, Jenkins, and Light and that prided itself on familiarity with Strindberg, Schnitzler, Shaw, Dostoevsky, and Ibsen. At Ohio State with Jenkins and Light in early 1916, under the tutelage of Ludwig Lewisohn, he translated Mann and

Flaubert and read Baudelaire and Nietzsche, Symons and Rimbaud, Mallarmé and Anatole France. Before and after studying at Ohio State he was reading and imitating French, English, and American practitioners of free verse.[2] And at Columbia he read Bergson and experimental poetry of various kinds. That Burke on moving to Greenwich Village referred to himself as "a Flaubert" was no accident, since Flaubert was the premier amongst a set of Continental writers whom he and many others associated with modernism. Despite his employment of certain realistic techniques, Flaubert was considered the prototypical modernist in fiction on account of his daring subject matter and his eschewing of moralizing rhetoric. By pursuing art for its own sake and modeling a bohemian lifestyle dedicated to the pursuit of art, Flaubert offered an example not just to Burke but to many young writers pursuing a modernist bent.

Burke's independent study was not confined to books or to the Continentals, however, for by moving to Greenwich Village Burke was gaining primary access to many of the most prominent American moderns, most notably those associated with the Provincetown Players, *Others* magazine, and the Stieglitz circle. Those groups were committed to serious study of drama, poetry, fiction, photography, music, sculpture, and painting, and to innovative productions within those genres in a uniquely American mode. Before 1920, then, Burke was taking up a conscious plan for self-study and literary practice—particularly poetry, at least at first—that was designed to make him not just conversant but fluent in the linguistic, theoretical, and artistic practices of European and American modernism.

The Others, under the leadership of Walter Arensberg and Alfred Kreymborg, were especially important to Burke, who was himself writing mainly poetry in the years 1915–18, the period of the Others' greatest reach. A product of the set of writers and artists centered around Arensberg's home, Kreymborg's Greenwich Village loft, and his Grantwood, New Jersey, collective (the set at this time counted as unofficial members Wallace Stevens, William Carlos Williams, Mina Loy, Lola Ridge, and Max Bodenheim, as well as artists Man Ray, Francis Picabia, Marcel Duchamp, Charles Demuth, Marsden Hartley, and Joseph Stella), *Others* began appearing in July 1915, a couple of months after Burke's arrival in Weehawken. It featured in its first number poetry by Stevens, Pound, Loy, Williams, Ridge, and Kreymborg; the second and third issues, published in the next few months, carried Stevens, Williams, Eliot, John Gould Fletcher, Bodenheim, and Arensburg. Later issues of *Others*, which appeared far more irregularly from 1916 through 1919, would feature Amy Lowell, Carl Sandburg, Edgar Lee Masters, H.D., and Marianne Moore.

Burke was from its inception among the enthusiastic and faithful patrons of *Others*, probably a thousand or so strong (the magazine had 250–300 subscribers).[3] By the end of 1915, Burke was submitting his own poetry to *Others* via Wilkinson, who asked on October 5 to show his "Metropolitan Light" and another poem "about music" (both now apparently lost) to Kreymborg, and who continued to pass along Burke's poetry until Kreymborg complimented "The Oftener Trinity" and accepted "Revolt" (Wilkinson to Burke December 19, 1915). While "Revolt" never actually made it into *Others* (for details, see page 29 in chapter 2, above), his free-verse "Adam's Song, and Mine" was published in *Others* in March of 1916. This was Burke's first publication. When Wilkinson left New York early in 1916, he gave Burke a letter of introduction to Kreymborg (Wilkinson to Burke, January 16, 1916), and apparently Burke made good on it by visiting personally with Kreymborg before going off to study at Ohio State in early March.[4] By taking up formal studies at Ohio State and later at Columbia, Burke for the time being lost the opportunity to mingle directly with Kreymborg, Arensburg, Stevens, and the rest of the group. He met Williams only a few years later, was a bit younger than the rest of the Others crowd as well, and regularly joined the Others group only after the set expanded to include Cowley, his wife Peggy, Hart Crane, Edna St. Vincent Millay, and Moore after 1918.[5] But in the course of his studies he certainly did continue to follow *Others* and the poets the journal sponsored. He seems to have particularly admired Arensburg's poetry, and he referred to the Others group both indirectly and directly while defending in his correspondence his enthusiasm for free verse (e.g., Burke to Cowley, May 27, 1916).

   Others was fervently committed to free verse and experimental poetry in the wake of the new poetry that was then coming onto the Anglo-American scene, especially, in the spring of 1912, when imagism was emerging from conversations among H.D., Aldington, and Pound. Pound in London, under the influence of Bergson, Nietzsche, T. E. Hulme, H.D., and Ford Madox Hueffer, began after 1910 developing and encouraging several varieties of experimental poetry that stressed novel language, imagery, subject matter, and form. H.D. was Hilda Doolittle, a Philadelphia poet living in England who married Richard Aldington (at least for a time) and who with Aldington and John Gould Fletcher before the Great War advocated a poetry that was objective, direct, and arhetorical—arhetorical at least in the sense that it avoided the sententiousness of the late Victorians. Pound tutored Amy Lowell in imagism in the summer of 1913, and he also discovered both Robert Frost, whom he helped to publish *North of Boston* (1914), containing the anti-romantic "Home Burial," "Mending Wall," "After Apple Picking," and other innovations; and, fresh from Harvard, T. S. Eliot, who published "The Love Song of J. Alfred Prufrock" in 1914, and *Prufrock and Other Poems* in 1917.

Pound's own subsequent vorticism, orientalism, and imagism all relied on experimental freshness and free verse. By the time Burke was settling in Weehawken, the two (and only) famous issues of Pound and Wyndham Lewis's vorticist periodical *Blast* had appeared in England (July 1914, July 1915), lobbying for free verse and heralding "the image":

that which presents an emotional and intellectual complex in an instant of time. . . . The image is not an idea. It is a radiant node or cluster; it is what I can and must call a vortex, from which and through which and into which ideas are constantly rushing. (from the vorticist "Manifesto" of 1914; quoted in Crunden 228)[6]

This was a formulation that grew out of earlier ones regarding method which were published as imagism's three tenets in March 1913: (1) "direct treatment of the 'thing,' whether subjective or objective," (2) "to use absolutely no word that does not contribute to the presentation," and (3) "as regarding rhythm: to compose in sequence of the musical phrase, not in sequence of the metronome" (Pound, *Gaudier-Brzeska* 83).

In America, the new poetry was simultaneously being taken up as a cause by a number of sympathetic experimenters. Edna St. Vincent Millay's poem "Renascence" in 1912 seemed to call for a new American poetry, and within three years Edgar Lee Masters had written *Spoon River Anthology*, Carl Sandburg most of his *Chicago Poems*, and Wallace Stevens "Peter Quince at the Clavier," "Disillusionment of Ten O'Clock," and "Sunday Morning." In the same year that "Renascence" appeared, Harriet Monroe in order to encourage modern verse started *Poetry* in Chicago, with Pound as her foreign editor; the poems in the first two issues, featuring Pound, H.D., and Aldington, eschewed the lush ornaments, inspirational sentiments, genteel commentary, and poetic diction that were typical of verse in *Harper's*, *Scribner's*, and *The Atlantic*. In 1913 *Poetry* carried H.D., Amy Lowell, John Gould Fletcher, Robert Frost, D. H. Lawrence, and Carl Sandburg, and printed Pound's famous definition of the image quoted above[7]; by 1920 it had published Stevens, Edgar Lee Masters, Floyd Dell, Marianne Moore, James Joyce, Edna St. Vincent Millay, and Sherwood Anderson, in addition to Eliot's "Prufrock." But Monroe also printed much traditional verse; she appreciated progressives as much as the moderns who were succeeding them (indeed, she was uneasy about the Armory Show[8]), so *Poetry* began soon to spawn imitators who were more vigorously experimental, among them *Glebe* and then *Others*.

Glebe, Alfred Kreymborg's first venture, was a monthly series of inexpensive editions of plays, stories, and poetry that died after ten months in 1914. The February 1914 number, entitled *Des Imagistes: An Anthology*, was the product of a packet submitted by Pound that included startling contributions by H.D., Pound, Aldington, Amy Lowell, Williams, and Joyce. Lowell's subsequent edition of *Some Imagist Poets* (1915) laid out (in a preface by Aldington) six principles of imagism—derived in large part from the three tenets noted just above—which are now frequently cited as hallmarks of modern verse in general: a reliance on the language of common speech; a commitment to the exact word, not the decorative one; the use of new rhythms; a free choice of subject matter; a focus on images—on particulars, not generals; and concentration (or intensity). In Lowell's hands (particularly in the two subsequent collections of *Some Imagist Poets* she put together in 1916 and 1917) imagism—from that point scorned as "Amygism" by Pound, who promptly disowned it— became more generally synonymous with free-verse poems that strove to avoid affected rhetoric, such as those in Kreymborg's *Mushrooms* (1916). Kreymborg, like Lowell, craved an American version of imagism, something comparable to his friend Stieglitz's turn to American artists after 1914 and something free of the orientalism and other international features that Pound was by then sponsoring in *Cathay* (1915) and else-where. For that reason Kreymborg had a special interest in Stieglitz's journal *291*, which during 1915 encouraged radical experiments in poetry as well as photography, and in Williams, who was, with Kreymborg, attached to The Provincetown Players and Stieglitz's gallery, and who was also developing his own unique and American brand of imagism, though it was one which employed several stock imagist tactics: nontra-ditional subjects and language, the rhythms of speech, and, above all, free verse.[9]

For whatever else they believed, the members of the Others group were committed to free verse. But this position was anything but universal, and controversy over the merits of the new poetry filled the pages of the literary periodicals that Burke was reading. Pound in the January 1916 *Dial*, for instance, excoriated genteel magazine publishers for resisting innovation, and six months earlier and through 1917 *The Dial* alternated genteel and proper objections to new poetry with defenses of it. "Great poetry must . . . breathe the air of high idealism. It must present life truly, but wholesomely," intoned one critic of Masters' *Spoon River* (*The Dial* 61 [1916]:325), while others defended Masters and the other composers of new verse. When in the summer of 1916 J. C. Squier in *The Dial* sneered at the imagists—"It is no more a school than I am" (318)—and one H. E. Warner ridiculed free verse, Amy Lowell responded with a learned and pointed defense of both in the September issue and with a tutorial on free verse, "Poetry as a Spoken Art," early in 1917. In December 1916 a *Dial* editorial took the side of free verse, but the Harvard *Advocate* (read by Cowley) claimed simultaneously that *vers libre* meant little more than "whimsical formlessness" and "sordid realism," and

Burke Meets His Match

Amy Lowell (in 1922) came to the Hotel Belmont and summoned Burke and me for an audience at five in the afternoon. We waited in the sitting room of her suite, at first standing by the windows and discussing architecture. After half an hour we sat down. A quarter of an hour later Miss Lowell's companion swept in and offered us Amy's cigars. We understood Miss Lowell was getting up for her day (which was night) in the next room. We finished the first cigars, waited some more, and started second cigars. At half past six Miss Lowell magestically entered and sat in a high capacious chair, her delicately modeled hand holding one of the famous cigars. She ordered Burke, a short man, to sit at her feet on a tiny stool. I was at her feet too, in a slightly higher chair.

She began imperiously. "The trouble with you young men is that you are too critical. You can't decide whether to be poets or critics. Look at Malcolm Cowley." A torrent of hearty defense opened out, for under the guise of dogmatic attack it was defense, as Miss Lowell's printed words on *Secession* later revealed. I watched Burke squirm on his footstool. His eyes blaze in an argument, his words come fast. But Amy would not let him cut in. She was reducing us to schoolboys, not arguing. Abruptly she closed the audience. Her breakfast was arriving. Burke and I walked over in the dusk to the West 42nd Street ferry, and I heard another torrential lecture. Vehemently Burke poured out all the things Miss Lowell had choked in his vocal chords.

—*from Munson's* The Awakening Twenties, *very slightly edited in the light of Munson's similar account in "The Fledgling Years"*

rejected the "undisguised unwholesomeness of the new manner of poetry" as "unfit for human consumption."[10] Padric Colum and Lowell therefore still needed to explain "The Imagists" and free verse in additional 1917 and 1918 *Dial* essays. While *The Dial* was supporting free verse and experimentation more consistently in 1917 and 1918, printing essays and reviews on and by Lola Ridge, Edna St. Vincent Millay, Conrad Aiken, Max Bodenheim, Foster Damon, and *Others*, other critics weren't so sure. Mencken and Lippman were ambivalent about experimental verse in *Smart Set* and *The New Republic*. And so was Cowley in Cambridge. On the one hand, Cowley approved of free verse in letters to Burke (e.g., November 9, 1915), sought out Amy Lowell in person (she lived near Boston), and composed free verse himself. On the other, he mocked Lowell (overweight and puffing on her famous fatima, "she look[ed] very much like a volcanic mountain in eruption. Focus on mountain," he reported to Burke on December 14, 1916), confessed to a personal aversion to free verse ("I don't like it, true, as a rule"), resorted to conventional verse in order to win a place in the Harvard Poetry Society, which produced *The Advocate*, and, since free verse appeared to him to be generating a disturbingly large number of bad lines, proposed that a law be passed prohibiting all but a few people from forsaking meter for *vers libre* (Cowley to Burke, undated, 1916).

But Burke was as unqualifiedly enthusiastic about the new measures as anyone in the Others group. As early as June 1915, Burke was sharing his free verse with Cowley, Light, and other friends. When Wilkinson commended some of those poems later in the same year and recommended him to *Others* (and *Others* to him) in the winter of 1915–16, he maintained his zeal. "Why do you go on so about *vers libre*," he scolded Cowley from Columbus in late May 1916. "Have you forgotten that *vers libre* is an accepted fact? . . . To object to free verse because it is free verse is stupid and superficial." Since Burke "hardly ever g[o]t a theme in terms of beats and rhymes" (letter to Cowley, May 27), his first serious poems, written from 1915 to 1917, are nearly always free verse in form even when they are not especially novel in theme. For instance, "Adam's Song, and Mine," the poem published by *Others*, expresses a conventional adolescent frustration in the new form:

> You pass me merrily.
> Your hair dashes back like the spray under a racing bowsprit.
> Your eyes are alight.
> You beckon me.
> You dare to beckon me
> Because you do not understand
> The baby rabbits at your feet.
> Virgin!
>
> You do not understand my quivering.
> Your legs are bare. I am ashamed!
> Yes,
> I am coming.
> I am coming to scramble with you
> Through the angry bushes.
> I shall race with you over the wet sand,
> And I shall bear with your innocence
> Until
> You feel how warm my breath is,—
> Virgin!

The same theme of frustrated love finds another free-verse form in "Spring Song," written in 1916—a lament in seven variable-length lines that juxtapose ubiquitous springtime sexuality with the persona's personal loneliness:

The soft spring night is smiling in its sleep,
And down here in the ponds the young frogs are chirping endlessly.
Today I saw two robins sporting on the lawn.
And just at dusk, when wistfulness was coming on, I watched a young girl
   swinging.
And now a flat yellow stage moon lies low among the trees,
And the spring near me is trickling toward the pond . . .
And I am without a beloved.

"Hokku,"[11] published in *Sansculotte* in January, 1917, reflects the vogue
for free-verse haikus that developed in the wake of Pound's own orientalism: "The gorgeous vase is shattered? I shall make pretty playthings of
the bits." Printed in two lines broken at a hyphen between "play" and
"things," instead of in the usual five-, seven-, and five-syllable consecutive lines, "Hokku" purposely confuses the distinction between poetry
and prose.

But "Hokku" also avoids the imagism that is often associated with
haikus; indeed in his early poems Burke seems to have skipped entirely the
vogue for strict imagism. More visibly an instance of free verse—in fact, as
visually formal and symmetrical as Williams's "The Red Wheelbarrow" or
Stevens's "Thirteen Ways"—Burke's "Ambulando Solvitur" (1916) is an
experiment in free verse in which the speaker's distress over the unnamed
but unmistakable "it" is underscored by a disarmingly simple diction and
syntax and an insistent free-verse repetition:

> It is solved
> by walking
>
> It is solved
> by walking very fast
>
> It is solved
> by the ambulance
>
> It is solved
> by the perambulator
>
> It is solved
> by a space-walk
> query
>
> It is solved
> by talking back and forth
> while going for a walk
> together

Many other free-verse experiments by Burke have been lost, never published. While his early poems are not especially distinguished, nor are they as visually experimental as the poems of Apollinaire or the Futurists or, later, the Dadas,[12] they demonstrate without question that Burke was reading free-verse practitioners deeply, following them carefully—Lowell lectured at Columbia while Burke was there in 1917 (Josephson 30)—and making a serious effort to master the form and to find a characteristic poetic voice. When Josephson first met Burke in November 1916, a couple of months before Burke's official enrollment at Columbia University, it was on the occasion of Burke's reading and defending his free verse passionately to a Columbia poetry society led by the then-genteel John Erskine (Josephson 30–31) and prepared to give its annual poetry prize to Sara Teasdale.

Not all modern poetry after 1910, and certainly not all of Burke's (as we will see in a moment), was radically experimental in form. As Cary Nelson has shown (*Repression* 23–27), traditional metrical and stanzaic forms continued to be employed in the Harlem Renaissance group and in other modernist circles to achieve distinctively vital and modernist effects. That is especially so since, in committing themselves to experimentation and free verse, the Others themselves were to a significant degree patterning their work and their social habits after the French Symbolists, a group of poets who often continued to employ traditional forms while pursuing untraditional ends. Arensburg, for instance, translated and imitated Laforgue, Verlaine, and Mallarmé; Stevens fancied them as well; Lowell credited the Symbolists with influencing imagism (Josephson, *Life* 59; Bourne 148) and in 1916 produced *Six French Poets*, a commentary on Verhaeren, Gourmont, Regnier, Fort, Samain, and Jammes; and Stieglitz had studied the Symbolists before establishing his famous gallery (Abrahams 136). Modernist free verse itself actually derived not so much from Whitman or Pound or Sandburg as from the Symbolists, either indirectly (through Arthur Symons) or directly: T. E. Hulme's famous January 1909 advocacy of free verse in his "Lecture on Modern Poetry," so influential to the experimental poetry of Eliot, Pound, H.D., Aldington, Lowell, and Fletcher, drew its inspiration directly from the *vers libre* practiced by the Symbolists; furthermore, Pound and the other poets he consorted with in London read the Symbolists themselves (Pondrom 8). As I'll indicate in chapter 6, Pound, Eliot, Lowell, and Aldington were particularly taken with Remy de Gourmont. As Cowley wrote to Burke on July 31, 1917, "As one reads from Baudelaire to Mallarmé, one gets the origin of all [contemporary] English verse movements . . . ten to twenty years later. A lecture of Amy Lowell's on Vers Libre and the strophe—I saw where she stole it: from an exercise for his own methods written by Gustave Kahn in 1897."

The Symbolists in poetry, like the Post-Impressionists in painting, were the French artists who were for Burke's generation associated most intimately with the genesis and character of modernism. As early studies by Edmund Wilson (*Axel's Castle*) and Marcel Raymond (*From Baudelaire to Surrealism*) indicate, the movement now designated by the term "modernism" was originally identified closely with the practices of the Symbolists and their own direct forebear, Baudelaire. Students of modernism still frequently tie its beginnings to the work of Baudelaire and his successors because of the Symbolists' influence on Eliot, Pound, Stevens, Yeats, Faulkner, and so many others. Burke from 1915 to 1920 accordingly immersed himself in Symbolist writing, particularly because Cowley was directed toward the Symbolists when he went to Harvard in 1915 and met Foster Damon (who presided over a group known as "The Aesthetes"[13]), because Burke's informal mentor Louis Wilkinson had also recommended French poets to him, and because at Ohio State he had come under the influence of Ludwig Lewisohn, a most knowledgeable enthusiast of German and French moderns whose *The Poets of Modern France* (1918) introduced readers, via his translations, to Charles Baudelaire, Paul Verlaine, Stephane Mallarmé, Gustave Kahn, Emile Verhaeren, Remy de Gourmont, Francis Jammes, Jules Laforgue, and other Symbolist poets. Encouraged by mentors and friends, and by his other reading, Burke began exploring modern French poetry on his own at the New York Public Library after dropping out of Columbia in the winter of 1917–18, just before he moved to 86 Greenwich Avenue (Cowley, *And I Worked* 72). He immediately encountered Pound's essay on Laforgue in the November 1917 issue of *Poetry*, as well as the special Symbolist issue of *The Little Review* (February 1918), which featured yet another Pound essay on Laforgue, in addition to a copious presentation of poetry by Laforgue, Jammes, Arthur Rimbaud, Gourmont, Verhaeren, and several others. When Burke began reading *The Dial*, he encountered defenses of free verse (from 1916 through 1919), reviews of Gourmont and Symons (1919), and, under Watson and Thayer's new leadership, Watson's translations of Rimbaud's *A Season in Hell* and *Illuminations*, a series of articles on French aesthetics, Pound's translation of Gourmont's prose poem *Dust for Sparrows* (1920–21), and other accounts of the Symbolists (all in 1920). In 1922 Burke was demonstrating an easy familiarity with Mallarmé in his review of Waldo Frank's *City Block* and in a subsequent letter to Frank, in which he quoted verbatim a Mallarmé sonnet to make a point (Burke to Frank, October 7, 1922). In sum, Cowley could claim with confidence in October 1921 that the Symbolists were among the central literary guides of "This Youngest Generation" of Burke, Cummings, Cowley, Dos Passos, and Damon: "They respect ideas that have characterized French literature hitherto, rather than English or American" ("Youngest Generation" 1).

Symbolism is no more monolithic than any other literary movement, and making generalizations about poets as various as the Symbolists is a hazardous assignment. But a look at Wilson's *Axel's Castle* and Symons' *The Symbolist Movement* (the famous 1899 volume, expanded in 1908, that first introduced the Symbolists to English readers) as well as Lewisohn's volume on the Symbolists does suggest how they were read and represented by Burke, his friends, and his mentors. Baudelaire, the forerunner of Symbolism, of course, in *Les Fleurs du mal* (1857, the same year as *Madame Bovary*) offered a prototypical new content and attitude to poets—the combination of self-revelation with an appreciation for strangeness and morbidity and the beauty in corrupt material. "Je cherche le vide, et le noir, et le nu!" he proclaimed in "Obsession," a signature line which no doubt contributed to his suppression and which, along with many other such lines, inspired Arthur Rimbaud (frequently cited as the first self-conscious modern), Paul Verlaine, and Stephane Mallarmé, the last "the acknowledged founder of the Symbolist school" (Lewisohn, *Poets* 17). To Mallarmé's salon in the 1880s came a generation of poets and writers—Kahn, Laforgue, Henri de Régnier—with a more-or-less coherent set of principles calculated to set them apart from the then-dominant schools of French poetry. Aloof and radically alienated from contemporary life (particularly from materialism and the pressures of industrialism), disgusted by traditional values and mores, repulsed by the conventional platitudes and techniques and subject matter they found in the poetry of their day, the followers of Baudelaire, Mallarmé, and Rimbaud after 1885 attempted to withdraw into an elitist realm of art, into an Axel's Castle abstruse and esoteric, dreamy and fantastical. Preoccupied with their private, inner sensibilities and nostalgic for myths and archaic civilizations and other remote refuges from contemporary philistinism, the Symbolists—like Swinburne, Pater, and Wilde in England—tended toward a radical aestheticism that expressed itself in an obsession with form and the determined pursuit of art above all. Convinced at least in theory that art could and should be separated from mainstream society (though Rimbaud for one denounced and renounced political quietism[14]), that art should somehow be self-contained and self-referential, refined and intensified such that everything inessential fades away—that art could be an event in itself rather than a rhetorical statement about a worldly event—they nevertheless took up illicit, notorious topics and poetic and political tactics that were chosen to horrify conventional society: sin and satanism, the unconscious and the bizarre, the morbid and depraved, free verse and fractured syntax, sensational scandals and bohemian lifestyles that proclaimed their high regard for personal freedom.

Symbolist poetry in theme was in large part a reaction against empiricism and scientific materialism. To the Symbolists, convinced of realities beyond the material, art was "a form of expression, at the best but approximate, . . . for an unseen reality apprehended by the consciousness" (Symons 3–4); "the poet is to use details of the phenomenal world exclusively as symbols of that inner or spiritual reality which it is his aim to project in art" (Lewisohn 19). "Evoking objects [only] in order to show a state of the soul" (Lewisohn 19), the Symbolists sought a private realm of The Beautiful that would "approximate the condition of music" (Wilson, *Axel's Castle* 13), that ideal of arhetorical art. That is, the poet's task—since "Nature is a temple [and] man goes through this forest with the familiar eyes of symbols always regarding him" (Baudelaire, "Correspondences")—was to convey through symbols (as opposed to through direct statements or objective descriptions) the intimations of his or her own special soul on its spiritual journey, the inner consciousness and emotion and subjectivity of a world-weary isolate: "Symbolist poetry seeks to clothe the idea in a sensible form which, nevertheless, shall not be its final end and aim, but shall merely serve to express the idea which remains subjective" (Mallarmé's Symbolist manifesto, published in *Le Figaro*, September 18, 1886; quoted in translation in Lewisohn 20). The British critic F. S. Flint offered this summation in 1912: "the Symbolist poet attempts to give you an intuition of the reality itself . . . by a series of images which the imagination seizes . . . in its effort to insert itself and express that reality, and to evoke at the same time the infinity of which it is the culmination point. . . . [Symbolism is] an attempt to set vibrating the infinity within us, by the exquisite juxtaposition of images" (355; reprinted in Pondron). The Symbolist poets inhabited an ineffable terrain between the mind and reality, and sought to invoke and evoke that space by subtle, indirect means.

Symbolist technique followed from Symbolist temper. While most of the Symbolists continued to express themselves in inherited forms, the new poetry also seemed to require new meters and a vocabulary stripped of poetic diction. Rimbaud, Laforgue, and Kahn developed *vers libre* to liberate the poet from rhyme and fixed line lengths, while others imitated the prose poetry written by Baudelaire. Consequently the second- and third-generation Symbolists too came to exhilarate in *vers libre*, new and "unpoetic" vocabulary, and fractured syntax, as well as to rely on indirection and mystical tones—on novel tactics designed to create a shadowy and dreamy feel that would be suggestive of the emotions of the poet ("the music of the soul" [Lewisohn 3–4]) and the realm of The Other. For "le suggérer viola le rêve": "poetic vision arises from suggestion," and not from direct naming (Mallarmé, quoted in Lewisohn 20). The artist, in touch with immediate experience, discerns new and arresting metaphors and associations that are designed to lead the reader to some higher realm. He or she presents personal emotions or moods, often brooding or otherwise meditative, or evokes sensuous reverie. Since the Symbolist poet aspires to music, that realm of pure art—"Music before all else / Music again and forever" (Verlaine, "Art poetique")—he or she relies on lyric forms or on alliteration and assonance and various kinds of repetition in the absence of rhyme and formal rhythm. Rimbaud, Mallarmé, and Laforgue were especially preoccupied with formal innovations. Of course, the Symbolists continued to exploit the possibilities of traditional tactics quite frequently, but by avoiding direct rhetorical statements, by relying on emotional suggestiveness, and by prizing experimentation, they influenced post-impressionists like Gauguin, Picasso, and Van Gogh and encouraged stylistic breakthroughs by later French moderns—most notably, for Burkeans, Apollinaire—and by Anglo-American poets like Pound, Yeats, and Eliot, H.D. and Fletcher, Lowell and Williams.[15]

The values and tactics of the Symbolists are reflected in Kenneth Burke's early poetry and criticism. Impressed by the Symbolists' respect for music, he decided while at Ohio State in the spring of 1916 "to take up exclusively the study of music," a resolution which, though it held up only briefly, may nevertheless have helped to confirm his decision to leave Ohio State for good. "I want to master another, and a far greater medium" than literature, he wrote. "Perhaps I shall be able to set free verse to music" (Burke to Cowley, May 1, 1916). During his months in Columbus Burke also became familiar enough with Baudelaire to be able to offer an amazingly faithful imitation of Baudelaire, in French, to the first issue of *Sansculotte*. Entitled "La Baudelairienne," the prose poem—still more prose than poem, if you ask me—was published in January, 1917. In it a Baudelairean beauty, "artificieuse et artificielle" as any of Baudelaire's heroines, possessed of the green eyes of Baudelaire's uncontrollable anti-bourgeois cats, and wearing a turquoise pendant like that of one of Baudelaire's mistresses and perfumed hair like the woman in his "La Crevelure," captivates a "fou garcon" who is ridiculed for his faithfulness and for the extravagance of his love as much as the narrator of Baudelaire's prose poems cynically ridicules virtuous actors and actions. When the woman becomes ill from her dissolute lifestyle, from the "jeux d'absinthe," and therefore loses her beauty—"Elle etait aussi laide qu'une religieuse, et sa face etait hideusement grêlée, . . . et les deux grosses pommes de sa piotrine s'etaient fort bien ridées"—the fou garcon becomes crazier still: he nurses her back to health ("sucait la fièvre de sa bouche"), bathes her with kisses, and, after she protests that his beauty will inevitably attract others who will win him away from her, morbidly disfigures himself with acid to show his eternal solidarity. Naturally—or rather unnaturally, in this faithful pastiche of Baudelaire—the woman is only repelled by his disfigurement, and shuns him "avec horreur." Designed to endow prose with musical effects, "La Baudelairienne" is somewhat reminiscent in form of some of the prose poetry in Baudelaire, in Gourmont, and even in Stein's *Tender Buttons* (1913), and anticipatory of later prose poetry in Pound's *Cantos*, Toomer's *Cane* (1923), and Williams' *Spring and All* (1923), all of which in one way or another seek to dissolve the dichotomies between poetry and prose. In content, of course, the fable is an ironic and wicked parody of the sentimental fiction that the moderns detested.

Burke's "The Oftener Trinity" is another free-verse poem that recalls Baudelaire (Light recognized it as such in a letter to Burke, November 19, 1915). The love poem (see excursus, "The Oftener Trinity") progresses not from winter to spring but from spring to fall and offers a series of shocking refrains in each of its three stanzas that are designed as ironic contrapunction to the elaborate opening lines of each stanza: e.g., "When the dirty snow softens the matted grass, / And Proserpina gathers up her garments / And prepares to return from the dull couch of Dis, / And the trees are busy with their fresh ornaments / In beautifying her path to Olympus . . . / My love is that same ugly thing / Which perpetuates the snakes."

And Burke's "Nocturne" (1916–17) is a free-verse reproduction of a Symbolist mood piece, an effort to recreate through images drawn from the natural world the speaker's inner condition:

> Did you hear the crickets chirping last night, Malcolm?
> The strawberries are hardly red,
> And you have yet to cradle your rye,
> But the crickets are chirping.
> Why should crickets chirp in Juneberry season?
> Last night it stormed, and after the storm,
> When the lightening was far away and the thunder still farther,
> I lay awake and listened to the crickets.
> We are both very young yet, Malcolm,
> And in July the crickets' chirping is very gay.
> Would you have wanted to cry too, Malcolm,
> Had you heard the crickets?

Several of Burke's poems in the Symbolist tradition, however, are more formally traditional. For example, instead of using free-verse or prose poetry, the 1915 poem "The Monster" ironically luxuriates in the traditional form of the sonnet while it describes in suggestive language a nontraditional, uncourtly subject: a lover come to "dare one cautious kiss, nor nothing more" from his innocent, dreaming mistress, asleep in

The Oftener Trinity

by Kenneth Burke

When the dirty snow softens the matted grass,
And Proserpina gathers up her garments,
And prepares to return from the dull couch of Dis,
And the trees are busy with their fresh ornaments
In beautifying her path to Olympus;
Then I love.
I am nobly desirous—
And as I seek my mate,
I keep one holy eye on Heaven.
But soar though I will,
My love is that same ugly thing
Which perpetuates the snakes.

When the green leaves are no longer glistening,
And the sap in me and in the trees is sluggish,
And the world becomes a dangerous velvet,
A lazy warmth;
Then I love.
Then Heaven slinks away before the prurient 'cellos wailing at my soul,
And swollen rhythms sway above my body.
Then I do not try to soar.
My love is that same ugly thing which rots great nations.

But when the chill leaps up,
And the leaves, with a beautiful melancholy,
Get out their silks to die in,
Like great lifeless vikings sent out upon the sea,
Majestic in their wealth-laden galleys;
Then I love—
Swimming in the moonlight,
Racing in the cold—
The prankish autumn moon,
And a healthy shivering
Catch me up in rough hands,
And trip me
And pummel me
And roll me over the hills.
My love is that same jolly thing
Which swilled new cider and danced in the barn.

—*from* Sansculotte *(February 1917); revised into "Three Seasons of Love" in* A Book of Moments her room. The lover is described as if he were a rapist, even a vampire, stalking innocence itself: "For through closed sleeping eyes she saw a form / Approach her, while its breath stirred like a storm. / She saw it crouch; it dripped black blood, and crept." And the poem as a whole seeks to recreate the mood of terror felt by the victim. The strangeness and morbidity of "The Monster," the product of a Symbolist mentality that has shaded into an 1890s-style decadence, is also apparent in the thematically and formally conservative poems about death that Burke wrote about this time: the four-line "Invocations" of mortality that showed up in the first *Sansculotte* ("Oh, melting snows, who bring the robins here! / Oh, youthful robins, harbingers of spring! / Oh, melancholy spring, faint overture, too sweet, of death! / O death . . ."); and "Hymn of Hope," in which the balanced, ironic title serves along with the cynical sing-song metrics to make the unhopeful contents more memorable:

> Or willy or nilly
> May this you remember;
> Your joy's in the past,
> And May smacks of November.
> Or willy or nilly
> Lest this you forget:
> Life is a plague
> And death's coming yet.

Perhaps out of respect for the Symbolists' frequent observation of regular measures, Burke also recast "Adam's Song, And Mine" into a more regular form for *Sansculotte*. The poem suffers so much by comparison with its free-verse counterpart that it would seem to confirm Burke's assertion that poems occurred to him most naturally in free-verse form:

> Willful hair and laughing eye,
> Beckoning me as you go by;
> Can't you see the world as I?
> Virgin! Virgin!
>
> You are light and passion-free,
> Beckoning to me guiltlessly.
> Shame! The thoughts that waken in me!
> Virgin! Virgin!
>
> I shall run and play with you.
> We shall laugh and leap, we two;
> Til my love has wakened you.
> Virgin!

A far fresher, though structurally still rather regular, version of the same general sentiment appears in "Ver Renatus Orbis Est." The speaker, at his New York window, alone, as springtime arrives (in other words, the speaker is in the same predicament as the speakers in "Adam's Song" and "Nocturne"), recalls "a pond now in Ohio / Where before bed some students are sitting; / Spring! calling us to the major cycle of conception." The final three-line stanza seizes upon the new poetic diction that the Symbolists encouraged in order to praise the sexual urge: "Deep buried wombs growing restless; / Dark sperm pressing against its prison; / Halleluia! Let cathode and anode be united." Note that all of these poems emphasize the personal and individual at the expense of the civic and political and conventionally moral. "Hymn of Hope," like "Spring Song," may have appeared in the reform publication *Slate*, but those poems and the others written by Burke before 1930 are personal and apolitical—far more aesthetic and Symbolist than the usual poetry of the *Masses* group.

The ironic tone of many of these early poems is particularly derivative of Jules Laforgue (1860–87), the Symbolist poet in whom Burke and his fellows evinced a special interest. The young Burke read carefully Laforgue's sparse but influential output—perhaps because he identified with Laforgue's unfortunate and bohemian lifestyle (Laforgue wrote his poetry while living in severe poverty for a time, and he and his wife died of consumption after just a year of marriage), perhaps because Laforgue's fresh diction and especially innovative free-verse style, formed out of his friendship with Gustave Kahn, influenced Eliot's early poems, or perhaps because Laforgue was drawn to themes that someone like Burke at this time of his life would have appreciated: urban life, adolescence, isolation, love and longing. As Cowley recalled in *And I Worked at the Writer's Trade*, Laforgue was also a particular favorite of Foster Damon, who imitated Laforgue and encouraged Cowley's own imitations (73–75).[16] Eliot, out of Damon's Harvard, not only admired Laforgue ("Prufrock" is routinely cited as the quintessential Laforgean lyric in English) but recommended him to Pound; in turn, Laforgue was picked up by Allen Tate, Hart Crane, Yvor Winters, Louise Bogan, and Burke. Burke "had been making his own explorations of modern French poetry at the New York Public Library . . . [and] after dropping out of Columbia in the winter of 1917, he had taken to writing Laforgean complaints and moonstruck rhapsodies in free verse" (Cowley, *And I Worked* 72). Instances of such moonstruck poems are "The Monster," "Spring Song," "Nocturne," "Ver Renatus," and "Rhapsody under the Autumn Moon"—the last a purposely elaborate apostrophe in which the speaker "in my bed" longs for "the hollow forests where . . . / Wild, crazy, alone, / I could tipple on heedless myths of Dionysoi and Persephonae / And moonstruck, flee from satyrs and druids, / And rejoice in the melancholy pleasure of soughing with the leaves," and so forth. In all these poems are the dreamy moonlit landscapes, adolescent longings, novel diction, free-verse forms, and emphasis on the inner consciousness of isolates that are associated with Laforgue.[17]

And in them is also what Cowley called Laforgue's "tangent ending"— a way of concluding a poem by moving away from it "at a tangent," as in the case of the ending of "Prufrock," when the sudden dream of the beach intrudes on Prufrock's thoughts (*And I Worked* 73). Similarly, Winters has called attention to the "double mood" that his generation saw as characteristic of Laforgue's voice: poems like Eliot's "Sweeney among the Nightingales" and Pound's "Hugh Selwyn Mauberly" have "alternating passages of two distinct and more or less opposed types of feeling. . . . One of them is usually ironic" (65). As Winters explains, it is a "formula for adolescent disillusionment: the unhappily 'cynical' reaction to the loss of a feeling not worth having" (67); one ironic voice or mood, often in an emphatic position at the end of the poem, cancels a sentiment expressed elsewhere in the poem. Winters is talking about the tactics apparent in something like Burke's "Revolt," in which the cynical final three lines puncture the hyperbole of the Tamberlaine-like would-be superman who dominates the rest:

> "Behold me, I am impregnable.
> "I am mighty and give no quarter
> "For I am filled with the might of justice.
> "Show me the bulwarks of tradition;
> "Show me them, that I may stick my fingers through them.
> "Show me the ponderous pyramids builded by the ages;
> "Show me them, that I may flick them away with boredom.
> "I will be free, I will bite in two the chains that bind me.
> "Quake before me, you shades of your forefathers,
> "For I am mighty and give no quarter."
>
> Bravo, my little man! Come over here
> And I shall ride you hobbyhorse upon my knee.
> Have you never noticed boys throwing stones at street lamps?

The same formula is apparent in the final lines of both stanzas in "Bathos, Youth, and the Antithetical 'Rather' ":

> To feel the grip of maddened, careless vice—
> To yield headlong when purple whims entice—
> To lose your soul upon a harlot's dice—
> Or rather, to have to be content with cheap poetry about it.
>
> In mighty self-respect to scorn the world—
> To shriek and pant—conceitedly be hurled
> To hell—to choke with life a tippling swirl—
> Or rather, to have to powder those damned pimples.

78

And the Laforguean formula also explains much of Burke's long "Rhapsody under the Autumn Moon." After rhapsodizing on those wild forests for seventy-odd lines, after dreaming up a fearless moon-companion Artemis to sport with and working himself into frenzied wishfulfillments like "I should be wild, now, in the forest / . . . I should be torturing myself deliciously with inspired lies / . . . I should have with me quick nervous youth . . . / [and] Soft, breathless cold-nosed girls," the speaker's reverie reaches its elaborate crescendo:

> Artemis! Artemis!
> Let me dream hideous dreams about you,
> And tell myself you are maddening me.
> Let me build altars to you,
> And elaborate dithyrambs to you,
> And be mightily awed by you,
> And rejoice when you have torn off every strip of your dark garments,
> And appear before me, chaste and naked.
> Drive me foaming among the weird bare trees I cannot name,
> Until I am as desperate as the daughter of the river god
> In flight to save her womb from the seed of Apollo.
> Bewitch me!
> Cast me back upon the rocks of Attica.
> Let me worship you as violently as the violet-weaving Lesbian could
> worship Aphrodite.
> Mystic moon,
> I would *live* my rhapsody!

All this is of course only a prologue to the brief Laforgean closure. The speaker, reminded of a sudden of his urban predicament, ends the poem with a second voice, a cynical second thought that in a sentence dismisses all the overstated enthusiasms that have just been uttered: "Dewy, perplexing wide-eyed moon / The traffic mumbles that you are not Artemis" at all.

As Armin Frank has noticed (122–23), Burke's ambitious late-1920s poem "From Outside" is also Laforgean. Written, carefully revised, and then published in *The Dial* on the occasion of Burke's 1928 Dial Award, which was announced in early 1929,[18] "From Outside" is an impressive dramatic poem in four contrasting blank-verse parts[19] during which yet another of Burke's isolates winds his way upstairs at the end of the day to a door where, before knocking, he recalls the life he has shared with his beloved and meditates on its meaning. Frank has written, with reason, that the speaker is a nephew of Prufrock's—a man both attracted to and fearful of life and love, a man who "sees his nearest step to happiness / In contemplation of another's splendor." As it turns out, the man "from outside" never does enter into human intercourse; instead, "as the day dissolves in nightfall," he notes

> How we must enter shivering from the mist,
> And find the match by touch, and light the lamp,
> And shed the silent downpour on the desk
> To dissipate the evening's tyranny—
> Affording that one thing which man has added:
> The articulate, analytic sound.
> Welcome! . . . Here again. . . . Here I am back—

The last line in this beautiful closing sequence is yet another "tangent ending"; in it this happier but still overly self-protective Prufrock, having in part three suspected his beloved of treachery and having decided to remain apart from her, finds (in part four) his only permanent consolation in language, in therapeutic retreat into "the realm of art" in which "we [can] find / The distant repetition of ourselves / In magnified comparison."

Burke's poetry, then, because it was so influenced by the Symbolists, is far more like Eliot's than Williams'—to use the comparison between two modernist poetic modes that I used in chapter 1. The product of study and consideration more than spontaneity, Burke's, like Eliot's, is a "classroom poetry" filled with Laforgean reminiscences and characters, and with the allusions, myths, and inherited symbols that Eliot and the Symbolists exploited even as they were inventing new rhythms to explore new subjects. Especially attracted to European writers and skeptical of the literary nationalists, Burke avoided writing the "objectivist poetry" (Williams' term) that emerged out of imagism, according to which the poem is "rooted in the locality which should give it fruit" and "formally presents its case and its meaning by the very form that it assumes" (Williams, *Autobiography* 175, 264). Williams, that is, after the war was striving for a less intellectual poetry, sometimes in an imagist mode (Williams was, after all, a close associate of the artists of 291—Hartley, Demuth, Marin, Dove, and Sheeler) and sometimes not (for the Others set was not dominated by Pound as much as the London scene was), but always with inventively fresh forms and rhythms. There are "no ideas but in things," he declared; as in imagism, where objects speak for themselves, the poem "is not a vehicle for thought, or for the recitation of events, but a physical object" (Breslin 79) in which the poet should strive above all to achieve "contact" with "the thing itself." As I mentioned in chapter 2 and as Williams perhaps most dramatically illustrated in *Spring and All* (1923), by "contact" Williams meant "direct, uncompromised writing" (175), primitive, new, indigenously American, as intensely in touch with the seeable world, and as fresh in its reformulations of the world, as a still life by Georgia O'Keeffe. Williams agreed with the imagists that the poet should see the object to its core; in the wake of the demise of *Others*, late in 1920 he began his own journal *Contact* as a medium for "man with nothing but the thing and the feeling of the thing," as Burke later put it in his early-1922 review of Williams' *Sour Grapes*.

While Burke, drawn to French poetry and thus repelled by Williams' nationalism, never wrote verse himself in Williams' mode, perhaps in part because he had given up writing poetry in favor of fiction by the time he met Williams in person, he did have plenty of personal affection and admiration for the older poet. On January 2, 1921, just as Williams was launching *Contact*, Burke met Williams for the first time (Josephson 72–75). The two would soon differ on the merits of "The Waste Land," but they shared an aesthetic commitment "to refine, to clarify, to intensify that eternal moment in which we live" through art, as Williams put it in *Spring and All*. By the end of the month, the two were corresponding routinely and warmly, sharing reading lists and ideas and local color. Burke was writing about Williams' poetry and offering his own work to Williams and *Contact*. Williams could not accept Burke's story "My Dear Mrs. Wurtelbach" (Williams to Burke, January 12, 1921), but he did accept for the fourth issue Burke's "Ver Renatus Orbis Est," a poem which, more than most of his verse, works in the concrete style that Williams favored for *Contact*. Even though Burke remained unenthusiastic about imagism[20] and "Ver Renatus" is hardly an instance of imagism, it did, Williams thought, retain a local particularity akin to Williams' own— "Noises from a distance without clarified meaning; / Hot flesh massed dissatisfied in the movies / Accepting the used-up breath in silence." (For that matter, so does Burke's "Two Portraits," the twelve-line regular-verse descriptions of fictional people that Burke placed in *S4N* late in 1922.) By March 1921, Williams was inviting Burke and his family to Rutherford for dinner. And their already rather intimate correspondence became firmly established when Burke began exchanging regular letters with Williams in late April from Monson, Maine, where Burke and his wife had repaired for the summer to work and write. The two were quickly intimate enough to trade scatological humor and for Dr. Williams to kid the hypochondriacal Burke when in one letter he asked worriedly about the symptoms of tetanus. Relax, Williams wrote, "you have a cold" (Williams to Burke, May 12, 1921).

In those first months of their acquaintanceship Burke also eagerly and repeatedly urged the Symbolists on Williams, in particular Laforgue. But the doctor remained leery: "I suppose I am somewhat influenced in my shyness toward Laforgue by a knowledge of what a too close study of his work has done to Eliot—and others, even Pound" (Williams to Burke, January 12, 1921). Absolutely committed to an expressly American and spontaneous art—he even engaged in "automatic writing," a practice directly opposed to Burke's studied habit (Burke to Williams, May 21, 1921)—and frustrated by Burke's continuing enthusiasm for the Symbolists and by his "damned theorizing" all the time (Williams to Burke, April 27, 1921), Williams nevertheless did agree to publish Burke's own essay on Laforgue in *Contact #3*. The article, which betrays Burke's familiarity with Laforgue's fiction and correspondence as well as his poetry, describes Laforgue as a "dilettante" and "adolescent" at heart whose "armor was handed down to him from Baudelaire and Corbière" in the form of unpoetic words that gave "a marionette nuance to his emotions." The "most moony of poets" had "a tendency to incorporate various voices in a poem," sometimes "as a tangent, a change in meter or stanza": Laforgue, "shout[ing] his dithyrambs to the L trains of Vibrant With Life, . . . writes in an endless succession of smirks, grins and grimaces, since the superadolescent does not have the courage of his tragedy." Williams approved of Burke's critique of a French poet and even considered Burke's final paragraph to be an instance of contact-style criticism.[21] But he seems to have paid no real attention to Laforgue's writing. Ever bordering on the anti-intellectual, he continued to struggle with the "bloodless" fiction Burke sent him during the summer of 1921: "So far, I feel these stories as cerebral brick a brack—to hell with them" (August 23, 1921). But he also remained encouraging. On the basis of Burke's "David Wasserman" (even though it included a long quotation from Gourmont) and some other stories, Williams could say by November 1921 that he found Burke "to be the only interesting character writing in America today" (November 19, 1921).

Burke's poetry, then, never really developed out of an allegiance to Williams, and Burke occasionally became exasperated with his friend's opinions—"Williams and his damned Contact . . . who in the hell cares what the noumenon is?" (Burke to Josephson, December 27, 1921)—but there is no question that the patronage of the older Williams also meant a great deal to Burke. For his part, Burke remained sensitive, loyal, and generous to Williams and his poetry throughout the decade and long after. He continued to share his work with Williams, listened attentively to Williams' critiques of his fiction, and reviewed *Sour Grapes* eloquently and presciently for *The Dial* (praising Williams as "a distinguished member of a miserable crew," the imagists, and explicating the concept of "contact" with reference to the magnificent "The Great Figure"). He generously outlined Williams' career when *The Dial* awarded Williams its annual prize early in 1927, and he recommended Williams' poems warmly to Cowley: "They represent excellence in an angle of approach which does not interest me per se. But even so one cannot be blind to their excellence. . . . I see now why I am interested in Williams: because he has frequently done to perfection just the sort of thing I do not want to do." In other words, just as Eliot's poetry helped Williams discover better what he wished to achieve himself, so too Williams' poetry helped Burke to discover his own beliefs: "In him I find a superb adversary, thus making one less likely to grow lax in his own productions" (Burke to Cowley December 23, 1921).

Burke also developed productive personal relationships with Hart Crane, Marianne Moore, and Allan Tate. Burke met Crane in the early 1920s, probably early in 1921 (when Crane was corresponding with Josephson) and certainly by 1922 when Crane's close friend Munson first collided with Burke in connection with *Secession*. By the spring of 1923, Burke was incorporating Crane into his circle of friends and entertaining Crane at Andover, and the two were thereafter lunching regularly, meeting with others over the fate of *Broom* (see chapter 4), listening to Stravinsky concerts together, conferring over the first drafts of *The Bridge*, and going to parties whenever Crane was in New York. At the most memorable one, Crane got drunk, smashed African carvings, threw musical recordings out a window, ripped up books—and found seventeen missing lines of his most famous poem, "fresh and clean" (Burke to Tate, October 17, 1929). During the winter of 1923–24, Burke sublet Crane's apartment on Grove Street.[22] Burke probably also met Moore early in the 1920s at one of Lola Ridge's open houses in the offices of *Broom*, though the two at first did not know each other well, since Moore lived with her mother and Burke was living at Andover. That gradually changed when Moore—a friend of H.D. from college who had moved into the Others circle in 1919 and 1920, who traded ideas with Stevens and Pound, and who captivated Williams and Kreymborg—fell more and more into the *Dial* circle after 1922,[23] particularly (as we will see in chapter 5) after she assumed the editorship of *The Dial* in the spring of 1925 and employed Burke as her assistant and occasional surrogate. The two remained friendly correspondents and mutual admirers until Moore's death in 1972. Tate, already acquainted with Crane and Munson, who was soliciting and rejecting Tate's submissions to *Secession* in 1922, no doubt met Burke on his first trip to New York in June of 1924.[24] By the end of the year Tate had married Caroline Gordon, settled in New York City (just in time to participate in the *Aesthete, 1925* caper), and joined Crane, Munson, Burke, Waldo Frank, the Cowleys, the Browns, the Josephsons, and the artists Gaston Lachaise and Edward Nagle in an informal group that was then meeting more-or-less regularly for literary discussions and refreshments. Though his literary interests were rapidly moving from the Continent back to the South, Tate remained in the group until September of 1928, when he traveled to England and then Paris. While finishing his biography of Jefferson Davis in Paris, Tate depended on Burke's regular letters for news of their common acquaintances, most often Crane. He sent

Burke critiques of "From Outside" and *Counter-Statement* (see chapter 6) and described the expatriate scene in Paris, including his lunches with Jean Toomer, Hemingway, Ford Madox Hueffer, and Crane. Meanwhile Burke asked Tate to assist Alice Decker, a young woman who had helped Burke ghostwrite publications on criminology for Colonel Arthur Woods before going to Paris to study art; enclosed photos of his newly constructed swimming hole; gossiped about Crane, Josephson, and Cowley; lamented (on October 17, 1929!) that he had not invested more in the stock market; and, of course, defended in detail his views on form. The friendly and always substantial correspondence between the two continued for decades after Tate returned to the United States, specifically Tennessee, in January 1930.

But despite his intimacy with four of the greatest American poets of this century—or perhaps because of it—Burke pretty much abandoned writing poetry during the 1920s.[25] Besides "From Outside," he published only three brief lyrics, "Ver Renatus," "Two Portraits," and a six-line comic "Psalm" in the decade (the last in *S4N* in 1923). Instead, he committed himself to critical study of and critical writing about the most important modernist writers and issues of the day. The 1921 essay on Laforgue was Burke's first analytical essay, and he quickly followed it with another, in *The Dial*, on Gourmont. Before the spring of 1922, he had placed other essays on modernist heroes Flaubert and Gide in *The Dial* and *The Freeman*, and begun to develop the critical and theoretical abilities that sustained him throughout his career.

But first, from early in 1919 until the end of 1922, he would try his hand at writing short fiction.

4

Thomas Mann,
the Little Magazines,
and Burke's Short Fiction

IT'S NOT THAT BURKE had never tried fiction before 1919. He wrote several stories in high school, and in 1917 he contributed "A Parabolic Tale, with Invocation," an irreverent, 300-word Aesopian parable dedicated to the wisdom of youth, to the first issue of *Sansculotte*. Later that summer he began and then abandoned a novel called *Fallow Ground*, and in November of 1918 he published a series of brief, aphoristic sketches called "Idylls" in *Smart Set*. He wrote several other short stories while still at Columbia, one of which, "A Man of Forethought," was good enough to get into *The Dial* three years later.[1] Still, Burke seriously took up short fiction only in the summers of 1919, 1920, and 1921, when he and his wife Lily repaired to one or another rural hideaway—Candor, New York, in 1919; the mountains around Asheville, North Carolina, in 1920; and Monson, Maine, from April 15 to September of 1921— to save on expenses, to live close to the land, and to concentrate on reading and writing and recreation. Having grown up accustomed to rural retreats like Cowley's place in Belsano, Pennsylvania, Burke was anxious to enjoy with his family healthy summers away from city heat and impurity and contagion. He was blessed with a spouse who was experienced and comfortable in the outdoors, so that, even though he had not yet acquired the place at Andover (which would permit him to live the rural life that he wanted from 1922 until his death over seventy years later), Burke with Lily during those summers was able to live close to the land and close to the vest while he wrote a series of stories through which he sought to break productive new ground in modernist fiction.

In the summer of 1919, the Burkes as newlyweds lived virtually rent-free in the same semi-abandoned shack that Jim Butler, a friend from

86 Greenwich Avenue, had first discovered, and that Burke, Cowley, Damon, Sue Jenkins, and Berenice Abbott had tried out for a couple of weeks, probably with Butler, the previous June. A marvelous outdoorsman, nature enthusiast, and primitive who reputedly could catch squirrels and trout with his bare hands, and an artist who learned his craft at the feet of his step-grandfather, Claude Monet, in Monet's hometown of Giverny, France, Butler proved by example that people could live for next to nothing in Candor during the summer.[2] When he offered "his" "cottage" once again for 1919, the Burkes and Josephson gladly accepted. According to Josephson, expenses that summer came to just fifty cents a day under the watchful stewardship of Lily, an experienced camper comfortable in the wilds ever since her North Carolina childhood. "We lived on grits, hominy, dried peas, and dried codfish," wrote Josephson, "our meals being sometime embellished with a little game we caught. . . . One day we smoked out a woodchuck and Burke slew him with an axe, so that Lillian was able to dish up a stew. On another occasion we made a rather crude job of butchering a big river turtle, which we consumed" (*Life* 67). Burke wrote to Cowley on June 21 about the satisfactions of rural life:

Everything at Candor is very plentiful this year—birds, flowers, berries, snakes, frogs, fish, etc. I have found a swimming hole which is up to my neck in one part, and the sunsets and storms are out-and-out Hearst editions. Not only are the strawberries and raspberries thick, but we have also found good blackberry patches, with some huckleberries and a few gooseberries. Indeed, even the poor old patriarchal orchard reacted somewhat to the mild winter, so that there are two or three trees with apples and about as many pears. Our garden has been doing so well that even the woodchucks were charmed with it, with the result that our proud little beans are much less proud, and our peas are razed to the earth. By some good luck, the kale, radishes, onions, beets, and carrots were spared. Five monster pink peonies are blooming in the yard, while our three rose bushes are just wilting. . . . What a place for an American Flaubert!

Burke used the opportunity to practice his Latin, to continue his study of Mann and Gourmont, to swim in Catatonk Creek, and to write "The Olympians," three new sketches that would later appear in *The Dial* ("Portrait of an Arrived Critic," "The Soul of Tajn Kafha," and "The Excursion"), "Victories" (never published and now lost), and, most ambitious of all, "Mrs. Maecenas." (He had finished a draft of "A Conjecture"—a short piece now lost—before his marriage in May.)

In 1920, the Burkes and their new-born daughter spent the summer with Lily's family in North Carolina. By the middle of May they were established in the Batterham's summer house in Beech, a dozen miles northeast of Asheville in the Blue Ridge mountains; from July 25 through September 20 they stayed at the Batterham house in Asheville. There

Kenneth Burke with his first wife, Lily Mary Batterham, and two of their daughters, *left to right,* Eleanor Duva (Happy) and Jeanne Elspeth (Dutchie), ca. 1924. Photograph courtesy of Elspeth Burke Hart.

Burke felt overwhelmed enough by the Batterhams that he never returned for such a lengthy stay: "My experience with many shades and nuances of Batterhams has convinced me that it is absolutely impossible for two independent units to exist as one amalgamated unit," he told Cowley (June 12, 1920). "This is a family of undercurrents, which is particularly distressing to my love of overcurrents," he wrote:

Never go out and piss without whistling, for you are sure to hear plotting behind one of the bushes. Sometimes, down here, I get the impression of myself as a little round hard rock; it is rained on, snowed on, sunned on, thrown, kicked, and yet it retains its identity as a rock, little, hard, and round. With the bullets flying and glances setting fire to the curtains, I march inexorably up the hill with Corona, and play on her *ad orgasmum*. I come home to dinner; my feet falter in the undercurrents, my fingers are scorched with the glances, my ears are singed with bullets, and after the second pipe, I trot out Corona again, and climb the hill, and replay her *ad orgasmum*. There is the possibility that I go on writing through sheer devilment, to taunt them silently with the plain evidence that they can't move me. (Burke to Cowley, July 18, 1920[3])

During those four months, whether out of drive or devilment Burke indeed worked hard with his Corona on assignments for *The Dial* (e.g., translating Mann's "Loulou" and writing an essay on Gourmont) and on the makings of various other essays and reviews. But, bouyed by the success of "Mrs. Maecenas," he still had the drive and the time to work on a number of short stories. He completed "David Wasserman," finished a substantial revision of his long "The White Oxen" (first begun early in 1918), and wrote his first version of "My Dear Mrs. Wurtelbach," the brief "Scherzando" and the lost "The Birth of Philosophy" (the last a part of a planned trilogy which never did get completed or published[4]). He also read Swift, listened to Josephson's and Cowley's reports on developments back in Manhattan, and continued to read and think deeply about the current state of modern letters.

Burke's most ambitious and extensive retreat to the country took place in 1921, when, eschewing expatriatism, he, Lily, and Jeanne Elspeth lived for next to nothing with their artist friend Carl Sprinchorn and the Josephsons from April 15 through September in very, very rural central Maine, near Monson, quite close to where the Appalachian Trail today passes into one of its most remote segments. As usual, Burke's letters to Williams and Cowley back in civilization (Cowley was working in Manhattan and then went off with the expatriates to France in July) were full of details about a "country lovely beyond your imagination" (Burke to Cowley, April 18): lakes and streams teeming with trout and salmon; woods populated by porcupines and bears, moose and deer, bluejays and owls; orchards full of apples and plums and wildflowers, and days filled with canoeing, fishing, mountain climbing, gardening, frog-catching, wood-chopping, swimming, and hiking, sometimes for days at a time, through endless woods. By September they were all "in the pink of perfection"; "there is not a spot on my body that I can't make as hard as a skullbone," Burke wrote to Cowley on September 12.

Burke described a typical day in a letter to Cowley on June 25–26. After killing bugs in the garden and scrapping plans for a day-long walk that would have taken them around their lake, into town, and past some slate works, the Burkes decided to spend the day at the lake and the nearby spring:

Arrived at the spring, we reconnoiter, finding the thickest strawberries we have seen to date. We simply cannot resist it. I go back for the baby, put her in the shade, and we begin. So far we have scared up two partridges; hens and peeps can be heard off in other parts of the patch; Lielie thinks she saw a deer; but the baby crawls into a thistle, and thereafter will not be comforted. Picking is over. We return to the spring, erect a canopy over the baby carriage, and she goes to sleep after much howling and much citronella. Mr. and Mrs. Burke eat; and then note that they are in the midst of the thickest mint patch in America. Simply cannot resist it, and add a pint of mint leaves to our quart of strawberries. Dutch awakes, and joins in the meal, shrieking at every ant that turns up for crumbs. After this is all over, and things are repacked, and tied, and put away, we move back to the lake. The baby plays half in the water and half out, shrieks at the leeches and the moose-flies, and beholds her parents swim with great awe and reverence. . . . After an hour and a half of this, home.

Burke also read and wrote, of course. He waded through the correspondence of Flaubert while preparing an essay on the subject for *The Dial*. By July he was packing off three ambitious new stories for Cowley to read on his passage to France, "The Death of Tragedy," "The Book of Yul," and "Odyssey" (which was later renamed "A Progression"[5]). And by the time he returned to New York he had completed "In Quest of Olympus" and "After Hours," had probably revised "Mrs. Wurtelbach," and had almost certainly begun "First Pastoral."

Burke's short fiction, unlike Fitzgerald's or Hemingway's, wasn't intended for a wide audience. In keeping with the values of his friends and of the avant-garde magazines that he and his friends read and that ultimately published the stories—those with a fairly wide circulation, like *Smart Set* and *The Dial* (the subject of the next chapter), but also magazines with very limited reach like *The Little Review*, *Broom*, *Secession*, *Manuscripts*, *1924*, and *S4N*—Burke was more interested in self-expression and in advancing the craft of fiction than in attracting a wide readership. As a writer of avant-garde fiction, Burke found Joyce a little tame[6]; but like Joyce and the Continental writers of fiction he had been reading since high school (notably Mann) and like the other members of "this youngest generation," Burke tried for new effects through the exercise of novel means. In particular, he pursued two general and related experimental lines, both congenial to the aesthete temperament that Burke cultivated through the mid-1920s.

The first he described in a letter to Scofield Thayer on March 15, 1921, in an (unsuccessful) effort to win *The Dial*'s acceptance of his first version of "My Dear Mrs. Wurtelbach":

> As the story ["My Dear Mrs. Wurtelbach"] is built upon a distinct theory of writing, perhaps you would be interested in a general view of the considerations which gave it shape.
>
> Perhaps the essential point is the use of criticism and the paraphernalia of criticism as an element in fiction. For a long time the world has been drifting away from the capacity to express itself in pure art. (To wit, Anatole France's claim that we are in a critical age rather than a creative one; the predominance which even so facile a writer of fiction as de Gourmont has given to ideology, interpretation, and erudition; the growth of the feuilleton, which is nearly always more interesting than the book under discussion. Indeed, I have always felt that so far as the needs of expression go, the most perfect representation of present tendencies would be a volume of critical appraisals of the life and works of a purely imaginary character. Also Spengler's pretty convincing testimony that we are in full skepticism.)

Burke's "critical appraisals of the life and works of a purely imaginary character" and his "use of criticism and the paraphernalia of criticism as an element of fiction" took form in the series of character studies, often signaled as such by their titles and often composed under the spell of Thomas Mann, that Burke mostly completed before the end of 1920: "A Man of Forethought," "The Excursion," "Portrait of an Arrived Critic," "Olympians," "Mrs. Maecenas," "David Wasserman," "The Soul of Tajn Kafha," and "The White Oxen." These stories typically interrogate the conflict between the bohemian and bourgeois ethos that Burke was feeling personally in Greenwich Village and that he observed in the fiction of Thomas Mann (e.g., in the novellas collected in *Tristan* [1903] and, of course, in *Death in Venice* [1912]). By means of theme and style, the stories also frequently gloss over hard distinctions between art and criticism in a way that anticipates the criticism-as-art in *Counter-Statement* and in much of Burke's other work not only in the 1920s but after. In fact, the very approach to fiction that Burke chose was ideally suited to his relentless exploration of a characteristically modernist theme that deeply interested him during the 1920s and that he would return to in *Counter-Statement* and *Towards a Better Life*: the place of the artist in society, the tension between the artistic temperament and the commercial, technological, and material imperatives of the age.

"The Excursion," "The Soul of Tajn Kafha," "A Man of Forethought," "Portrait of an Arrived Critic," and "Olympians" all illustrate the principle in miniature. While "The Excursion" and "Tajn Kafha" are fables as well as critical character sketches (and hence anticipate in some ways the more fantastical stories Burke wrote a year or so later), each of the others amounts to a critical portrait of a character that is painted by a narrator who is common to the stories and who speaks with a knowing, satirical voice. Even though "A Man of Forethought" was written rather early, in 1917, it contains the mocking edge of the character sketches Burke would compose a couple of years later. The story concludes with a "smart" plot twist appropriate to *Smart Set*, where it was published in May 1919, a few months after Burke's "Idylls" appeared there—*Smart Set* and "smartsetism" having shaped Burke's taste since high school: Carter, the "deucedly cautious" protagonist, having sighed for years for an unattainable married object, gives her up at last—only to learn from her husband that she's run off with another man.[7] More important, through the knowing and none-too-subtle irony of a narrator who retains a critical and omniscient distance on his subject, the story critiques a man who eternally forethinks everything so carefully that he ends up substituting thinking about life for life itself. Characteristically, for example, at the very end, Carter "promptly left the room, bought a revolver and some cartridges, loaded the revolver, put it to his head, and, being a man of forethought, didn't shoot himself."

Burke's "Portrait of an Arrived Critic," written two years later, shows more literally the "use of criticism and the paraphernalia of criticism as an element of fiction," since the protagonist is an actual critic captured right in the midst of writing an article. The sketch shows the same critical distance and the same narrative voice as "A Man of Forethought," only this time the narrator is critiquing a critiquer. Alfred, the Arrived Critic, the "compleat gentleman," hypersensitive to lilies, arcane diction, and the pursuit of aesthetic perfection, the rarified opposite of his hard-drinking fellow critic Flannagan, sets out to ridicule artists as "precocious crybabies" who utter "ineffable innuendoes, slashing blindly, without discrimination or dignity," but in the process the Arrived Critic ironically only reveals himself to be ridiculous in insulating himself against life while all the time deluding himself that "he had gripped it."[8]

"The Olympians" is a critical but fairly sympathetic depiction of J. J. Beck, a sickly musician reduced to making the best of the genteel realities of the Methodist Church, the Boy Scouts, and local athletics by offering piano lessons to teenagers and homilies on "The Appreciation of Music" to civic groups. One of his pupils, fifteen-year-old Dorothy, arouses The Olympian in Mr. Beck—that is, makes him stir "along with the sap in the trees outside." But when Dorothy proves too immature and insensitive to respond, Beck is left to himself. Aroused mainly by music and opera, he puts himself into self-exile from a town that offers only a dull contrast to art, a town with "houses, shutting away all manner of things; houses that stood out frankly and openly, but within their walls, what slinking possibilities; houses with black corridors, with furniture and people in the shadows. These were sleeping houses, and as secret as caves."[9]

"A Man of Forethought," "Portrait of an Arrived Critic," and "Olympians" are brief sketches of themes and tactics that Burke would develop more completely in "Mrs. Maecenas," "David Wasserman," and "The White Oxen." "Mrs. Maecenas" is the first full-length illustration of his "use of criticism as an element of fiction" that Burke was able to get into print, and he considered it, for good reason (as I'll indicate at the beginning of chapter 5), his first major publishing achievement. The picture of Mrs. Maecenas, the young widow of a college president who remains within the college community as a patron of the arts and who is portrayed through all the meticulous, symbolically charged description that an admirer of Flaubert might summon, stands as a pure instance of a "critical appraisal of the life and works of a purely imaginary character." After having persisted for several years at the parochial college, which is satirically depicted in stereotypically modernist fashion as a bastion of smug gentility, and after having tried to bring culture to the genteel masses as much as Mr. Beck had, Mrs. Maecenas "was getting weary. She had seen ten semesters of the university, and her hopes of mothering a little renaissance out here in the wilderness had gradually pined away as the engineering and agricultural schools grew steadily more vigorous. Everywhere, everywhere, typical young Americans were springing up, sturdy tough daisy-minds that were cheerful, healthy, and banal. How could art thrive here, she asked herself, in a land so unfavorable to the artist's temper!" Although Warren believed, not implausibly, that the college in the story was created out of Burke's memories of Ohio State (227), the story actually includes most of the recognizable features that many moderns catalogued as a means of ridiculing the universities as refuges for smug gentility and that finally sent Burke away from Columbia to Greenwich Village[10]: "The great machine of the university could dump its annual output of standardized 'leaders of America,' could ship them off every commencement day labelled 'with all the advantages of a college education'; the alumni could put up a sun-dial or a gate, or an iron railing, every year in sacred memory of their dear Alma Mater; the great auditorium could tremble with cheering and shouting when big Dick Halloway, handsome, blonde-haired Dick, the hero of the university, shot the winning goal; all this could go on if it would—but Mrs. Maecenas got farther away from it all, and nearer to her books and her piano." This classic bourgeois/bohemian conflict resolutely in place in part one of the story—"Mrs. Maecenas found herself entertaining uncharitable feelings toward these fine young men and women"—Burke in part two introduces another Dorothy-figure to his suffering Beck-like Mrs. Maecenas: one seventeen-year-old Siegfried, a student whom Mrs. Maecenas ushers happily and hopefully into her world of books and music, French and Latin, Flaubert and Gourmont and Huysmans. "You must come here often, Siegfried, and we shall kneel together before the clandestine altar [of art]," she offers, and Siegfried is pleased to oblige.

The focus of the story having moved from the college scene to these two principals, no real plot, no real conflict ensues. Rather, Burke leaves readers of "Mrs. Maecenas" with critical sketches of his two characters. Instead of juxtaposing them further against the genteel and hostile college setting, Burke turns to an explication of Mrs. Maecenas, her young charge, and their relationship. Part two is therefore composed of scenes of an upper-middle-class version of bohemian life, scenes reminiscent of ones in Decadent fiction, as Mrs. Maecenas entertains Siegfried in her library, loans him her rare and sometimes obscure Continental classics, listens critically but responsively, even breathlessly, to Siegfried's poetry and to his Latin translations, discusses Aristotle with him, and through it all "delivers him" in general from his philistine "American captivity." By part three Mrs. Maecenas has become ready to throw her arms around Siegfried and kiss him for promising to "redeem America in the eyes of the world," while, for his part, Siegfried "contented himself with the conclusion that the general was leading to the specific," that his need for Experience was soon to be satisfied by a sexual tutorial from Mrs. Maecenas. The story, then, is Flaubertian in its realistic and symbolic detail—Mrs. Maecenas is familiar with de Gourmont's *Oraisons Mauvaises* and with the "glorious unhealthiness" of Baudelaire, among other things—and through it all the narrator retains a gently satiric distance, a tone of Flaubertian *impassibilité*, of detachment and mild irony.[11]

The final pages of the story place Siegfried against Mrs. Maecenas rather than the two of them against the college philistines; Burke's description of the two of them takes over so completely that the narrative becomes a sketch more than a story. Mrs. Maecenas emerges as the willing object of Siegfried's devotion, while Siegfried becomes a proto-Symbolist, a would-be Gourmont, basking in an irreligious religion of love and art that motivates him to resist the temptation to grope his patroness: "We no longer have religion," he says, "if by religion one means the hierarchy of angels, and a Janitor Coeli, and a God to sit massively on his throne, but ah! . . . how appealing the instincts of religion still are to us! I could take the vows of an anchorite, not to attain some ultimate Kingdom of the Blessed thereby, but merely through a vague urge towards aestheticism." The story is impressive not only in demonstrating Burke's mastery of an original approach to fiction but also in showing his critical distance on the aesthete lifestyle that he was both describing here and enacting in his own life.

The ending to "Mrs. Maecenas"—a Laforgean tangent end adapted here to fiction, just as Burke had done in "La Baudelairienne"—arrives very suddenly. Just as Mr. Beck awakened with a start from his infatuation with young Dorothy, so too Mrs. Maecenas's aspirations for her juvenile are shaken suddenly by an abrupt show of pimples on the chin of Siegfried, pimples that break into mortal view just as she feels particularly Olympian towards him. The spell thus broken for Mrs. Maecenas as it was for Mr. Beck, she determines, without the hint of a struggle, to forget Siegfried utterly. Siegfried is meantime annoyed "that she should react so to pimples!" With that the story of their relationship ends. Unresolved, forgotten, is the original conflict between bohemian and bourgeois, between the artist and philistine society. The reader is left with the two critical portraits, with a "critical appraisal of the life and works of two purely imaginary characters," more than with a traditional narrative.[12]

As effective as "Mrs. Maecenas" is, an even more successful illustration of Burke's habit of offering in his fiction critical appraisals of imaginary figures is his outstanding and inventive "David Wasserman." The title character this time is in fact quite literally the object of analysis, for Burke devises a continuing metaphor of psychoanalysis to give his readers the experience of listening firsthand to a splenetic, misanthropic, misogynistic, relentlessly self-absorbed, and neurasthenic would-be artist who is once again confronted by a tiresome, clueless, philistine society that asks nothing more than a safe conformity.[13] Through a minimum of narrative event and a maximum of concrete, self-revelatory monologue—nothing much really "happens" in the story—Burke lets Wasserman expose himself to the reader as someone paranoid about the oppressive gentility (a literal gentility this time, since Wasserman is a Jew) that isolates and frustrates him almost completely. That the bohemian Wasserman is so completely unattractive—one of Burke's friends referred to him as "your bastard"[14]—again reflects Burke's critical distance from the Mannian bohemian/bourgeois choice. Both alternatives are depicted unsympathetically, the vaguely realized life of the hamletian writer that Wasserman imagines for himself as well as the inevitable job as Jewish clothier that his father holds out to him as an only alternative and that Wasserman finally accepts.

In technique the story is extremely original and eloquent; it is an instance of the point Burke would make in "Psychology and Form" that eloquence can generate form. In place of narrative events and in place of the Flaubertian narrator he had employed in many of his earlier stories, here Burke gives his readers a series of powerful dramatic monologues that stand in relief against the succession of sketchily described scenes out of which the monologues are delivered. First there is a feverishly one-sided "discussion" in his girlfriend Cynthia's Brooklyn house during which Wasserman tries to win Cynthia's sexual consent; the scene juxtaposes Wasserman's frustrated contemplation of a wild sexual conquest of Cynthia with her own impassive, conventional disapproval and the presence of genteel, eavesdropping family members upstairs. Next comes a later-that-night coffee-shop "conversation," equally one-sided, between Wasserman and his analyst Wright, who counsels customary, bourgeois forbearance in a way that allies Wright with Cynthia. Then a barroom discussion with Wright juxtaposes Wasserman's bohemian quotations from Gourmont (in French, naturally) with his sputtering expostulations that he and his genius are only being crushed between Cynthia's and Wright's respect for propriety. Another such discussion in the same location gives Wasserman an opportunity to recount his rejection as a member of the radical group Red Flag when he will not cede his independence to the requirements of the group[15]; the episode leads to Wasserman's renunciation of leftist politics as just another repressive source of his stultification. Despite Wasserman's rage, however, the final couple of vignettes resolve his choice in anything but a bohemian way. First, the acuteness of his sexual frustrations drives him to an offhand proposal of marriage to Cynthia ("women demand some sort of ceremony"), and then he determines to accept a conventional position with the Wasserman Clothing Company. Through it all Wasserman maintains an inspired, paranoid invective that is nearly as hilarious as Jason Compson's perverse monologue in *The Sound and the Fury*.

From the perspective of "Olympians," "Mrs. Maecenas," and "David Wasserman," it is easy enough to recognize the first and longest story in *The White Oxen*, the title story, as yet another dramatization of the tension between an insensitive society and a sensitive youth, his sensitivity this time signaled by his continuing and conspicuous identification with a herd of white oxen that he encounters by chance one day at the local zoo. While the emphasis on the symbolically charged white oxen and the otherwise realistic manner of the story identify it as in keeping with Flaubert and Huysmans, two of Burke's central guides when he began the story early in 1918 (he returned to it during the summer of 1920 in North Carolina [Burke to Cowley, February 18, 1918; July 18, 1920]), its focus on an exposition of the protagonist also places it in keeping with Burke's other critical studies of imaginary characters.[16] Matthew Carr, Burke's tender young protagonist, projects his affection for the white oxen onto his friends until they all prove unfaithful. Edward Carroll, Matthew's high school buddy, is at the end of Part Two identified as "one of his [Matthew's] white oxen," but he only betrays Matthew's trust. A "woman of the streets" also becomes one of Matthew's white oxen until "she approached [him] in a way that neither god nor devil had ever meant for man." And Gabriel Harding befriends Matthew in college, even rooms with him, until turning on Matthew and robbing him for no real reason. Ultimately, then, it is Matthew who proves to be the white oxen, to remain innocent and set apart: "They [the oxen] had none of these painful tilts with life; to them the supreme gift of God was to sleep and to know that one is sleeping. He yearned to see things with their dull, slow-blinking eyes, to retire into their blissful sloth of semi-sensation. He yearned to be one of these white oxen—he, the purest of the white oxen."[17]

In all of these stories, in "A Man of Forethought," "Tajn Kafha," "Mrs. Maecenas," "Portrait of an Arrived Critic," "The Olympians," "David Wasserman," and "The White Oxen," Burke shows a continuing critical interest in an artist or artist-prototype who lives apart from society, usually in the Mannian manner of the protagonists of *Death in Venice* and "Tonio Kroger." The conflict between modernist bohemians and the materialistic society that surrounds them is played out through the depiction of sensitive young men who are exiled or self-exiled from society by their craft and/or their conduct but who nonetheless long for some kind of passionate engagement in life. Burke had been noticing Mann's work since his high school days in Pittsburgh as well as during his time at Ohio State and Columbia, and his high regard for Mann expressed itself in any number of ways. *The Dial* in April of 1921 published the translation of "Loulou" that Burke made in North Carolina the previous summer. That same summer, having translated others (Mitchell to Burke, August 8, 1920), he offered to translate a volume of Mann's stories for Boni and Liveright. Mann's "Tristan" appeared in the December 1922 and January 1923 *Dial*, having been translated by Burke with the help of Scofield Thayer. A translation of Mann's *Death in Venice* that Burke had begun in Columbus he later revised thoroughly into the version of Mann's classic that *The Dial* published in the spring of 1924; the volume also includes "Tristan" and "Tonio Kroger." When Mann signed on to do *The Dial*'s "German Letter" in 1922, it was Burke who was conscripted to translate it.[18] Burke would also translate passages from *Buddenbrooks* for the November 1924 *Dial*, and Mann's "Pariser Rechenschaft" for *The Dial* in 1927. References to Mann recur familiarly in Burke's critical essays and reviews and correspondence in the postwar period and after, and Burke's essay on "Mann and Gide" would appear in *The Bookman* in 1930 and later in *Counter-Statement*. Consequently, in "Olympians," J. J. Beck, the fragile, retiring musician, longs like Mann's Aschenbach for the "agitations" of life, represented by fifteen-year-old Dorothy Howardell, as sure an image of human beauty as fourteen-year-old Tadzio is in *Death in Venice*. In "A Man of Forethought" Burke contrasts the interior life of the cerebralist with the life of action that such a man of forethought inevitably misses, while "Portrait of an Arrived Critic" offers readers a critical choice between the rarified aesthete Alfred and his hard-living bohemian antagonist Flannagan. In "Mrs. Maecenas," Burke after the first pages turns completely away from the bourgeois/bohemian conflict to gain a critical distance on the lives of two bohemian aesthetes.[19] And in "David Wasserman," Burke experiments with a series of sustained dramatic monologues in order to create a critical portrait of a would-be bohemian torn by a bourgeois desire for sex and safety. In all of these tales, Burke before his twenty-fifth birthday shows a precocious ability, gained no doubt in part from his immersion in Mann and certainly continuing (as we shall see) through *Counter-Statement* and *Towards a Better Life*, to appreciate both the enchantments and the perils of living the aesthetic life.

In some respects, Burke's "My Dear Mrs. Wurtelbach" fits the same theory of fiction that generated his first stories. In fact, it might indeed be seen as the prototypical "critical appraisal of the life and works of a purely imaginary character" that Burke billed it as in his letter to Scofield Thayer quoted earlier in this chapter; it, too, in several ways uses "criticism and the paraphernalia of criticism as an element of fiction" in that the story satirizes commercial American lives and life by holding up for critical scrutiny not only the dearly departed Mr. Wurtelbach but also the Chamber of Commerce mentality that dominates the scene around him. While it is impossible to know for sure, it is also very conceivable that the version of "Mrs. Wurtelbach" that Burke enclosed with the letter to Thayer was more similar to "Olympians" and "Mrs. Maecenas" than it is to the version of the story that we now have. Burke's correspondence, at any rate, speaks of a "shorter version" of "Mrs. Wurtelbach" (e.g., Burke to Cowley, September 27, 1922); this is the one that appears in *The White Oxen*, the one which he first submitted to Williams for *Contact* (see Williams' letters to Burke of March and April 1921). But when "Mrs. Wurtelbach" never appeared in *Contact* or in *The Dial*, Burke probably decided to return to the story during his summer at Monson, this time with a somewhat different approach to fiction in mind.

In any event, the published version of "Mrs. Wurtelbach" is rather different indeed from Burke's earlier stories. By the time Burke completed his first stories for *Smart Set*, *Contact*, *The Dial*, and *The Little Review*, by the time he turned back to "Mrs. Wurtelbach" during his summer in Monson, he had come to an even more avant-garde theory of fiction that was suited to radically experimental forums like *Secession* and *Broom*, where "Mrs. Wurtelbach" finally appeared in January of 1923. That is, a second, more daring theory of art, albeit one related to the first, directs the stories that Burke wrote beginning with the remarkable "My Dear Mrs. Wurtelbach," which Burke considered a "turning point" in his approach to fiction (*Complete White Oxen* xii).[20] Raving over the success of the story, Cowley saw "My Dear Mrs. Wurtelbach" as following a distinctively "'modern note' that distinguishes authors of the present 'advance guard.' . . . The modern note at present is the substitution of associational for logical thought. Carried to its extremity among the Dadas, the modern note is the substitution of absurdity for logic" (Cowley to Burke, January 6, 1923). And indeed, "Mrs. Wurtelbach" does proceed not by means of linear development but by means of a stream of associations. It opens with the musings of Charles, the narrator, in response to the death of his college friend Wurtelbach. Charles's letter of condolence to Mrs. Wurtelbach, beginning "My Dear Mrs. Wurtelbach," leads him to a series of recollections and reconsiderations of his and his friend's life, ending with the shockingly cynical conclusion that "if there is one pure joy left with us, it is to pass a tight jobby." In other words, the entire story becomes a letter of condolence gone wrong and grown big: the cynical cliches offered to Mrs. Wurtelbach as the story begins grow into more scathing assessments of larger matters, as Charles ponders first the world of commerce and then the cosmos in general. "THE WORLD IS WITHOUT A TOY," concludes Charles at last, sounding now something like the author:

Romance, realism, the inquisition, the City of God, geo-centricity . . . they have left us nothing . . . nothing but a wobbly art trying to hit us on the head with a club. Is there some life beyond the mucous membrane? Is there some significance beyond a little suburban home? As an adolescent, I carried vague possibilities in my groins; and now there is nothing left but to look at people. Christ, they have even burned out our pessimism!

Ah! to have gotten up in the night, and to have noticed the door open and the light lit. And to have passed down the corridor . . . and nothing . . . nothing . . . to have returned, unchanged.

What are we to do with the growing trees? And Mrs. Buckhorn yelling down the dumb-waiter shaft? Let me rise above . . . let me maintain . . . let me affirm . . . There is the epigram, and there is the epic . . . and I have squeezed big theoretic tears. If there is one pure joy left with us, it is to pass a tight jobby.

David, my little man, sling your pebble at the universe. (ellipses in the original)

The story, then, passes from satiric vignette to stream of associations. Cowley, in the midst of his enthusiasm for Dada, seized upon the Dadaist "substitution of absurdity for logic" and the "nothing, nothing" of the conclusion as evidence that "Mrs. Wurtelbach" was especially "most modern" in displaying a Dada temper: "The transposition from the speech to THE WORLD IS WITHOUT A TOY ha[s] an absolute emotional rightness. I still think that the speech should have mentioned Wurtelbach, or that Wurtelbach should have delivered the speech. But Gawd it's a fine story. Critically the thing that surprises me about it is the way in which you anticipated several literary developments of the next two years" (Cowley to Burke, January 6, 1923).[21]

98

"My Dear Mrs. Wurtelbach," "The Book of Yul," "In Quest of Olympus," "Scherzando," "The Death of Tragedy," "First Pastoral," "A Progression," and "Prince Llan" all substitute other formal principles, chiefly association and variations on theme, as in music, for a reliance on traditional narrative logic. Written as his friend Robert Coates was conceiving of a Dada novel, two years before John Dos Passos would devise the deliberately amorphous narrative known as *Manhattan Transfer* (1925), and well ahead of *Finnegans Wake*, these stories are all highly original, even unique experiments in narrative form, many of them subsequently appearing in *Secession*, that were influenced by modernist developments in abstract painting and music and that develop in ways that are free of the representational and referential and chronological. "Narrative is no more an organic necessity to fiction than melody is to music," Burke wrote to Thayer in the same letter that outlines his theory that fiction might be seen as a "critical appraisal of the life and works of a purely imaginary character":

[Narrative] must come to be taken simply as one of the elements which can be brought in when aesthetically justifiable. Literature and music, because they exist in time—in contradistinction to painting, sculpture, and architecture, which exist in space—had accepted this arbitrary thread of progress because it was the simplest method of establishing a temporal gradation which, while being graded, also retained the feeling of unity. An essentially artistic progression, however, would have its basis in something more exact than this mere illusion of development. (such as for instance a sequence of form-units, expositional, argumentative, oratorical, narrative, or to look at it another way, lugubrious, brilliant, matter-of-fact, sullen, agitated, remote, chaotic, etc.) Surely, this method of composition would have more aesthetic compulsion than the present prevalent accident of having chapter eight deal with Harry at the age of twelve years and six months because chapter seven dealt with said Harry at the age of twelve years and three months. . . . In this way the elements of a prose fiction would be juxtaposed like the colors on a canvass: because one quality called forth another. (Burke to Thayer, March 15, 1921)

In these lines Burke was beginning to shape concepts of artistic form that he would set down in *Counter-Statement* and that he would enact in *Towards a Better Life* later in the decade. As I will indicate soon enough, the passage actually describes "A Progression," "The Death of Tragedy," and even "First Pastoral" as much or more than it does "Mrs. Wurtelbach." What is important to note here is that Burke was announcing his intention of experimenting rather radically with form in fiction, experimenting such that other aspects of form besides narrative chronology might be emphasized. "Mrs. Wurtelbach," as I have noted, achieves form not via narrative continuity but through the stream of associations that the protagonist offers in contemplation of his dead friend, e.g., "The time he and Wurtelbach had . . . dead. Like lead, in bed, his dull, dull, head (pause) . . . dead (one, two, three) . . . 'Hello . . . yes . . . oh, hello, Alice. I hoped you'd call. Yes, I got home all right . . . dead . . . rather late of course but I had a good night.' Now, concerning this matter of the Chicago Awto-Lite Company. . . ."[22] Consequently, when the revision of "Mrs. Wurtelbach" was completed and when it was clear that it couldn't be published in either form in *The Dial* or *Contact,* the latter now defunct, Burke sent it to *Broom* in the fall of 1922, which was now a recognized place for the most successfully experimental material then being developed.

Burke further articulated the concepts behind his most avant-garde fiction in a letter to Gorham Munson, now lost, that Munson quoted in part in his *Destinations* (see excursus, "Burke on Fiction"). In the letter, which refers explicitly to "Prince Llan" but which also reflects Burke's approach to other stories, Burke claimed that the form of his fiction cannot be described by the form that arises from conflict, as it had in the fiction of the past. Just as in music or in abstract painting form emerges at times not from conflict, so too in Burke's 1921 stories form derives not from conflict but from a focus on the hero, from a stream of psychological associations, and from a reliance on experimental "minor organisms"—dream visions, allegorizing, dialogue, and so forth,[23] much of it difficult to predict. Yes, fiction would open with a "challengelike beginning" and include a "coda ending"—and indeed "Scherzando," "Metamorphoses of Venus," and "Prince Llan" do end with explicitly named Codas, by analogy with music. But in the middle might come just about anything: "diversity of attack, turning here and then there." Moralizing, even in the gentle manner of his earlier satiric stories, of course, would be anathema. And in place of the Flaubertian narrator would come a variety of narrative overseers and first-person voices. But other than that, the only thing predictable is unpredictability. In keeping with avant-garde modernism and the playful spirit of Dada, then, Burke in the later stories of *The White Oxen* offers not a representation of experience but a new way of seeing and forming. Out from under the shadow of Flaubert and Mann, he like his fellows was now striving for innovation for its own sake, out of the modernist conviction that inherited forms are worn out, in need of reinvigoration and replacement.

Burke's letters to and from Cowley and Josephson in 1920, 1921, and 1922 are rife with references to Burke's radical experimentalisms in fiction, particularly to ones in which he builds form not on narrative or conflict but on some other principle. Remembering their summer in Maine, Josephson later wrote, "We must experiment or die. We evolved plans for stories without plots that assumed the form of sonatas, or novels having the form of symphonies" (*Life* 68). Or, in Munson's

Burke on Fiction

Here is why there is so much searching for a definition of form at the present time. Once [i.e., in the past] the plot always centered around a conflict. The scene was set, the conflict began, the big moment was the drawing together of the threads. This was form. It is the form of all drama. In "abstract" writing there is no conflict of this nature. The movement is usually a simple straight line or curving line. There is no conflict because the plot is the hero; and a plot either does things or does not—it cannot baffle itself, for even baffling itself is a simple plot. Thus, like Joyce, we must turn to the Odyssey, or some such, instead of to the tragedy (the psychological novel turned to tragedy). A challengelike beginning, and a coda end—and in between the main thing is diversity of attack, turning here and then there. With, of course, somewhat of a splurge right before the coda. Then one must devote his time to minor organisms, trying if possible to make each paragraph a microcosm, with its own formal developments. But aside from the beginning, end, and coda, there are, it seems to me just now, no other major functions. The rest are simply relationships between the parts, such as ending a conversation chapter with some speechless act growing out of it, or following a letter with an image, and so forth. While, of course, the letter or conversation should have gone through some still smaller curve in themselves.

—*Burke to Munson (no date); quoted in Munson's* Destinations, *147.*

words: "With Burke we enter the workshop of fiction and he shows us the structural elements of good stories functioning without concealment. There are certain mathematical propositions, psychological concepts, and problems in mechanics which can be best explained by a blackboard demonstration" ("Workshop" 136). Or, as Harold Loeb writes: "Kenneth Burke, stimulated by research in plastic mediums for what Clive Bell calls 'significant form,' has been studying its elusive equivalent in writing. His stories, which discard the old binding of plot or narrative, obtain unity by what he calls a super-plot: 'the structural framework which appeals to us over and above the message of the line,' or paragraph."[24]

Thus, when Munson started *Secession,* Burke was ready with a folder filled with experiments so unusual that they might otherwise never have been published, so strange that they are sometimes difficult to read today. Munson, with the encouragement of Cowley and Josephson, had founded *Secession* with the explicit aim of featuring the "youngest generation" of most experimental moderns, people like Williams, Damon, Brown, Cummings, Moore, Stevens, Dos Passos, Toomer, Tate, Crane, and Yvor Winters, all modernist writers one generation more daring (Munson felt) than Dreiser, Bourne, Mencken, Masters, Sherwood Anderson, Sinclair Lewis, and Van Wyck Brooks. All of those members of Munson's youngest generation contributed to the eight issues of *Secession* that appeared between April 1922 and April 1924, as did avant-garde Dada artists secured for *Secession* by Josephson and Cowley (against Munson's better judgment)—Hans Arp, Philippe Soupault, Louis Aragon, and Tristan Tzara.[25] From its inception *Secession* was militantly avant-garde in conception and execution, a "hard two fisted affair . . . for the youngest generation of American writers . . . [who were] defining a new position from which to assault the last decade" (Munson, "Fledgling" 31). It was designed explicitly, that is, as a journal for the most esoteric experiments in English that could be appreciated by a few readers who were themselves in a coterie dedicated to recharting the direction of modern literature. So when Munson approached Burke by letter with the idea of *Secession* in the last days of 1921, and when he arrived in Andover in the spring to ask personally not only for Burke's editorial help but also for his contributions, Burke could offer "The Book of Yul" (published in issue 2), "First Pastoral" (issue 3), "In Quest of Olympus" (issue 4), and "A Progression" (issue 7). Burke's remaining unpublished stories from 1921 would go to equally experimental other little magazines—"The Death of Tragedy" to *The Little Review*, "The Metamorphoses of Venus" to *S4N*, and "Prince Llan," Burke's latest written story of this period, to the final issue of *Broom*.

"The Book of Yul" and "The Death of Tragedy" are both constructed on the same general experimental principle of "associations" that operates in "Mrs. Wurtelbach."[26] Instead of logical or temporal progressions, Burke in both stories provides "natural progressions" and "variations" of theme from episode to episode (Burke to Cowley, June 30, 1921). "Yul" is a complicated dream vision that emerges out of a realistic setting (Part 1) which dissolves into an increasingly odd fantasy through the intercession of a blinding "snow ecstasy." That is, a character leaves his companions for a walk into a realistic, tangible snowstorm and then in the snow dreams up a traveller named Yul who, as per nightmare, wanders through a strange city and through stranger events—each one associated with the next—until he witnesses the story's powerful climax: In a church, Yul observes a terrible parody of a religious ceremony that is recreated through progressively frenzied and insistent language—long, paratactic sentences with rising cadences, clipped and combined fragments of sentences that breathlessly foreshorten the action, the recreation of primitive chants through various Dadaesque typographical experiments:

102

LET THE NAILS BE DRIVEN INTO THE HANDS AND THE FEET OF THEM AND THEIR
SIDES TRANSFIXED WITH SPEARHEADS UNTIL BLOOD MIXES WITH THE SWEAT OF
THE EXECUTIONERS AND REJOICE NOW THAT THEY ARE ALIVE OH UNFOLDING OF
THE REVELATION OH ECSTACY OF BLOSSOMING INTO A WORLD OF ETERNITY OH
ASTONISHMENT. . . .[27]

"The Death of Tragedy" follows a similarly novel sequence of unpre-
dictable events. A series of realistic opening vignettes, connected only
through associations, satirize contemporary American culture (the Standard Oil Company, ethnic rivalry, middle American bumpkinisms, current
politics, "the clean dead houses on a terrace, with the father returning a little after five"). As Burke himself accurately summarized the opening part,
it "opens with a kind of formal essay on America, trusts, poolrooms, boys
in a tent in the back yard sitting around with their peeties hanging out,
laxatives, . . . jumbled together quite brokenly" (letter to Cowley, May 1,
1921). Against this background, Part 2 then offers the particular and sad
details associated with one Clarence Turner, a novelist contemplating a
play on Broadway and confounded by a tedious love affair with a poet.
In Part 3, any semblance of sequential action dissolves completely when
Clarence dreams the reader into asides, qualifications, illogicalities, and
even the vision of a Maine landscape. At last the narrator breaks into a
kind of parodic prayer: "Oh vomit of loveliness! Let us rise in the night
and give thanks for the pure horizons that remain to us"—horizons that
presumably serve as an antidote to the urban and religious squalor that
the story emphasizes.[28] As these summaries suggest (actually, the stories
quite resist summary), both "narratives" again reveal Burke's attempt to
forge fiction out of something besides logical and chronological action.

That same general approach to fiction distinguishes "In Quest of
Olympus," "A Progression," "Metamorphoses of Venus," and "First
Pastoral." "In Quest of Olympus" develops out of several sources of
form, none of them particularly literary. Josephson understood it to be
arranged after the parts of a symphony, and Armin Frank contended
that it imitates "the cubist form of collage" (38–39), both conclusions
reinforced by Burke's own statement that " 'In Quest of Olympus' [is] in
five parts, the first three on one plane, the fourth on a second, and the
last in the third" (Burke to Cowley, June 30, 1921). The first three planes
develop the not-so-coherent adventures of a first-person narrator who
experiences the cycle of life in an obliquely allegorical fashion: finding
himself washed ashore in uncertain surroundings, he emerges from a
womb-like cave and encounters his strange old friend Treep, who grows
up—quite literally—by chopping down an old, fatherly oak that then falls
upon him, crushes him, and transports him (in Part 2, which now follows
Treep as protagonist) to "a kind of Nordic warrior's heaven," where, a

giant now among giants, he usurps the throne (and the name) of the evil Arjk and becomes a follower of Wawl, the senior god. In Part 3, he tries gallantly but unsuccessfully in the service of Wawl to rescue the goddess Hyelva, who is ravished by the Blizzard God so that a snowstorm erupts in New York. In the second plane, the snowstorm takes the reader into New York City and into the lives of James Hobbs and Esther MacIntyre and then Hobbs's friend Harowitz until, in the third movement, Burke somehow offers a sorrowful second coming of Christ (including, among other oddities, attendance at a Broadway play and a tour of New York and its environs). These topsy-turvy events and characters appear to attempt some sort of perspective by incongruity, judging from the juxtapositions of weirdly different matters. Then again, there is also an allegorical and dreamlike element to the story, something vaguely Jungian, when a "little guy becomes a Giant by felling a tree"—an event which Burke later interpreted as the ritual slaying of a maternal tree and which appears to parallel the cycle of life: birth (the narrator works his way out of a cavern into the sunlight), maturation (the protagonist becomes magnified by the chopping down of the parental tree), adulthood (the protagonist acquires a new name and encounters sexuality).[29]

As its title implies, "A Progression" also works through a meandering stream of associations. A real Mr. Dougherty, typecast as the arrogant industrialist, walks toward the end of his day into a conventional commuter train—when, in the space of a paragraph, he is suddenly attacked by Indians in airplanes, transported to a South Sea island, and devoured. That incident reminds the narrator to offer a commentary on progress, which in turn reminds the narrator of Ellery Smith, a farmer who lowers a gate and discovers himself wandering in "an unknown country," which then reminds him of the possibility of ghosts and "the case of M. Henri Basle, a member of several learned organizations in France"—and then of the fantastic child Argubot, who initiates the fable of Big-Eyes, Medium-Sized-Eyes, and Little-Eyes, until at last the "story" closes with Argubot's apotheosis into heaven. Somehow this collage of events, this "progression" from realistic setting through fabulous action—a reenactment of the fantastic pattern of several of Burke's tales of travelers and traveling from 1921—adds up to a modernist attack on the conventional notions of predictability, rationality, and, as the punning title indicates, Progress itself. Burke worked a similar vein in "Metamorphoses of Venus," a collage of sometimes realistic, sometimes unrealistic vignettes—various "metamorphoses" of tales about love—that is unified by theme rather than by character or sequential action. The "coda" in the end is a tip-off that here again Burke is constructing a story formally by analogy with music. Part 1, as in "The Death of Tragedy" or "In Quest of Olympus" or "A Progression," offers a general theme in the persons of Paul and Virginia and in the images of rock and flame. Part 2 provides the episodic variations on the theme, and then the coda recapitulates. Burke in these stories is working what he would call "qualitative progression" in *Counter-Statement*: "Instead of one incident in the plot preparing us for some other possible incident of plot . . . the presence of one quality prepares us for the introduction of another. . . . We are put into a state of mind which another state of mind can appropriately follow" (124–25). The tales anticipate experiments in narrative by Toomer (in *Cane*, 1923), Williams (*The Great American Novel*, 1923), Dos Passos (*Manhattan Transfer*, 1925), and Cummings (in his untitled collection of stories published in 1930) in their inventive playfulness and in their relinquishment of chronological sequence, causal progression, and the continuous presence of leading characters as unifying elements in fiction.[30]

But "First Pastoral" is even more tract-like than "A Progression" and "Metamorphoses of Venus," even though it moves in fictional territory something akin to the fable or parable. "First Pastoral" involves the reader in the philosophical musings of Brother Angelik, who meditates upon the heresies of early schismatics and the rarified theories of neo-Platonists like Bembo during an absent-minded stroll that takes him outside the monastery walls and into proximity with the shepherd John and shepherdess Jocasta, "the two of them lying earnestly interlocked on the sod." This stark juxtaposition of the intellectual and the physical is resolved when Brother Angelik trades in his cassock for pastoral garb and, disguised as Theodoce, uses his philosophical musings to attempt a seduction of Jocasta himself. When that seduction fails, Angelik in frustration commits suicide. The story's classical setting and intellectualisms reflect the influence of Burke's associations with Richard McKeon and with the New Humanists (see Burke to Josephson, December 27, 1921: Josephson replied to the letter by urging Burke to be less classical and less bookish [Josephson to Burke, February 4, 1922; May 9, 1922]).

"Prince Llan" also betrays the effects of Burke's contemplation of Paul Elmer More and the New Humanism. While in form the story is as surreal and fantastic and tract-like as any of the 1921 stories, in content this final short story, the only one written by Burke during 1922, displays the same conflict between spirituality and sensuality that is in "First Pastoral." A key dogma of Paul Elmer More was that the soul has a dual nature, that people are torn between an evil, sensual lower self and a higher, controlled, rational self.[31] Consequently, in "Prince Llan" Burke explores the possibility of reconciling these opposites in a "dualism not of strife but of mutual completions," what Armin Frank calls "reaching the salvation of quietude by going through the passional stage" (36). As Austin Warren has noted (234), Llan is a kind of modern-day Rasselas, a philosopher in search of the ideal life. Llan mortifies his flesh, eschews sexuality—he wanders for a time with a couple of willing, nubile virgins, but sends them on their way at last, "little unsealed things, little unplumbed possibilities, little fields unplowed"—and intellectualizes relentlessly, ever on the lookout for immutable essences. His foil is Gudruff who counsels in a letter the pleasures of the flesh—"every channel of sensation." Gudruff offers Llan just those temptations that his contemplations have been ridding him of. The possibility of a reconciliation of these opposites is figured in the coda in the person of Joseph. As the "Programme" affixed to the coda indicates,[32] Joseph might be conceived as "the marriage of Prince Llan and Gudruff, a dualism at one with itself, a dualism not of strife but of mutual completions." "If you have a garden and a library, you have all," offers Burke by way of Cicero. "Prince Llan" as "an ethical masque" advises its readers to reconcile opposites, to merge dualisms into a harmony of reason and passion, intellect and emotion, sense and sensibility.[33] The story resonates with Burke's own story, with his own ability to reconcile opposites, to live with and accommodate seemingly irresolvable differences.

Having resolved things thematically, Burke closes "Prince Llan" by abruptly killing off his narrator: "I, Morducaya Ivn, the respected chronicler of these meditations and events," merges with the Nebula, with Futurity, and dies. The death in retrospect seems auspicious, for with Morducaya Ivn also died Burke's efforts in short fiction. With the exception of "The Anaesthetic Revelation of Herone Liddell," written over thirty years later, the publication of "Prince Llan" marked the end of Burke's experiments with short fiction. Ending with "Prince Llan" seems appropriate, for, as Munson noted in the passage from *Destinations* that I quoted from above, "Llan" is the purest instance of Burke's mature experimentalism in the short story form. It proceeds not so much by plot and character as by a conflict of ideas and qualities; the modern allegory has "a challengelike beginning and a coda end, and in between the main thing is diversity of attack, turning here and then there, with, of course, somewhat of a splurge right before the coda" (147). But if "Prince Llan" marks a logical conclusion for Burke, it is also something of a beginning, for half a decade later Llan's pilgrimage "towards a better life" would be reenacted in other terms in Burke's novel.

In the sense that "Prince Llan" is a dramatization of ideas, in the sense that its coda counsels its readers toward a merging of its binaries,[34] "Prince Llan" might, I suppose, be said to be one of the most "rhetorical" of the stories in *The White Oxen, and Other Stories*, at least in the sense of "rhetorical" that one associates with Burke's famous pronouncement a decade and a half later that literature is "equipment for living"—that stories and poems and plays are "strategies for dealing with situations" rather than "pure" and arhetorical expressions (*Philosophy of Literary*

Form 296). Actually, as I'll indicate in chapter 6, Burke arrived at a mature appreciation of the rhetoricity of art by the end of the 1920s in the final essays of *Counter-Statement*. "Prince Llan" does seem to be something of an effort at persuasion, something of an effort to convince readers to adjust their thinking and conduct their affairs in certain ways, and in that sense it anticipates the final chapters of *Counter-Statement* and the rhetorical concept of literature as equipment for living.

But most of the stories in *The White Oxen* are hardly rhetorical in that way. True, Burke's words in the preface of *The White Oxen* are frequently quoted to indicate his early commitment to rhetoric: "I see these stories as a gradual shifting of stress away from the realistically convincing and true to life; while there is a corresponding increase of stress upon the more rhetorical properties of letters. It is a great privilege to do this in an age when rhetoric is so universally despised." And indeed, as I've indicated, the progress of the stories in *The White Oxen* is certainly away from the "realistically convincing." But that progress is hardly in the direction of literature as persuasion, as equipment for living. By "the more rhetorical properties of letters," Burke meant something much more aesthetic than persuasive, something closer to "form" and "eloquence," those key terms in his 1924 essay "Psychology and Form": "Eloquence [is] the essence of art, while pity, tragedy, sweetness, humor, in short all the emotions which we experience in life proper, as non-artists, are simply the material on which eloquence may feed. . . . Eloquence is simply the end of art, and is thus its essence" ("Psychology and Form," in *Counter-Statement* 40–41). Thus in the preface to *The Complete White Oxen* Burke indicated that in his stories he "mainly had in mind an interest in formal and stylistic twists as such, as well as their entanglements in character and plot" (ix). In that very aesthetic sense, in the sense that they demonstrate form and eloquence, the stories of *The White Oxen* do become more "rhetorical" even as they become more experimental. They are more eloquent in that they "bristle with disclosures, contrasts, restatements with a difference, ellipses, images, aphorism, volume, sound-values, in short all that complex wealth of minutiae which in their line-for-line aspect we call style and in their broader outlines we call form" ("Psychology and Form," in *Counter-Statement* 38). In most of the stories of *The White Oxen*, and certainly in the final stories of the volume, Burke is concerned less with affecting readers than he is with expressing himself and solving aesthetic problems, far less with satisfying the expectations of his readers than with foiling those expectations in novel ways that would delight him and his fellows within his coterie of modernist readers. In William Rueckert's words, *The White Oxen, and Other Stories* is "writing that is more interested in itself—in what it is doing—than it is in saying something" ("Field Guide" 9); "the progression in the book is toward symbolic and fantastic stories which are primarily vehicles for achieving a variety of stylistic and formal effects. Toward the end of the collection, the stories approach the condition of music" (*Drama* 9). Or, as Malcolm Cowley claimed in his review of Burke's stories in the December 1924 *Dial*, "his progress [throughout *The White Oxen*] is in the direction of personal expression" (520).

From 1918 to 1922 Burke moved from one theory of fiction, from quasi-realistic "critical appraisals of the life and works of purely fictional characters" in the manner of Flaubert and especially Mann, to far less realistic, more fantastic experiments in narrative form. But the two approaches to fiction were related.[35] Both engaged Burke in working out aesthetic problems, in inventing new theories and practices of fiction for his own satisfaction and for the benefit of a small audience of similarly inventive moderns. As he would often do in his career, Burke wrote a book that merged his dual interests in art and criticism. *The White Oxen, and Other Stories* investigates the fictional lives of writers and critics, artists and artist-prototypes; the stories "use criticism and the paraphernalia of criticism as an element of fiction" in a way that anticipates not just *Towards a Better Life* but also *Counter-Statement* and the art of Burke's later criticism, even *A Rhetoric of Religion*. In evincing a sustained interest in aesthetic matters—in theoretical possibilities as well as artistic craft and experiment for their own sake—Burke was keeping faith with the aesthete values he held and shared with those around him, including the colleagues and mentors that he was now coming to work with at *The Dial*.

"A Great Date in History"? October 19, 1923

Literary rivalries don't always remain confined to the written word. Sometimes fisticuffs are involved too, and some humor.

Even as the spectacular contents of its all-American issue were arriving in the hands of its patrons in January 1923, *Broom* and its editor, Harold Loeb, were in the midst of a financial crisis. Loeb's inheritance was running low, printing costs were escalating in Europe, and production and delivery problems were frustrating Loeb and his American editor, Lola Ridge; it was becoming impossible to manufacture a product in Europe and distribute it on time to subscribers mostly in the United States. Loeb visited New York to seek financial backing, but when his relatives were not forthcoming with additional financing, he determined to abandon *Broom* after the March 1923 issue (Loeb, *Way*, chapters 9, 10, 11). Loeb felt that he could take some satisfaction in having published four magnificently printed volumes, i.e., sixteen issues, of the most stunning avant-garde modernist art of the era—fiction by Stein, Toomer, and Dos Passos; poetry by Williams, Moore, Apollinaire, Cummings, Stevens, and Crane; criticism by Yvor Winters and Loeb himself; and reproductions of work by Lipchitz, Mogdiliani, Picasso, Gris, and Matisse.

Matthew Josephson and Malcolm Cowley were not ready to give up so easily on such an important venture, however. Josephson had been working as an associate editor since leaving *Secession* and accepting Loeb's offer in Berlin in the fall of 1922, and soon after Cowley had signed on too, as a translator, writer, and liaison to potential contributors (Loeb, chapters 9 and 10). Now the two proposed to take over *Broom* themselves and to convert it to a quarterly; they "hoped to make it an organ for good prose, experimental verse, and violent polemics," mostly written by "the youngest generation" of American writers (Cowley, *Exile* 190). Backed by his brother-in-law, Josephson purchased a two-thirds ownership of *Broom*, and Loeb was relegated to contributing editor (Loeb to A. C. Barnes, Loeb Papers, September 21, 1923). Josephson and Cowley launched the "new" *Broom* with an August 1923 issue (vol. 5, no. 1) that included fiction by Cowley and Toomer, an essay on Gris and cubism by Loeb, and reviews of new, young writers by Josephson, Toomer, and Loeb. For future issues they lined up other items by Burke, Slater Brown, E. E. Cummings, William Carlos Williams, Glenway Wescott, Isidor Schneider, Charles Sheeler, Joseph Stella, and Wallace Stevens, not to mention Virginia Woolf, Robert Graves, Philippe Soupault, and Louis Aragon. In the summer of 1923 Josephson and Cowley returned to New York from Paris, determined to make *Broom* a success.

In their strategy of emphasizing younger American writers, Josephson and Cowley were poaching more than a little on the territory of Gorham Munson's *Secession*, but it seemed to them that more than enough publishable material existed to nourish both periodicals. Burke, though an editor of *Secession*, had indicated precisely that to Loeb back in January 1923 (Loeb, *Way* 173). Cowley and especially Josephson didn't mind offending Munson anyway, for the two had broken with Munson in the summer of 1922. Munson had been incensed at Josephson, and to a lesser extent at Cowley, for maliciously intervening in the contents of *Secession* 3 and 4 (they printed a Josephson story over Munson's veto and cut all but two lines of a long poem by Munson's friend Richard Ashton), and for other real or imagined insubordinations during Josephson's tenure on *Secession*. For their part, the increasingly Dadaistic Cowley and Josephson were finding Munson more than a bit old-fashioned and overbearing (Cowley, *Exile* 189–93; Munson, "Fledgling" 39–45; Josephson, *Life* 230–35).

Problems with *Broom* persisted for the new editors, however. In October of 1923, Cowley called a meeting of New York modernist writers in order to chart a successful path for *Broom*. One possibility was to effect a merger of *Secession* and *Broom*, since both were committed to "the youngest generation." Josephson had even offered Munson Ridge's place as American editor a few months before, but Munson was too angry at Josephson at the time to accept (Josephson, *Life* 232; Munson, "Fledgling" 40). Another option was to let *Broom* die. Another was to shift *Broom*'s direction in some productive way. Still another was to ask those present to make a renewed commitment to *Broom* in the form of monetary and literary contributions. "If we can get together in one room," wrote Cowley to Burke, "we can at least define our separate positions, whether or not we can make plans to go ahead. Eternal Jesus. The people who can be content with art-for-art, three issues of a harmless little magazine and an occasional glass of synthetic gin will continue to be content. For God's sake let's brew some stronger liquor" (quoted in Cowley, *Exile* 189).

Not everyone could attend the meeting, as it turned out. Williams, Stevens, Brown, Edward Nagle, Waldo Frank, and Jean Toomer couldn't make it, though Brown and Nagle sent letters of support for *Broom*. Munson, recovering from an illness and living with Toomer in Ellenville, New York, a hundred miles away, also sent a statement. But Cowley and his wife Peggy, Josephson and his wife Hannah, Burke, Wescott, Hart Crane, Schneider, Jim Light, Bob Sanborn (a member of the *Others* group), and apparently some others all did gather on October 19, 1923, in an Italian restaurant/speakeasy on Prince Street in Greenwich Village to "determine what we were going to do this winter, and whether people wished to work together or persist in their feuds" (Cowley to Loeb, October 30, 1923).

Apparently they wished to persist in their feuds; the meeting turned into a raucous fiasco. After reading the letters of support, Cowley turned to Munson's statement. Having just received a letter from John Brooks Wheelwright, who blamed Cowley and especially Josephson for the latest round of errors in *Secession* 5 and 6, Munson was angry (Munson to Burke, October 17, 1923; Munson to Cowley, October 15, 1923). He deemed *Broom* to be unworthy of support on account of the leadership of Josephson, whom he called dishonest, treacherous, irresponsible, self-seeking, and an "intellectual faker" (Cowley, *Exile* 190). Apparently Munson calculated his attack on Josephson to be a sort of test for Burke and Cowley: "I wanted to give you and Cowley a chance to take the leadership" of *Broom*, he later told Burke. Munson wondered whether Burke would go public with his artistic distaste for Josephson when Burke was a personal friend of Josephson's (Munson to Burke, November 2, 1923).

But the idea backfired. As Cowley proceeded through the statement, he "was overcome with a sense of absurdity and began to declaim it like a blue-jawed actor reciting Hamlet's soliloquy" (*Exile* 191). That quickly brought objections from Munson's loyal friend Crane, who shouted insults at Cowley. Others shouted back. Bottles were overturned and glasses spilt. Hannah Josephson tried to call for order. Light shouted, "They're stomping us down, they're pressing us into the dirt!" Wescott attempted to quiet things by asking, "How can you people hope to accomplish anything when you can't even preserve ordinary parlor decorum?" But a defense of parlor decorum, of course, inspired only derision. Wescott then stormed out. A gang of teenagers, hearing the ruckus outside, came in to bait the feuding writers. Josephson and Crane came to blows. "It turned into a riot drunk party after a while. Attempts by Cowley and me to control it were pathetic," wrote Josephson. "Attempts by the members to discuss their common problems concertedly failed through the inertia of intoxication."[36]

Through it all Kenneth Burke was "generally useless" (Josephson to Loeb, October 20, 1923). Apparently he had spent the afternoon drinking, and only gradually came around to his senses during the evening. Cowley says that during the hubbub Burke told listeners a hilarious story about a neighbor's dog (192), and Munson says that Burke escaped his test of loyalty by being drunk. In any case, the chaotic meeting dissipated. Limericks were recited, some people left, others stayed to eat or socialize. Both Josephson and Munson interpreted the affair as a Dada prank (Josephson to Loeb, October 20, 1923; Munson to Burke, January 8, 1924), Josephson with satisfaction and splendid approval for "the great date in history, a turning point for . . . the History of Literature in America," Munson with sarcastic disapproval for Dada's "cult of action in life."

The future of *Broom* went unresolved, however. And ultimately the failure of the October 19 meeting doomed it. Cowley and Josephson left the meeting with the conviction that the two of them, plus Brown and Burke, had to take control of *Broom* and exert leadership. Burke probably never fully and formally joined the editorial team—although Josephson took a copy of the yet-to-be-released November *Broom* to Andover for inspection (Josephson to Burke, October 26, 1923) and though Burke on *Broom* stationary did ask Toomer to contribute to *Broom* (March 9, 1924). But informally he took a very close interest in its affairs (along with Cummings, Williams, Brown, Nagle, Cowley, and Josephson) and contributed a story to it. The group decided to use for future issues a cheaper format (newsprint) instead of the lavish appointments of earlier *Brooms*, and to publish only sporadically, when enough material had been gathered. They would contribute their own funds to *Broom* and seek other financial underwriters (Josephson to Loeb, November 30, 1923). The first of these downsized numbers, volume 6, number 1, appeared in January, 1924.

It turned out to be the last official number, however. Burke's story "Prince Llan" offended the postal inspectors who had been eyeing *Broom* with suspicion since its November 1923 issue included Charles Durboraw's "An Awful Storming Fire," a "primitive" tale about the pick-up of a street girl, a story added, ironically, when Loeb withdrew at the last moment his own piece of fiction. When Burke's story included an abstract description of copulation and a hero "buying women" who had "sitters [that] undulated" and "breasts . . . that stood out like pegs" (according to Cowley's rendition of the tale in *Exile's Return* [194], only one breast was permitted in a story), the post office refused to permit the issue to be mailed.[37] The suppression created considerable financial trouble for the *Broom* overseers, although it also won them notice in *The New York Times* and in the Associated Press. The ACLU offered to help for free (Josephson, *Life* 266), and it is possible that the occasion could have been turned to *Broom*'s gain. But in fact

111

it discouraged the group too much to continue: "The editors, battle-weary and dead broke, felt unable to take advantage of the sudden newspaper fame their magazine had achieved, or even to answer the many letters of sympathy from readers" (Josephson, *Life* 273). Burke for one had had enough. He left a meeting early, in disgust, when the subject turned to how to respond to the suppression: "I realized that most everything in the world was involved [in the discussion] except the art of storytelling, and a tremendous pudency overcame me. Publicity, vice, censorship. . . . The vocabulary suddenly became unmanageable, then distasteful" (letter to Cowley, January 18, 1924). Burke took the train to North Carolina for a six-week visit to his wife's family. On the train he wrote a long letter to the censor (which does not survive), and there the matter ended. Two months later Josephson had taken a job on Wall Street and given up on *Broom*, his backer (and brother-in-law?) Maxwell Geffen having withdrawn his support and his potential buyers Knopf and Liveright (and someone else in Knoxville) having decided to withdraw as well (Cowley to Loeb, March 14, 1924; Josephson to Loeb, October 20, 1923). Cowley got distracted by the "Aesthete: Model 1924" affair, which had broken late in December. For a time the possibility of more issues remained alive (Burke to Toomer, March 9, 1924; Crane to Burke, February 23, 1925), and a year later the *Broom* group would reconvene to produce *Aesthete, 1925* (see chapter 2). But in early 1924 *Broom* had in effect ceased to exist.

Secession was also killed by the October 19 meeting, because Munson was now effectively isolated from many of "the youngest generation" that *Secession* was built around. Brown and Cowley and of course Josephson determined not to contribute further to *Secession* (Cowley to Loeb, October 30, 1923). Burke resigned his *Secession* editorship right after the October 19 meeting because he wished to remain neutral in the dispute between Josephson and Cowley and Munson and because he characteristically felt more comfortable being unaligned with either the Dada school of Josephson and Cowley or the nationalists now so closely associated with Munson; but he remained on good terms with Munson and contributed impartially to both magazines while they lasted (Cowley to Loeb, November 22, 1923; Munson to Burke, October 23, 1923). Burke's story "A Progression" took up a third of the winter 1924 issue of *Secession*, which also included poems by Yvor Winters and Hart Crane, an essay by Waldo Frank, a notice of Burke's resignation, and explanatory notes assigning blame to Josephson for errors in previous issues. With its eighth issue in April 1924 composed entirely of Winters' twenty-page essay "Testament of a Stone," *Secession* completed its two-year run as a sponsor of "the youngest generation." Munson, who had intended that *Secession* would last only for a few years anyway (he had announced the intention in the first issue), took some consolation from the fact that he had outlasted *Broom* by a few months.

The real aftermath of the October 19 drama, though, took place earlier, on or about November 10, 1923, when Josephson traveled to Munson's retreat to confront his insults directly. (Josephson had gone to the area to see Brown, who lived about a mile from where Munson was convalescing from his illness with the art historian William Murrell Fisher.) After trading insults, the two decided to settle the matter by means of a fistfight. Who won? Josephson publicly claimed a draw, shading into a narrow victory: "Munson . . . had become very fat, outweighing me by about fifty pounds. His fists felt like pillows. He stood still; I hauled off and hit him with a first roundhouse blow in the mouth that left a slight scratch. The slow-moving Munson, after a few exchanges, clinched with me and we fell to the wet ground, rolling about awhile and becoming well covered with mud. I struggled to break with him. We were both out of breath as we got to our feet and could scarcely swing at each other. . . . Fisher told me later that I was sitting on Munson's chest when we stopped" (*Life* 266). Privately he took even more credit for giving Munson "a sound thrashing" (letter to Loeb, November 16, 1923): "I assure you I beat him severely; I roared at him for twenty minutes before I finally bullied him to come out of the house. . . . I failed to knock him out [only] because I don't know enough, but I did other things, and with a cut mouth and eye, he was not a pleasant, and quite a muddy, sight. . . . I came out unscathed . . . but G. B. M. thereafter wrote letters to all he knew, claiming a draw (!)—a truly preposterous and suspicious enough gesture" (letter to Loeb, November 30, 1923). Munson indeed had scored the bout rather differently. In print he too claimed a draw shading toward victory: "All that need be said in public print is that the scuffle was brief, not bloody, and at one moment exceedingly funny. It ended inconclusively" ("Fledgling" 52); "it was a scene in the theatre of the absurd. . . . Josephson was ignorant in boxing as well as unathletic in build. The encounter was more nearly a scuffle than a fight. Its high point—or better, the low point—was reached when the Dadaist lay supine under the rump of the Secessionist, his body writhing beneath the weight of a convalescent, . . . his arms pinioned by the knees of the critic. . . . 'Let me up' was the Manifesto of this upsetting moment" (*Awakening* 185–86). But elsewhere Munson was less modest. "Matty's attack was a body one, but as his hitting power was light, it didn't matter much, and I enjoyed the entry to his exposed face, swelling his eye, etc. At one time we somehow fell to wrestling, and I threw Matty, and hugely enjoyed pinning his arms down with my knees, resting my derriere on his tummy and gibing at him" (Munson to Burke, November 10, 1923).

No one will ever know who ended up sitting on whom. The only other observer of the fight, Fisher, summed up the fistfight (and, in effect, the entire October 19 fiasco) in one simple sentence: "That was the poorest boxing exhibition I ever saw" (Munson to Burke, November 10, 1923). Josephson saw it all as the end of an era:

Several of us who were in the first wave of literary tourism in Europe had returned to the United States with the hope of putting our Great Young New American Movement into high gear. . . . But there were as yet no helpful social arrangements by which the artist

113

himself might escape the peril of being caught up by the assembly lines. At any rate, our affirmations had won us too little public support; our amusing perturbations had raised up only some small tempests.

Now in their middle twenties, the men in our sector of the Young Generation turned to mending their own fences. We dispersed to take jobs in Madison Avenue or Wall Street or wherever opportunity led us; for it was time to make a home, beget a child, and plant a tree. (*Life* 274)

5

At *The Dial*—and
Up against Dada

URKE'S FICTION BROUGHT him to the attention of a small group
of committed modernists who were just beginning the venture of
creating a new version of *The Dial* as a place dedicated to modern
arts and letters. The publication of "Mrs. Maecenas" was an auspicious
event for Burke. "I date my beginnings, decidedly, from the time when
The Dial took my story 'Mrs. Maecenas' and from the several eventful
years of my association with the magazine thereafter," he wrote in a letter
to Nicholas Joost on November 3, 1958.[1] The "new" *Dial*, an auspicious
event itself, dated its own beginnings from about the same time, for Sibley
Watson and Scofield Thayer had barely published one number when it
accepted "Mrs. Maecenas" and "Portrait of an Arrived Critic" in January
of 1920.[2]

The Chicago-based *Dial* had been a serious, and seriously leftist,
political and literary review (it dubbed itself "a fortnightly review of
literary criticism, discussion, and information") after it was acquired in
1916 by Martyn Johnson.[3] Progressive politically—it carried commentary
by Dewey, Veblen, and Randolph Bourne—the magazine was only a bit
more conservative in aesthetics, for it included notices of Frost, Pound,
Eliot, Williams, Joyce, and the Provincetown Players alongside ones for
Booth Tarkington, John Galsworthy, and Zane Grey. On June 6, 1918,
in the midst the Great War and the financial trouble associated with the
high cost of paper, and probably in response to the demise of the leftist
review *Seven Arts*, *The Dial* announced that it was moving operations
to New York City and becoming a more overtly political publication.
Thus, late in 1918 it reviewed Trotsky's *The Bolsheviks and World Peace*,
published the controversial liberal historian Charles Beard, carried the
Original Decrees of the Soviet Government, and installed Veblen and
Dewey on its masthead as editors. In Greenwich Village *The Dial* was

subsidized by Scofield Thayer and Sibley Watson, two wealthy young men who had taken an interest in the magazine while it was still in Chicago, and when the journal continued to struggle financially in the face of postwar conservatism, Thayer and Watson took the opportunity to purchase the magazine when it was offered to them late in 1919. The November 29, 1919, issue carried the news that Watson was now president of *The Dial* and Thayer its new editor.

The very first issue of the new *Dial* indicated that under Watson and Thayer *The Dial* had changed, fundamentally and famously, into a magnificently produced, far less political monthly, one committed to the cause of modern art and literature. Thayer, born in 1890, was the product of great wealth and a privileged education. He attended Milton Academy with T. S. Eliot, and then, with Cummings and Foster Damon, studied at Harvard, where he worked on *The Harvard Monthly* until his graduation in 1914. Thayer developed a taste for Continental Post-Impressionists and writers; a poet of sorts himself, he particularly venerated Picasso, Joyce, Freud, and a number of German writers. Watson, born in Rochester in 1894, came from Thayer's same economic and social mileau. After six years at Groton, four at Harvard, and some months in Chicago, he found himself in Greenwich Village in 1917 because he had decided to take up medical study at NYU, where he received his degree in 1921. (His interest in film ultimately expressed itself in his specialty, radiology.) A student of the Symbolist poets, Watson published essays under the name W. C. Blum and played an anonymous but generous role in encouraging *The Little Review* during its years in New York City (Anderson, *Thirty Years' War* 188–89).[4] But of course his most important sponsorship of modernism came in the form of his collaboration with Thayer, as well as with other Harvard acquaintances like Stuart Mitchell and Gilbert Seldes, on *The Dial.*[5]

Anyone who has examined, or even glanced at, *The Dial* of Thayer and Watson easily appreciates Burke's enthusiasm, at the age of twenty-two, for placing his stories there. Since, in chapter 2, I have already described the stupendous contents of *The Dial* from 1920 to 1924, there is no need to repeat here the fantastic litany of successes in "the greatest American magazine of arts and letters of [the] century" (Joost, *Scofield Thayer* 267). Suffice it to say that Thayer and Watson gratified their taste for modern art by publishing the very best work they could find, and that their judgments about what constituted outstanding work have proven to be extremely cogent. Since Watson especially appreciated the work of Americans, the two leaders of the magazine quickly established relationships with outstanding writers and artists affiliated with Greenwich Village— Cummings, to be sure, but also Williams, Stevens, Millay, Waldo Frank, Djuna Barnes, Lola Ridge, Edmund Wilson, Van Wyck Brooks, Marianne

Moore, Sherwood Anderson, Stieglitz, O'Keeffe, Demuth, Stuart Davis, Edward Nagle, and Marsden Hartley. Since Thayer was enthusiastic about British and especially Continental moderns (e.g., Yeats, Brancusi, Bertrand Russell, Santayana, and Schnitzler), *The Dial* developed several European connections, sometimes with the help of Ezra Pound,[6] who, as *The Dial's* agent, brokered the publication of "The Waste Land" as well as writing by himself, H.D., Hueffer, Proust, Anatole France, Unamuno, Croce, Wyndham Lewis, and Remy de Gourmont (Sutton 4). Thayer personally visited Europe himself from July 1921 until mid-1923 to secure contributions from Mann (as well as to receive psychiatric treatment at the hands of Freud). As a result, *The Dial* was able to publish and reproduce all of the above as well as Picasso, Rimbaud, Matisse, Lawrence, Lachaise, Joyce, Conrad, Woolf, Pirandello, Chagall, Toulouse-Lautrec, Hardy, and the many others who helped make it famous. And all of this represents only the primary art and not the reviews and criticism/commentary of *The Dial*, which in magnificent fashion considered everything from Eliot's *Sacred Wood* and *Ulysses* to Dada, film, and jazz.

Thayer and Watson were fairly eclectic in their modernist tastes.[7] Writers of various nationalities were welcome, including those recent "enemies" from Axis Germany. Leftists like Stuart Davis, Louise Bryant, and John Dos Passos as well as political conservatives and reactionaries like Eliot and Wyndham Lewis all found space in *The Dial*, as did cosmopolitans like Joyce and literary nationalists like Williams and Frank; the less tolerant literary nationalists found the magazine too international, while doctrinaire socialists mocked its conservatism (Wasserstrom, chapter 4). While many of the artists were already so well known that *The Dial's* more experimental rivals *Broom* and *Secession* saw it as a bit staid and that today it appears in some ways as an anthology of so-called "high" modernism, many of the people Thayer and Watson published, like Mann, Eliot, Cummings, Crane, Moore, and Burke, to mention a few, were still rather obscure figures to Americans when they first appeared in *The Dial*. *The Dial* as a matter of policy attempted to make publication judgments on esthetic, not political grounds. "We have never published anything or anybody for any reason but the one natural reason," read a *Dial* editorial in June 1923: "because the work was good" (638). A rather reclusive (and, as we will see, unfortunately rather paranoid) aesthete, an enthusiast of Beardsley and other *fin-de-siècle* decadents, Thayer in an early editorial Comment promised a *Dial* that would be explicitly "non-political" (April 1920). While he claimed to vote for socialists, Thayer had little use for the explicit political orientation of the old *Dial* (Joost, *Scofield Thayer*, chapter 1), and so he resolved to avoid explicitly political essays and commentary almost completely. From the perspective of three-quarters of a century, *The Dial* therefore now looks pretty conservative politically, especially by comparison with the "old" *Dial*, though to be fair it should be added that in the increasingly conservative 1920s Thayer and Watson were operating in a climate of overt censorship (recall, among other things, the *Masses* trial of 1918, the suppression of *The Little Review* over *Ulysses*, and the demise of *Broom* in early 1924, all of which took place in New York)[8] that made it imprudent to take political and artistic chances, especially when the financial consequences of a suppressed issue would have been grievous. In addition, *The Dial's* commitment to international modernism and artistic experimentation tended to encourage apolitical contents emphasizing aesthetic quality above all. That is particularly so since modernism itself before 1930 was still "undecided, unfixed, still exploring its potential and possible alliances" (Nelson, *Repression* 230). "What *The Dial* sought was aesthetic perfection, perfection in form, and it expressly decried a preoccupation with politics and social reform," notes Nicholas Joost (*Scofield Thayer* 103). The magazine sought "to consolidate the [modernist] revolution . . . [so that] what had seemed shatteringly novel in 1920 was acceptably orthodox in 1929" (23). Itself intended as a work of art, *The Dial* preached the aesthetic doctrine of autonomous art (at least until Burke began to chip away at that doctrine after 1925, as I'll show in the next two chapters) and fielded an aesthetic criticism based on an apprehension of form and a deemphasis on politics. Gilbert Seldes' words on the occasion of Cummings' *Him* are representative: Seldes claimed to be upholding "the Aristotelian practice of keeping one's eye on the object, of criticizing the thing criticized and not the grandfather of the artist nor his taste in haberdashery nor his private opinions" (July 1928).[9] Thayer and Watson hoped to make money by their new venture, but, as evidenced by the huge deficits they ran up and the generous subsidies they gave to writers in the form of payments and under the aegis of the Dial Award, what they hoped for most was increased public acceptance for the artistic revolution known as modernism.

The aestheticism of *The Dial* made it an ideal place for the aspirations of Kenneth Burke, himself committed above all in the first years of the 1920s to a rather pure aestheticism. While Burke was establishing ties with Williams, Frank, Crane, and others among the literary nationalists, his tastes still ran more toward Continental writers and toward the consideration of aesthetic values. As a member of "This Youngest Generation," he defined himself, as I've indicated, in opposition to the older generation, most of them literary nationalists, and identified with the aestheticism of the Symbolists and Flaubert. Thus, heartened by the success of "Mrs. Maecenas," by the prestige of *The Dial*, and by what he perceived as a congenial aesthetic position, Burke contributed several other early pieces to *The Dial*. As I indicated in chapter 4, above, his short sketches "The Excursion" and "The Soul of Kajn Tafha" appeared in the July 1920 issue, and "Portrait of an Arrived Critic" in April 1922, though the more experimental "David Wasserman" and "My Dear Mrs. Wurtelbach" were rejected. In February of 1921 and 1922, Burke placed his first major critical essays in *The Dial*, one an ambitious and sympathetic overview of the French aesthete Remy de Gourmont and the other an article on the correspondence of Flaubert, both of which (as I'll indicate in the next chapter) displayed a decided attraction for art for art's sake that was most congenial to *The Dial*. Perhaps in part because of his friendships with other Harvard men like Cowley and Damon, Burke also obtained assignments to complete a number of *Dial* reviews—of John Cournos's *The Mask* (published in the April 1920 issue); of Virginia Woolf's *Night and Day* and *The Voyage Out* (in May 1921); of James Oppenheim's poetic autobiography *The Mystic Warrior* (August 1921); of Arthur Schnitzler's *Casanova's Homecoming* (December 1921); of Stefan Zweig's *Romain Roland* (January 1922); of William Carlos Williams' *Sour Grapes* (February 1922); and of Paul Elmer More's *The Religion of Plato* (May 1922).[10] In addition, he translated Mann's "Loulou," a short story about a woman who humiliates her foolishly and conventionally genteel husband, for the April 1921 issue.

Then came Burke's big break. Impressed, no doubt, by the ability and versatility he had already displayed, and facing the problem of covering for Thayer and assistant editor Sophia Wittenberg while they were abroad, Watson asked Burke to serve as an assistant editor for *The Dial*, possibly on the recommendation and certainly with the approval of Alyce Gregory, Thayer's secretary and also an assistant editor.[11] "There is the possibility that I shall work for the *Dial* from July to November, filling Sophie Wittenberg's place," wrote Burke to Cowley on his twenty-fifth birthday, May 5, 1922. "In fact, it is already settled between Watson, Seldes [now managing editor], and me, but the thing seems too good. Christ, what a chance! I should get thirty-five dollars [a week] and pay for all contributions. Not a great pile, perhaps, but with my present low expenses it would leave me in positive affluence." Burke was very glad for the work not only for the literary opportunities it offered but because it appeared, providentially, just as he and Lily were preparing for the arrival of their second daughter and just after he had borrowed the money to buy the place at Andover, where he had moved about April 1, 1922, in time to install a garden and begin making the house livable. Munson would be dropping by in May to recruit Burke to help with *Secession*, a responsibility Burke kept while working at *The Dial*, but it paid no stipend, and so Burke was beginning to wonder how he would make ends meet when he got the offer from *The Dial*. Beginning his work on June 27, 1922 (Seldes to Burke, May 9, 1922), Burke stayed on not just through November but for fifteen months, until the end of September 1923.

Kenneth Burke in the 1920s. Photograph courtesy of Michael Burke.

For, once he took up his duties at *The Dial*, Burke quickly made himself indispensable by doing just about everything and doing it well. He was responsible for things like proofreading, page design, and the set-up of each issue, for example. One of his first such tasks was to set "The Waste Land" into print so that it could appear for the first time ever in the November issue.[12] Oftentimes, as in the case of Eliot's poem, the work required great precision, especially since Burke was struggling under the directives of the exacting Thayer, a stern and fastidious editor even from as far away as London and Vienna, whence he sent Burke cable after cable on *Dial* business in 1923. Burke also continued to do book reviews—a workman-like critique of Evelyn Scott's novel *Narcissus* for the September 1922 issue (he found the book derivative of Joyce and Waldo Frank); an assessment of Frank's *Rahab* and *City Block* for October (a review that instigated a rejoinder from Frank)[13]; a study of J. Middleton Murry's *Still Life* and *The Things We Are* for December (another articulation of Burke's aestheticism, of his preference for formal achievement over realistic content); a dutiful account of Giovanni Gentile's tract *The Reform of Education* (January 1923); and an analysis of Gertrude Stein's radically experimental *Geography and Plays* (April 1923), which, as I'll indicate soon enough, Burke deplored as an extreme instance of Dada disrespect for language.

Having set Mann's "Loulou" into English, Burke was also assigned to take up additional translations for *The Dial*. Even before Burke arrived for full-time work, Seldes had assigned him to translate Hugo von Hofmannsthal's "Vienna Letter," which appeared in August and October of 1922,[14] and for the July 1922 issue, he translated Hans Purrman's "From the Workshop of Henri Matisse," a fascinating narrative recollection of Purrman's encounter, through the intercession of Gertrude and Leo Stein, with Matisse and his salon in 1905. The August issue contained Hofmannsthal's "Lucidor: Characters for an Unwritten Comedy," and in September *The Dial* published Burke's translation of Richard Specht's German-language portrait of "Arthur Schnitzler," begun in April. By the time of the December issue, Thayer had signed on Mann to do a regular German Letter, all eight of them subsequently translated by Burke (December 1922; June and October 1923; January and November 1924; October 1925; July 1927; and July 1928). Thayer had also convinced Mann to contribute several stories, so Mann's "Tristan" appeared in December and January, the product of a collaboration between Thayer and Burke,[15] and in the same month Burke began the laborious and exhilarating process of preparing *Death in Venice* for an English-reading public, an effort that consumed much of Burke's time during 1923 and that was published in *The Dial* and separately as a book in the spring of 1924.[16] Burke was also responsible for helping out on the translation of Gerhart Hauptmann's "Heretic of Soana," published in April, May, and June of 1923 (Burke to Thayer, May 19, 1923); for Stefan Zweig's lengthy essay on Dickens (January 1923); for Julius Meier-Greafe's article, "German Art after the War" (July 1923); and for Arthur Schnitzler's story "The Fate of the Baron von Leisenbohg" (December 1923). When Pound was dismissed by Thayer in late March 1923, Paul Morand took over the Pound's task of writing the Paris Letter, and so it also fell to Burke to translate those too; they appeared a dozen or so times from August 1923 through April 1929.[17]

By the end of 1922, Burke, having filled in while Seldes vacationed in New Hampshire in September, was so obviously capable of additional responsibilities that Seldes felt comfortable reducing his own hours at *The Dial*, first to work on a book and then to go on an extended trip to Switzerland. From January until the end of July 1923, therefore, Burke served as acting managing editor—arranging for reviews of books, overseeing the preparation of issues, attending to Thayer's exacting, even tyrannical editorial directives, and writing letters to contributors (one of them, at Thayer's insistence, to reject Pound's Malatesta cantos, another to justify the exclusion of a contribution by Freud).[18] Though he managed to squeeze in a week off each month in the summer of 1923 to attend to things at Andover (Burke to Thayer, May 19, 1923), he was kept extremely busy by his job. He even was pressed into doing an editorial Comment for July 1923, one that offered a surprising but resolute support for classicism as a source for pure art that would effectively counter the "commercial code" then so dominant: "The classical spirit would be so inimical to the spirit of modern business that when all its ramifications have been followed through we learn that classicism would be nothing other than howling rebellion" (104).[19] By the end of the summer of 1923, Thayer and Seldes were back in the country and back on duty, and so, as October began, Burke was content to give up full-time work (though he also expressed his willingness to pick up again whenever he was needed [Burke to Thayer, August 24, 1923]) and to occupy himself at Andover with other projects. These included completing *Death in Venice* (and the Mann stories "Tonio Kroger," "Cemetery Road," and "Tobias Mundernickel" that would fill out the Mann volume[20]), preparing his own stories for the press (he entertained offers in December for what would become *The White Oxen, and Other Stories*), reviewing Djuna Barnes's *A Book* (*The Dial*, April 1924), translating Heinrich Mann's story "Virgins" (*The Dial*, January 1924), and seeing to the affairs of *Broom* and *Secession*.

In January 1924, just days after "Prince Llan" was getting *Broom* suppressed into oblivion, Burke and his family left for a visit to his in-laws in North Carolina. The place at Andover was still not ready for winter occupancy, so a trip south seemed advisable. While he was in winter quarters in Asheville, Burke continued to do piecework for *The Dial*. At the request of Alyse Gregory and for the sum of two dollars each, he did a number of "Brief Mentions"—short notices of a hundred words or so of books that *The Dial* wanted to recognize without supplying a full review (Burke to Gregory, January 20, February 11, and February 20, 1924); no doubt he had done many others during 1922 and 1923. On January 23, 1924 (Burke to Gregory, Burke Papers), he mailed *The Dial* the final installments of *Death in Venice* and turned his attention to translating Schnitzler's "New Song" (finished February 11 and published in November 1925). He also wrote a review of devotional poems by Solomon Ibn Gabirol that would appear in August 1924.[21]

But by February 27, 1924, Burke was back in Greenwich Village working regularly at *The Dial*. Sophia Wittenberg was preparing to fly the country for the spring months, and Alyce Gregory, now serving as managing editor, was planning to marry on the last day of September. So Gregory asked Burke to return as assistant editor during March, April, and May, and again in October, for fifty dollars a week (Gregory to Burke,

February 2, 1924; Burke to Gregory, Burke Papers, February 6, 1924). During June, July, and September, Burke occupied himself with the farm, but he was also a de facto *Dial* employee, since he did a great deal of *Dial* piecework during those months. There were more Brief Mentions, the beginnings of the essay that would become "Psychology and Form" (see chapter 6), a respectful review of Glenway Wescott's *The Apple of the Eye*[22] that underscores the value Burke placed on aesthetic innovation and experimentation, a review of Brownell's *The Genius of Style*, and a review of Mann's *Buddenbrooks* that appeared in November. Burke's review of *The Genius of Style* was submitted to Gregory on December 23, 1924, and published the following March; it defended Brownell's plea for "aesthetic prose" and contained a last-sentence gibe at Mencken that is very much in the spirit of *Aesthete, 1925*. Burke's *Buddenbrooks* review absolutely gratified Thayer, who wrote, "We have not published a better review" (Thayer to Burke, November 19, 1924).

Of course, there was also more translating to do, most notably the introductory sections of Spengler's *Decline of the West*, published in *The Dial* in November and December 1924 and January 1925 as *The Downfall of Western Civilization*. Burke began working on Spengler on July 1 and kept at it through the first days of November, when he mailed the final installment to *The Dial*.[23] Thayer was by now so impressed by Burke's talents that he invited Burke and his family to join him at his place on Martha's Vineyard for the month of August 1924. For fifty dollars a week plus room and board Burke worked about six hours each day as Thayer's secretary (Thayer to Burke, July 27, 1924), but that still left plenty of time for sailing, fishing, and beachcombing (Burke to Thayer, September 2, 1924; Burke to Josephson, August 12 and 24, 1924).

By the end of 1924 it was obvious that Burke had made himself essential to the fortunes of *The Dial* as an assistant editor, managing editor, critic, fiction writer, and translator. And *The Dial* was useful to Burke as well. It provided him with a more than adequate income, with substantial artistic and critical freedom and security (enough to permit the radical aesthetic experimentation of *The White Oxen, and Other Stories*), and, just as important, with steady exposure to the most powerful modernist personalities and texts of the day. Burke fit well with *The Dial*'s commitment to aesthetic excellence, and *The Dial* fed Burke's taste for Continental moderns, particularly those with refined aesthetic temperaments, like Gourmont, Flaubert, and the Symbolist poets. Burke was now consorting on a daily basis with talented New Yorkers, directly or indirectly associated with *The Dial*, who were obsessed with aesthetic concerns—Thayer and Watson and Seldes, of course, but also Edmund Wilson,[24] Marianne Moore, Slater Brown, Allen Tate, John Peale Bishop, Hart Crane, Gorham Munson, Jean Toomer, Isidor Schneider, Lewis

Mumford, Van Wyck Brooks, Malcolm Cowley, Matthew Josephson, and William Carlos Williams (Burke to Wheelwright, September 27, 1925). As 1924 turned into 1925, several of these were cooperating in putting together the *Aesthete, 1925* caper (see excursus, "Aesthete, 1925," in chapter 2).

The depth and nature of Burke's aestheticism at this time, as well as his characteristic independence, are visible in his contributions to *Aesthete, 1925* and to *The Dial*. But Burke's commitment to aestheticism can be understood even better if it is placed against his attitudes towards Dadaism, that brief and perplexing moment within modernism that in the half decade after the Great War nonetheless captured the fancy of Burke's friends Cowley and Josephson and the pages of *Broom* and *Secession*, though not *The Dial*.

Dadaism isn't easy to define. One of its best chroniclers, especially of its American manifestations, describes it as a "deliberately incoherent movement" (13), as "neither a school nor a movement but rather an essentially chaotic phenomenon that cut across art forms and national boundaries" (Tashjian, *Skyscraper* xii).[25] Like modernism itself, which spawned Dadaism as one of its many incarnations, Dadaism followed from both Symbolism and the Great War; and like modernism, its definitions and manifestations shift with individuals and national boundaries. Though an American version of Dada (without the nomenclature) was already evident in the art and activities of Marcel Duchamp, Francis Picabia, Man Ray, and others in the Stieglitz circle in 1915 and though its essential qualities had been formulated even before then, Dadaism was officially declared (or so the story goes) in the Café de la Terrace in Zurich on February 8, 1916, by Tristan Tzara, a Rumanian writer appalled by the massive human destruction being wrought by World War I. Tzara and a number of other internationals set themselves in radical opposition to the war and to the old culture that created it. With Hans Arp, the Alsatian poet and artist, and the German painter Max Ernst, Tzara in Zurich produced the *Bulletin Dada* through the end of 1918 as a means of expressing the negation and protest that they all felt toward virtually every aspect of conventional European culture. Like the Symbolists, who were deeply repulsed in the second half of the nineteenth century by what they perceived as the mindless cultural philistinism of the West, the Dadas broke completely with mainstream morality, epistemology, religion, politics, and art. But unlike the Symbolists, the Dadaists did not retreat into a rarified private world of art and abnegation, inaction and ennui. Instead, they engaged in highly public mocking demonstrations—street theatre, written declamations, mock trials, weird costumes, insults, fisticuffs, vaudeville— all sorts of "significant gestures," informal and spontaneous nonsense events, that might ridicule any kind of traditional propriety and that might dramatize for the public the decadence of conventional Western values, manners, and behaviors.

Since some of those values and behaviors were artistic, the Dadaists also rejected artistic conventions of every kind. While the Symbolists respected some literary and artistic traditions, Dada art was a highly anarchic and deeply individualistic public critique (albeit a frequently obscure critique) of traditional and conventional artistic decorum. In radically seeking to free art from all Victorian sincerities and all "classical rigidities" (as Tzara put it in a 1922 *Vanity Fair* essay), the Dadas embraced novelty and experiment. (Tzara, for instance, violated syntactical and typographical conventions in a way that borrowed from, and then in turn influenced, the Futurists and the Stieglitz circle and the writers of advertising copy, a development that also influenced E. E. Cummings.[26]) The Dadas depicted "unartistic" subjects, particularly the artifacts associated with the urban scene, with great enthusiasm (e.g., Man Ray would photograph arrangements of ball bearings, watch springs, and kitchen matches) and in so doing blurred the distinction between art and non-art and forced audiences to become as self-conscious about the media as about the messages of art. (For example, Marcel Duchamp exhibited ready-mades; other Dadas touted the artistic value of steam shovels and skyscrapers; and Max Ernst cut illustrations from mail-order catalogs, shuffled them, and exhibited the result as a painting.) And in their writing they flirted with extreme obscurity and radical self-expression. While much Dada art was calculated to bring laughter—Dada artists certainly displayed a sense of humor—all of these activities were nevertheless intended to excite disgust and revulsion; all were designed as a way of saying "no" to established social norms. "DADA means nothing," proclaimed Tzara. "We spit on humanity. . . . Dada is the abolition of all logic. . . . We must sweep everything away and sweep clean" (quoted in Josephson, *Life* 108). Tzara's March 1918 Dada Manifesto emphasized negation, anarchy, protest, and the abolition of hierarchy and logic. His followers even played chess without rules (Loeb, *Way* 59–60).

After the war, the Dadas returned to their homelands and spread their doctrine throughout Europe. A particularly vibrant group of Dadas consorted in Paris under the leadership of André Breton, Louis Aragon, Phillipe Soupault, Paul Eluard, and, fresh from New York, Duchamp's friends Man Ray and Francis Picabia. There they observed together the full range of Dada practices and genres: the collage and the mock trial, experimental poetry and nonsense prose and prose poetry, Rayograph photography and automatic writing (unpatterned, free-associational, Freudian-inspired prose that helped to generate surrealism). Like the Italian Futurists before the war, the Paris Dadas were fascinated by machines and technology, though unlike the Futurists, the Dadas could be critical as well as enthusiastic about technology.[27] They also espoused playfulness, spontaneity, naivete, and primitivism—Breton patronized African art, most attended to jazz, and others touted in various ways the childlike and "savage" and untutored. Together they embraced the ephemeral, the throw-away, the novel, and the ridiculous. In January 1920 Tzara himself arrived in Paris and took up residence with the expatriate literary crowd around the *rive gauche*. Although a rivalry within the established group eventually developed when Tzara undermined (in Dada fashion) an international congress on Dada that Breton had organized in Paris during the summer of 1922—the rivalry was probably inevitable, given the nature of Dada—Paris became the most notable and notorious Dada stage, at least until the whole movement fizzled, seemingly all at once. By December 1924 *The Dial* was carrying an epitaph for Dada in the Paris Letter that Burke translated for it.

It was this Parisian brand of Dada that Josephson and Cowley found themselves in the midst of during 1921, 1922, and 1923. Josephson at first found Dadaism somewhat ridiculous: "Dadaism is an attempt to throw cubism into the discard, and is more amusing than important as a movement," he wrote Burke on September 10, 1920. But once he arrived in Paris himself in the middle of 1921 and met some of the Dadas personally (Ray, Breton, Aragon, Soupault), he found them "young and stimulating" and "joined the[ir] camp" enthusiastically (letter to Burke, December 10, 1921). Josephson's letters to Burke in the next few months are filled with details of his tutorial at the hand of Aragon, so that by February 1922 he had rejected all set forms, all inherited artistic traditions: "As for me, I am over with the old leper. His time is over," he told Burke (February 4, 1922). By springtime Josephson declared himself completely for the new—for "ad copy, not syllogisms," for "spontaneity, aggression, humor, vigor, and choler" as opposed to the "penumbrated despair and wistfulness of the nineteenth century" (to Burke, April 20, 1922; May 24, 1922). He also enthused after Apollinaire, who had "urged the poets of this time to be at least as daring as the me-chanical wizards who exploit the airplane, wireless telegraphy, chemistry, the submarine, the cinema, the phonograph, what-not."[28] Harold Loeb, editor of *Broom*, was just as enthusiastic: Once he got himself situated in Paris, Loeb rid himself of Kreymborg's American nationalist bent after a couple of issues and set out to cast *Broom* in a more Dadaist light. "Our idea is to recognize new beauties," he declared. "It is the policy of *Broom* to examine contemporary phenomena, from movies to jazz, to billboards, advertising slogans, skyscrapers, etc. and using them as bases to create that significant form of which our genius is capable. . . . Our bent in this direction has been misnamed 'skyscraper primitivism' by several contemporaries including *The Dial* [in September 1923]" (Loeb to A. C. Barnes, Loeb Papers, September 21, 1923). Josephson was the natural one to preside with Loeb over this "skyscraper primitivism"; as editor and associate editor of *Broom*, Loeb and Josephson made a place, among the other moderns they published, for Soupault, Ray, Gertrude Stein, and Apollinaire, not to mention for their own essays and art on Chaplin, American cinema and music, and other subjects amenable to the Dadaists. Josephson's own "Made in America" (June 1922), "After and Beyond Dada" (July 1922), and "The Great American Bill-Poster" (November 1922) and Loeb's "Foreign Exchange" (May 1922) and "The Mysticism of Money" (September 1922) disseminated Dadaist values. The last offered a particularly articulate summary defense of American art developing out of America's "religion of money"—art such as dredges, threshing machines, airplanes, comics, advertising copy and formats, skyscrapers, bridges, and jazz.

Munson for a time and Cowley for a longer time also became Dada converts. Munson befriended Josephson and several of the Dadas in the summer of 1921. He wrote and published some poems "making use of the multiplication tables and the mention of forbidden things, and being properly idiotic" ("Fledgling" 28). And he published three numbers of *Secession* with a decidedly Dada cast to them: he accepted prose by Josephson (under the name of "Will Bray") on new Dada writers as well as near-nonsense verse by Aragon and Tzara and Josephson himself for the first number; Tzara's nonsense story "Mr. AA the Antiphilosopher" for the second; and Josephson's prose-poem "Cities II" and "poems" by Soupault and Arp for the third—before becoming exasperated with Josephson and Dadaism in the summer of 1922. And though he claimed to stand apart from them, Cowley quite literally made Dada a way of life, especially after befriending Aragon in the autumn of 1922. He changed his poems to satisfy Dada aesthetic values, placed his experimental work in *Broom* ("A Young Man with Spectacles," "Young Mr. Elkins"), patronized other Dada writers and secured them for *Broom*, watched as his friend Robert Coates composed a Dada novel, and even engaged in some rather notorious Dadaist "significant gestures." The latter included a Dada prank in the pages of *Secession* number 4 (with Josephson, he mutilated a poem by Richard Ashton[29]); a book-burning episode during which traditional works were consigned to the flames by Cowley and then doused by Cummings' urination; and a barroom brawl during which, more or less on a whim, he punched the proprietor of the Rotonde and after which he had to bribe his way out of prosecution (*Exile* 158–70; Loeb, *Way* 168–69; Bak 264–65). The final episode finally sent Cowley back to New York in the late summer of 1923, determined to open another Dada front in New York (see the sidebar on the October 19, 1923, caper in chapter 4, above).[30] As Tashjian shows, Cowley was a bit late in bringing

Dada to New York: Dada had already influenced Stieglitz, Dove, Sheeler, Ray, Demuth, and Stella, as well as Williams, Cummings, and Crane, all of "whose [art] developed out of their response to Dada" (Tashjian, *Skyscraper* 5; see also Naumann). These artists either took in Dada with enthusiasm (e.g., Ray), were influenced by it to some degree (e.g., Crane), or generally opposed it (e.g., Williams).

Burke, too, developed his early aesthetic values partly through a dialogue with Dada. Certainly he was well acquainted with Dadaism; even though he remained in New York, he was well enough informed about its Parisian and other manifestations[31] to write an essay describing and evaluating it in February 1921, well before Josephson fell in with the Dadas in Paris. In "Dadaisme Is France's Latest Literary Fad," Burke indicated by way of definition that Dadas in Paris "have inaugurated the first true chaos in the world's history. . . . Each Dadaiste masterpiece must remain a puzzle to its owner, as it is a puzzle to anyone. For the Dadaiste masterpiece is produced by something beyond the mere laws of appreciation; Dadaisme is a stab, a haphazard thrust." Burke associated Dada with Symbolism, Futurism, and the end of the war ("the younger generation which spent five formative years in that long holiday of misery can never settle down again to such a docile existence as that which comes of polite words, proper punctuation and pretty stories"). He identified its chief organs of expression (*Littérature, 391,* and *Cannibale*), named its ringleaders (Picabia, Tzara, Aragon, Soupault), noted its chief premises ("Their byword is 'rien', which means nothing"), and offered instances of Dada art.

The article indicates that in some ways Burke sympathized with Dadaism. He appreciated the Dada fetish for novelty, its modernist revolt against the staid and conventional—especially in matters of form did Burke appreciate Dada experiment and innovation. He also appreciated the "complete affirmation of the creative" that underlay all the negation in the movement; in sweeping away the old, in committing completely to the new, "[the Dadaist] has distilled individualism to its quintessence, and the brew is decidedly intoxicating" ("Dadaisme"). Moreover, as I have already indicated in chapter 4, Burke's "My Dear Mrs. Wurtelbach" certainly articulates a Dada "rien" on its closing page in a way that excited Cowley, who also contended, with reason, that the story was built on the substitution of absurdity for logic. The spirit of playful experimentation evident in the later stories of *The White Oxen*, like the typographical maneuvers in "Scherzando," "Yul," and "After Hours" and like the fanciful "plots" of "The Death of Tragedy," "In Quest of Olympus," and "Prince Llan," are also in keeping with Dada values. Similarly, in his 1925 "Dada, Dead or Alive," Burke rather elaborately countered Waldo Frank's contention that Dada is not right for the American artistic scene

Kenneth Burke in mock academic garb, late 1920s. Photograph courtesy of Elspeth Burke Hart.

by testifying eloquently to the value of the "spirit of the contemporary" that exists in both America and Dada. Instead of trying to rein in Dada in favor of a more controlled, philosophical, "saintly" art, as Frank recommended,[32] Burke instead endorsed "Dada aggrandized." He supported, in other words, an inclusive art that embraces every sort of subject, even those in radical opposition—"stately kings and runny-nosed populace, supernal beauty and brass bands, affirmation and actuality" (23–26).[33] Burke also no doubt appreciated the Dadas' rebellion against the old order at just the time that he was identifying himself with the "youngest generation" and apart from Frank, Brooks, Dreiser, and Anderson. And he certainly appreciated the Dada spirit of playfulness, expressed in the *Aesthete, 1925* publication that accommodated "Dada, Dead or Alive" and evidenced in Burke's participation in other literary pranks.[34]

But despite some areas of agreement, Burke finally remained rather apart from Dada. For one thing, its radical individualism struck him as anarchic and uncritical; in approving everything novel and prizing the spontaneous and irrational, Dadaists were aesthetically undiscerning: "Here at last art is beyond the critics, even to the extent, perhaps, that the intoxicated creator . . . finds that he cannot approach his own recent production. The approach is impossible, because a finished work must be approached critically rather than creatively, and critically it is unintelligible" ("Dadaisme"). When Cowley commended "Mrs. Wurtelbach" as a Dada masterpiece, Burke quickly corrected him ("I insist that . . . the associated ideas cannot be put down in the Dada manner"), for, skeptical of the city and the wonders of technology, he never became as enthusiastic as the Dadas about urban modernity or about the machine as a subject for celebration in art: "The arrant and sterile modernity which we get out of Dadaism is founded entirely on a complete obliviscence to about nine-tenths of the facts. It is all city products" (Burke to Cowley, January 18, 1923). For that matter, in his own art he eschewed Krazy Kat, Chaplin, ad copy (except in his mock ads), skyscrapers, machines, and other novel Dada subjects: "The Dadaistes have simply carried our present-day neo-mania to its furthest conclusion" ("Dadaisme"); "I do not find [the promise of America] in advertising, or penny slot machines, . . . or city atrocities" (Burke to Cowley, January 18, 1923). Later he insisted that he was never the fellow "skyscraper primitive" that Josephson claimed Burke was in *Life among the Surrealists*: "On that point he and Munson were much closer to each other than I was to either of them" (Burke to Loeb, November 23, 1959). Never could Burke accept the Dada attack on language itself; scandalized by the nonsense diction, he called Dada poetry "masturbatory" (see Josephson to Burke, February 28, 1922): "You have failed to sell me the Dadaists, in spite of your unmistakable enthusiasm. . . . I am scandalized by this: That words of all things are used in a way that denies their essential property, the property of ideological clarity" (Burke to Josephson, December 27, 1921).[35] While praising *Broom* and Loeb's "The Mysticism of Money," he nevertheless continued to advocate instead an aesthetic elitism that was rather contrary to the Dadaist egalitarianism expressed by Loeb:

The question still remains as to whether the artist must build his excellence upon the foundation of this democratic manure, or whether he is entitled to pass up the matter entirely, accepting de Gourmont's rather enticing idea of the two currents of art, one for the populace and one for the elect. Latent in your article is the complete acceptance of democracy, the acceptance of the *vulgus* as the *vox domini*; why should artists start with this handicap? (Burke to Loeb, October 20, 1922)[36]

"I believe that art is the possession of the initiated," Burke wrote to Cowley. "The great bulk of the world remains as insensitive to aesthetic values as an ape does to Cezanne" (February 6, 1922). Instead of accepting nearly everything novel in America as a Dada good, as he had implied in the hyperbolic "Dada, Dead or Alive" (his contribution, after all, to the gag publication *Aesthete, 1925* composed after the demise of Dada), Burke typically remained critical of—even alienated by—the contemporary American scene:

You are right in looking at America as "a land of promise, something barbaric, and rich." But alas! I feel that in your admiration (theoretical, . . . strengthened by Matthew Josephson) you have neglected to distinguish between a qualitative and a quantitative richness. . . . It is a fight against mass, a fight which you used to combat along with me: the fight for quality. . . . [In America] there is . . . not a trace of that really dignified richness, the richness that makes for peasants, household gods, traditions. America has become the wonder of the world simply because America is the purest concentration point for the vices and vulgarities of the world.

I can only say to you what I said to Matty months ago: We *will* build a literature out of advertising, we *will* build a literature out of economy, directness, psychological salesmanship, and the like. But in the refined artist the use of this material will be so subtilized, so deepened, that the ad writer would not even suspect that this artist is thinking in the ad writer's set of terms. That is the thing you do not take into account. And to me it is the only important thing. (Burke to Cowley, January 18, 1923)

Instead of sweeping away everything old, instead of embracing completely Josephson's enthusiasm for "spontaneity, exuberance, aggression, and choler," Burke preferred to respect some classics, even to defend classicism (as in his July 1923 *Dial* Comment), and, at least to an extent, to respect an attitude of aestheticism-as-withdrawal.[37] In his pursuit of the foundations of aesthetic form, he studied the classics, consulted with McKeon and the New Humanists, and read Flaubert as an aesthete. Early in 1924, he showed to Cowley his impatience with the movement and his "sudden nauseabund realization that you and Matty are doing your best to turn literature into a sandpile with buckets and shovels"; and he offered Cowley a "Credo" for the "next phase" of Dada:

> Against raw-rawism
> In favor of beauty, dignity, sanctity of criticism
> For a passionate apprehension of life
> Spinoza rather than Souppault
> God rather than dada
> Against the purely representative, the symptomatic
> For aesthetics, called such (Burke to Cowley, January 7, 1924)

"Burke was hell bent on leading American literature back to the true path of Spinoza and Goethe, his literary idols of the moment," wrote Josephson (*Life* 233). Burke helped convince Munson to back *Secession* away from Dada—the two rejecting an experimental prose contribution from Gertrude Stein in the process. In short, with respect to Dada Burke retained a characteristic individualism.[38] Committed to no particular school and yet connected to all of them, he maintained what he called in the preface to *Counter-Statement* "an equilibrium of his own." His thinking comes through clearly in a letter he wrote to Cowley: "The trouble with Dada is that there are no first-rate Dadaists. They are swine lying in a whole bed of pearls. I refuse to hear more of them. YET AT THE SAME TIME I ADMIT THAT IF ANY OF US DOES ANYTHING OF LASTING IMPORT, IT WILL BE DONE WITH THE SAME EQUIPMENT WHICH THE DADAISTS ARE USING" (January 18, 1923).

Burke would show an "equilibrium of his own" toward the aestheticism of Thayer and Watson and *The Dial*, too. By the end of 1924 he was composing two key essays, "Psychology and Form" and "The Poetic Process," the first published in *The Dial* in July 1925, that (as I'll indicate in the next chapter) begin to offer an alternative to pure aestheticism and to the doctrine of the autonomy of art. As 1925 wore on into the later years of the decade he continued to forge his own independent direction in criticism. In addition, in the summer of 1925 he had a personal falling out with Thayer that actually confirmed his independence from the magazine even as he remained closely associated with it for the rest of the decade.[39]

The Dial was experiencing considerable instability early in 1925. Thayer's sessions with Freud hadn't ameliorated his mental illness, and so he was contemplating another trip to Europe to write and recuperate. Sophia Wittenberg had now left the magazine for good. Alyse Gregory, managing editor since late in 1923, was busily nursing her husband, the Englishman Llewelyn Powys, near Woodstock, New York, where he'd gone with a case of tuberculosis (Joost, *Scofield Thayer* 83), and the two were planning to move to his home on the Dorset coast as soon as it was feasible—in June, as it turned out (Gregory to Burke, March 19, 1925). Aware of these difficulties and willing to help, Burke offered to work full time at *The Dial* early in 1925 (Burke to Gregory, *Dial*/Thayer Papers, February 25, 1925; Watson to Burke, February 27, 1925). During February and early March the problems grew more serious as Watson was attending to affairs in Rochester, where he had returned to live in October of 1924, and to his medical career. Then, in response to the crisis, Thayer and Watson decided to appoint one of their favorites, Marianne Moore, as acting editor, a position she assumed—permanently, as it turned out— about the first of April.[40] Kenneth Burke was secured as her full-time associate editor (Watson to Burke, March 9(?), 1925), reporting to work officially on April 22 (Burke to Josephson, March 16, 1925).

Together Moore, Watson, and Burke got *The Dial* through 1925. Fortunately, there was a backlog of manuscripts on hand. While Moore and Watson decided on additional acceptances and while Moore did reviews and editorials, Burke contributed "Psychology and Form" as the lead essay in the July issue. He reviewed V. F. Calverton's *The Newer Spirit* in time for August[41]; struggled over a review of Denis Saurat's *Milton, Man and Thinker*, a book that he loathed ("the only thing in the world I detest more than this review is the book about which it was written": Burke to Moore, September 21, 1925); and in another review showed considerable (and, in retrospect, surprising) sympathy, after the aesthete example of Remy de Gourmont's *Esthetique de la Langue Française*, for the efforts of the aptly titled Society for Pure English. He also did more Brief Mentions, including one of I. A. Richards' *Principles of Literary Criticism*. And he translated Mann's German Letter (October), Morand's Paris Letters, Hofmannsthal's essay on Balzac (May) and Schnitzler's story "Lieutenant Gustl" (August). When Moore went to Maine on vacation in September, Burke served as acting editor; then, until after the middle of December, he worked half-time (Burke to Moore, September 15, 1925).

But a difficulty arose when Thayer in the midst of his paranoia inexplicably accused Burke of some act of disloyalty. Exactly what upset Thayer I have been unable to discover—it may have been that an error in *The Dial* drove the exacting Thayer to suspect a deliberate sabotaging of the magazine (Moore to Watson, November 30, 1925)—but the real cause was Thayer's unfortunately distracted personality, which was driving him to suspect the loyalty of several *Dial* staffers, even Watson himself (Sutton 288). In any case, Thayer demanded Burke's dismissal. The affair must have developed in June, for by June 30, Gregory was asking Burke sympathetically for details about "these reverberations which reach us [about *The Dial* which] do shock me" (Gregory to Burke, June 30, 1925), and by mid-July Burke was writing to Thayer to explain why

133

he could not go to Europe as Thayer's secretary because of Thayer's previous accusations (July 15, 1925).[42] Moore and Watson refused to act on Thayer's demands, and the two of them stoutly defended Burke for the rest of the year. Watson wrote to Burke to reassure him that Watson retained his own full confidence in Burke, a letter which "much cheered" Burke (Moore to Watson, November 30, 1925). As late as December 28, Moore was still defending Burke resolutely: "I could not have retained my office [as editor] had I been asked to concur in his [Burke's] dismissal," she wrote to Thayer. "As it is, convinced though I am of his affection for you and of his pride in *The Dial*, I must needs acquiesce in his leaving, since this was the plan originally agreed on."[43] "The thought of turning away loyal dependents who revere you and Dr Watson—who have done their work as well as if they had done it for love rather than for bread, is sickening," she added on January 16, 1926, just as Thayer in Prerow, Germany, was on the verge of the complete breakdown that would result in his hospitalization the following month.

And so Burke left *The Dial* in 1926 and sought other employments. "He is leaving," Moore explained to Watson, "because the situation is too unpleasant for him to care to stay on. He is not leaving as a therapeutic measure and does not believe his going will be of any assistance to the patient. He shares your opinion that S. T. has not sufficient contact with the world" (Moore Archive, November 30, 1925). With his third daughter expected in June 1926, Burke took full-time employment with the Laura Spelman Rockefeller Memorial Trust, where until August 15, 1927, he did research on drug addiction for Colonel Arthur Woods. About a year later, in October 1928, Colonel Woods again hired Burke, this time to study connections between drug addiction and crime at the Bureau of Social Hygiene in New York, where he continued until mid-1930; Burke ghostwrote Woods's book *Dangerous Drugs* (1931). During and in between those assignments Burke accepted a number of translating jobs for Harcourt, Brace, *The Little Review*, and *Vanity Fair*,[44] tried to persevere on the work of fiction that developed into *Towards a Better Life*, explored (for some reason) the possibilities of writing a *History of Love* (Burke to Josephson, November 11, 1927; the project never got very far), and kept up his freelancing as much as his other jobs would permit.

He still remained close to *The Dial*, however. By late February of 1926, Thayer having officially severed editorial ties with *The Dial*, Watson was asking Moore if Burke's feelings toward *The Dial* were "restored" enough "that we can ask him for book reviews again" (Watson to Moore, February 25, 1926), so Moore assigned him to review T. V. Smith's *Notes on the American Doctrine of Equality* (Burke to Moore, April 15, 1926); and by the end of May Moore was awaiting Burke's review essay on Spengler and asking Burke to substitute for her once more while she went on vacation for two weeks in July (Moore to Watson, May 27, 1926; Moore to Burke, June 28, 1926). Burke also faithfully continued his translations of Morand's Paris Letters and Mann's German Letters. When his friend Williams won the Dial Award for 1926, Burke wrote the essay surveying Williams' career that was published in February 1927. In the summer of 1927, Burke was even more involved, particularly when he was substituting again for Moore while she traveled, this time to Europe. Burke continued to work full-time for Colonel Woods, but he somehow also managed *The Dial* during June, July, and August.[45] Besides overseeing the office and attending to correspondence and negotiations with contributors, Burke also translated a piece by Mann ("Pariser Rechenschaft," which appeared in June 1927), reviewed Paul Radin's *Primitive Man as Philosopher* for the November 1927 issue (in his review Burke resisted the modernist taste for primitivism by denying the distinction between the primitive and the civilized), prepared the translation of Hofmannsthal's Vienna Letter that appeared in August 1928 (Burke to Moore, May 26, 1928), and reviewed Van Wyck Brooks's *Emerson and Others* for January 1928. Finally, Burke also served *The Dial* as its last music critic. Moore found herself in a jam when Lawrence Gilman turned up ill just as he was succeeding Paul Rosenfeld (Moore to Burke, September 21, 1927; Burke to Josephson, October 11, 1927), and so Burke wrote fourteen Musical Chronicle columns, surveys of serious modern musical performances in New York City, from October 1927 until *The Dial* ceased production in mid-1929.[46] Moore always retained her admiration for the loyalty, ability, and versatility Burke displayed during the final years of *The Dial*. "How was Mr. Burke to work with at *The Dial*?" she repeated when she was asked the question years later. "He could do *any*thing—and do it with a springy step and the light touch. It's now that I realize how exceedingly rare that is" (recounted to Burke in her letter of July 19, 1944).

But *The Dial* became a diminished thing under Marianne Moore, though probably not because of Marianne Moore, who worked faithfully and capably as editor even to the complete neglect of her own poetry. When Thayer became too ill to continue securing manuscripts and to guide the magazine on a daily basis, and when Watson became more interested in medicine than the arts, *The Dial* began to lose some of its luster. With Watson's influence now far outweighing Thayer's, *The Dial* grew much more American, losing some of its compelling Continental flavor. Moore was forced to publish Thayer's own rather dreary poems at the expense of others more deserving, and, without his deep pockets, she also was forced to scale back somewhat on some of the magazine's regular features, the Letters from European capitals, for instance. Moore was a strong editor working under difficult circumstances, and her decisiveness in restorating relations with Pound permitted her to publish a number of his cantos, criticisms, and translations. *The Dial* under Moore also patronized Williams, Rilke, Yeats, Crane, Eliot, and D. H. Lawrence, and so, judged by any standard except for its own achievement before 1925, *The Dial* remained a stunning production. But it still wasn't the same. Moore also made some celebrated misjudgments, including the notorious editing of Hart Crane's "Wine Menagerie" into "Again" (Joost, *Scofield Thayer* 93–99) that infuriated Crane and his friends, and her refusal to publish 34,000 words from *Finnegans Wake* ("Anna Livia Plurabella") on the grounds that it was too long, too obscene, and not very good.[47] She also carried her special favorites—most notably, the venerable but hardly very modern George Saintsbury wrote extensively for *The Dial* under her direction—so *The Dial* came to have an insider's feel to it rather than a cosmopolitan one when Moore, Pound, Watson (as "W. C. Blum"), Burke, Thayer, Seldes, Cummings, Cowley, Stewart Mitchell, Alyse Gregory, and the artists associated with Stieglitz appeared more and more frequently as contributors. The contents were still outstanding, but they were also more familiar and predictable. "The Dial is getting Awful," complained Cowley to Burke as early as July 26, 1926; protested Williams to Pound: "It almost means that if you are 'one of The Dial crowd' you are automatically excluded from perlite society as far as influence [with the publishers] in N. Y. goes" (Williams, *Selected Letters* 103–4). In 1927 *The New Republic* claimed (January 5, October 12), with only some exaggeration, that *The Dial* hadn't encouraged a single interesting new American writer for years. Subscriptions were slipping too. By the spring of 1929, Watson finally decided to give up the effort. The final issue appeared in July.[48]

Burke's most significant contribution to the last years of *The Dial* was in the form of his fiction. Marianne Moore published six of Burke's "Declamations," six segments of what would become *Towards a Better Life*, in 1928 and 1929. As I'll indicate in the next two chapters, *Towards a Better Life,* together with the late-1920s essays that found their way into *Counter-Statement,* contains Burke's most mature and independent contributions to the modernist conversation that he would offer before the Great Depression settled in; they amount to an articulation of his second thoughts on modernist aestheticism. Before I turn to that, it is worth recalling that for the "Declamations" and for his other fiction, for his criticism, his translations, and no doubt for his many other contributions to *The Dial*, Watson and Moore presented Burke with the final Dial Award, for 1928.[49] The announcement on the last page of the January 1929 issue commended Burke's commitment to aesthetic values above all by quoting Burke himself: "The artist, as artist, is not a prophet; he does not change the mould of our lives: his moral contribution consists in the element of grace which he adds to the conditions of life wherein he finds himself."

6

Counter-Statement as
Counter Statement

*C*OUNTER-STATEMENT, too, like many of Burke's essays in *The Dial*, can be seen as the product of an aesthete sensibility, as a document with clear links to the Symbolists as well as to other modernist groups and doctrines. It takes up standard modernist artists, texts, topics, and controversies—Cezanne and Gide and Baudelaire and Verhaeren; *Death in Venice*, *R. U. R.*, and "The Waste Land"; psychology, aesthetics, form; the artist's confrontation with industrialism; the grounds of artistic merit and appeal; and the relations between art and society, artists and observers. But the book is not easily or simply modernist, for if Burke in *Counter-Statement* incorporates some doctrinaire aesthete and modernist notions into his understanding of art, he also counters some others. To put it another way, in *Counter-Statement* Burke from a position squarely within the modernist conversation nevertheless destabilizes certain key modernist assumptions—and in the process destabilizes *Counter-Statement* itself.

The general aim of *Counter-Statement*, to delineate the essential character of art and the relationships that exist between art and society, is certainly a modernist staple. In the preface to the second edition Burke explicitly described the book as a study of "wherein the worth and efficacy of a literary work reside" (xvi).[1] As such, the collection of essays, which were arranged generally in the order in which they were composed[2] and revised for the occasion of book publication, participates in one way or another in the tradition of analogous collections such as the multi-authored *Criticism in America: Its Function and Status* (1924), Foerster's *Humanism in America* (1930), Grattan's *A Critique of Humanism* (1930), Croce's *Aesthetic* (1902), Joel Spingarn's *Creative Criticism* (1917, 1925, 1931), Irving Babbitt's *Rousseau and Romanticism* (1919), Clive Bell's *Art* (1913), I. A. Richards' *Principles of Literary Criticism* (1924), V. F. Calverton's *The*

Newer Spirit (1925), Van Wyck Brooks's *Emerson and Others* (1927) and *Sketches in Criticism* (1932), Eliot's *Sacred Wood* (1928), and Wilson's *Axel's Castle* (1931), as well as in the tradition of critical statements and reviews by Spingarn, Pound, Wilson, Mencken, Brooks, Munson, Winters, Cowley, Joseph Wood Krutch, Granville Hicks, and others in periodicals like *Seven Arts, The Dial, Contact, The Bookman, Secession,* and *The New Republic.* As its title suggests, *Counter-Statement* is in a complex dialogue with these and other modernist critical texts, and, since it is a revision of a number of earlier essays and since one of its essays ("Lexicon Rhetoricae") is subtitled in part a "correction" of two earlier essays in the book, it also enters into a dialogue with itself. The result is a book which promotes a unique, if sometimes elusive and even contradictory, modernist account of the place of the artist and art in the early twentieth century.

Burke begins *Counter-Statement* by dealing with established modernist topics essentially as an aesthete or Symbolist would: that is, in a way that positions the modern artist as radically alienated and aloof from society, working in a realm of pure art that is insulated against the philistine masses. The "Three Adepts of 'Pure' Literature" from a departed generation whom Burke describes in his opening to the volume were all modernist heroes, and Burke had originally written about all three Europeans in the early 1920s while in the midst of his most committed rendezvous with aestheticism.[3] Flaubert, whom Burke had "dragged away [from the realists] into our [aestheticist] camp early in 1922" (Burke to Cowley, February 6, 1922), "had always looked upon art as an existence-in-itself" (1); Walter Pater, whom Burke admired for his "superior adjustment of technique to aesthetic interests" (9), was of course the most notable of the British aesthetes; and Remy de Gourmont, who "made one think of literature as a risk, a kind of outlawry" (64), was the Symbolist critic who was perhaps most admired by the most influential modernist image-makers during the first few years after World War I.[4]

Burke's Flaubert is truly an aesthete at heart, withdrawn from the world, adopting early in life (and never renouncing) a decadent interest in things illicit, striving monomaniacally after beauty rather than after the personal status or wealth pursued by Balzac, trying to conceal his art in pure form though ultimately failing in that because of his commitment to the novel form, a form ill-suited to the concealment of art. It would be an exaggeration to say that in its description of Flaubert the essay paints an uncritical portrait of the ideal life as something akin to the ones dramatized in *Axel's Castle* or *A rebours*—the ideal life as a purposeful retreat in the course of which an estranged solitary tries to give himself or herself as many pure moments of individual artistic satisfaction as possible. But the pronounced tendency toward that stance is certainly there, for

Burke does not reprove Flaubert's residence in "the *tour d'ivoire* school of writers" (1) or his singleminded devotion to his art—singleminded to the extent that Flaubert "read one thousand five hundred books to produce one" (3), looked "continually for an ideal form" (7), and delayed "seeing Louise Colet [his mistress] for even months, until he had 'finished a chapter'" (5). For Flaubert, according to Burke, the good life amounted to the deliberate multiplication of private and sublime emotional experiences that are produced mostly by contact with art; the ideal is something akin to the "poundings of the heart" Flaubert once "felt on beholding a bare wall of the Acropolis" (6), an intensity of feeling that he hoped to evoke through and in his writing. "I may never know again," says Burke's Flaubert, "such *eperduments de style* as I got for myself during those eighteen magnificent months" of composing the *Tentation de Saint-Antoine*. And good art for Flaubert was just as radically separated from public, civic action and from utilitarian ends: "What seems beautiful to me, what I should most like to do, would be a book about nothing, a book without any exterior tie, but sustained by the internal force of its style, a book which would have no subject, or at least in which the subject would be almost invisible, if that is possible. The most beautiful books are those with the least matter" (6).

Far from reproving this attitude, Burke was identifying strongly and personally with it and with Flaubert, whom he admired greatly for his artistic innovations and achievements, and also for his attitudes. Not only did Burke exclaim the identification in his letter to Cowley of January 6, 1918—"I shall get a room in New York and begin my existence as a Flaubert. Flaubert is to be my Talmud, my Homer, my beacon"—he also betrayed it in a revealingly personal sentence in the version of the Flaubert essay published in *The Dial* in February 1922 (a sentence deleted from *Counter-Statement*): rather like Burke himself or like some of his closest friends Crane and Cowley, "Flaubert at eighteen had all the earmarks of a promising young genius in revolt against Ohio, destined to come to New York and get a job with some advertising agency."

Burke's words on Pater reveal just how thoroughly aestheticized is Burke's account of Flaubert, for Burke's Pater is indeed the prototypical aesthete. Locked away in an artistic "cloister" so restricted that "he derived the characters and environments of his fiction by research" (10) rather than through experience, Pater is appreciated for the innovation of placing style and artistic technique above everything. "Art to Pater was 'not the conveyance of an abstract body of truths' but 'the critical tracing of . . . conscious artistic structure.' He thought of a sentence as a happening, [and] . . . his preference for artifice was consistent" (12). Residing in "the Immutable, the Absolute" world of Beauty, placing aesthetics above ethics, Pater "proclaim[ed] the dignity of man in art" (15). For Pater, art was its own reward, and artists first and foremost should seek Beauty rather than private virtue (let alone civic amelioration, except insofar as aesthetic refinement itself serves as a benign and constructive force in society). "Ideology in Pater was used for its flavor of beauty, rather than of argument. He treated ideas not for their value as statements, but as horizons, situations, developments of plot, in short, as any other element of fiction" (14).[5] Burke's tone here is reportorial rather than explicitly epideictic, but the patience and sympathy in his account still essentially mirror his sympathy for Pater's project.

Moreover, Burke's sympathy for Pater shows up further when his account is seen as being in general opposition to the New Humanists' disapproval of Pater, on the grounds that Pater's criticism was impressionistic, based only on shifting and emotional sensations rather than on firm aesthetic foundations.[6] By crediting Pater with residing in that "Immutable and Absolute" world of Beauty rather than in a lower world of impermanent flux, and by emphasizing Pater's fiction rather than his criticism, Burke countered the New Humanists' demonizing of Pater's alleged subjectivism. Burke's approval of Pater's reverence for The Beautiful thus allies him with the Symbolists as well as with Croce and Spingarn, whose own aestheticism may well have influenced Burke's views before 1925.[7]

But it is Burke's portrait of Gourmont that is the most revealing one among the "Three Adepts." Though Gourmont is barely remembered today, he was greatly admired by influential early moderns for his broad and deep learning, for his many plays, poems, stories, novels, and works of criticism, for his Symbolist literary values, for his editorial efforts on behalf of the Symbolists in connection with the periodical *Mercure de France* (which he founded and edited), and for leading a radically cloistered personal life that seemed committed to art above everything. *The Little Review* devoted a special hagiographic number to Gourmont in February/March 1919. Cowley in 1921 mentioned Gourmont, with Flaubert, as one of two basic introductions to French literature for "this youngest generation." T. S. Eliot considered Gourmont a formative influence on his life and art, as references and ideas in the essays in *The Sacred Wood* and *Selected Essays* attest. Amy Lowell and Richard Aldington considered Gourmont a pioneer in *vers libre* and imagism, Aldington publishing a lavish, two-volume, illustrated edition and translation of selected works by Gourmont in 1928. And Ezra Pound not only contributed a cranky review of Aldington's edition to *The Dial* while Burke was working there as music critic—it was cranky towards Aldington's work but not Gourmont's—but he also translated for *The Dial* all the epigrammatical quasi-poetry in Gourmont's previously unpublished *Dust for Sparrows* in eight consecutive issues of *The Dial* in 1920–21. Pound was indeed a great admirer of Gourmont as early as 1912. He communicated with

Gourmont until Gourmont's death in 1915 (at the age of 57), appropriated Gourmont's ideas into his own views of poetry and criticism, and included several essays on Gourmont in *Pavannes and Divisions* (1918).[8] He also wrote tributes to Gourmont on the occasion of his death for both *The Fortnightly Review* (1915) and *Poetry* (January 1916), and edited the special *Little Review* number on Gourmont (February/March 1919). Indeed, Sieburth in *Instigations* puts it this way: "Between 1912 and 1922 he was to devote more pages of enthusiastic appreciation and translation to Gourmont than to any other single contemporary" (1).

Burke's fascination with Gourmont is not unusual, therefore, particularly given his early enthusiasms for Continental writers in general and for the Symbolists in particular. Like Gourmont's other admirers, Burke personally appreciated Gourmont's disgust for social and artistic convention and his reclusive lifestyle—one spent in devoted service to art.[9] In that Gourmont served as a role model, then, he was "almost a 'traumatic' experience in my development," Burke later recalled (Fogarty 59). He also appreciated Gourmont's advocacy for a refined aristocracy of art and for an equally refined style—"a refinement [that] can do nothing but put to shame the brass of a Dell or Sherwood Anderson" (Burke to Henry Canby, March 21, 1921). Burke's letters reveal that as early as 1916 he was reading Gourmont (Wilkinson to Burke, March 13, 1916) and that the enthusiasm continued for some time. Three years later he was still discussing Gourmont with Josephson (see Josephson to Burke, March 27, 1919), and quoting him in his fiction ("Mrs. Maecenas," published in March 1920). And in the early 1920s he was sending Gourmont's books to William Carlos Williams to study. In fact, the nationalist Williams (as one might expect) expressed misgivings about Burke's enthusiasm for the aesthetic and ascetic Parisian Gourmont (Williams to Burke, January 12, 1921; March 22, 1921), even as he noted his admiration for Burke's essay on Gourmont that had recently appeared in *The Dial* (February 1921)— which essay was the basis for the essay on Gourmont that later appeared in *Counter-Statement*.[10] Accordingly, then, Burke devotes half of "Three Adepts" to this one figure, and he describes Gourmont in keeping with the received wisdom on him—as a prototypical Symbolist and modern.[11]

Gourmont, that is, like Pater and Flaubert, "remained until his death a man closed in his study, seen by a few intimates, living almost exclusively with books" (18); like Burke's Flaubert and Pater, Gourmont "had much too strong a detestation of democratic standards to be anything but a disciple of Art for Art's Sake" (16). A follower of Mallarmé, like Mallarmé a "leading apologist of symbolism" (21), a person who pursued throughout his life the intensely felt "exclusively personal experiences which are important so long as sensation endures" (20), an agnostic who was interested in the Catholic Church as an artistic pageant, Gourmont also had a Symbolist weakness for illicit subjects and a modernist "fever for innovation" and originality (16):

This attitude manifested itself in the experimental nature of both his critical and imaginative writings. His one imperative was to be venturesome. Since art, by becoming an end to itself, became a matter of the individual—or by becoming a matter of the individual, became an end in itself—he was theoretically without external obligations, at liberty to develop his medium as he preferred. (17)

This radical individualism, a staple of Symbolist decadence, was at the center of Gourmont's work.

Burke's overview of that work, an overview that shows the detail in Burke's knowledge of Gourmont, underscores Gourmont's enthusiasm for pure style, for the "complete lubrication of phrase" (17) that insulated Gourmont, as it had Pater, from philistine society: Gourmont had "little time for those perfect systems of government wherein the aggregate of humanity is to be made happy at the expense of each individual" (20). And Gourmont's innovation in thought was, appropriately, his "dissociative method," a "companion discovery to symbolism" (23)—that is, a suitably modernist method of invention designed to liberate words and beliefs from the conventional associations that have through time fossilized around them. An effort to rejuvenate knowledge, the dissociative method was designed to free thinkers from inherited dogma by offering a critique of inherited commonplaces and by generating for inquirers new associations for words and concepts. Burke illustrated the dissociation of ideas in *Counter-Statement* by quoting Gourmont's own examples— the associations between Byzantium and decadence and the associations that the English and French have held for Joan of Arc—both of which Gourmont had dissociated productively. With obvious enthusiasm, then, Burke concludes one segment of "Three Adepts"—and that conclusion was added on the occasion of *Counter-Statement*, by the way[12]—by crediting the concept of dissociation of ideas with influencing modernist prose experiments by Stein and Joyce and by speculating on possible extensions of the concept to literary criticism: "Any technical criticism of our methodological authors of today must concern itself with the further development and schematization of such ideas as de Gourmont was considering" (24).[13]

While the artistic heroes cited and discussed in *Counter-Statement*— Flaubert, Pater, and Gourmont in the opening chapter, Mann and Gide in a later one, and Cezanne, Shakespeare, Goethe, Eliot,[14] Joyce, Dostoevsky, Baudelaire, and assorted others elsewhere in the book—tie *Counter-Statement* intimately to the discourse of modernism, an even closer tie is forged by the book's preoccupation with a central modernist topic, the nature of form. From the beginning readers have noticed the centrality of this issue in *Counter-Statement*,[15] and Burke himself emphasized the importance of form to *Counter-Statement*: in the preface to the second edition, for instance, where he describes his theory of form as "the gist" of his book, and in his interview with John Woodcock, where he asserts that " 'Psychology and Form' . . . is really the center of that book" (704). *Counter-Statement* in general—and "Psychology and Form," "The Poetic Process," and "Lexicon Rhetoricae" in particular—presents Burke's fullest elaboration of thoughts about form that he would continue to develop throughout his career and that he had begun to formulate in earnest at least as early as 1921, when Cowley was identifying Burke and the other members of "This Youngest Generation" as writers obsessed with form.

"Psychology and Form," the best-known essay in *Counter-Statement*, does contain of course Burke's most quotable contribution to a theory of form: "Form is the creation of an appetite in the mind of the auditor, and the adequate satisfying of that appetite" (31). As I will indicate soon enough, Burke deserves enormous credit for this formulation because in it he reconceives form such that it is far less a static textual feature and far more a dynamic act of cooperation among writer, reader, and text that is more broadly rhetorical and social than purely aesthetic. In establishing "so perfectly the relationship between psychology and form, and so aptly illustrat[ing] how the one is to be defined in terms of the other" (30), Burke's theory of form is a tremendous innovation.

Nevertheless, it would be wrong to overstate the extent of Burke's innovation, to exaggerate his distance in "Psychology and Form" from modernist dogma. First, Burke's very use of psychology as a grounding for aesthetic form is consequent upon the modernist appreciation for the new science; considering the Symbolists' and the other moderns' powerful interest in Freudian and Jungian systems and explanations, and considering his own experiments with psychological arrangements in his short stories, Burke's interest in psychology and form in *Counter-Statement* in some ways seems less startling, almost inevitable. Indeed, in his 1932 review of *Counter-Statement* Harold Rosenberg noted explicit parallels between Burke's views and ones propounded in Paul Valéry's Symbolist *Introduction to the Method of Leonardo da Vinci* (1894): "Poe has clearly established his appeal to the reader on the basis of psychology and probable effects. From this angle . . . the work of art becomes a machine designed to arouse and combine the individual formulation of these minds" (120). Second, as you would expect of someone who described himself as "completely in the aesthete tradition" (Woodcock 708) until his composition of "Psychology and Form," Burke confines his account of form in that essay almost completely to form in art. Non-artistic discourse is regarded as a lower species, as mere "information" that trades in "facts," the kind of form deriving from mere surprise and suspense that one perceives in the daily newspaper (37).[16] Burke's examples in the chapter are accordingly drawn from drama, from Goethe's rather rarified prose, from Shakespeare's *Hamlet, Much Ado,* and *Julius Caesar,* and from that purest, most autonomous of art forms, music, which "is by its very nature least suited to the psychology of information. . . . Here form cannot atrophy" (34).[17]

In addition, Burke intimately involves in his discussion of psychology and form the terms "intensity" and "eloquence," two staples drawn from the aesthetes. The modernist desire for intensity, for those moments of ecstasy when the artist and his audience might burn alike with something akin to a hard, gemlike flame, derives from form when form is somehow created by eloquence, which "is the minimizing of this interest in fact, per se . . . until in all its smallest details the work bristles with disclosures, contrasts, restatements with a difference, ellipses, images, aphorism, volume, sound-values, in short all that wealth of minutiae which in their line-for-line aspect we call style and in their broader outlines we call form" (37–38). In other words, if Burke's theory of form is innovative in incorporating audience psychology, audience expectations, it also backs away at certain points from too profound a move from the text by collapsing text, audience, and author once more and "mak[ing] three terms synonymous: form, psychology, and eloquence. And eloquence thereby becomes the essence of art" (40). The remainder of "Psychology and Form" enlarges not so much on psychology as on eloquence, on "the exercise of propriety, the formulation of symbols which rigidify our sense of poise and rhythm" (42). Much of that remainder is in close keeping indeed with the assumptions of the Symbolists and particularly with the rarified and refined attitudes toward style that are associated with Gourmont.

Burke's theory of form is also developed elsewhere in *Counter-Statement,* in "The Poetic Process" and in "Lexicon Rhetoricae." "The Poetic Process" was in fact first composed as a companion piece to "Psychology and Form." After *The Dial* accepted "Psychology and Form" in December 1924 (Gregory to Burke, December 15 and 19, 1924; Burke to Gregory, November 20 and December 23, 1924) for publication in July of 1925, Burke in February offered *The Dial* "The Poetic Process" as well because he had designed the latter as the second of three projected essays on "the laws of artistic effectiveness . . . , the nature of audiences, and the problem of artistic permanence" (Burke to Gregory, February 4, 1925). When "The Poetic Process" was nonetheless quickly and summarily rejected by *The Dial* (Gregory to Burke, also February 4, 1925), Burke published it in *The Guardian*[18] in May 1925, and apparently abandoned the notion of completing the third essay until he could incorporate his

ideas into his "Program" and his "Lexicon" in *Counter-Statement*—
"Lexicon," after all, is Burke's "codification, amplification, and correction" of "Psychology and Form" and "The Poetic Process" (123)—and, in very different terms, into his later essay "The Philosophy of Literary Form."[19] Appropriately, "The Poetic Process" is restored therefore right after "Psychology and Form" in *Counter-Statement* as part of a coherent core statement about exactly how form is psychological in nature—how form in a work of art derives from an artist's need to express his or her inner emotions in a way (that is, in a symbol) that appeals to the predisposition for perceiving form that inheres in every human brain.[20]

For if "Psychology and Form" gives the impression that form is somehow relative, inhering not on the page but in the apparently ephemeral raising and satisfying of variable audience expectations, in "The Poetic Process" Burke is emphatic in giving form an anything-but-relative foundation: The psychological processes that operate within people to permit an apprehension of form are eternal and universal. "Certain psychic and physical processes . . . in the human brain" make it possible to perceive formal patterns "which are at the roots of our experience"; thus, certain recurrent patterns in nature—"the accelerated motion of a falling body, the cycle of a storm, the procedure of the sexual act, the ripening of crops," and so forth—strike humans as having formal resonance "because the human brain has a pronounced potentiality for being arrested, or entertained, by such . . . arrangement[s]" (45). An artist (like Thomas Mann) can offer a crescendo (like the progress of a cholera epidemic in *Death in Venice*) in order to produce form because the pattern of a crescendo is inherent in nature and in the wiring of the brain: "Throughout the permutations of history, art has always appealed, by the changing individuations of changing subject-matter, to certain potentialities of appreciation which would seem to be inherent in the very germ-plasm of man, and which, since they are constant, we might call innate forms of the mind" (46).[21] The forms of the mind, "the potentiality for being interested by certain processes or arrangements," make possible the apprehension of eloquent patterns such as crescendo, contrast, comparison, balance, repetition, disclosure, reversal, contraction, expansion, magnification, series, and so on, all of them subdivisions of the major forms, unity and diversity.[22] Analogous to Plato's sense of "certain archetypes, or pure ideas, existing in heaven" (47), Burke's archetypal "psychological universals" are thus the root source of form: "For we need but take his [Plato's] universals out of heaven and situate them in the human mind" (48) in order to have a grounds for artistic form that is as observable as gravity, the cycle of a storm, or the maturation of crops (45).

In this way the opening pages of "The Poetic Process" offer Burke's solution to a dilemma that he and other modernist critics had been wrestling with during the early 1920s. Are the foundations of aesthetic form and aesthetic judgment relative and in flux, as Bergson had offered? Are they radically personal, as in the impressionistic criticism of Croce, Anatole France, and Paul Rosenfeld? Are they therefore influenced inevitably (as Freudians held) by the variable drives and predispositions of the critic? Or are there fixed and eternal grounds for form and critical judgment, as the New Humanists insisted? Burke proposes his own compromise in "The Poetic Process." "At bottom I believe that the laws of artistic effectiveness remain the same, while the subject matter embodying these laws changes from culture to culture, age to age, and individual to individual" (Burke to Gregory, February 4, 1925, referring to "Psychology and Form" and "The Poetic Process"). It was a brief that he articulated in greater detail in sections 11 through 18 of "Lexicon Rhetoricae," detail that he once again summarized in section 18:

The various kinds of moods, feelings, emotions, perceptions, sensations, and atti- tudes discussed in the manuals of psychology and exemplified in works of art, we consider universal experiences. . . . The[se] universal experiences are implicated in specific modes of experience. . . . The range of universal experiences may be lived on a mountain top, at sea, among a primitive tribe, in a salon—the modes of experience so differing in each instance that people in two different schemes of living can derive very different universal experiences from an identical event. The hypochondriac facing a soiled glove may experience a deep fear of death to which the trained soldier facing a cannon is insensitive. The same universal experience could invariably accompany the same mode of experience only if men's modes of experience were identical. (149–50)

Literature, then, as a "verbal parallel to the pattern of experience" (152), as a symbol, is in one sense permanent, transcendent, ahistorical: "the formal aspects of art appeal in that they exercise formal potentialities of the reader" (142), potentialities that are as tangible as universal biological processes like systole and diastole, inhalation and exhalation (140). In so stating, Burke sides with those moderns who saw literature as offering a fixed foundation against contemporary flux and confusion. But in recognizing that different people experience art from differing modes of experience, that "each work re-embodies the [universal] formal principles in different subject matter" (142), he also acknowledges the perspectives of the Bergsonians, impressionists, Freudians, and Dadaists who were more skeptical about the universality and timelessness of art.[23]

If Burke's meditation on form in "Psychology and Form," "The Poetic Process," and certain parts of "Lexicon Rhetoricae" ties him to the Symbolists, to the Freudians, and to other moderns, then so does his emphasis on symbol itself—on the link between the artist's inner emotions and the audience's emotions that is supplied by what Burke here calls Symbol. In "Psychology and Form," "The Poetic Process," and "Lexicon

Rhetoricae," Burke does shift interest from the emotions of the writer to the emotions of audience. But he doesn't discard the emotion of the author as a source of "the poetic process." Far from it. As the rest of "The Poetic Process" makes clear, and as Burke further clarified in the sections of his "Lexicon" which garnish "The Poetic Process" (i.e., 150–66), while the apprehension of form does indeed depend on the psychology of the perceiver and on the characteristics of the object being perceived, form in art also derives ultimately from the artist's emotional need to articulate emotional states. Burke writes, for instance, that some "psychic depression" within a person might "translate itself into the invention of details which will more or less adequately symbolize this depression" in the same way that a sleeper depressed for some reason might, as Freud offered, through a dream invent details that symbolize that depression. "The poet's moods dictate the selection of details and thus individuate themselves into one specific work of art" (49–51; see also the amplification of "The Poetic Process" in section 19–24 of "Lexicon Rhetoricae").

Thus, while the poetic process might end with audience, it certainly begins, as modernists in the tradition of Bergson, Croce, Bell, and the Symbolists would have it, with the artist's deeply emotional need for self-expression, for a means of articulating symbolically his or her inner emotional world. True, Burke differs from the Symbolists and Freudians in contending that artists do not stop with expressing their emotions but also seek a form through which to evoke emotion in their audiences: in his view, the artist "discovers himself not only with a message but also with a desire to produce effects upon his audience" (54).[24] Nevertheless, as Gorham Munson contended in quoting from those essays even before their *Counter-Statement* versions were published (*Destinations* 153), Burke in "Psychology and Form" and "The Poetic Process" does associate himself both with Symbolism and with "the purest aestheticism." He does so by arguing that "the poet steps forth, and his first step is the translation of his original mood into a symbol" (56); and that "the artist begins with his emotion, he translates this emotion into a mechanism [or symbol] for arousing this emotion in others, and thus his interest in his own emotion transcends into his interest in the treatment" (55). Burke's identification of himself with the Symbolists is particularly evident when, at the end of "The Poetic Process," he goes to some lengths to explain how artists painstakingly refine their symbols through style and technique until they attain the status of the Beautiful (58). Granville Hicks therefore agreed with Munson's assessment of Burke's aestheticism when he reviewed *Counter-Statement* late in 1931. The editor of the leftist *New Masses* and biographer of John Reed objected in *The New Republic* that Burke was too "principally concerned with eloquence" and with technique at the expense of the social aspects of art; Burke was keeping writers and their work "as far removed as possible from the controversial and important issues of the day" (75–76). In this judgment Hicks was joined with Malcolm Cowley, who also complained from a Marxist perspective that Burke was giving too much emphasis to technique.[25]

In a very real sense, then, Burke developed central chapters in *Counter-Statement* by working from orthodox modernist premises. After presenting as models Flaubert, Pater, and Gourmont, after introducing them as heroes who maintained a sympathy for the illicit, a stomach for analysis, an exuberance toward excess, and an attachment toward the odd and insane (2–3), and as ones who lived for art in an elite opposition to mainstream society,[26] Burke offered innovation and form and stylistic refinement as the defining concerns of critics and artists alike. Understanding "eloquence" and "intensity" as central terms in aesthetics, and self-expression as implicated "in all human activities" (52), Burke sought to account for all the sources of form. Convinced with the Symbolists that the emotion of the artist is the generating force behind the poetic process, Burke also offered that form is the result of the artist's desire to produce effects on an audience: "He attain[s] articulacy by linking his emotion to a technical form," to a symbol (56) refined into eloquence through stylistic technique. *Counter-Statement* depicts The Good Life as a multiplication of private emotional experiences that are produced by aesthetic retreat with art. The opening chapters in most respects take up "matters of purely aesthetic judgment" (31) or identify art and aesthetics or wall off aesthetics from morality and truth as thoroughly as had Croce and his American disciple Spingarn and the artists who enacted their views.

And yet *Counter-Statement* truly articulates "the purest aestheticism" only if one ignores the qualifications on pure aestheticism that Burke placed in "Psychology and Form," "The Poetic Process," and "Lexicon Rhetoricae" (in each of which Burke is at pains to stress that "the self-expression of the artist, qua artist, is not distinguished by the uttering of emotion but by the evocation of emotion in others" [53]), only if one ignores the essays written for the book after 1925 (which Munson had not read when he made his comment), and only if one ignores the changes Burke made even in essays originally published before then. Indeed, particularly in those chapters of *Counter-Statement* composed last, Burke was offering his own original and rather social-rhetorical contribution to modernism, one very different from what Munson and Hicks saw in *Counter-Statement*. For *Counter-Statement* ultimately upholds art not as self-expression but as communication, not as self-contained and autonomous object but as moral and civic force. Even as early as the late 1920s Burke was staking out his position on literature as "equipment for living"—as social and rhetorical action.[27]

The "Mann and Gide" chapter expresses Burke's growing alienation from the radical aesthetes. Originally published in *The Bookman* in June 1930, after being turned down by Marianne Moore and *The Dial* in its final months (Moore to Burke, October 1, 1931), "Mann and Gide" revisits two writers whom Burke had considered many times before.[28] Thomas Mann and André Gide, probably the most famous living Continental moderns, Burke understood as drawing certain traits directly from the aesthetes, particularly an appetite for the repellant, the sick, and the illicit, an identification with "outsiders," and a fascination with "the non-conforming mind's constant preoccupation with conformity" (93). Gide's earlier work, including *The Immoralist*, displayed "the same rotten elegance as characterizes Wilde's *The Portrait of Dorian Gray*" as well as a "Baudelarean tendency to invoke Satan as redeemer" (93–94), while Mann aggrandized dissolutes like Aschenbach and articulated the "notion that the artist faces by profession alternatives which are contrary to society" (95). Original and experimental and innovative, Mann and Gide belong in these senses with the "Three Adepts" who open the book.

But unlike the aesthetes of the previous generation, Burke's Mann and Gide were fundamentally moralists and rhetoricians, Burke now argues. As the second half of the essay emphasizes, instead of living with art and pursuing beauty inside an Axel's castle, Mann and Gide devised in their fiction a rhetoric that was fundamentally moral in its thrust. "One need not read far in the writings of Gide to discover the strong ethical trait which dominates his thinking"; even when it contains the weird sex and violence of *Lafcadio's Adventures*, his art is full of "categorical imperatives," "scruples," "moral sensitiveness," and the like (100–101). Mann too considered moral problems to be the subject of his work—"moral chaos" and "moral vacillation" (101–2). Misunderstood as morally bankrupt, when actually his subject is moral uncertainty and his technique irony, Mann to Burke in 1930 was socially responsive and responsible: "Society might well be benefitted by the corrective of a disintegrating art, which converts each simplicity into a complexity, which ruins the possibility of ready hierarchies, which concerns itself with the problematical, the experimental, and thus by implication works corrosively upon those expansionistic certainties preparing the way for our social cataclysms" (105). Mann and Gide were to Burke (as to everyone else) anything but conventional, but they maintained as well the role of "praeceptor patriae" (106), haranguing people in their own way toward virtues of their own defining.

The social effects of literature on "the reader" and "society" are easy enough to discern in "Mann and Gide." But even "Three Adepts of 'Pure' Literature" itself, in retrospect, can be seen as setting up Burke's social and moral views on the effects of art. For by the end of the 1920s Burke had gained a healthy moral distance on all three objects of his undeniable respect. The quotation marks around the "pure" in his title indicate his knowing irony, his cool awareness of the impossibility of such a thing as purely asocial art. From the perspective of 1930, it is easy to see that not even Burke's Flaubert is fully and completely an aesthete, for although he certainly longed for refinement and withdrawal, he "never succeeded in arriving at an aesthetic amenable to his temperament" (5), particularly in that he chose a medium—the realistic novel, as opposed to criticism or poetry—whose social outlook was at odds with his aesthetic tendencies. Flaubert wished to write with attention to pure form, to compose "a book about nothing, a book without any exterior [i.e., social] tie, but sustained by the internal force of its style, . . . a book which would have almost no subject" (6), but he in fact worked in a medium that would not permit such a thing. He ultimately "suppress[ed] the verbalistic side of his interests" in favor of expressing concrete experience (9). By the time he came to prepare a reprint of the Flaubert essay for *Counter-Statement*, Burke understood the social nature of art well enough to delete a paragraph meditating on Flaubert's "art-for-art's sake doctrine" (153–54), as well as his original concluding paragraph, which indicated his earlier strong appetite for "pure technique," for technique as "the profoundest element of art" (155). Instead of that original conclusion (which would have given Hicks even more cause to complain of Burke's emphasis on technique), Burke for *Counter-Statement* composed four new paragraphs (7–9) which disclose the difficulty of pursuing a pure aestheticism in fiction. "A distinction between 'pure form' and 'pure matter,' " he now wrote, "may enable one to speculate about books which talk beautifully about nothing, but it provides no hints at all about specific matters of methodology" (8–9). The late revisions in the Flaubert essay show Burke backing off his earlier aestheticism—even though he was still sympathetic with Flaubert's effort at an art so artistic that it concealed its art. And he made similar revisions to the Gourmont portion of "Three Adepts," too. The 1922 admiration for Gourmont remains, but by 1931 Burke could leaven his admiration for Symbolist aestheticism by inserting three new paragraphs (16–19) which place aestheticism itself in a social and rhetorical context.[29]

Burke elsewhere in *Counter-Statement* critiques Flaubert's wish (one he shared with other moderns, of course) that some sort of pure form might be possible in art, that "a book which would have no subject" might be somehow producible. As I have already indicated with respect to "The Poetic Process" and the corresponding glosses of "The Poetic Process" in "Lexicon Rhetoricae," Burke by 1931 held that subject matter is impossible to divorce from artistic form. Indeed, it is only through subject matter that an artist can achieve form, can embody form for the apprehension of the reader or observer. Universal form on the page ultimately corresponds to and derives from the variable capacity to perceive form that exists in an audience whose circumstances change from time to time and place to place; "there are no forms of art which are not forms of expression outside art" (143). In arguing that variable content as well as permanent form determine the reaction of an audience, Burke was challenging not just a Flaubertian ideal but Clive Bell's more immediate—and certainly no less aesthetic—view that form alone creates aesthetic response. Bell's *Art* (1914), an avant-garde treatise on the modern visual arts, depicted the artist as radically detached from life, pursuing a "significant form" that is divorced from content, a pure form "behind which we catch a sense of ultimate reality. . . . In the moment of aesthetic vision, [the artist] sees objects not as means shrouded in associations, but as pure form" (45–46). Burke had disputed Bell on the relation between form and content in literature as early as his June 1923 review of Gertrude Stein's *Geography and Plays*, a work which attempts (Burke felt) a pure formalism in literature but which inevitably fails to achieve it; and that critique of Bell reappears in section 10 of "Lexicon Rhetoricae"—the tip-off is the use of Bell's phrase "significant form" as a header—a section which initiates a lengthy technical argument on the relation between form and content in literature. In that argument, which continues through section 14, Burke emphasizes that in literature form must always be joined to (or counterpoised with) content to create an aesthetic response. While content or "information" in art should never overwhelm form, lest artfulness be diminished (the "right proportion" between form and content is the subject of section 14), content can never be eliminated either, as Flaubert and Bell were wishing. "The forms of art are not exclusively 'aesthetic,' " then, concludes Burke. They "can be said to have a prior existence in the experiences of the person hearing or reading the work of art. They parallel processes which parallel his experiences outside art" (143).[30]

Burke began rethinking Flaubert and Gourmont's aestheticism early in the 1920s, then, and began adding audience to his aesthetic at least as early as the winter of 1924–25. True, since "Psychology and Form" and "The Poetic Process" were still both published rather early in Burke's career, Burke's sense of "the audience" in those essays is rather uncomplicated. His "audience" is still the stable and perceptive and rather passive individual reader or observer, still a qualified and predictable "we" (30)— someone rather like The Critic, who, if informed and sensitive, will respond as others do to the same artistic experiences. The psychology of the audience becomes really the trained and coherent psychology of individual experts from relatively homogeneous backgrounds who are sensitive and accomplished and experienced enough to perceive the subtleties of form and the distinctions between art and mere information. Note for instance how frequently audience in "Psychology and Form" and "The Poetic

Process" is described in singular terms or as an unproblematical and homogeneous "we": in the 1925 essays, artists write in order to move elite individuals and not heterogeneous groups. Cultures may change— "The Poetic Process" emphasizes that—but within cultures audiences are stable and coherent and passive and unproblematical.

But Burke's view of form in these early essays is still a major advance over most modernist conceptions of form for at least three reasons. First, during a period when new interest in psychology was generating new psychological analyses into literary characters and their creators (e.g., Brooks's *Ordeal of Mark Twain* and Charles Baudouin's *Psychoanalysis and Aesthetics*, both mentioned by name in "Psychology and Form"), Burke was instead pushing towards a consideration of the psychology of readers and how their perceptions are manipulated by artists to achieve certain effects: "Modern criticism, and psychoanalysis in particular, is too prone to define the essence of art in terms of the artist's weaknesses. It is, rather, the audience which dreams, while the artist oversees the conditions which determine his dream" (36). Second, Burke thereby shifts emphasis from art as mere self-expression of personal emotions to art as inducing emotions in an audience. Where Bell could offer that artists "do not create works of art in order to provoke our aesthetic emotions, but because only thus can they materialize a particular kind of feeling" (44), Burke was to emphasize the reverse: "If it is a form of self-expression to utter our emotions, it is just as truly a form of self-expression to provoke emotions in others. . . . the self-expression of the artist, *qua* artist, is not distinguished[31] by the uttering of an emotion but by the evocation of emotion. . . . We will suppose [in opposition to other critics] that the artist . . . discovers himself not only with a message, but also with a wish to produce effects upon his audience" (53–54). Third, in doing both of these things Burke was laying the groundwork for the even more expansive notion of audience and the even more rhetorical conception of art that he would express in "Lexicon Rhetoricae" and "Program." Rather than confining form to structural features, as Bell had, Burke in those essays in *Counter-Statement* was adding a rhetorical dimension to form; he was indeed in the midst of "shifting from self-expression to communication" as a way of viewing art.

"Lexicon," then, is a major contribution not so much in acknowledging audience (for Richards was doing the same at about the same time), but in pointing to new conceptions of audience and art. In keeping with its subtitle—remember, it is billed not just as a codification and amplification of "Psychology and Form" and "The Poetic Process," but also as a "correction" (123)—"Lexicon" emends those earlier chapters in a number of ways. For instance, audience in "Lexicon" is conceived not as the simple, passive, relatively monolithic, and unproblematical collection of individuals of "Psychology and Form," but as complex and heterogeneous. There is no such thing as the "perfect reader": "Aristotle points out in his *Rhetoric* that there are friendly readers, hostile readers, and simply curious audiences" (179); some real readers may even have "contrary patterns of experience" (177); and "the actual reader is obviously an indeterminate and fluctuant mixture of the [hysterical and connoisseur]" (180)—though the artist still remains "expert" enough to "reduce the recalcitrant reader to acquiescence," even to "overwhelm the reader and thus compel the reader to accept his interpretations" (176). The reader, less than self-contained now, is (like the writer and the art object) part and parcel of a culture.[32] As sections 15 and 25 make clear, anything-but-autonomous readers are situated in a cultural setting or "ideology" that directs their experience—"Othello's conduct would hardly seem 'syllogistic' in polyandrous Tibet" (146)—and audience expectations, similarly shaped by culture, are anything but purely personal and idiosyncratic. Indeed, "an ideology is the nodus of beliefs and judgments which the artist can exploit for his effects . . . [and] in so far as its general acceptability and its stability are more stressed than its particular variations from person to person and from age to age, an ideology is a 'culture' " (161). The artist, in other words, manipulates ideological assumptions for persuasive purposes, and thereby "persuades" and "moves" and "contributes to the formation of attitudes, and thus to the determining of conduct" (163). Art is political and moral. A Symbol not only "interprets a situation" (154), but it serves as "the corrective of a situation"—as "an emancipator" that persuades active readers in search of transformation to alter their values and attitudes and conduct (155–56). Already in 1931 literature for Burke is "equipment for living": the phrase later made famous in *The Philosophy of Literary Form* is a foreshortening of an important sentence from the penultimate paragraph in "Lexicon Rhetoricae": Art, far from being walled off from life in the manner of the aesthetes, is "an equipment, like any vocabulary, for handling the complexities of living" (183). In keeping with Burke's essay in the 1930 *Critique of Humanism* (see chapter 2, above), Burke's "Lexicon" involves art indelibly in life, conduct, ethics, and morality. (At the same time, Burke makes it clear that to defend art as implicated in life and morality is not to align it with the genteel, conventional morality that the moderns so despised and repudiated.[33]) In the final pages of *Counter-Statement*, Burke by way of summary concludes with a call for the rehabilitation of rhetoric. For "effective literature could be nothing else but rhetoric, . . . [which is] the use of language in such a way as to produce a desired impression on the hearer or reader" (210).

Building, then, on the same assumptions he had formulated for "Lexicon," "Psychology and Form," and "The Poetic Process" (art is eternal in that "it deals with the constants of humanity," while it is also social and situated in that it is "a particular mode of adjustment to a particular cluster of conditions"), Burke in "Program" turned to the attitudes and material conditions which he felt ought to be addressed by artists in the midst of the crisis of the Great Depression. In 1931 Burke wanted artists and critics to address the fundamental tensions of American society: the stresses between the "new" industrial ethos and traditional agrarian values, the inevitable conflict between the "bourgeois" practical and the "bohemian" aesthetic worldviews, the emerging collision between decentralized democracy and statist fascism, the problems of unemployment, the requirements of the dole. That Burke offers just such a list should not be surprising, for a major and perennial problem for modernist artists was and is what to do with and about new technology, industrialism, and urban life—witness, for instance, the Dadas. And that this list of Burke's is increasingly political and social is surely by design: in proposing these concerns, Burke was placing art and artists and critics in close relation to society, resisting any temptation toward aesthetic remove or elitism. In juxtaposing art and politics, art and non-art (the chapter is distinguished from others in *Counter-Statement* by its avoidance of now-canonical modernist works), Burke was now seeking to heal the modernist alienation between artist and society in a way that the Dadas and the Leftists of *Seven Arts* (and, for that matter, the New Humanists) would have appreciated.

True, the contemporary artist was never to lose his or her aesthetic temperament or oppositional stance toward all political positions. Burke's artist characteristically retains a modernist appreciation of beauty and suspicion about all orthodoxies: e.g., "his sensitiveness to change must place him at odds with the moral conservatism of the agrarians . . . , but the industrialist elements likewise will meet his innovations with resistance" (109). But as the chapter continues Burke's voice becomes prophetic and portentous, not only in registering his frank distrust of the fascists (recently come to power in Italy) but also in seeking "the dole as a norm" and "the redistribution of wealth by some means" (115), as well as in recommending that artists "become subversive" in dramatizing "the miseries of a[n economic] system which . . . has caused so many physiological needs to be perverted in so many people" (119). By the end of the chapter, Burke chooses between his opposites and adopts explicitly the language of the radical reformer: "Let us not pamper . . . a 'philosophy' of efficiency which makes overproduction a menace"; "let us attempt to bring to the fore such 'Bohemian' qualities as destroy great practical enterprise"; "let us reaffirm democracy (government by interference, by distrust) over against Fascism (regulation by a 'benevolent' central authority)" (119). Burke's economic views led him to imagine a radical restructuring of American industrialism based on the concept of the dole, for " 'Inefficiency' is required as the counter-principle to prevent the machine from becoming too imperious and forcing us into social complexities" (120–21). Most of all, Burke was now emphasizing "the function of the aesthetic as effecting an adjustment to one particular cluster of conditions, at this particular time in history . . . , for this gloomy reader's present ill-starred hour" (121–22). The urgent cadences of "Program" articulate an aesthetic position very different from the one proposed by the earliest-written chapters of *Counter-Statement*. Here, in the chapter he wrote last for his book,[34] Burke opts for an absolutely committed position for art and the artist. For good reason he could say in his preface to the second edition that "Program" is an "attempt to translate aestheticism into its corresponding political equivalents" (xiii). Art and criticism for Burke have now become part of a political attitude, "part of an intervention into history" (Jay, "Kenneth Burke" 72), part of an understanding of aesthetics that hearkens back to the reformers at *The Masses* and that anticipates the Marxist aesthetics so powerful during the 1930s. And for good reason he could call upon "Program" to "counter-blast" Granville Hicks's charge in *The New Republic* that *Counter-Statement* was a book by an aesthete, a book whose "emphasis is so unmistakably on technique . . . that the reader is bound to realize that it is technique alone that interests [Burke] the author" (101).[35]

At the same time that he was being criticized by Hicks (from the left) for being excessively aesthetic and insufficiently concerned with social amelioration, then, Burke was voicing opinions about the social value of literature that were leaving him vulnerable to attack (from the right) for just the opposite reasons. Just how much Burke's aesthetic in "Program" was a departure from what came to be known as "high" modernist tenets can be seen in Allen Tate's reaction to *Counter-Statement* in letters to Burke written from 1931 to 1933. Tate, surprisingly enough (considering how close Tate's politics and cultural values were to the substance of his own poetry and prose), felt that the autonomous artist wasn't so much shaped by culture and ideology that he couldn't command those forces through a Nietzschean expression of will. After commenting approvingly on what he saw as Burke's "agrarianism" in "Program," a position that Tate considered to be in keeping with his own politics and the politics of the other "twelve Southerners" who were then putting forth the agrarian manifesto *I'll Take My Stand* (Tate to Burke, April 9, 1931), and after sharing some initial misgivings about other aspects of *Counter-Statement* that prompted Burke to complain half-seriously that Tate was "mad and bitter" to deny "the fairly rational idea that books are written to produce effects on readers" (Burke to Tate, August 19, 1933), Tate was moved to defend directly and explicitly his commitment to the doctrine of the

155

autonomy of art. Yes, Tate admitted, there are such things as writers and readers. But "literature is not written for the explicit purpose of moving anyone," he insisted. "High Literature is nothing less than a complete qualitative and quantitative re-creation of the Very Thing-in-Itself. If some of its properties incidentally lead us to cut throats, seduce a virgin, or give all our goods to the poor, that is our responsibility. But because this may be so, there is no reason to . . . conclude that the whole function of literature is persuasion. A great poem is great whether anybody reads it or not" (Tate to Burke, August 30, 1933; for Burke's counter-salvo of September 27, 1933, see the excursus, "Burke Refutes Tate"). Tate's words constitute a frank, unqualified re-articulation of the doctrine of the autonomy of art, a view ultimately traceable to the Kantian notion that art is a self-contained object whose beauty is a matter of internal formal relations and a view so consistent with the opinions of so many moderns that Perloff has identified it as one of four-teen central modernist assumptions. I have already noted, for instance, Williams' belief that the true artist creates a self-contained "new object," as independent of morality and truth as "a table" (see the final pages of *Spring and All*). The motto of Margaret Anderson's *Little Review*— "No compromise with the public taste"—also reflects the opinion that art should be concerned less with reforming genteel society and more with creating purely aesthetic emotions that only the refined artist and critic can apprehend.[36] The revolutionary language of the "Manifesto" printed in *transition* in 1929 (see excursus, "Manifesto") betrayed the similarly aesthete notions that "pure poetry is a lyrical absolute," that artists "are not concerned with the propagation of sociological ideas," and that "the writer expresses, he does not communicate." Spingarn and Croce's aestheticism similarly assume the autonomy of art. And a dismissive, telling sentence from Ezra Pound—"Rhetoric is the art of dressing up some unimportant matter so as to fool the audience for the time being" (Pound, *Gaudier-Brzeska* 83)—sums up the view of many moderns that literature is something "high" and "pure" and absolutely apart from the often rough-and-tumble tactics of rhetoric and persuasion that Burke was linking it with.

Burke in "Program" thus puts certain tendencies of the moderns— to regard art as autonomous and autotelic and to understand art as the product of a sensitive elite divorced from the rough and tumble of impermanent daily life (tendencies visible in Burke's thinking in the early 1920s)—into juxtaposition with a different modernist view, one that looks back to the attitudes toward art of Randolph Bourne, John Reed, and John Dos Passos, and forward to the socially committed artists and critics of the 1930s. While remaining respectful of canonical writers and skepti-cal of Dada hyperbole, Burke nevertheless retained an appreciation for

Burke Refutes Tate

In this letter of September 27,1933 (slightly edited for length), Burke patiently and sometimes humorously tried to correct Tate's misguided opinions about the autonomy of art—opinions that Tate had expressed in a letter of August 30 (the phrases enclosed here in Burke's quotation marks originated in that letter) and that Burke had first tried to straighten out in *Counter-Statement*.

Andover, New Jersey
September 27, 1933

Dear Allen:

'Tis late. Outside my study, all the sounds are night sounds. The poisons of rotted grapes unfit me for the more burdensome tasks which even now I should be performing. Instead, I shall converse. Sentence for sentence conversing.

"This question of the writer-reader relation." I see no qualitative difference between a sentence, a letter, and a book. The sentence is usually addressed to someone in front of us, the letter to someone absent, and the book to someone indefinite.

"It is perfectly obvious that there are readers and writers." Then it is equally perfectly obvious that at least *one* way of discussing literature would be by considering both readers and writers.

"High literature . . . is not written for the specific purpose of moving anybody." What! Does this lad not try to make his verse appealing? Has he not even *omitted* things which he considered significant but the significance of which he felt would not be apparent and moving to others?

"Specific purpose." Ah! Perhaps that is the trouble. What is a *specific* purpose? If someone writes a joke, is it for the specific purpose of making some hypothetical reader laugh? I hold that a joke is to be laughed at.

"Specific purpose." Maybe Allen read that article by Hickville Grannie. Hickville Grannie said that I said that "literature should make the reader go out and do some specific thing." If Allen got his interpretation of my thesis from that source, then oh my God, for the same man who said that I said that literature should make people go out and do some specific thing also informed us in the same article that my esthetic system divorced literature from life. Even goodwill advertising does not guaranty that the reader will "go out" (Hicks actually used that stylism on me) and buy the product advertised. Even advertising but hopes to turn the reader in its favor. Trust me, please.

"Thing-in-itself." At that I grow uneasy. If I am a fat burgher traveling on the highway, and Robin Hood takes my purse, I know that Robin Hood is a thief. If I am humble and starving, and Robin Hood gives me money, I know that he is a benefactor. But as for what Robin Hood an-sich is—I am a little uneasy.

"Thing-in-itself." Though some commentators are doubtful, others stress the fact that Kant held the moral impulse to be the one evidence of the noumenal world that came through pure into the world of phenomena. Maybe Allen means that. However:

"High Literature (which is usually mixed with certain incidental impurities)." Yes indeedee, but the trouble is that *English* is one of the incidental impurities of Shakespeare.

"Truth One and Eternal . . . incidental impurities . . . let's not indulge in romantic irony." I hold that if it were One and Eternal that two and two is four, we should proclaim this One and Eternal Truth differently if our age said two and two is five than if our age had said two and two is a pumpkin. Romantic irony is one way of pointing. There are other ways.

"The time of Truth should not be wasted." I invite you to refer me to any doctrine of the One and Eternal Truth which was not balanced by the qualification *that in this life* it is symbolized by impermanent, temporal images. We must "translate back" from the multiplicity of our given social texture. We cannot say merely I-It-Both, Onely and Eternally.

But the edge of our wine has vanished. We have several times stifled a yawn, in the very midst of the discussion. We shall turn of[f] the tap. Greetings, good South—and a pleasant if undeserved slumber to both of us.

KB

---

the Dadas' overt rhetoricality—of their intuition that the Enlightenment distrust of rhetoric and belief in the transparency of language in the face of right reason could not be sustained in a period professing a Nietzschean skepticism toward Western conceptual systems. The experience of reading *Counter-Statement* recalls Calinescu's and Poggioli's measured observations that a central tension within modernism is the one between two kinds of avant-garde, the aesthetes and the social activists—one repelled by the philistinism of the masses into ascetic withdrawal, the other stressing the artist as committed forerunner and prophet. Within Burke's revisionist modernism, neither the doctrine of the autonomy of art nor the view of the artist as prophetic leader is precluded. In *Counter-Statement*, Burke represents and juxtaposes both positions in a manner that both recognizes and denies extremes. *Counter-Statement* begins by assuming an aesthete stance, by aestheticizing morals, by declaring the existence of "matters of purely aesthetic judgment," and by emphasizing music as a prototype for ideal art; but by the time it closes, Burke without discarding his respect for technique and eloquence and form has ceased to organize ethics and morals under aesthetics and has begun to consider drama as the central terrain of modernism—a drama that quickly brings to mind "roles" and "play" and "audience" and rhetoric, a drama that Burke encountered in his first days in Greenwich Village with The Provincetown Players, and, of course, a drama that Burke would later develop into his most famous explanatory metaphor.[37]

The same tension (or perhaps I should say complementarity) between the aesthetic and the social animates "The Status of Art" and "Applications of the Terminology," two of the other latest-composed essays in *Counter-Statement*.[38] "The Status of Art" intrudes directly on a "tempest" involving the aesthete critics among the moderns (who in anticipation of the New Critics wished to attend to works of art "from within," "on their own terms," as a form of self-expression) and the geneticists (who approached art from the perspective of one or another theory of causation).[39] Consequently the chapter on one hand defends the inutility of art in a way that the aesthetes would have approved,[40] offers in passing a measured but sympathetic further commentary on Flaubert and Gourmont, and critiques Freudians (like Brooks) and Spenglerians who were understanding literature as *merely* the reflection of internal drives or "contemporary political and economic issues" (79) or irresistible historical cycles. On the other hand, the chapter also emphasizes once again Burke's insistence that literature be considered "as a means of communication" with definite social utility. For all their protests that "ethics should be a subdivision of esthetics" (68), Pater, Baudelaire, Wilde, and other aesthetes were also social critics attempting to amend mainstream society through shock tactics and radical critique; while constituting a distinct minority, even experimental *tour d'ivoire* writers can nevertheless influence millions (70–72). "Far from being 'in retreat,' [the artist] must master ways of exerting influence on the minds and emotions of others" (74).

"Applications of the Terminology" also steers between aesthetic and ideological positions. Like "Lexicon Rhetoricae," which it names or echoes at several points, the chapter on one hand traces several implications of the points Burke had made in "Psychology and Form."[41] In drawing those implications—for classic and romantic, objectivity and subjectivity, art and life, poetry and illusion, and convention and originality—Burke insisted once more that artists should never forget to seek aesthetic beauty. Artists should never become so excessively "proletarian" in seeking "to eradicate certain forms of social injustice" (189) that they forget to appeal to those universal components of form detailed in "Psychology and Form": "The most 'unreal' book in the world [even Lyly's *Euphues*] can properly be said to 'deal with life' if it can engross a reader" (192). On the other hand, Burke in "Applications" is equally insistent that "effective literature [is] nothing else but rhetoric" (210) in that it seeks to move audiences and change attitudes. Literature as a form of action resists removal from life.

159

PROCLAMATION

TIRED OF THE SPECTACLE OF SHORT STORIES, NOVELS, POEMS AND PLAYS STILL UNDER THE HEGEMONY OF THE BANAL WORD, MONOTONOUS SYNTAX, STATIC PSYCHOLOGY, DESCRIPTIVE NATURALISM, AND DESIROUS OF CRYSTALLIZING A VIEWPOINT...

WE HEREBY DECLARE THAT :

1. THE REVOLUTION IN THE ENGLISH LANGUAGE IS AN ACCOMPLISHED FACT.

2. THE IMAGINATION IN SEARCH OF A FABULOUS WORLD IS AUTONOMOUS AND UNCONFINED.
(Prudence is a rich, ugly old maid courted by Incapacity... Blake)

3. PURE POETRY IS A LYRICAL ABSOLUTE THAT SEEKS AN A PRIORI REALITY WITHIN OURSELVES ALONE.
(Bring out number, weight and measure in a year of dearth... Blake)

4. NARRATIVE IS NOT MERE ANECDOTE, BUT THE PROJECTION OF A METAMORPHOSIS OF REALITY.
(Enough ! Or Too Much !... Blake)

5. THE EXPRESSION OF THESE CONCEPTS CAN BE ACHIEVED ONLY THROUGH THE RHYTHMIC " HALLUCINATION OF THE WORD ". (Rimbaud).

6. THE LITERARY CREATOR HAS THE RIGHT TO DISINTEGRATE THE PRIMAL MATTER OF WORDS IMPOSED ON HIM BY TEXT-BOOKS AND DICTIONARIES.
(The road of excess leads to the palace of Wisdom... Blake)

7. HE HAS THE RIGHT TO USE WORDS OF HIS OWN FASHIONING AND TO DISREGARD EXISTING GRAMMATICAL AND SYNTACTICAL LAWS.
(The tigers of wrath are wiser than the horses of instruction... Blake)

8. THE " LITANY OF WORDS " IS ADMITTED AS AN INDEPENDENT UNIT.

9. WE ARE NOT CONCERNED WITH THE PROPAGATION OF SOCIOLOGICAL IDEAS, EXCEPT TO EMANCIPATE THE CREATIVE ELEMENTS FROM THE PRESENT IDEOLOGY.

10. TIME IS A TYRANNY TO BE ABOLISHED.

11. THE WRITER EXPRESSES. HE DOES NOT COMMUNICATE

12. THE PLAIN READER BE DAMNED.
(Damn braces ! Bless relaxes !... Blake)

— *Signed* : KAY BOYLE, WHIT BURNETT, HART CRANE, CARESSE CROSBY, HARRY CROSBY, MARTHA FOLEY, STUART GILBERT, A. L. GILLESPIE, LEIGH HOFFMAN, EUGENE JOLAS, ELLIOT PAUL, DOUGLAS RIGBY, THEO RUTRA, ROBERT SAGE, HAROLD J. SALEMSON, LAURENCE VAIL.

Manifesto for "The Revolution of the Word" published in transition, *June 1929*

In short, Burke in *Counter-Statement* both borrows from and critiques modernists of every stripe. He could appreciate Spengler's critique of the myth of progress as much as the author of "The Waste Land" did (see Burke to Munson, February 17, 1924), while simultaneously being critical of "genetic" criticism inspired by *The Decline of the West*. He could capitalize on the Symbolist enthusiasm for Freud while tempering extravagant psychological explanations for the appeal and genesis of art. He could appreciate the New Humanists' insistence on fixed standards while criticizing their inflexibility and their demonization of Pater.[42] He could remain apart from the Dadas while still understanding that their appreciation of the radically new and mechanical and urban could be the basis of a new American literature. He could agree with Hicks and other leftists that art must have a social agenda while reminding them that art has a commitment to aesthetic form as well. And so on. Burke, in sum, could state that he "stands for nothing" (91) except the integrity of his own responses to and formulations about modernist concerns, responses and formulations that try to remain faithful to both the aesthetic and social wings of modernist thought.

Thus, I disagree with Heath's statement that "not until the mid-1930s did Burke incorporate political philosophy into his aesthetic" (11) and with Rueckert's recent assessment that *Counter-Statement* "remains . . . a work by a literary critic who has not yet developed a real sense of the larger social context" that is found in his later work (Rueckert, "Field Guide" 10). That social context is indeed present in an emphatic way in the dramatic internal dialogues of *Counter-Statement*. True, Burke would go even further in associating art with culture and politics in his next critical book (e.g., "The Rout of the Aesthetes" is one of the subtitles of *Auscultation*) and in later works. But *Counter-Statement* already shows Burke's substantial movement in that direction—as well as the desire (which he never lost) not to rout the aesthetes entirely. Therefore I appreciate Greig Henderson's argument that "Burke's aestheticism [in *Counter-Statement*] is a strategy for encompassing a sociohistorical situation; moreover, it aims to have a corrective or corrosive effect upon that situation and is thus practical; art, for Burke, is anything but useless" (175). And I prefer Rueckert's earlier conclusion about *Counter-Statement*: the book is a "both/and" document that "is equally concerned with two seemingly contradictory areas of investigation: the purely aesthetic and the sociological" (*Drama* 32):

Counter-Statement is actually a kind of dialogue, with three speakers apparently contradicting each other. One of the speakers defends pure art by arguing that the end of poetry is eloquence . . . ; the second speaker defends art as revelation by arguing that the end of poetry is wisdom; and the third speaker defends art as catharsis. . . . The dialogue is resolved by transcending the contradictions; all three attitudes can be accepted if one adopts an attitude of critical openness which permits many angles of vision. (*Drama* 10)

That *Counter-Statement* is meant as a dialogue, as an exploratory discourse calculated to stimulate the active reader's thinking, not to resolve it, that, unlike most critical tracts, it is meant not to close off debate but to generate further dialogue, accounts for the book's difficulty as well as its continuing interest. And that *Counter-Statement* is an internally conflicted, even contradictory document, self-reflective and critical of its own codifications, marks it as modernist, too, of course, for the hybrid, polyphonous text is a modernist staple—witness Toomer's *Cane*, Faulkner's *The Sound and the Fury*, and Cage's *Empty Words*. Like other such documents, *Counter-Statement* is itself an instance of "perspective by incongruity," an experiment itself in form. Rather than raising and fulfilling expectations in any conventional way, its chapters make coherent arguments that tend to parody or correct or undermine the arguments contained in previous chapters; containing chapters linked by emotional and intellectual associations, it is an instance of "qualitative form" (Warnock 66). Rather like other modernist texts such as *In Our Time*, *Go Down, Moses*, *Dubliners*, *Winesburg, Ohio*, or even Burke's own *White Oxen* and *Towards a Better Life*, *Counter-Statement* is something of a collage, a collection of more-or-less self-contained items that nonetheless cohere uneasily, experimentally, yet undeniably and invigoratingly, into a whole book.[43] Instead of scoring Burke for "fail[ing] to advance a coherent and sustained critical standard" (Heath, *Realism* 10–11), instead of expecting internal consistency and conventional form from a book with chapters that were written over a period of nearly a decade, and instead of growing impatient with Burke's decision not to smooth out inconsistencies, a reader of *Counter-Statement* is better advised to make the inconsistencies a virtue, and to gain perspective by the incongruities Burke offers. *Counter-Statement* might be read as the record of the Growth of the Critic's Mind, and as an instance of Burke's "debunking attitude"—of his characteristic skepticism toward and resistance to just about everything, including systems of his own making.

In *Counter-Statement* Burke tries all sorts of things, floats all manner of trial balloons. He writes two chapters ("Lexicon" and "Applications") to extend and "correct" two others ("Psychology and Form" and "Poetic Process") that are already in conversation with each other—and then undermines all of those with "Program." He experiments with strange chapter titles and with a parenthetical remark long enough to require a paragraph break. And he orchestrates a variety of voices into a modernist polyphony. In addition to the serious expository and clinical voices, there are the evangelistic hortatories of "Program," unpretentious asides and witticisms ("The artist, whom we have left for some time at the agonizing point of expressing himself" [54]), sarcastic swipes (e.g., at Hoover's "football discipline" [67]), informal intimacies (e.g., "whatever our reservations as to Walter Pater" [9]), pedantic meditations and indirections (on scholastic philosophy or German linguistics or the prose of Thomas Browne), and frank directness ("Here form cannot atrophy" [34]). And all of this is balanced by Burke's notorious and confounding elusiveness and by his memorable and famous aphorisms: "The method most natural to the psychology of form is eloquence" (37); "Artistic truth is the externalization of taste" (42); "A system of aesthetics subsumes a system of politics" (113); "Tragedy as a mechanism is based on a calamitous persistence in one's ways" (202); and "When in Rome, do as the Greeks" (119). Deadly serious and yet playful and theatrical, *Counter-Statement* in modernist fashion calls attention to itself as form.

Kenneth Burke's *Counter-Statement*, then, is a "counter" statement in at least three overlapping ways. Most obviously, it resolutely counters the genteel poetics and cultural practices that all the moderns were combatting. In championing new modern writers, in advocating experimentation, in anatomizing form, and in understanding art as "naturally antinomian" (preface), Burke was placing himself and his ideas counter to the writers and critics of genteel, mainstream culture. As he once told John Woodcock: "I was raised in a tradition that was based on the concept of an art that ran counter to the general nature of things, as a kind of counterprinciple. . . . It was a time . . . when all the writers we most wanted to read were on a shelf in the library marked MINOR RESTRICTION. It certainly goes back to Ibsen and Shaw and all their battles" (705). On a second level, *Counter-Statement* also counters certain prevailing notions within the modernist community. "Each principle it [the book] advocates is matched by an opposite principle flourishing and triumphant today," Burke noted in the preface. That does not mean that the book is an explicit, tract-like counter-attack or systematic refutation of a set of dogmas. Although Burke on occasion did use the term "counter-statement" as a synonym for refutation (e.g., "I answer you with definitions rather than counter-statements" [Burke to Munson February 23, 1924]), he notes in the preface that *Counter-Statement* "deals only secondarily and sporadically with refutation," except for the chapter on "The Status of Art." "My solution is to attempt a more constructive type of criticism," he wrote to Cowley on his twenty-fifth birthday, "not merely to attack the existing but to build up a counter-structure" (Burke to Cowley, May 5, 1922). If the book is not a systematic refutation, it is nevertheless directed to fellow members of the modernist community— a community that is able to sponsor and contain and accommodate a surprising range of views about the nature of art and the relationships between art and society.

Finally, *Counter-Statement* is internally conflicted: it "counters" itself. The sentiments in "Three Adepts" are subtly countered by another chapter on literary adepts, "Mann and Gide." "Psychology and Form" and "The Poetic Process" (which work together) are both supplemented and corrected by "Lexicon Rhetoricae" and "Applications of the Terminology." And all of these are countered to a greater or lesser degree in "Program." Operating as a "counter-statement" on all three levels, then, *Counter-Statement* amounts to a particularly interesting and internally conflicted instance of modernist criticism; it is a characteristically Burkean statement within modernism of what its values, and what its range and possibilities, might be.

7

Conclusion: Conversing with Modernism in *Towards a Better Life*

B URKE'S *Towards a Better Life; Being a Series of Epistles, or Declama-tions*, written over several years from 1927 to 1931 and published in the first days of 1932, is as difficult to overview as Burke's other fiction. The book jacket copy that Burke composed for his experiment describes the novel accurately enough as a "portrait of a secular anchorite," the anatomy of a tempestuous, rather despicable man "who deliberately courts disaster, voluntarily places himself in jeopardy," by making a series of cynical and self-destructive life choices. For its form the book relies only superficially on action, but it does proceed generally according to three chronological phases that correspond to the three parts and eighteen chapters (six chapters per part) of the novel. Nearly every chapter is a self-contained "declamation" or "epistle" that the protagonist John Neal writes (but never actually sends) to his rival Anthony, a wealthy would-be idealist who claims for a time the heart of Florence, a woman Neal has also desired. In the first part of the book, John Neal *in medias res* recounts the recent and not so recent events of his life that have placed him in the small country town where he has flown to make a new start as a result of his original self-absorbed, unsuccessful, and rather contradictory pursuit of Florence—contradictory because it is Neal who actually brings Florence and Anthony together and because Neal actually seals his rejection by Florence by stealing from her the money he needs in order to impress her. In Part 2 his "structure of cynical repose" in the rural village collapses when Florence, now separated from Anthony, reappears suddenly in Neal's life, only to be dismissed ruthlessly by him when he learns that she has been discarded by Anthony; to Neal, Florence

165

is only to be hunted, not attained. Having renounced Florence, Neal also abandons his family (he has married for money) and returns to New York. There, in Part 3, he has an opportunity to restore relations with another lover, Genevieve, who assists Neal at several points in the story but who is also cruelly repudiated by Neal in the end. The novel closes with more of Neal's self-destructiveness as he cuts himself off from friends and from Genevieve, collapses into himself, and, mad or very nearly so, tries to make sense of his life.

This account of its plot far overestimates the role of narrative event in *Towards a Better Life*, however. The "story" is actually told, notes Burke on the book jacket, "less from the standpoint of psychological documentation than from the standpoint of its potentialities as 'ritual.' [The author] has tried for a maximum of concentration, avoiding that 'watered stock' kind of prose which arises when a writer jots down every casual bit of gossip about the doings and sayings of his characters."[1] In other words, as the preface indicates, Burke was explicitly resisting the characteristic moves of the realistic novel. Regarding his plot as "peripheral," as "little more than a pretext" that would enable him to achieve his larger goal, namely to "lament, rejoice, beseech, admonish, aphorize, and inveigh" in the voice of John Neal, Burke sought a highly aesthetic form for his novel that places eloquence and emotion well before event. As Isidor Schneider noted in his review of *Towards* in 1932, "Realism assumes that given the events, emotions will follow. Mr. Burke assumes that given the emotions the events will follow" (101–2). Thus "a different framework [than the realistic novel] seemed imperative," wrote Burke in his preface: "[I] emphasiz[ed] the essayistic rather than the narrative, the emotional predicaments of my hero rather than the details by which he arrived at them. . . . In form the resultant chapters are somewhat like a sonnet sequence, a progression by stages, by a series of halts; or they might be compared to an old-style opera in which the stress is laid upon the arias whereas the transition from one aria to the next is secondary" (xii–xiii). Of course, even sonnet sequences and operas usually move sequentially, whereas *Towards a Better Life* moves not so much sequentially as psychologically; John Neal's epistles, because they are never sent or even intended to be sent, are less epistles than "declamations"—personal expressions of the narrator's state of mind, "merely a device used by Neal to help him explain himself to himself" (Rueckert, *Encounters* 135). The effect is a highly concentrated and elusive series of expostulations that "certainly make the reader work," as a writer-friend of Cowley's, Ivan Beede, wryly understated as the book was taking shape (reported in Cowley to Burke, September 30, 1929). Denis Donoghue has even resisted calling the book a novel—"It is certainly not a novel, nor was meant to be" (482)—designating it "an anatomy" and comparing it instead to a dance designed "not to tell a story but to give the accomplished bodies an occasion to disclose their resources," the resources in this case being a succession of eventful and artfully crafted sentences (480).

What does one make of such a book? It is typical, if not stereotypical, to read *Towards a Better Life* in one of two related ways, either as an autobiography of sorts or as a cultural product of the 1930s that reflects a state of national and authorial depression. A great many commentators indeed have seen the book as a thinly fictionalized autobiography, as a representation of Burke's personal and emotional troubles during the first years of the 1930s, when his first marriage was breaking up, when he was arranging his marriage to Lily's sister Libbie, and when the Great Depression may well have seemed not just an economic designation but a psychological one. In a foreword to *Auscultation, Creation, and Revision*, Burke himself said that *Towards* was "about a man cracking up" and that he, Burke, "didn't feel so safe [then] himself" either (in Chesebro, *Extensions* 45). William Rueckert on one occasion observed that *Towards* reenacts in Neal the abandonment of Burke's literary career (*Drama* 34), and he observed elsewhere ("Field Guide" 12) that "Burke has said many times that the book names his number." In a fine review, Rueckert also mentions that "Burke wrote his novel at a time of deep personal trouble, [a factor which] too is in the novel" ("Burke's Other Life" 648), and he recently completed a lengthy exposition of the novel as "Burke's symbolic action, his fictional ritual of rebirth, resurgence, and transcendence" (*Encounters* 157). Indeed, Burke did say that he worked out "the trouble" of his marriage in his novel. "I couldn't go to a psychoanalyst," he reported, "because I was too pigheaded. So I used my novel" (Yagoda 67). In a similar vein he confessed to Olivia Skinner, "I was in bad shape myself [at the time he was writing *Towards*], but too pigheaded to see a psychiatrist. I was fictionalizing actual situations, and it scared the life out of me. But I got it all down, and analyzed those situations—and got better. But for years I didn't try fiction again" (Skinner). Paul Jay, who has carefully studied Burke's letters to Cowley, has concluded that Burke was close to a nervous breakdown by the end of 1932 (Jay, *Selected Correspondence* 153) and that his novel indeed reflects his personal disarray; and Burke thirty-five years after the publication of *Towards* wrote about it as a "perversely idealized self-portrait" of a man under great stress: "[When he wrote it,] the author was in a state of acute internal conflict owing to maladjustments in his personal affairs" ("On Stress" 91).

Thus the consensus, encouraged by Burke's testimony in "On Stress" and elsewhere, is that Burke wrote *Towards* as a form of homeopathic personal therapy in order to purge himself of certain traits and hence make himself worthy of Libbie (Rueckert, "Field Guide" 13–14; *Encounters*

133). "I rely upon the Declamations to burn away certain very uncomfortable parts of me. 'If I could, by a ritual, like the old Jews, load my sins upon a goat, I should beat it mercilessly and drive it into the wilderness to die.' Each man can, out of the depths of himself, invent but one new aspect of vice—and no wonder he prizes it so greatly that he makes it the cause of the destruction of his hero," wrote Burke to Cowley just as he was engaged in finishing *Towards* (August 9, 1931; the quotation within the letter is from the last chapter of the novel). When it is read autobiographically, Burke's novel tends to confirm the frequently articulated view of Kenneth Burke as the Strangely Inspired Hermit of Andover that I have been working to counter in this book.

I don't know enough about Burke as a person to be sure how appropriate it is to read *Towards* as an autobiography. It may well be. Not only does Burke's own testimony point in an autobiographical direction, but the book does in general describe a man vaguely torn between two women, a man whose infidelities drive him at last to internal contradiction. John Neal writes letters that he never sends, just as Burke was in the habit of doing, and, having trouble sleeping, he enjoys taking night rambles through fields and woods as the insomniac Burke himself did. Neal in Part 3 frequents the New York modernist scene that Burke knew so well. Like Burke he enjoys and criticizes music, plays the piano, and meditates on death, and he seems to have developed expertise on the use and effects of drugs, expertise that Burke was gaining from his work with Colonel Woods at the time he was composing *Towards a Better Life*. Like Burke, Neal is drawn toward interpreting the world on the model of drama. Given these parallels, I don't care to oppose this biographical reading too strenuously until an authoritative biography of Burke is on hand, because the book may well contain these and other autobiographical aspects.[2] It is worth pointing out, however, that Burke also sometimes complained that people were looking too strenuously for the autobiographical in *Towards*,[3] that I am personally hard pressed to discover resemblances between Florence and Lily or Genevieve and Libbie, that I also fail to see many, if any, significant biographical parallels between the events of the book and the events of Burke's life, and that Burke's contemporaries did not read the book as veiled biography. None of the reviewers of the first edition mentions autobiography, for instance, and Austin Warren in 1933 was claiming that "Burke's hero . . . is in no sense himself; Burke breaks with the Anglo-American tradition of autobiographical novels, and no more writes his own life than he essays the broad sociological canvas of a Balzac, Tolstoi, Sinclair Lewis, or Dos Passos" (347). *Towards a Better Life* may have been a therapeutic exercise for Burke, but it apparently wasn't drawn directly from his life in any material way.

Indeed, if anything it seems to me that Burke's letters of 1930 and 1931 actually reflect a stable, sociable, and even doggedly optimistic personality that is quite unlike that of John Neal. In the face of the early Depression, during those months when Burke was completing *Towards*, he was apparently still quite balanced. As his own testimony about his condition indicates, Burke was only too aware of the desperate case of the national economy and of the threat it held for his own economic circumstances. But he wasn't personally devastated. He retained his job with Colonel Woods until summer 1931, felt secure enough—and bohemian enough—to resign from it in order to finish *Counter-Statement* and *Towards*, and benefitted from the fact that the farm was already paid off. In fact, Burke actually seems to have been elated as often as he was stressed. On the one hand, he felt acutely the "trench morale" associated with "the greatest debauch of financial gloom in all history" (letter to Cowley, April 29, 1931); on the other hand, in the same letter he boasted that he could "compensatorily frisk" at his situation: "Even this morning I frisk, though I should be sour with hangover. And it is clear at least that our definitions of human decency were made in bad times, for people are better in bad years than in prosperous ones." As challenging as circumstances must have seemed from a national, political, and even personal perspective, the summer of 1931 was nevertheless also stimulating and rewarding for Burke as he worked to see *Counter-Statement* through the press and to complete *Towards a Better Life*. "The gardens flourish, the grass is already two feet high," he reported happily to Cowley on June 1. "So there is a summer— there is enough for a 'pure present'—and as I did with considerable success in Maine some years ago, I shall devote myself merrily to my [writing] tasks and my bodily exertions, thinking of nothing beyond the season." "Life goes on [amid the economic uncertainty]," he told Cowley on August 9; "each weekend there are boisterous throngs about. Rice wine is cheap but effective. The pond continues to flourish. Seven oil lamps in one room give the illusion of blazing splendor. Thus do we, by going through the motions, conceal from ourselves the steady march toward zero."[4] The same emotional doubleness is reflected in Burke's letters of 1930. "I am, as a matter of fact, in a mood of rather irritating complacency at present," he wrote Josephson on August 7: "There are itches, but no gnawings." On September 14, he wrote Cowley about his "joyous nightmare" of a situation: "I am unable to say whether I have gone to seed [in my work] or am about to reap a harvest. Many motionless days, many sullen days in the same room, many days without horizons, have made me a dynamo not at all—yet at the same time they have enabled me to catalogue my papers and arrange my materials so that now the minimum number of my notes are [indecipherable]. . . . This should prevent my getting too soon again into that anarchic condition which makes one's ideas amount to least."[5]

In sum, perhaps the repellant John Neal does resemble Kenneth Burke in ways that I am unable to appreciate—although, thoroughly self-absorbed, self-destructive, humorless, and anti-social, Neal seems to me about as unlike as one could be from the affable, gregarious, anything-but-monastic Kenneth Burke that I met (as it were) in the course of my research for this book. In fact, the distance between Burke and Neal would be understood as much more pronounced if Burke had acted on an interesting artistic hunch he had, to employ a technique not all that much different from the set of framed narratives that Faulkner would soon adopt for *Absalom, Absalom!*:

I have been thinking of another simple mechanism—namely, of enclosing the entire set [of Declamations] within the frame of a prologue and epilogue, written not by this gloomy and unclean fellow, but by a very kindly, charitable, and typically sweet-minded Kenneth Burke. For reasons we shall not stop to detail, he chances upon these documents, and becomes interested in their author. . . . Then, in an Epilogue, the sweet-minded myself goes to pay the author of them a visit. He is now an old man, dirty, surly, uncommunicative, living with his pigs. . . . The story ends with sweet-minded KB very comfortably visiting friends, in an atmosphere of intimacy and mutual confidence, of graceful compliments, etc. Say it to no one. It must be carefully done. (Burke to Josephson, August 7, 1930)

So although Neal may perhaps represent something that Burke feared becoming at some future time, whether for good reason or not, and although the melancholia that Neal displays at the beginning of Part 3 may be something copied from Burke's personal experience, *Towards a Better Life* is much more than an autobiography. As for whether the book should be classified as a 1930s item, as Rueckert classifies it (*Drama* 34), that is, whether it is a reflection of the economic, artistic, and political tensions that the nation was negotiating along with Burke, that too seems to me only part of the truth at best. The title of the book points not to societal amelioration but to a personal and private one.[6] Leaving aside the question of whether Burke was actually suffering professionally or psychologically in the 1930s, the fact remains that much of *Towards a Better Life* was not written in the 1930s at all.

On the contrary, the novel was largely conceived and executed well before the demise of *The Dial* in the summer of 1929 and before the deep economic crisis that was initiated by the stock market crash of late October, 1929. Burke had developed specific plans for the novel at least as early as June 29, 1927, when he told Josephson that he "would try the ruse of allied parts, stories capable of being taken individually but also capable of pulling together as a whole. . . . I like tableaux, presented as such, and they don't seem to fit well into the standard novel."[7] Less than a year later Burke was far enough along to begin publishing portions, and on May 23,

1928, Marianne Moore agreed to publish "A Declamation"—which was to become the first chapter of *Towards*—in *The Dial* that August. Just as "A Declamation" was appearing, Burke submitted to Moore a final draft of the Second Declamation, and he was telling Josephson of his plans to work seriously on additional chapters that coming fall, when his other jobs would permit (Burke to Josephson, August 8, 1928). By the end of June 1929 he had completed seven Declamations (Decker to Burke, June 30, 1929), six of them appearing in *The Dial* and the seventh, upon *The Dial*'s demise, headed for *Hound and Horn*, then edited by R. P. Blackmur.[8] Before the end of August the eighth was finished and also dispatched to *Hound and Horn*, where it appeared in November (Burke to Blackmur, August 29, 1929). Burke and Cowley discussed the ninth declamation on September 30 and October 3, 1929, and Burke laid out his plans for the tenth a few days earlier (Burke to Cowley, September 24, 1929). Progress stalled a bit after the stock market crash because Burke had recently returned to full-time work under Colonel Woods at the Bureau of Social Hygiene, but by the end of the year he had placed the ninth declamation, which appeared in the March 1930 *Hound and Horn*, and worked more on the tenth. All these Declamations found their way, with relatively small embellishments and occasional deletions, into *Towards a Better Life*, so in effect Burke had written a little more than half of *Towards*, ten of its eighteen chapters, before the beginning of the Depression.[9]

Burke completed the book over the next two summers, during 1930 and 1931, before the economic collapse was fully complete and according to the plans he had already devised. He worked especially hard to finish *Towards a Better Life* during the summer of 1931,[10] submitted his novel to Harcourt, Brace around Labor Day, and learned on October 7 that it would be published (C. A. Pearce to Burke). "Offensively proud" of his work, Burke was positively ebullient at the news of its acceptance. "There is not a god-damned barb that can pass through the hippopotamus hide of [my] self-delight," he told Allen Tate (October 16, 1931). In any case, *Towards a Better Life* is as much or more a 1920s book than it is a product of the 1930s.[11] In form the novel is in close partnership with the experimental modernist short fictions that Burke himself was concocting in the early 1920s. And in content, like *Counter-Statement*, the novel attempts to come to grips with central modernist values of the 1920s, particularly with the notion of the autonomy of art and the artist.

In form the book is indeed highly experimental. Its novelty, obscurity, and difficulty put it in the company of a great many modernist novels, and not just celebrated ones like *Finnegans Wake*, but also ones like André Gide's *Les Faux-monnayeurs* (1926), a book which required nothing less than the issuance of a companion volume containing the critical theory and experimentation on which it depended, and one to which Burke referred in connection with Williams' highly experimental, plotless, even arbitrary collage *The Great American Novel* in his *Dial* essay on Williams of 1927. Ostensibly an epistolary novel in a tradition reaching back before *Pamela*, Burke's *Towards a Better Life* stretches that form beyond its limits in that his narrator's letters are never dated, signed, sent, or answered. Yet neither is the book an extended personal diary of John Neal, because the Declamation format makes Neal nearly always conscious of the fact that he is addressing Anthony. While it bears analogies to *Mrs. Dalloway* (1925)—another record of the inmost thoughts and emotions of a distracted protagonist, another alternation between action and contemplation that emphasizes contemplation—the declamatory format of *Towards a Better Life* makes it very different as well from Virginia Woolf. Rather like the surrealists who wrote so feverishly under the influence of Freud during the 1920s, Burke's protagonist seems to be using writing as a means of self-analysis. Cowley, thinking no doubt of Burke's reclusive narrator, considered its prototype to be an earlier precursor of the modern novel, *A rebours*, while Burke himself mentioned a tie to Pater's esthete novel *Marius the Epicurean* (Parker and Herenden 95). Impressed by the plotlessness of the novel, Josephson considered it to be an instance of Unanimism, a movement within modernism calculated to free the novel of plot (*Life* 98).[12] As Yvor Winters offered, "Instead of giving us the progression of a narrative, [the novel] endeavors to give us a progression of pure feeling. Frequently there is not even progression; we have merely a repetitious series of Laforguian antitheses" (72). Examples of these antitheses abound in this novel built around contrasts: Neal vs. Anthony; Neal vs. his Alter Ego; Florence vs. Genevieve; urban vs. rural; the lyrical lie of Part 2, chapter 5, and its antidote in the next chapter; and so forth.

Almost by temperament and certainly by his artistic environment, Burke seemed incapable of succumbing to the usual tactics of fiction—building of suspense, creating verisimilitude in language and dialogue, creating consecutive action. Like some other moderns after Freud, Burke was seeking to create a non-prosaic zone of "surreality" strictly apart from everyday reality and the fiction of the realists. As he had in the latter stories of *The White Oxen*, Burke in his novel was once more "shifting away from the realistically convincing and true to life [and stressing instead] the more rhetorical properties of letters"—those more rhetorical properties, recall from chapter 4, being stylistic tropes and schemes associated with elegant eloquence that he identified in the preface to *The White Oxen* and that he argued for in "Psychology and Form." "As for he who . . . wants 'a good story,' whomsoever he be, he will despise me," he told Cowley (September 2, 1931). What Burke wanted instead of story was something similar to what he sought in his later short stories: an expressly and intensely artistic novel constructed as a vehicle for stylistic display. "All my cronies," he wrote to Tate in defense of his Declamations, "though they in their poems write for years as no man ever spoke, seem to feel that it is a crime to write fiction in any other speech than they use in ordering groceries. . . . But though I grant that there is much giving of information in literature, I think there is also a ritualizing of information given— and merely because newspapers so ably perform that service for which they were designed, I see no reason why all prose should be modeled after them" (April 6, 1931). Or, as he put the same sentiment in the preface (xx):

[I]n realizing by comparison with the present how much of the 'eventfulness' of a prose sentence is omitted from our prevalent newspaper and narrative styles, we are furnished with authority enough for a 'return' to more formalized modes of writing. There is no reason why prose should continue to be judged good prose purely because it trails along somewhat like the line left by the passage of a caterpillar. Why should an author spend a year or more on a single book, and end by talking as he would talk on the spur of the moment? Or why should he feel impelled to accept as the 'norm' of his elucubrations that style so admirably fitted for giving the details of a murder swiftly over the telephone and rushing them somehow into copy in time for the next edition of the news? The two billion such words that are printed daily in the United States (to say nothing of the thousands of billions that are uttered) would seem to provide the public with enough of them—and if only through modesty, an author might seek to appeal by providing something else.[13]

In that such words distinguish once more literature from life, and in that (in keeping with the custom of the esthetes) they place literature on a higher plane than "communication," *Towards a Better Life*—at least in technique and at least to the extent that it is intertextual with prior aesthetic experiments in modern literature and with some of the more plotless tales in *The White Oxen*—is in form most definitely a 1920s book. It is an aesthetic experiment by an avant-garde novelist with a developed sense of style for its own sake.

The sentences I have just quoted from the preface to the first edition of *Towards a Better Life* come immediately after Burke pays extended homage to one of his other long-standing artistic exemplars, Thomas Mann. Mann, of course, is himself a writer who offers stylistic analogues to *Towards a Better Life*; Burke always regarded Mann's meticulous prose as an ideal to strive after. Just as Mann conceived of his novels as aspiring to the condition of music, so Burke contended, as I have indicated, that *Towards a Better Life* holds together rather "like a sonnet sequence" or a series of "arias in an opera" (xiii): each chapter, while advancing the total effect of the book, is an eloquent instance (or instances) "of lamentation, rejoicing, beseechment, admonition, sayings, and invective . . . [which]

mark, in a heightened manner, the significant features of each day" (xii).[14] But that is not the only way that Burke's book once again recalls Mann. Like several of the stories in *The White Oxen*, *Towards* is a "critical appraisal of the life and works of a purely fictional character"; it is as much an occasion for the "use of criticism and the paraphernalia of criticism as an element of fiction" as any of the stories Burke wrote before 1924. Just as "Portrait of an Arrived Critic," "The Olympians," "Mrs. Maecenas," and "David Wasserman" (as I indicated in chapter 4) repeatedly interrogate the conflict between the bohemian and bourgeois ethos that Burke had observed in Mann's fiction, just as they offer opportunities for Burke to explore the place of the artist in contemporary society, *Towards a Better Life* presents the portrait of a bohemian artist-figure, John Neal, who lives his life and understands his life in relation to a bourgeois society that he considers banal and contemptible. Neal is another Mannian artist-outsider only too aware of the distance between himself and his neighbors.

But *Death in Venice*, Burke's short stories, and *Counter-Statement*—all of them dramatizations of the fundamental modernist tension between the self and society—offer no easy, uncomplicated affirmations of the artistic life, no simple imitation of *A rebours*, no fervent celebrations of an esthete at war with philistinism. And so it is with *Towards a Better Life*. Neal, the prototypical modernist, the embodiment of the autonomous artist and disinterested critic who is alienated from his surroundings, satirizes his philistine environment all right. But he is anything but celebrated. His unsent letters reveal far more about him and his shortcomings than about his society. Whether Neal is a portrait of Kenneth Burke is disputable, but it is indisputable that *Towards* is in its way another *Portrait of the Artist as a Young Man*, a portrait this time of a modern who lives his life faithfully but finally regretfully according to doctrinaire modernist values. Burke used Mann and other moderns as formal guides to the construction of *Towards a Better Life*, but in portraying those values in so uncompromising a manner and so destructive a manner, Burke mounts from within a sharp criticism of the artistic stance of moderns who conceived of themselves and their work as autonomous and radically alienated from society.

Neal is definitely, by temperament as well as by trade, an artist-critic, and a modern artist-critic at that. The very first sentence of the book proclaims Neal's artistic proclivities, and the final words of that introductory chapter name his central occupation as a writer-critic always "busily at work upon my utterance, . . . plac[ing] antinomies on the page, . . . reduc[ing] every statement by some counter-claim to zero" (12). Neal has "openly identified [him]self with literature" and made a "bold-faced claim to art" (35), and so he repeatedly uses metaphors and critical categories borrowed from art to understand his world. As a writer he consequently writes the dozen-and-a-half epistolary declamations that make up *Towards a Better Life*, piling up glittering, discerning aphorisms by the score, after the fashion of Nietzsche and Gourmont. Neal patronizes the drama[15] and writes a play himself. He takes up the tools of the sculptor in Part 3 and in the same section writes a short story, another quasi-epistolary piece within this epistolary novel that, befitting Neal, juxtaposes a lonely writer, a dummy policeman, and Blake's poetry. Bohemian to the core, Neal supports himself not with a job but with family income, small handouts, petty thievery, and a financially remunerative marriage to an unnamed woman who owns a farm. Neal "is busy," Burke said in his preface, but "busy not in ways that will add a single car to our thoroughfares" (xvii).

As this description of his vocation suggests, Neal's values have been gained through traffic with modernism. As a bohemian in New York he consorts with the artistic crowd and ignores politics (except insofar as artistic remove is itself a political position, an implied corrective). He patronizes Bach's Passion, and makes the rounds of the coffeehouses and parties of the avant-garde. His "letters" to Anthony are constructed as self-expressive moments, as beautiful sentences that create their own world, divorced from readers. Neal appreciates fiction that is unassisted by conventional plot (76), and he values plays when they are less conventional and predictable than the one he actually composes to accommodate the bourgeois tastes of his townsfellows. As a walking critic he disdains conventional art, not just the sonnets of conventionally disaffected artists but his own play and the version of *The Merchant of Venice* that he brings to the provinces in Part 2, chapter 4. His sculptures are crude, unfinished, unmimetic modernist experiments in form that he creates out of himself and then bashes as first drafts, as self-expressive "creations without revision" (135). His Alter Ego, another dismal shadow of Neal himself, in Part 3 plays the piano as a modern might, "often devoting many consecutive hours to moody pieces, at other times preferring music in which there was much ingenuity" (166). Accordingly Neal the modern understands himself as fundamentally autonomous, as a Great Individual constructing his own life as a defiant act of Nietzschean independence. Neal explicitly defines himself against the rest of the world: "When finding that people held the same views as I, I persuaded myself that I held them differently" (3). He also understands personal relationships as the expression of aesthetics, such that his rivalry with Anthony, for instance, should be understood as and through an "ars poetica" (11) and such that he can excoriate conventional artists and critics, and even not so conventional ones (78). Anthony, who is thoroughly conventional, generally respectable, predictably idealistic, interested in social amelioration, and economically fortunate, is his opposite. Neal scorns the "competent brood" that he associates with Anthony, "pledg[ing him]self to examine their accomplishments until I have made clear all insufficiencies in them, pursuing them with pamphlets, pasquinades, scurrilities, [and] obstrectations from the sewers" (114)[16]; and he ridicules Florence's regard for "order, arrangement, and husbandry" (109). Neal, in short, has what Burke would call in *Permanence and Change* a "trained incapacity" or "occupational psychosis": it is the psychosis of modernism, a perspective on the world that makes him see it only partially, and as diseased. Neal's epistolary musings are especially relevant to one of his implied audiences—an artistic community conflicted by the place of art and the artist in the world.

As bohemian artist-critic, Neal naturally execrates the communities around him. His early life established the pattern for the rest: after an idyllic childhood, his mind somehow became "transformed, plunged into stridency, with [his] mind henceforth an intestine wrangle not even stilled by the aggressions of external foes" (34). From then on "[his] converse became a monologue . . . ; [he] came by preference to talk most intimately with strangers, and to correspond with my friends on postcards" (5). Like a gargoyle spouting words instead of rainwater (9), Neal excoriates the general population for ignorance and lack of discernment, for making mortgages and voting Republican, for working hard and cherishing their ethnicity: "So great is their desire for conformity," he says of the complacent citizenry, "that in an environment of geniuses they might even have shown talent. They are all men of honor when their interests are not at stake—and as their indifference spreads to many areas, the vocabulary of justice still flourishes and exerts influence. On doing them a kindness, if one is too modest in accepting thanks, he finds them prompt to join in the belittling of his services. . . ." (63)—and so on for two more pages of eloquent invective against the conventional small town mores despised by so many moderns.

Not that Neal has actually done many of those kindnesses. Thrown into temporary congress with Anthony, Neal comes to scorn him as a "moralistic dog—admitting a hierarchy in which you are subordinate, purely that you may have subordinates; licking the boots of a superior, that you may have yours in turn licked by an underling" (9). The vituperation spills onto the next page and into many of the following chapters. Having later (in Part 1, chapter 5) come to identify briefly with an "unintended colleague," a fellow sufferer-from-love, he nonetheless frankly distances himself at the friend's suicide: "It was like the cutting from me of some parasitically feeding thing" (46). Neal rebukes Anthony for lacking his own introspectiveness (16), for misusing and deceiving a young woman (18–21), even for selflessly dreaming up a scheme for "a better life" in the form of a utopian community (for Neal in his misanthropy and paranoia assumes that the scheme is only a ruse to win Florence). "Led by a kind of moral pedantry" (18), he lectures all about everything—art, ethics, human relationships, small town life. His celebrated aphorisms, not to mention his invective and lamentations and admonishments, derive from his sense of moral, artistic, and intellectual superiority. For a time he speaks with admiration of "a mouse-faced man who chewed briskly, and who [held] . . . a general aversion" toward the world: "[The man] hated his employer, his clients, and in particular all laughter which possessed the unthinking ebullience of health." But after some weeks Neal "tore at him like a fiend, and [the two] parted company for ever" (29–30). Neal pitches over Florence when she is juxtaposed to an all-too-banal hotel room, and he regards Genevieve as a kind of pet who can be kicked with impunity: "What harm have I done in bringing anguish into a life which was so well able to surmount it?" (31). Genevieve's selfless decency, loyalty, and generosity only marks her, to the anti-conventional Neal, as common— and thus despicable and disposable. Having managed to survive in Part 2 through a financially fortunate marriage, he is offered a place of some honor in his rural community—which he naturally refuses. "*Me flendo vindicabam*" might be his motto: "My vengeance lay in complaint" (37). Neal is a notable instance of the satiric railer, the Nietzschean Hamlet or Timon cynically aphorizing and inveighing about the shortcomings of his society: "The world is made more tentative if all sagacious things are said by despicable people, and all stupid things by the lovable" (14). Burke thus calls his Neal "a John the Baptist" (xvii), a zealot crying out at his world from the margins of society, a man who satirizes his community in some of the choicest invective in English.

But this John is no saint. Though blessed with intelligence, wit, eloquence, and perspicuity that attracts attractive people, he persists in a radical misanthropy that separates him from them. It doesn't occur to Neal that most of his judgments about Anthony, Florence, Genevieve, and his other acquaintances also redound on his own head. Capable of duplicity whenever it suits, disloyal, scornful of just about everyone, he nevertheless sees himself as superior to his surroundings. Furthermore, his moral ineptitude seems to be the direct consequence of his aesthetic credos. When he meets Anthony, he erects a wall of splenetic hatred that grows proportionately as Anthony prospers out of bohemianism and into respectability. Neal pursues Florence, but only from the pleasure of the chase; determined to remain autonomous, he actually pairs her up with Anthony, steals from her in order to seal his separation from her, and finally rejects Florence completely when she appeals to him so openly in that squalid hotel room at the end of Part 2. When Genevieve in Part 3 attends him generously, he rejects her even more cruelly, sending her off to sell her body for money. Radically aloof by virtue of his perspective on life,

Neal has "tried to look upon people as little more than the proof of a thesis, like blackboard drawings to illustrate a proposition in Euclid" (50).[17] Finding himself for a time married and a father (it is unclear to me whether he is a step-father or biological one), he nonetheless feels no familial or community bonds; like a "fugitive" or "exile" or "fresh-cut stump, bleeding its sap into the sunlight" (65), he remains radically removed from everything and everyone. When Neal is thrown into the company of like-minded artists in Part 3, he simply drives them away with everyone else. Taking autonomy to an extreme, defining himself now not just against bourgeois society but all society, bohemian as well as bourgeois, he drives his artist friends away by his self-righteousness. Though the bohemians support him in the city (144–45), he still refuses willfully to connect, preferring instead to keep people distant: "If a person whistles or calls," he advises, "give no evidence of hearing" (192). As the novel concludes, Neal is locked in his own world, quarantined completely against his society. All he has are his own words and, as his only companion, an Alter Ego. In the final chapter, even his declamations grow fragmentary, disjointed, unconnected; as Austin Warren has said, "The last chapter stammers its last utterances before the silence closes down" (348). In the final chapters of *Counter-Statement*, Burke renounced self-expression for communication as an end, renounced pure aestheticism in favor of the social aims of art; Neal's tragedy is that he has missed that lesson. Locked at last in the insular cell of his own consciousness, able to utter but unable to communicate, he can only declaim madly and disjunctively to his isolated self.

Towards a Better Life is no spiritual autobiography of John Neal, but it is still possible that Burke's St. John is reborn, at least to an extent, in the end. Several readers, judging from the final chapters and from Burke's own comments about his novel, have understood Neal as to some degree regenerate. According to this line of thought, Neal's disintegration and insanity, the product of his radical isolation, actually prepares him for something of a rebirth. As Burke himself apparently wrote on the book jacket, with a quotation from the final chapter, "If [Neal's] absolutism brings him to disaster, it also brings him compensatory insight. He is routed, yet gratified to think of himself as one who 'became bat blind, that he might have bat-vision.' "[18] Denis Donoghue and William Rueckert concur. Building on Burke's hint that *Towards* is a "ritual of rebirth," Donoghue offers that "the aim of the book is to get [Neal] to put up with things in the spirit of comedy," to renounce the critical attitude that isolates him, to "learn to kneel" in pursuit of "A Better Life" (483–84). Rueckert too offers that the novel points the way to a better life not only "by showing [us] how not to get there" but also in teaching Neal what he needs to learn. To Rueckert the novel is a ritual of purgation and purification ("Burke's Other Life" 649) and its ending something of an epiphany ("Field Guide" 13). "Neal at the end of the novel points ahead, is a portender, as the title suggests, and is thus a hopeful character under the aegis of Burke's favorite tutelary deity, the Comic Muse" (*Encounters* 136).[19]

On the other hand, Burke's own comic interpretation of the book was developed retrospectively, and there is good reason to read the conclusion far less hopefully. The book does end, after all, with Neal's jabbering madness; his flirtation with the Mad Girl in White is only too representative of his state of mind. Neal also remains completely and tragically isolated in the end; if he does experience some sort of epiphany, there is no comic episode, no reintegrative communion with another human being, attached to the ending to confirm it. No one is there anymore to listen to Neal's invective, lamentations, and aphorisms, and his language itself grows ever more fragmented and idiosyncratic, trailing off into the unconnected observations of the final chapter. To the extent that he uses it at all, Neal is now confined to a prisonhouse of language, writing his story-within-a-story with no way out in the third last chapter and intoning the disjointed mad *sentientia* of the final chapter. The last words of Neal the writer-critic, fittingly, promise silence: "Henceforth silence, that the torrent may be heard descending in all its fullness" (219). As Burke commented later, Neal rather than betraying the markings of an epiphany actually "choos[es] to fold up within himself, as though he were encased in his own internality, . . . [having completed] an ideal regression to the 'infantile' " (*Language as Symbolic Action* 338).

Whether the ending of the novel is comic or not—and Burke himself, characteristically, ultimately invited his readers to look at the ending of the novel in both ways[20]—*Towards a Better Life* concludes, as *Counter-Statement* does, with a renunciation of one version of modernism and the implicit acclamation of another. Although Burke employs a modernist, experimental form, he uses that form to dramatize the material consequences of the pose of the autonomous artist. Malcolm Cowley in his 1932 review of the novel reduced it all to his own aphorism: "There is no salvation apart from society" (24); the radical artistic individualism of *Axel's Castle* leads the protagonist not so much to insight as to ruin. The social and rhetorical do not exactly triumph in *Towards a Better Life*, but their opposites surely fail, and fail utterly. Radical individualism leads to ruin. *Towards* is quintessentially modern in technique, but in content it counters those among the moderns who would aestheticize literature and its makers away from life and into a palace of art. As he had also done in the case of *Counter-Statement*, Burke from a position within modernism firmly problematizes some of its central tenets.

Towards a Better Life, then, is a book of theory and criticism as well as a novel. As he had in *Counter-Statement*, Burke created a new form that borrowed from both the critical and the literary, a form demonstrating Burke's "habit of developing fiction out of essays rather than essays out of fiction."[21] In his later years Burke was fond of recommending *Towards* as an introduction to his theoretical work and conceptual systems,[22] and for good reason. Thematically the novel offers Burke's belief in social intercourse and the conversation of mankind as antidotes to sterile, autonomous art and contentious argument. Theoretically it begins to look toward dramatism as an approach to understanding every sort of human behavior: Neal uses drama to explore human motives in Part 1 (25) and in the beginning sentences of Part 3: "Though lives rarely have the conformity of entire plays, there are possible subdivisions corresponding to the acts of a play. A cycle or constellation of events separates itself from the general clutter—and since it can be classified, we can note its subsidence. The curtain descends upon a partial close, a converging or resolution of some factors" (131). Technically *Towards a Better Life* works by mixing art and criticism and by offering perspective through incongruity, by juxtaposing a Self against one after the next sharp opposite. As William Rueckert has noted, Burke's novel also looks toward his future concerns by dramatizing the need to move beyond factional disputes and to keep "moving towards": "Almost every Burkean proposition is a process/towards one. He has had a lifelong concern with moving on, with purification, with dialectic, with locating and taking on new antagonists," with progress through dialectic and irony (*Encounters* 242). The Laforgean pose of the narrator of *Towards*, in other words, is characteristic of Burke's own pose.

Towards a Better Life is also a good introduction to Burke's criticism because it offers his considered response to modernism. As 1931 turned to 1932, Harcourt, Brace threw a party on the occasion of its publication, on January 28, 1932 (Burke to Williams, January 18, 1932; Williams to Burke, January 19, 1932; Burke to Wheelwright, January 11 and 21, 1932). Burke was still hugely proud of his novel, the hippopotamus hide of his self-delight still fully intact. And so, no John Neal, Burke characteristically felt it appropriate to observe the event with his friends, to celebrate heartily and sociably with a group of his intellectual and artistic companions. From there he would be going on to The Next Phase, as Burke liked to say, to new problems and intellectual circles and sets, to *Auscultation, Creation, and Revision*, *Permanence and Change*, *Attitudes toward History*, *The Philosophy of Literary Form*: to the 1930s.

An Informal Chronology
Notes
Works Cited and Consulted
Index

An Informal Chronology

The following is an unsystematic listing of events in the life of Kenneth Burke between 1915 and 1931. The chronology derives chiefly from evidence in correspondence to and from Burke, some of it published in Jay's *Selected Correspondence*. But it also makes use of biographical information scattered in Skodnick, Woodcock, Rountree, Bak, and Warren, bibliographies by Frank and Thames, and memoirs such as Munson's *Awakening*, Cowley's *Exile's Return* and *And I Worked at the Writer's Trade*, Brown's *Robber Rocks*, Day's *Long Loneliness*, and Josephson's *Life*. The chronology also includes references to certain public and publishing events that seem likely to me to have been important to Burke.

1915

Van Wyck Brooks, *America's Coming of Age.*
Robert Frost, *North of Boston.*
Wallace Stevens, "Sunday Morning."
Genteel *Pollyanna* and *Pollyanna Grows Up* (by Elinor Porter) are bestsellers.
Amy Lowell and Richard Aldington edit *Some Imagist Poets. The Egoist* publishes
    a special imagist issue.
Carl Sandberg, *Chicago Poems.*
D. W. Griffith produces the film *Birth of a Nation*, and Charlie Chaplin appears
    in *Work.*
Parts of what would become Sherwood Anderson's *Winesburg, Ohio* begin to
    appear in *The Masses* and *The Little Review.*
Alfred A. Knopf establishes a publishing house dedicated to modern literature.
Jazz and ragtime are going strong in the Storyville section of New Orleans.

Having recently graduated from Peabody High School in Pittsburgh (where he read English and Continental writers such as Shaw, Meredith, Ibsen, Mann, Strindberg, Schnitzler, Hauptmann, Chekhov, Dostoevsky), Burke is living with his parents at 989 Boulevard East in Weehawken, New Jersey (across the Hudson from 42nd Street in New York City and near the mouth of the Lincoln Tunnel, then under construction), where his father has taken a new job. He has been circulating among his friends a story called "Analysis of a Cerebralist," now lost, which features a sensational plot involving incest.

183

May 6: A day after his eighteenth birthday, Burke begins a long correspondence with the English writer Louis Wilkinson, who soon begins to introduce him to various writers.

May 7: A German submarine sinks the S.S. Lusitania.

Others magazine (dedicated to the "new" poetry) is founded, edited by Alfred Kreymborg and funded by Walter Arensberg; the loose *Others* circle includes at various times Kreymborg, Dorothy Kreymborg, Arensberg, Arensberg's wife Louise, Wallace Stevens, William Carlos Williams, Lola Ridge, Mina Loy, Malcolm Cowley, Maxwell Bodenheim, Louise Bogan, Max Eastman, and artists Marcel Duchamp, Francis Picabia, Charles Demuth, Marsden Hartley, Joseph Stella, Charles Sheeler, and Man Ray. The group produces *Others* until May 1919 and organizes informal get-togethers until 1921. Burke is reading *Others* as well as *Poetry* and *The Little Review*. He is also writing free verse, such as "Adam's Song, and Mine," "Rhapsody under the Autumn Moon," "Revolt," and "The Oftener Trinity" (all later published).

Summer: The Provincetown Players, led by George Cram Cook and Susan Glaspell, are germinating in Provincetown, Massachusetts.

June 15: Marcel Duchamp arrives in New York City, and stays.

July: Pittsburgh friend Jim Light suggests that Burke read *The Masses* and try to meet *Masses* writers and editors like John Reed. The Vorticists Ezra Pound and Wyndham Lewis issue the second and final issue of *Blast*.

August: Lifelong friend Malcolm Cowley encourages Burke to join him as a student at Harvard, but instead Burke works as a bank clerk while living with his parents.

November 5: At a party Burke meets Theodore Dreiser. Burke is writing lots of verse, some stories, and a play (the last never completed).

Wilkinson is hoping to help Burke get his free verse into *The Little Review* and *Others*.

1916

John Dewey, *Democracy and Education*.
Einstein formulates his General Theory of Relativity.
T. S. Eliot gives up philosophy for a literary career.
Greenwich Village saloneer Mabel Dodge is psychoanalyzed and thus reinforces the Freud vogue.
Max Weber, *Essays on Art*.

January: Burke is reading Edgar Lee Masters' new *Spoon River Anthology*. He is in love with Sue Jenkins (who later marries Jim Light and then Slater Brown); he visits Malcolm Cowley at Harvard.

In late January or early February he meets Alfred Kreymborg, editor of *Others*.

February: In Columbus, Jim Light launches his experimental literary magazine *Sansculotte*.

February–June: Burke studies at Ohio State University with Jim Light and Sue Jenkins; they've chosen Ohio State because Ludwig Lewisohn, teacher of a high school mentor, is now on the faculty at OSU. Address: 151 West 10th Street, Columbus. Lewisohn introduces Burke to Remy de Gourmont and Thomas Mann, and Burke likes Mann so well that he translates *Death in Venice*—the basis for the translation later published in *The Dial* and in The Modern Library series. Perhaps he meets two Batterham sisters—Margaret and Lily—who are enrolled at Ohio State.

February 2: Henry James dies in London.

March: Burke's first publication appears in *Others*: the free-verse poem "Adam's Song, and Mine."

April: Easter Rebellion in Dublin.

Burke defends free verse in a letter to Cowley and writes quite a bit of it as well.

May: "I am going for certain to take up exclusively the study of music," he writes to Cowley.

Dadas form in Zurich, led by Tristan Tzara.

Summer: Burke visits Pittsburgh after school is out in June, and visits Cowley at the Cowley family country place in Belsano, Pennsylvania, near Altoona. Burke spends the summer in Weehawken; he hopes to visit Europe if he can manage to save the money.

July 1: Somme Offensive begins on Western front.

Seven Arts magazine is organized to encourage indigenous American culture, with Randolph Bourne as its spiritual center (as well as Waldo Frank, Paul Rosenfeld, Van Wyck Brooks, and Oppenheim). Its first issue appears in November.

Burke decides not to return to Ohio State.

September 4–5: Having spent the summer developing an experimental theatre on Cape Cod and having added Eugene O'Neill to the group, The Provincetown Players resolve to present plays back in Greenwich Village, under the leadership of Cook and Glaspell. The group includes Reed, Louise Bryant, Kreymborg, Mabel Dodge, Max Eastman, Charles Demuth, William Carlos Williams, and Marsden Hartley.

Burke's poems are well received when Cowley reads them to a literary society at Harvard.

November: Burke meets Matthew Josephson after reading his experimental poems to a Columbia University literary group that meets under the guidance of John Erskine.

O'Neill's "Bound East for Cardiff" opens in Greenwich Village.

185

Still promoting his charge, Wilkinson tells Dreiser about Burke's writing.

Woodrow Wilson is re-elected President.

1917

T. S. Eliot, *Prufrock and Other Observations*.
William Carlos Williams, *Al que quiere*.
Jung, *The Unconscious*.
Edna St. Vincent Millay, *Renascence*.
James Joyce, *A Portrait of the Artist as a Young Man*.
The Little Review moves from Chicago to Greenwich Village.
Albert Boni and Charles Liveright open a Greenwich Village publishing firm and
    soon begin The Modern Library.
The "Stieglitz Circle" of modern artists, centered around Stieglitz's gallery 291,
    now includes Georgia O'Keeffe, John Marin, Hartley, Williams, and Charles
    Dove.

January: Burke contributes to *Sansculotte* (a translation of Mombert's "Lullaby,"
a story "Parabolic Tale," and poems "Revolt," "Hokku," "La Baudelairienne,"
and "Invocations"). His poem "Spring Song" appears in the Greenwich Village
progressive magazine *Slate*.

January 23: Artists John Sloan, Marcel Duchamp, Gertrude Drick, and Charles
Ellis climb the Washington Square Arch and declare Greenwich Village a free
state.

February: Light and Jenkins encourage Burke to return to Ohio State, and Cowley
urges him to come to Harvard (which he visits and looks over; on the same trip
he visits Wilkinson in Cambridge). But instead Burke enters Columbia University,
where he studies for the rest of the year. He continues to live in Weehawken and
publishes poems in *Sansculotte*: "The Oftener Trinity," and "Bathos, Youth, and
the Antithetical 'Rather.' "

Burke encounters the work of William James and Bertrand Russell in a philosophy
course at Columbia, led by Professor Frederick Woodbridge; he reads Bergson; he
studies English literature with Erskine. He takes the ferry to classes with Richard
McKeon.

March: Burke publishes poems "Nocturne" and "Adam's Song, and Mine" in
Sansculotte. (The latter is a more fixed-form version of the poem with the same
name published earlier in *Others*.)

The Russian Revolution is in progress; eventually Lenin and the Bolsheviks assume
power in November. John Reed reports the action.

April: Society of Independent Artists show opens; Duchamp's notorious ready-
made "Fountain" is removed but creates a sensation anyway. Columbia suspends
two faculty members for espousing pacifism and American neutrality. History
professor Charles Beard resigns in protest.

April 3: Georgia O'Keeffe exhibit opens at Stieglitz's 291 Gallery in New York.

April 6: The United States enters World War I. Slater Brown, Cowley, Cummings, Hemingway, and Dos Passos enter the ambulance corps.

The Espionage Act permits the prosecution of radicals.

Summer: George Cram Cook and Susan Glaspell spoof Freudianism in their Provincetown Players play *Suppressed Desires*. The Players again move to Greenwich Village in the fall and are joined by Edna St. Vincent Millay and her sisters.

During the summer Burke works in a shipyard, experiments with a later-abandoned novel, *Fallow Ground*, and spends much time in Greenwich Village with his friend Josephson. He writes short fictional sketches—"A Man of Forethought" (later published in *The Dial*), "When the God's Laugh," and "The Laying Down of Lives." (The latter two, whose titles suggest that they may have been written under the cloud of the war, were never published and are now lost.) In July Burke and Josephson attend meetings of the Guillotine Club, a socialist anti-war group. Burke returns to Columbia in September. Not unsympathetic to the German side, he avoids service in World War I probably because of physical shortcomings (his size and his trouble hearing out of one ear).

August 18: Mabel Dodge remarries, and her New York modernist salon shortly thereafter begins to wind down.

September: Jim Light suddenly quits Ohio State when, during the war frenzy, Lewisohn is fired for his German heritage. Light asks Burke to find him and Sue Jenkins a place in New York. Light takes lodging in Greenwich Village with OSU friend Charles Ellis and is soon involved with The Provincetown Players.

December: With its editors under indictment, *The Masses* suspends publication; it later returns in tamer form as *The Liberator*.

1918

Willa Cather, *My Ántonia*.
Oswald Spengler, *Decline of the West*.
Ezra Pound, *Pavannes and Divisions*.
Luigi Pirandello, *Six Characters in Search of an Author*.

First week of January: Burke once and for all resolves to quit Columbia because it requires students to complete prerequisites before enrolling in advanced courses and because he wishes to involve himself as a writer more closely in the modernist scene in Greenwich Village. He is still living in Weehawken.

January 8: Wilson proposes his "Fourteen Points."

Columbia University awards a poetry prize to genteel Sara Teasdale.

February: Burke is writing his short story "The White Oxen" and reading Baudelaire, Gourmont, Huysmans, Flaubert, and Pater.

March 15 (roughly): Burke moves to 86 Greenwich Avenue house ("the Clemenceau Cottage") with Light and Jenkins, who are now intimately involved with

The Provincetown Players; other tenants of the house include George Cram Cook, Susan Glaspell, and perhaps Eugene O'Neill (the principals of The Provincetown Players) as well as the photographer Berenice Abbott, painter Charles Ellis (later the husband of Norma Millay), and writer and artist Djuna Barnes—all of whom also participate in Players' productions. Burke, having resolved to be a writer, lives on oatmeal and milk (according to Josephson) and drenches himself in Greenwich Village life, including the new experimental theatre. He befriends other Players, including Percy Winner and possibly Dorothy Day.

March: *The Little Review* begins to run segments from Joyce's *Ulysses* (through 1920).

April: Van Wyck Brooks, "On Creating a Usable Past," is published in *The Dial*. Americans fight at Belleau Wood and Chateau-Thierry.

April 15: Arthur Eastman, Floyd Dell, and Art Young of *The Masses* are tried for conspiracy to obstruct recruitment; the trial results in a hung jury (as does the retrial in October).

June (last half): Burke spends a few weeks at a nearly abandoned house in Candor, New York, with Foster Damon, Malcolm Cowley, and Berenice Abbott (and with Sue Jenkins and Jim Butler). Damon, Cowley, Burke, and Abbott cooperate in a ruse to concoct and then promote poetry under the name of Earl Roppel.

July and August: Burke apparently works in a shipyard.

November 11: Armistice ends World War I.

Burke's brief story "Idylls" appears in Mencken's *Smart Set*.

Burke is living on Patchin Place in Greenwich Village; he has been reading Flaubert, Huysmans' *A rebours*, and Pater's *Marius the Epicurean*.

The world-wide flu epidemic claims Randolph Bourne in New York in the final days of the year.

1919

Sinclair Lewis, *Main Street*.
Sherwood Anderson, *Winesburg, Ohio*.
John Reed, *Ten Days That Shook the World*.
Bergson, *L'energie spirituelle*.
Waldo Frank, *Our America*, a manifesto for a new American literature.

January: Burke is probably living back in Weehawken.

February: Burke is in love with Lily Batterham, who is living at 3 Bank Street in Greenwich Village.

April: Burke sends his story "A Conjecture" (which was never published and is now lost) to Louis Wilkinson for comment.

May 19: Burke marries Lily Batterham. He places a story, "A Man of Forethought," in *Smart Set*.

Summer: The Burkes and Josephsons spend the summer reading, writing, gardening, entertaining visitors (and subsisting on fruit, berries, vegetables, trout, game, and grits), at a dilapidated farm near Candor, New York. Burke concentrates on improving his Latin and writing fiction: "Olympians," "Portrait of an Arrived Critic," "Mrs. Maecenas," "The Soul of Kajn Tafha," "The Excursion," and "Victories" (the last, never published, is now lost).

Versailles peace conference; a treaty is signed in June and rejected by the U.S. Senate on November 19.

September: Boston police go on strike. Burke moves into 24 Charles Street in Greenwich Village.

Winter: Strikes in the steel and coal industries.

December: Emma Goldman and 248 others are deported by Attorney General A. Mitchell Palmer.

1920

T. S. Eliot, *The Sacred Wood.*
Van Wyck Brooks, *The Ordeal of Mark Twain.*
Sinclair Lewis, *Main Street.*
Provincetown Players present *Emperor Jones.*
Ezra Pound, *Hugh Selwyn Mauberley.*
Edith Wharton, *The Age of Innocence.*
F. Scott Fitzgerald, *This Side of Paradise.*
Charlie Chaplin's "The Kid."
January 1: Prohibition begins.
The Nineteenth Amendment extends suffrage to women.
Commercial radio begins.

January: Burke moves to 143 Waverly Place, Greenwich Village. Scofield Thayer and S. Watson, having acquired controlling interest of it the year before, transform *The Dial* into a magazine of the arts. A signal event: *The Dial* rejects "Victories" and "A Conjecture" but accepts four other Burke stories—"Mrs. Maecenas" (which appears in March), "The Soul of Kajn Tafha" and "The Excursion" (which appear in July), and "Portrait of an Arrived Critic" (which appears in April 1922).

February: First child is born to the Burkes (daughter Jeanne Elspeth "Dutchie").

March: Burke is working on an essay on Remy de Gourmont and has begun a story, "David Wasserman."

April: Burke's review of Cournos' *The Mask* appears in *The Dial.*

Mid-May: The Burkes move for the summer to Lily's family's summer residence in Beech (Buncombe County) in the mountains of western North Carolina; from July 25 through September 20 he is at the Batterham home in Asheville. Burke spends his time translating Mann ("Loulou") and Gourmont for *The Dial* and working on his fiction: a substantial revision of "The White Oxen," the completion of "David Wasserman," "The Birth of Philosophy" (never published and now lost), "My Dear Mrs. Wurtelbach," and "Scherzando." Through the mail, Burke and Cowley talk of founding a modernist "school" (christened "Courve" by Burke) that would integrate poetry, painting, and sculpture and incorporate Futurist elements of city life and the machine.

August: Burke's story "David Wasserman" is rejected by *The Dial* and submitted to *The Little Review*, which accepts it but doesn't publish it right away for fear of suppression. Burke proposes to translate a volume of Mann's stories for Boni and Liveright.

Sacco and Vanzetti are arrested amid a "Red Scare," which is fanned September 16 when a bomb explodes outside J. P. Morgan's on Wall Street and kills 33.

September: Burke's review of Huneker's *Painted Veils* appears in *The Literary Review*. He considers accepting a position writing ad copy for World's Market.

October 17: John Reed dies in Moscow.

November: Warren Harding elected President. The Provincetown Players present "The Emperor Jones," November 1. Burke's review of Waldo Frank's *The Dark Mother* appears in *The Literary Review*. He meets William Carlos Williams late in the month or early in December.

December: William Carlos Williams and Robert McAlmon produce the first issue of their periodical *Contact*. Burke's review of Floyd Dell's *Moon-Calf* appears in *The Literary Review*.

1921

January: Burke, now living at 50 Charles Street in Greenwich Village, receives his first letters from Williams.

January 2: Burke offers Williams his stories "My Dear Mrs. Wurtelbach" and "The White Oxen." He also meets Robert McAlmon, who with Williams is putting out *Contact*.

With rents rising in New York and Greenwich Village and with Burke looking for healthier quarters, the Burkes begin looking for a farm in the New Jersey countryside. Burke publishes reviews in *The New York Times* (January 9).

The avant-garde magazine *Broom* is conceived in New York by Harold Loeb and Kreymborg; the first issue will appear in November.

February: Burke's essay "Approaches to Remy de Gourmont" appears as the lead article in *The Dial* (and later in *Counter-Statement*); he places a review of Flynn's *The Influence of Puritanism* in *The Literary Review*; his essay "Dadaisme Is France's Latest Literary Fad" is published in *The New York Tribune*.

February 21: Margaret Anderson and Jane Heep appear in court on obscenity charges stemming from their printing in *The Little Review* of episodes from Joyce's *Ulysses*: they are fined a total of one hundred dollars.

March: *The Dial* rejects "My Dear Mrs. Wurtelbach."

April: Burke spends a day at Williams' home; on the 27th Williams offers to publish in *Contact* his poem "Ver Renatus Orbis Est." "The White Oxen" is being considered for *Contact* by McAlmon. Burke's translation of Mann's "Loulou" appears in the April *Dial*.

A major expatriate exodus to Paris is under way. Many of Burke's friends join the exodus, including Barnes, Cowley, Brown, Dos Passos, Day, Cummings, and Josephson.

April 15: The Burkes move for the summer (until September) to Monson, Maine, northwest of Bangor, accompanied by Josephson and the artist Carl Sprinchorn. There Burke works on his fiction: "The Book of Yul," "A Progression" (first known as "An Odyssey"), "In Quest of Olympus," "The Death of Tragedy," and probably "After Hours." Williams is a regular correspondent.

May: Burke places reviews of Virginia Woolf's *Night and Day* and *The Voyage Out* (in *The Dial*) and Jammes's *The Revolt of the Rabbit* (in *The Freeman*).

May 21: The first trial of Sacco and Vanzetti begins.

June: Dadaism is at its height in Paris, around Tzara. Cowley engages in the Dada scene at the Rotonde Cafe and Dome Cafe in Paris. Munson and Josephson are also part of the Dada vogue.

August: Burke's essay "The Armour of Jules Laforg[u]e" appears in *Contact*; a review of James Oppenheim's autobiographical poetry (*The Mystic Warrior*) appears in *The Dial*. Burke completes his essay on "The Correspondence of Flaubert."

September: Burke's story "David Wasserman" appears in *The Little Review*. "Olympians" and "Yul" are rejected by *Broom*. Burke has begun developing his story "First Pastoral."

October: The Burkes are still living at 50 Charles Street.

October 18: Cowley's essay "This Youngest Generation" (featuring Burke and four other young writers) appears in *The Literary Review*, a supplement to *The New York Evening Post*.

November: Burke completes an article on Pater.

December: Burke publishes reviews of Schnitzler's *Casanova's Homecoming* in *The Dial* and of Sprinchorn's painting in *The Arts*.

December 26: In a letter to Burke, Gorham Munson proposes to begin a new magazine (later named *Secession*) that would feature Burke and the other members of "this youngest generation."

1922

Strikes in the coal and rail industries.
Ku Klux Klan revival.
During the summer, Mussolini becomes dictator of Italy.
The first issues of *Secession*, *The Fugitive*, and *The Criterion*.

John Marin paints "Maine Islands."
T. S. Eliot, "The Waste Land."
Provincetown Players present *The Hairy Ape*, directed by James Light.
Harold Stearns, editor, *Civilization in the United States*.

January: Burke's review of Zweig's *Romain Roland* appears in *The Dial*. He finishes an essay, "Some Aspects of the Word," which may never have been published.

February: Burke's article "The Correspondence of Flaubert" (later collected into *Counter-Statement*) and a review of W. C. Williams' *Sour Grapes* appear in *The Dial*. His fiction ("Scherzando" and "Olympians") is printed in *Manuscripts*. Kreymborg resigns as Loeb's partner on *Broom* and is soon replaced by Josephson.

March 1: George Cram Cook and Susan Glaspell sail for Greece, and The Provincetown Players enter a one-year hiatus, after which Light emerges as their premier director.

April 1 (roughly): With the help of a loan from Burke's father, the Burkes make a down payment on and move to a seventy-acre farm (later expanded by an additional acquisition) near Andover, New Jersey; by the middle of the month they have already planted peas, onions, tomatoes, lettuce, carrots, and radishes, and have invited people to visit.

April: Burke's story "Portrait of an Arrived Critic" appears in *The Dial*, and his essay "André Gide, Bookman," appears in *The Freeman*.

May: Burke publishes a review of Paul Elmer More's *The Religion of Plato* in *The Dial*. (He has taken an interest in More's "New Humanism.") The first issue of *Secession* appears, and Gorham Munson visits Burke on May 20 to ask him to be a third editor (with Munson and Josephson). Consequently, Burke helps on *Secession* for the next seventeen months, conferring frequently with Munson.

June: The second issue of *Secession* comes out with Burke's story "The Book of Yul." Burke and Cowley are working on a poetic drama spoofing popularizers of Freudianism such as Floyd Dell; the play is never completed.

July: Burke's translation of Purrman's "From the Workshop of Henri Matisse" is printed in *The Dial*.

July 1–December 31: Commuting from Andover and also keeping a room at times in New York City, Burke works full-time at *The Dial* as an assistant editor (he has worked sporadically there previously) and as acting managing editor while Gilbert Seldes is on vacation and Sophie Wittenberg is on leave. Among other things, he spends long hours carefully setting "The Waste Land" into print for its first publication in the November issue. Burke fraternizes in the American office of *Broom* with Lola Ridge, her assistant Kay Boyle, William Carlos Williams (in town from September to January), and the rest of Ridge's circle.

July 2: A second daughter is born (Eleanor Duva "Happy").

Under the influence of More, he writes his story "Prince Llan."

192

August: Burke publishes a poem ("Eroticon") and story ("First Pastoral") in *Secession*, and the article "The Younger Generation" in *The New York Evening Post*'s "Literary Review"; his translation of Hofmannsthal's story "Lucidor" appears in *The Dial*.

September: In *The Dial*, Burke publishes a review of Evelyn Scott's novel *Narcissus* and a translation of Specht's "Arthur Schnitzler." Burke is reading *Ulysses*; he submits "Mrs. Wurtlebach" to *Broom*.

October: Burke reviews fiction by Waldo Frank (*Rahab* and *City Blocks*) in *The Dial. Broom* accepts "My Dear Mrs. Wurtelbach." About this time Burke has an "audience" with Amy Lowell.

November: Burke's story "After Hours" is printed in *S4N*. About November 15, *Vanity Fair* publishes his "Art and the Hope Chest" (on Van Wyck Brooks's *Ordeal of Mark Twain* and Freudian criticism) in its December issue. In a letter to Brooks, Burke claims membership in "The Youngest Generation." In person and in correspondence he confers with Loeb about *Broom*, with Munson about *Secession*, and with Frank, Williams, Cowley, and Josephson.

December: Burke publishes a review of Middleton Murry's books on Dostoevsky in *The Dial. The Dial* also carries the first part of a translation of Mann's "Tristan" that Burke has done with the assistance of Scofield Thayer, and Burke's translation of Mann's German Letter. So that it might later appear in *The Dial*, late in the month Burke begins thoroughly revising a translation of Mann's *Death in Venice* that he first began at Ohio State. He and Lily close the Andover house for the winter and spend it in New York (as they did for the next few years); Burke's family apparently spends some of the final months of the year in North Carolina and the first months of 1923 in New York City. *Dial* revenues soon permit the Burkes to pay off completely their mortgage in Andover.

1923

D. H. Lawrence, *Studies in Classic American Literature.*
William Carlos Williams, *Spring and All.*
Jean Toomer, *Cane.*
Surrealism "develops" in Paris.
Book-of-the-Month Club founded.

January: Burke publishes a review and his story "In Quest of Olympus" in *Secession*. "Mrs. Wurtlebach" appears in *Broom. The Dial* publishes a review as well as Burke's translations of Zweig on Dickens and the second installment of Mann's "Tristan."

Burke again begins full-time work at *The Dial* until September 29. As an assistant editor he handles many of the business and production details while Thayer is in Vienna and London. While Gilbert Seldes visits Switzerland in the spring and summer, Burke acts as managing editor. In order to work in New York, he commonly rents a room and returns to his farm and family on weekends. In winter, when work in New York is only part-time, he usually commutes from Andover.

On his train rides he works on the translation of *Death in Venice* and on other projects.

February: *Broom* is on the ropes when Loeb withdraws from it after disputes with Josephson and money shortages; Josephson and Cowley, with Loeb as titular editor, try to keep it alive as a quarterly (which next appears in August). Burke reviews Gertrude Stein's *Geography and Plays* for *The Dial*.

French troops occupy the Ruhr when Germany cannot pay war reparations. The threat of more war worries the expatriates.

March: Burke begins to think seriously about publishing a book of his stories. *Broom* is in financial difficulty, and its control passes to Josephson and Cowley.

Spring: Throughout this season (and the rest of the year), Burke works hard on his translation of *Death in Venice*. He rejects some Pound "Cantos" and a contribution from Freud that had been submitted to *The Dial*. Williams writes to him about Europe.

May: Burke's poem "Psalm" is in *S4N*. He finishes a translation of Hauptmann for *The Dial* and entertains Hart Crane at Andover. Cowley performs a famous Dada "gesture" in Paris at the Rotonde Cafe and then returns to the United States in July.

Hitler is arrested after an attempted coup d'etat fails in Munich.

June: Burke is translating Mann's monthly "German Letter" for *The Dial*. In the first week of the month, Burke, Brown, and Josephson barely escape a gang of toughs who disrupt one of their frequent informal meetings at a Sullivan Street speakeasy.

June–October: *Secession* runs into trouble when Wheelwright takes over production responsibilities in Europe.

July: As managing editor of *The Dial*, Burke composes the editorial Comment that appears this month and translates Meier-Graefe's "German Art after the War." He also places his essay "Chicago and Our National Gesture" in the New Humanist magazine *The Bookman*.

August 2: Harding dies, succeeded by Coolidge.

October: Burke attends a famous meeting on October 19 to determine the future of *Broom* and *Secession*. After the meeting he resigns from the editorship of *Secession* but remains on good terms with Munson—who ends up in a fistfight with Josephson a few days later. He becomes part of an informal group attempting to keep *Broom* alive. Burke signs a contract for his translation of *Death in Venice*, which is now nearly complete. And his translation of Mann's latest German Letter is in *The Dial*.

December: Burke entertains offers for the publication of his book of stories, later named *The White Oxen, and Other Stories*. His translation of a Schnitzler story appears in *The Dial*. Burke sublets a place at 45 Grove Street in Greenwich Village from his friend Hart Crane. Burke remains very much involved in the disposition of *Broom*.

H. L. Mencken begins *The American Mercury* magazine; the first issue (dated January 1924) contains Boyd's essay "Aesthete: Model 1924," which infuriates Cowley.

1924

George Gershwin's "Rhapsody in Blue."
Ernest Hemingway, *In Our Time*.
Marianne Moore, *Observations*.
Eugene O'Neill, *Desire Under the Elms*.
Thomas Mann, *The Magic Mountain*.

January: Burke publishes his story "Prince Llan" in the final issue of *Broom*. When the issue is suppressed by the Post Office, probably because of sexual references in Burke's story, *Broom* ceases publication. *The Dial* carries another German Letter from Mann, translated by Burke.

January 15 or so through February: The Burke family visits the Batterhams in Asheville, North Carolina. Burke's translation of Heinrich Mann's "Virgins" appears in *The Dial*. He is putting the finishing touches on *Death in Venice*, translating Schnitzler's "New Song," and doing reviews and Brief Mentions for *The Dial*.

March: Burke is back working at *The Dial*. He is employed off and on throughout the year, especially in March, April, May, and early October, as Thayer and Watson begin to withdraw from daily involvement with the magazine (since January, Alyse Gregory has been functioning as managing editor, assisted by Burke). The rest of the Burkes return to Andover on March 23. Burke has now finished all the revisions to his translation of *Death in Venice*, which will appear in *The Dial* in March, April, and May and then be published in Knopf's Modern Library Series; he's also translating Mann's "Tonio Kroger," "Tristan," "Cemetery Road," and "Tobias Mindernickel" for inclusion in the Knopf book (the last two never appear).

April: Burke's story "A Progression" is printed in *Secession* (which soon ceases publication). He reviews Djuna Barnes's *A Book* for *The Dial*.

May: Spring planting in Andover. Burke completes three upstairs rooms in the house. The Provincetown Players offer Paul Robeson in *The Emperor Jones* and *All God's Chillen Got Wings*.

Summer: Burke is reading Schopenhauer, Kant, and Spengler; he'll translate the introduction of *Decline of the West* for *The Dial* (for $120). *The White Oxen, and Other Stories* is being prepared for the press. Burke is also doing Brief Mentions and reviews for *The Dial*.

July: Peggy Cowley is bitten by a copperhead during a party at the Burke farm; she recovers.

August: The Burke family spends the month at Scofield Thayer's home at Edgartown, on Martha's Vineyard. Burke is working there as Thayer's secretary for five or six hours a day, five days a week. Burke's article "Notes on Walter Pater," later to appear in *Counter-Statement*, is published in the magazine *1924*, and *The Dial* prints his review of the poems of Solomon Gabirol.

September: *The White Oxen, and Other Stories* is published by Boni and Liveright about September 20; the first reviews appear in the following month.

Fall: Burke continues work on a meticulous translation of Spengler and does Brief Mentions for *The Dial*.

November: Calvin Coolidge is elected President. The Provincetown Players open O'Neill's *Desire under the Elms* on November 11. Late in the month Burke's friends conceive of the idea for *Aesthete, 1925*, a magazine satirizing Mencken and Boyd, and begin fleshing out its contents. Burke's translation of a section of Mann's *Buddenbrooks* appears in *The Dial*.

Spengler's *The Downfall of Western Civilization* (a.k.a. "The Decline of the West") appears in *The Dial* in November and December, and in January 1925. Burke composes "Psychology and Form," accepted in December by *The Dial*.

December: Burke's review of Wescott's *The Apple of the Eye* and Cowley's review of *The White Oxen* are printed in *The Dial*. Burke does more Brief Mentions.

Winter, 1924–25: Burke, quartered in the Village for the winter, belongs to "an informal talking and tippling club" in New York City. Other "members" are John Bishop, Hart Crane, Slater Brown and Sue Brown, Edmund Wilson, Alfred Kreymborg, Gilbert Seldes, Paul Rosenfeld, Jean Toomer, Lewis Mumford, and Van Wyck Brooks. Other friends include John Dos Passos and Dorothy Day, who soon moves in with Burke's brother-in-law Forster Batterham.

1925

Scopes trial, Dayton, Tennessee.
Gropius's Bauhaus is built in Dessau.
Adolph Hitler, *Mein Kampf*, volume 1.
Theodore Dreiser, *An American Tragedy*.
F. Scott Fitzgerald, *The Great Gatsby*.
Alain Locke, *The New Negro*.
Virginia Woolf, *Mrs. Dalloway*.
Brancusi's sculpture "Bird in Space."
William Carlos Williams, *In the American Grain*.
I. A. Richards, *The Principles of Literary Criticism*.
Countee Cullen, *Color*.
John Dos Passos, *Manhattan Transfer*.
The New Yorker begins publication.

January: On a Saturday night and most of the following day (and/or on November 30, 1924), Cowley, Burke, Slater Brown, Allen Tate, Isidor Schneider, Peggy Cowley, Charles Sheeler, Jack Wheelwright, Hart Crane, and Matthew Josephson compose most of *Aesthete, 1925*. William Carlos Williams mails in his contribution. Burke contributes "Dada, Dead or Alive" and a last-page pseudo-ad ridiculing Mencken.

Burke is completing work on "Psychology and Form," later to appear in *Counter-Statement*. Burke's translation of *Death in Venice*, including "Tristan" and "Tonio Kroger," is published by Knopf.

February: In the first week of the month, six hundred copies of *Aesthete, 1925* are distributed to bookstores and old *Broom* subscribers. Burke finishes "The Poetic Process," which is rejected by *The Dial* before being accepted elsewhere.

March: Burke publishes a review of Brownell's *The Genius of Style* in *The Dial*. Burke and Watson (who is interested in experimental film) discuss making a motion picture of Burke's "In Quest of Olympus" (the project never materializes).

March–December: A transition period at *The Dial*. Watson and especially Thayer withdraw further from daily involvement, and Thayer is planning an extended trip to Europe to secure manuscripts, write, and rest and recuperate from a psychological disorder. Alyse Gregory, recently married, is moving to England. As a result, Marianne Moore becomes associate editor in early April and then assumes control as acting editor (working half-time) on April 27; she chooses Burke as her assistant editor, and so Burke works steadily from April 1 through December 20 or so, when again he quits in order to write in Andover. When Moore vacations in September, Burke takes over her editorial duties. Some of Burke's time is made uneasy when Thayer irrationally calls for Burke's firing at some real or imaginary slight, perhaps exacerbated by Burke's refusal to accompany Thayer to Europe as his private secretary, but Moore and Watson defend Burke's loyalty and the quality of his work. Burke maintains a room at 40 Morton Street in The Village, and he spends weekends and other available times at the farm. (Libby Batterham is a frequent visitor now at the farm.)

May: Burke publishes "The Poetic Process" (later included in *Counter-Statement*) in *The Guardian* and translates for *The Dial* Hofmannsthal's "Honore de Balzac."

July: Burke's "Psychology and Form," later published in *Counter-Statement*, appears in *The Dial*. Burke again refuses when Thayer asks him to serve as Thayer's private secretary on his European trip. Lily Burke and the Burke children are visiting her parents in Asheville.

July 4: A party at Slater and Sue Jenkins Brown's includes Crane, Tate, and Burke.

August: Burke is ill in Andover with the flu. His translation of Schnitzler's "Lieutenant Gustl" and review of Calverton's *The Newer Spirit: A Sociological Criticism of Literature* appear in *The Dial*.

September: While she vacations in Maine, Moore leaves Burke in charge of *The Dial*. Burke's review of I. A. Richards' *Principles of Literary Criticism* is published in *Saturday Review*.

October: Burke visits friends at the artist's colony in Woodstock, New York.

November: Burke's translation of Schnitzler's story "New Song" is in *The Dial*. He also reviews there a book on Milton.

December: Burke's translation of de Mare's "Swedish Ballet" is in *The Little Review*.

1926

Georgia O'Keeffe's "Black Iris."
Fritz Lang's film *Metropolis*.
The New Masses begins publication as successor to *The Liberator*.
Hart Crane, *White Buildings*.
Ernest Hemingway, *The Sun Also Rises*.
Langston Hughes, *The Weary Blues*.
National Broadcasting Corporation creates nationwide radio network.

January: Burke reviews Robert Bridges and Logan Pearsall in *The Dial*.

February: Burke turns down yet another offer to come to Europe as Thayer's secretary. He publishes a review on Williams in *The New York Times*.

March: Burke is reading Williams' *In the American Grain* and I. A. Richards.

During 1926–27, Burke works for the Laura Spelman Rockefeller Memorial Trust, doing research on drug addiction for Colonel Arthur Woods. Although the work reduces his literary activity, and though he speaks in letters to Cowley of an inability to write fiction (of a "tentativeness [so] complete [that it] makes any statement abhorrent"), he also is at work on a novel. His New York address remains 40 Morton Street.

April: Burke's translation of "Georges Papazoff" appears in *The Little Review*. He freelances for *The Dial* (e.g., Brief Mentions and translations of Morand's Paris Letters) and begins a review of Spengler's *Decline of the West*.

May: A Hart Crane poem published in *The Dial* (as "Again") creates a stir when it is revealed that Moore extensively revised the poem, submitted as "Wine Menagerie."

June: Third daughter, Frances Batterham ("Jake"), is born. Burke is experimenting with a perpetual-motion machine.

July: Burke's article on Smith's *Notes on the American Doctrine of Equality* appears in *The Dial*.

Burke works sporadically at *The Dial* for two weeks in July (when Moore is on vacation) and in August (when he replaces another employee on vacation).

September: Burke's lengthy review of Spengler's *Decline of the West* is printed in *The Dial*; parts of it appear later in "The Status of Art" chapter of *Counter-Statement*.

December: Burke visits Washington, D.C., on business for Colonel Woods.

An Informal Chronology

1927

Charles Demuth's "My Egypt."
Virginia Woolf, *To the Lighthouse.*
First "talking movie": Al Jolson in *The Jazz Singer.*
Hound and Horn and *transition* begin publication.

February: Burke publishes an article on Williams in *The Dial.* He continues to work this year for Colonel Woods at the Laura Spelman Rockefeller Memorial Foundation through August 15. He also continues to work on his novel, but his literary production is diminished by his salaried work. He remains at 40 Morton Street while working in New York.

Burke also spends June, July, and August looking after *The Dial* while Moore travels in Europe. His days are very full—he does *Dial* work from 6:30–7:30 A.M., does his Rockefeller work until 5 P.M., does more *Dial* work until 6, eats dinner, does translations for *Vanity Fair* and *The Dial* until 10 P.M., and finishes up *Dial* work from 10–11 P.M. On weekends he gardens at Andover. He also finds a bit of time to do research on an abortive *History of Love.*

June: Burke's translation of an excerpt of Mann's speech "Pariser Rechenschaft" is published in *The Dial.* He translates Mann's German Letter for *The Dial.*

June 13: Lindbergh is welcomed in New York after his transatlantic flight.

Burke's translation of Emil Ludwig's *Genius and Character* is accepted by Harcourt, Brace, and Company (after first apparently falling through); the collection of biographies is published later in the year.

August 22: Sacco and Vanzetti are executed.

September: Moore asks Burke to write the monthly music column for *The Dial.* Burke's review of Brooks, Kreymborg, Mumford, and Rosenfeld's *The American Caravan* is printed in *The New York Herald.*

November: Burke's review of Radin's *Primitive Man* is printed in *The Dial.* He continues to research *A History of Love.*

December: Burke's first music column appears in *The Dial. The New York Herald* prints his review of Molnaar's *Paul Street Boys.* Lily is in the hospital for an operation, and Burke is still doing translations, including *The Dial*'s Paris Letter.

1928

Ravel's "Bolero."
William Butler Yeats, *The Tower.*
Final two books of Proust's *Remembrance of Things Past* are published.
Fugitives: An Anthology of Verse is published.
Trotsky exiled from Soviet Union.

Burke's music columns in *The Dial* appear in January, February, March, April, May, June, July, and December. He continues to hold a room at 40 Morton Street and to commute regularly to Andover.

199

January: Burke reviews Van Wyck Brooks's *Emerson and Others* for *The Dial* and Wasserman's *World's End* for *The New York Herald*. He, Slater Brown, Robert Coates, Matthew Josephson, and Malcolm Cowley reenact a scene from *Aesthete, 1925* by producing a series of satires on contemporary culture; under the title "New York: 1928," it is published in nineteen pages in the summer 1928 issue of Jolas' "international quarterly for creative experiment" *transition*. Burke's contributions are three satires in the form of quasi-ads: "Cheat the Censor," "She Brought the Wrong Book," and "Important Communication to the Editor."

February: Burke reviews Thiess's *The Gateway to Life* for *The New York Herald*.

March: Burke reviews Schicke's *Maria Capponi* for *The Herald*.

April: E. E. Cummings' play *Him* is produced by Provincetown Players in Greenwich Village.

May: Moore agrees to publish excerpts ("Declamations") of Burke's *Towards a Better Life* in *The Dial*. The three Burke children have the measles. Burke finishes a Hofmannsthal translation of 4400 words.

June: Burke has an automobile, and erects a garage in Andover with a study above it.

August: Burke's "A Declamation" appears in *The Dial*. He continues work on his novel. He also is negotiating the purchase of additional acreage at Andover so that he can build a four-acre lake behind a nine-foot dam.

September: Burke is translating Baumann's *St. Paul*.

October: Burke's "Second Declamation" is in *The Dial*. The Andover dam is under construction. Late in the month Burke begins work editing a journal and researching drug addiction and criminology at the Bureau of Social Hygiene, again for Colonel Woods; the office is on the thirtieth floor of a building at 61 Broadway. The pay is good enough that he quits doing freelance translations for *Vanity Fair*. The job continues until at least June 1930.

November: "Third Declamation" appears in *The Dial*. The "Fourth" is almost completed.

Herbert Hoover elected President.

December: Watson offers Burke the Dial Prize ($2000) for 1928.

1929

Robert Lynd and Helen Lynd, *Middletown*.
John Dewey, *The Quest for Certainty*.
Robert Frost, *West-Running Brook* and *Selected Poems*.
William Faulkner, *The Sound and the Fury*.
Ernest Hemingway, *Farewell to Arms*.
Erich Maria Remarque, *All Quiet on the Western Front*.
Thomas Wolfe, *Look Homeward, Angel*.

I. A. Richards, *Practical Criticism*.
Founding of Museum of Modern Art.

January: Burke's Greenwich Village address is now 65 Bank Street. He continues to write a music column for *The Dial* (January, February, March, April, May, June) and prepares Baumann's *St. Paul* for publication by Harcourt, Brace. "Fourth Declamation" appears in *The Dial*.

February: Burke's poem "From Outside" is published in a special "tribute to Burke" issue of *The Dial*, in honor of his award. He is still working full-time at the Bureau of Social Hygiene.

March: Burke's "Fifth Declamation" appears in *The Dial*.

May: "Sixth Declamation" is printed in *The Dial*.

July: The demise of *The Dial* takes place. Burke visits Cowley's family place in Belsano, Pennsylvania.

August: *The Bookman* publishes Burke's essay "A Decade of American Fiction"; he reviews Cowley's *Blue Juniata* in *The New York Herald*.

September: Burke's "Seventh Declamation" is printed in *Hound and Horn*. Burke, Cowley, Berenice Abbott, Bill and Sue Brown, Bob and Elsa Coates, and others enjoy a Labor Day party at which Hart Crane goes into a drunken rage, smashes furniture, rips apart books and artworks—and finds seventeen missing lines of "The Bridge." Late in the month, Burke returns to work for Colonel Woods at the Bureau of Social Hygiene, where he ghostwrites a book on drugs and crime.

October 29: Stock market plunge begins economic depression. A few days before, Cowley begins a job at *The New Republic*.

November: "Eighth Declamation" appears in *Hound and Horn*. Burke's review of Maurice Barres's *The Sacred Hill* is in *The New York Herald*.

December: Burke continues to work at the Bureau of Social Hygiene.

December 11: Harry Crosby and his mistress commit suicide.

1930

Empire State Building opens.
Freud, *Civilization and Its Discontents*.
C. S. Johnson, *The Negro in American Civilization*.
Black Sun Press in Paris publishes Hart Crane's *The Bridge*.
Katherine Ann Porter, *Flowering Judas*.
Allan Tate and others, *I'll Take My Stand*.

January: Still commuting to and from Andover, Burke begins negotiating with Harcourt, Brace on the publication of *Counter-Statement*.

February: Burke is working on an essay on Mann and Gide.

March: "Ninth Declamation" appears in *Hound and Horn*.

May: Burke's essay "Three Frenchmen's Churches" is published in *The New Republic*.

June: Burke's essay "Mann and Gide" (later a chapter in *Counter-Statement*) appears in *The Bookman*. Burke's job at the Bureau of Social Hygiene probably concludes about this time.

July: In *The New Republic*, Burke publishes his essay "Waste: The Future of Prosperity," which is reprinted in the October 1930 *Reader's Digest*. Living at Andover are Alice Decker (an acquaintance from the Rockefeller job) and Libby Batterham.

August: Burke adds a large room onto his Andover house. He is also reviewing Dewey's *Quest for Certainty* and *Experience and Nature*.

September: The Burkes host their annual Labor Day Weekend party in Andover: swimming, diving, tennis, food and drink, dancing, talk. *Pagany*'s first issue carries Burke's "Tenth Declamation." Burke works steadily on his "Declamations" and continues to plan the collection that would become *Counter-Statement*.

November: Burke's New York address is now 58 Perry Street in Greenwich Village.

1931

Pearl Buck, *The Good Earth*.
Yale publishes Colonel Woods's *Dangerous Drugs: The World Fight against Illicit Traffic in Narcotics*, a product of Burke's efforts.

February: Burke's essay "Boring from Within" is in *The New Republic*.

March: In letters to various literary friends, Burke is considering starting a new literary magazine (to be financed by Sibley Watson as a kind of successor to *The Dial*); because of internal squabbles and financial shortages, the enterprise never materializes.

April: Burke signs a contract for the publication of *Counter-Statement*. He spends the next few months finishing and revising its chapters and preparing the final manuscript.

May: With Cowley, Wheelwright, Coates, Josephson, and Evan Shipman, Burke visits Yaddo, the artist's colony near Saratoga Springs, New York, because Cowley has organized a gathering to hammer out a collective memoir of the 1920s. While the others enjoy themselves, Burke works on *Towards a Better Life* and Cowley continues work on what would become *Exile's Return*.

June: With *Counter-Statement* in production, Burke moves to complete and publish his novel *Towards a Better Life*.

July: Burke's essay "Redefinitions" (revised into *Counter-Statement* as "Applications of the Terminology") appears in the July, August, and September *New Republic*.

August: Burke is working to complete *Towards a Better Life* and is negotiating with a publisher.

September: *Counter-Statement* comes off the presses, and *Towards a Better Life* is completed. Burke publishes a review of Ouspensky's *A New Model of the Universe* in *The New Republic*.

October: On the 6th, Burke's daughter Happy undergoes successful surgery of some kind; on the 7th, Harcourt, Brace agrees to publish *Towards a Better Life*. On Halloween, Burke speaks before the John Reed Club in New York. Burke's New York address is 381 Bleeker Street.

November: Reviews of *Counter-Statement* begin to appear; Burke responds to one of them in his "Munsoniana," published in *The New Republic*.

December: In *The New Republic* Burke publishes a "Counterblast" to Granville Hicks's review of *Counter-Statement*.

Notes

CHAPTER 1. INTRODUCTION

1. Perloff, Malcolm Bradbury ("Nonhomemade"), Monique Chefdor, Astradur Eysteinsson, and a number of others have remarked in recent years on the diversity within modernism. (For contrasting approaches to modernism as a coherent and unified movement, see for instance Kenner, *The Pound Era*; Howe; Jameson, *Fables*; Vendler; Ellman and Fiedelson; and Levinson.) Perloff, in "Modernist Studies," offers a list of fourteen characteristics of modernism as it has been traditionally defined, among them "the replacement of representation of the external world by the imaginative construction of the poet's inner world," "the artist as hero," "the autonomy of art and its divorce from truth or morality," "the depersonalization and 'objectivity' of art," "ambiguity and complexity," "the fluidity of consciousness," "the importance attached to the Freudian unconscious," "the alienated self in the urban world," and "internationalism" (158). As this book will indicate, however, few if any of these tenets were accepted unanimously or uncritically by the moderns themselves.
2. For a discussion of gender, sexuality, and modernism, see in particular Scott's *The Gender of Modernism* and Carolyn Burke's "Getting Spliced: Modernism and Sexual Difference." For an account of the Harlem Renaissance from a modernist perspective, see Houston Baker's *Modernism and the Harlem Renaissance*.
3. For an account of the contradictions inherent in modernist politics, see chapter 3 of Raymond Williams' *The Politics of Modernism*.
4. The scholarly literature on the subject of modernism is of course vast. My sense of modernism in these pages has been shaped especially by Perloff's "Modernist Studies," *The Futurist Moment*, and *The Dance of the Intellect*; Nelson's *Repression and Recovery*; Calinescu's *Five Faces of Modernity*; Eysteinssen's *The Concept of Modernism*; and the essays in Chefdor, Quinores, and Wachtel. Two early summaries of modernist aesthetics that I especially appreciate are Cowley's *After the Genteel Tradition* and Wilson's *Axel's Castle*; both offer instructive narratives of modernism that were formulated before 1935.
5. Quoted in Frederick J. Hoffman's *The Twenties*, 244.

6. Both are quoted in Schwartz's *The Matrix of Modernism*. James in "The Pragmatic Method" (1898) offered that truth is colored by circumstance, made true by pragmatic actions, rather than true forever: "The ultimate test for us of what a truth means is indeed the conduct it dictates or inspires." Nietzsche in "Truth and Lie" had also meditated on truth as a human creation.

7. This backward-looking strain within modernism is the emphasis of Jeffrey Walker's *Bardic Ethos and the American Epic Poem*.

8. "*Ulysses*, Order, and Myth," *The Dial* 75 (1923): 480–83.

9. In his chapter on the avant-garde in *The Five Faces of Modernity*, Matei Calinescu contends that the avant-garde in this century has always been defined by these two contending strains—the withdrawal into aestheticism and the drive to social activism. Interestingly, the same two strains were identified in Munson's *Destinations* in 1928. See also chapter 2 of Renato Poggioli's *The Theory of the Avant-Garde* and Calinescu's "Modernism and Ideology."

10. Two other fine memoirs of the period that are especially instructive to students of Kenneth Burke are Munson's *The Awakening Twenties* and Josephson's *Life among the Surrealists*.

11. Indeed, the year 1913 has been seen as an international watershed (see Breon-Guerry's *L'année 1913*). The Armory Show and the Patterson Pageant are described in Abrahams' *Lyrical Left*, Munson's *Awakening*, and Milton Brown's *American Painting*, "Armory Show and Its Aftermath," and *Armory Show*.

12. In a January 24, 1913, letter to Gertrude Stein, Dodge wrote: "There is an exhibition coming off [i.e., the Armory Show] which is the most important public event that has come off since the Declaration of Independence. . . . There will be a riot & a revolution & things will never be quite the same" (quoted in Abrahams, *Lyrical Left* 3–4). For an overview of Dodge's salon, see Crunden, 383–98.

13. In fact, a number of recent studies have attempted to redress the traditional emphasis on Paris by emphasizing Greenwich Village as a modernist crucible. See Nelson's *Repression and Recovery*; Tashjian's *Skyscraper Primitives*; Crunden's *American Salons*; Wertheim; Martin's *Marianne Moore*; Homer; Davidson; Fishbein; Churchill; Heller and Rudnick; and Abrahams, *Lyrical Left*.

14. Melia is quoted in Foss, Foss, and Trapp, 187.

15. Frank Lentricchia, quoted by Hayden White in the Preface to *Representing Kenneth Burke*, viii.

16. For a summary of criticisms of Burke as autodidact, as someone who writes only for himself, and as someone interested in being a gadfly more than an advocate of his own system, see Harris, 452–53.

17. In his edition of the Burke-Cowley correspondence, Jay misidentifies the book as *Permanence and Change*.

18. *Criticism and Social Change* as a whole does indeed frame Burke as a critical Marxist, as a "critical theorist of society" (86), but I also want to acknowledge that in a secondary but important way in his discussion of *Counter-Statement*,

Lentricchia does understand Burke as "a charter member of the modernist avant-garde" who wrote for other moderns.

19. Stanley Fish notes that "deconstruction is a programmatic and tendentious focusing of ways of thinking that have already come to be regarded as commonplace and orthodox. That is why, when deconstructionist doctrine began to be promulgated, one of the first things people did was to proclaim that so-and-so—usually Kenneth Burke—was a deconstructionist before there was a name for it" (155). But see also Denis Donoghue's *Ferocious Alphabets*, which treats Burke as an anti-deconstructionist, and Lentricchia's *Criticism and Social Change*, which poises Burke against Paul de Man. A recent volume of essays edited by Bernard Brock, *Kenneth Burke and Contemporary European Thought*, places Burke in relation to the thought of Habermas, Grassi, Foucault, and Derrida.

20. But only one of the contributors to Grossberg, Nelson, and Treichler's massive *Cultural Studies* mentions Burke as a cultural theorist.

21. As early as 1922 Burke had claimed that "if man was not the measure of all things, he was at least the measure of all things human" (letter to Waldo Frank, May 8, 1922).

22. See for instance my own "Burke's *Permanence and Change* and Contemporary Social Constructivism" as well as the cultural studies critics previously mentioned. Chesebro's *Extensions of the Burkean System* makes very sparing references to Burke's work before 1932.

23. Gunn and Lentricchia also view "conversation" as a central metaphor for Burke. While I prefer the metaphors of conversation, dialogue, and drama, I also fully appreciate the appropriateness of more agonistic metaphors that are sometimes summoned up in discussions of modernism, metaphors that implicitly acknowledge the contentiousness of the modernist conversation. Eysteinssen, for example, defines modernism as "a struggle" over the meaning of significant changes that started at the end of the nineteenth century (5): modernism is "a scene of aesthetic, cultural, and ideological conflict" (51). As I will demonstrate, agonistic metaphors are indeed appropriate to describe the tone of some of the controversies Burke was involved in within modernist circles.

CHAPTER 2. OVERVIEW: A FLAUBERT IN GREENWICH VILLAGE

1. Warren's account of Burke's Ohio State days was apparently approved by Burke himself. See Warren to Burke, August 22, August 27, September 8, and November 15, 1932; the last letter explicitly mentions Burke's corrections of a Warren draft, which Burke had pronounced "accurate and independent."

2. Light to Burke, January 22, 1916; March 18, April 17, 1917.

3. My guess is that the Peabody High instructor was the "Kirk"—i.e., Mr. Kirkpatrick—referred to in Burke-Cowley correspondence before 1920.

4. For a summary of Lewisohn's life and work, see Gillis's *Ludwig Lewisohn: The Artist and His Message*. At least one of Lewisohn's stories had appeared in *Smart Set*. His first books were *The Modern Drama* (1915) and *The Spirit of German Literature* (1916); *Poets of Modern France*, an account of the

Symbolists and their legacy, would appear in 1918. He later published over forty other books. Inspired by Lewisohn, Burke at Ohio State translated *Death in Venice*, a translation he would later revise for *The Dial* and The Modern Library. The Espionage Act that sanctioned certain abridgements of the first amendment in the interest of promoting American military interests was passed in the spring of 1917. For Lewisohn's personal account of the incident and for his perspectives on the setting at Ohio State in the year when Burke was there, see his *Up Stream*. (Of course, Lewisohn was not the only one to be victimized. Professor Leon Fraser at Columbia was dismissed for opposing American intervention, an action protested by the resignation of the eminent historian Charles Beard. Penn fired radical professor Scott Nearing. And similar incidents occurred at other universities.)

5. Keidel must have been another Ohio State professor Light and Burke knew.
6. Cowley in a letter to Burke, October 13, 1917, mentions Burke's September 24 letter about Light and Jenkins in New York.
7. That Cook, Glaspell, and O'Neill were frequent visitors to 86 Greenwich Avenue is the testimony of Matthew Josephson in *Life among the Surrealists*. Josephson also describes other occupants of the rooming house and provides a memorable description of Burke just before his twenty-first birthday. A sample: " 'I've burned my bridges,' he said at the time. Having borrowed a small sum from his father in lieu of college tuition, he lived on iron rations of oatmeal and milk twice a day and worked at stories and essays which he was very eager to publish before his funds gave out" (41). Burke's correspondence indicates that he moved for good to 86 Greenwich Avenue about April 1, 1918. See also Susan Jenkins Brown's memories of the "Clemenceau Cottage" at 86 Greenwich Avenue (so named because the French statesman had lived there in exile during the late 1860s) in *Robber Rocks*, 10–15.
8. Cowley reported to Burke in a letter of May 11, 1917, on his visit to a Paris little theatre called The Modern.
9. My summary of The Provincetown Players is based on histories by Churchill, chapter 8; Deutsch and Hanau; Gelb and Gelb; Hapgood; Sarlos; Shaeffer; Crunden, 398–402; and Wertheim, chapter 10. See also Matthews; Heller.
10. Barnes's role is detailed in Fishbein's *Women of the Left Bank*.
11. Even before Burke moved formally to 86 Greenwich Avenue about April 1, 1918, he knew well the people mentioned in this paragraph. A letter from Cowley to Burke dated March 9, 1918, for instance, mentions familiarly Ellis, Dell, Davis, "Edna," and "Berenice." In his later interview with Woodcock (707), Burke mentioned "what a dream [Edna St. Vincent Millay] was" when she arrived in the Village. Later, in 1919, Butler set up Burke, Josephson, and Burke's new bride for the summer in an abandoned cottage in Candor, New York, where they all read, wrote, and scavenged off the land (Josephson, *Life* 67). Sue Jenkins recalls Day as a frequenter of the Clemenceau Cottage (Miller 137); a letter from Lily Burke to her husband of July 9, 1919 (she had left Candor for a short medical trip to New York), speaks familiarly of "Dorothy," and Cowley also mentions her in a letter of June 10, 1919; and Day grew even closer to the Burkes in the next few years. A friend of Peggy

Baird (with whom she was arrested during a demonstration for women's suffrage in 1918), Day came to know Burke and his wife fairly well after Baird became engaged to marry Cowley in the summer of 1919 (after her divorce from the *Others*-associated poet Orrick Johns). After the Cowleys returned from a time in France, and after Day had returned from several absences from New York, the Burkes, the Cowleys, and Day socialized regularly from 1923 to 1926, particularly after Burke's unconventional brother-in-law Forster (pronounced "Foster") Batterham became Day's common-law husband and father to their daughter in 1925–26 (see Day, *Long Loneliness*; and Miller, 166). A brief recollection of Forster Batterham is included in Wheaton, 168, because Forster had roomed at Georgia Tech with Fred Wolfe, Thomas Wolfe's brother, and because the Batterhams and Wolfes were acquainted in Asheville, North Carolina. (For tipping me to the connection between Forster Batterham and Day, I am grateful to Sarah Sinopoli.) For the record: Miller also quotes Sue Jenkins as remarking that Rose, Lily, and Margaret Batterham were with her at Ohio State, so Burke possibly met his future wife in Columbus even before she moved to Greenwich Village. Indeed, records in the Ohio State University Archives indicate that "Lily M. Batterham of Asheville, North Carolina," was enrolled during the 1915–16 academic year as well as the following year. Having received a degree in education from North Carolina Normal, she then also received a B.A. from Ohio State in 1916 and an M.A. in 1917. Margaret lived with Lily both years. In 1917–18, after Lily left, Margaret lived with Rose before receiving her B.A. in 1918. Elizabeth (Libbie) Batterham, it should be noted, received a B.A. from Ohio State in 1921.

12. Cary Nelson, in *Repression and Recovery*, has recently commented on *The Masses* as an occasion for leftist modern art and for its influence on later such art.

13. Fishbein, chapter 2, gives a good account of *The Masses* spectacular trials, and the remainder of her book is a thorough account of its history. My account of *The Masses* is indebted to Fishbein, to my own survey of the publication, and, to a lesser extent, to Wertheim, chapters 3–5; Churchill; Humphrey; Leach; Zurier; Aaron (18–30); and Nelson, *Repression and Recovery*. A convenient and generally reliable (emphasis on "generally") reference book offering short descriptions and histories of most of the magazines discussed in this chapter is *American Literary Magazines: The Twentieth Century*, edited by Edward Chielens.

14. Light to Burke, July 1915.

15. E.g., Light to Burke, April 21, 1917; Josephson to Burke, June 7, 1920; Cowley to Burke, March 9, 1918; Jenkins to Burke, May 17, 1916. As the last letter and one from Light (on June 5, 1917) indicate, a friend of Jenkins, Light, and Burke, Nan Apotheker, published some of her poetry in *The Masses*. Later letters indicate that Burke's relationships with *Masses* figures continued, if not always smoothly. "Max" is referred to in Burke letters from Matthew Josephson (July 8, 1919; August 5, 1920), and Dell in letters from Cowley (July 12, 1923; February 21, 1924; November 8, 1924). Munson (*Awakening*

161) records Dell's enthusiasm for the work of Burke in 1921, though the two apparently later quarreled. Burke seems to have used Dell as the prototype of the protagonist of his satiric "Portrait of an Arrived Critic" (Burke to Cowley, February 1, 1920), and in a letter of March 24, 1921, William Carlos Williams ridicules "Floyd Dell's dislike for you."

16. Wertheim 25; Hoffman, Allen, and Ulrich 253. Judging from its contents, *Slate* was very likely associated as well with Mabel Dodge's salon, which "tested the limits of modernism" by offering a continuing forum for social agitators, sexual liberators, educational reformers, and artists (Crunden 387).

17. Jenkins' letter to Burke, November 13, 1916, indicates that she was working at *Slate* (which was just then getting organized), that "Jess" was seeking poems and stories, that *Slate* expected to receive material from Eastman, and that Dell had submitted "an article on rebellion." Light, in a letter to Burke of January 15, 1917, reported that *Slate* had rejected "Revolt" (which Light in the same month published in *Sansculotte*). Cowley mentioned sending his poetry to *Slate* in a letter of November 21, 1916, and wondered to Burke about "Jess's venture" in a letter of January 10, 1917.

18. Burke to Cowley, September 18, 1917.

19. Stevens' "Peter Quince at the Clavier" appeared in the second issue of *Others*, and Eliot was introduced in the third. The fourth issue was given over to a "choric school," whose attempt to tie dancing to poetry was explained in a foreword by Ezra Pound (Munson, *Awakening* 35).

20. See also Wertheim, chapter 7; Tashjian, *Williams*; and Naumann's *New York Dada*, which contains a chapter on Arensburg and his circle.

21. See Williams' *Autobiography*, chapter 23; Deutsch and Hanau's appendix; Sarlos, chapter 5.

22. Jenkins to Burke, January 29, 1916 (misdated 1915 by Jenkins); Wilkinson to Burke, September 22, 1915; October 5, 1915; December 6, 1915; December 19, 1915; December 31, 1915. Louis Wilkinson was an English novelist who responded when Burke must have sent him "fan mail" early in 1915. The two exchanged dozens of letters through the spring of 1921 and were still occasionally corresponding as late as September 1926. Wilkinson's first letter offers Burke and his generation encouragement ("You [and your generation] are infinitely more free of formulae . . . and you have no temptations to waste time over Victorian Christianity or Victorian morals"), though their correspondence fell off after Wilkinson, a generation older, later resisted Burke's enthusiasm for the moderns: "The real trouble with all your new people [i.e., new writers] is that they're inferior; and they're a damned sight too conscious of 'modern tendencies' and whether they're carrying them out or not. You absurdly overestimate James Joyce. . . . His obscurity is often tedious to the last degree. . . . I'm sick to death of the whole blasted lot of them" (Wilkinson to Burke, March 31, 1921). Wilkinson critiqued generously Burke's early poems and stories and gave Burke reading assignments (Anatole France, Maupassant, Gourmont), and he helped introduce Burke to members of the New York literary set, including Theodore Dreiser (see Wilkinson to Burke, November 15, 1916). It was Wilkinson who submitted Burke's

first poetry to *Others* and to *The Little Review*. And it was Wilkinson who confirmed Burke's decision to quit Columbia in January of 1918: "I advise you emphatically to leave college and to take that room you think of in New York. You are frustrating yourself by going on with this kind of 'schooling.' . . . I feel on fairly secure ground in advising you in this [because I did the same thing and have never regretted it]" (Wilkinson to Burke, January 4, 1918).

23. Wilkinson to Burke in Columbus, March 22, 1916.

24. Crane and Moore also frequently corresponded with Burke. Later, during the winter of 1924–25 (and possibly 1925–26), Burke and Kreymborg belonged together to an informal meeting group; see Burke to Wheelwright, September 27, 1925.

25. See Tashjian's *Skyscraper Primitives* for an accessible account of Dada influences on Stieglitz and his circle. Tashjian especially emphasizes what Stieglitz learned from Duchamp, Ray, and Picabia: a blurring of art and non-art, and of art and nature (as, for instance, in Duchamp's ready-mades); a Dadaesque questioning of the relation between art and the real; an appreciation of new, urban subject matters; irreverence in tone; and the involvement of the viewer in art. See also Naumann's *New York Dada 1915–1923* (which I encountered after completing this chapter); Kuenzli, *New York Dada*; and Dawn Ades, *Dada and Surrealism Reviewed*.

26. See Tashjian, *William Carlos Williams*, chapters 1–3; Munson, *Awakening*, chapter 1; Williams' *Autobiography*, xii–xiii; Crunden, 339–82; and Wertheim, chapter 8. The most thorough treatments of Stieglitz are in Abrahams' *The Lyrical Left*, in Lowe, and in Whelan's recent biography. Wasserstrom, 27–55, traces the influence of Stieglitz's "organicism" on Greenwich Village artists, writers, politics, and publications.

27. This aspect of Stieglitz is the emphasis of Dorothy Norman's adoring biography *Alfred Stieglitz: An American Seer*, but it is perhaps most dramatically on display in the reverential homages to Stieglitz that are collected in *America and Alfred Stieglitz*, edited by Waldo Frank and others.

28. The magazine *291* is described in Nelson, 78 and 274. Nelson credits the contributors to *291* with pioneering techniques in collage, typography, and the use of page space that are normally associated with later European moderns.

29. Burke in the summer of 1922 began working for *The Dial*, which in 1921 and 1922 reproduced work by Demuth, Marin, Max Weber, and O'Keeffe. Burke wrote to Cowley on June 2, 1922, that "the Stieglitz group has paid attention to me." Munson, in a letter to Wheelwright of December 14, 1922, mentions a five-hour discussion with Stieglitz over the magazine *Secession*, a discussion his friend Burke may well have also taken part in. Many letters in the *Dial*/Thayer Papers at Yale indicate that Burke carried on personal negotiations with Stieglitz on behalf of *The Dial* (e.g., Burke to Thayer, March 8 and April 13, 1923; and Thayer to Burke, February 15, 1923). A letter from Crane to Stieglitz on December 5, 1923 (in Weber), mentions Burke's admiration for Stieglitz, and in a November 11, 1923, letter to Waldo Frank, Burke indicates a familiarity with Stieglitz's "school." In February 1922, Burke published his

short stories "Scherzando" and "Olympians" in *Manuscripts,* a short-lived experimental publishing effort sponsored and financed by its contributors that paid special attention to the art of Stieglitz and his circle (Hoffman, Allen, and Ulrich, *Little Magazine* 267; Lowe 243–44).

In a letter to Burke of June 28, 1925, Stieglitz commends Burke's "Psychology and Form" and offers "heartiest greetings from O'Keeffe and myself." In 1925 and 1926 *The Dial* featured Stieglitz favorites in nearly every issue, including Demuth, Sheeler, Hartley, O'Keeffe, Cummings, Picasso, Rousseau, Cezanne, and Matisse. Burke may also have met Sheeler through the *Aesthete, 1925* affair (see excursus, "Aesthete, 1925"), which they both worked on later in 1924. A 1933 letter to Burke from Toomer comments offhandedly that "Georgia O'Keeffe . . . thinks you are a pretty fine fellow."

30. The words quoted are from the first issue of *Soil*. In an essay entitled "American Art" in the second issue of *Soil* (quoted in Tashjian's *Skyscraper*), Coady explained that "by American Art I mean the esthetic product of human beings living on and producing from the soil of these United States." Despite its name, *Soil* promoted mostly urban aspects of American life and had special enthusiasm for new technologies, in a way reminiscent of the Futurists. In Coady's words (Tashjian, *Skyscraper Primitives* 82; Hoffman, Allen, and Ulrich 31),

> New York! New York! I should like to inhabit you!
> I see there science married
> To industry,
> In an audacious modernity,
> And in the palaces,
> Globes,
> Dazzling to the retina
> By their ultra-violet rays;
> The American telephone,
> And the softness
> Of elevators. . . .

And so forth.

31. E.g., "We are, perhaps, the back-to-the-soil movement in American letters" (Burke to Cowley, June 1, 1922).

32. "The Wildflower" rather explicitly recalls O'Keeffe's still lifes. Demuth composed a famous painting from Williams' "The Great Figure," and Williams sent *Secession* a poem dedicated to Demuth, one of his oldest friends (Williams to Burke, undated). In his *Autobiography* (171), Williams recalls that he "loved" Hartley and was close friends with him.

33. In a February 1922 review of Williams' *Sour Grapes*, published in *The Dial*, Burke defined "contact" this way: "I take Contact to mean: man without the syllogism, without the parode [*sic*], without Spinoza's Ethics, man with nothing but the thing and the feeling of that thing. . . . Contact might be said to resolve into the counterpart of Culture, and Williams becomes thereby one of our most distinguished Neanderthal men."

34. A fifth twelve-page issue of *Contact* appeared, dated June 1923, though "no one bought it" (Williams, *Autobiography* 175). The exceedingly rare copies

of *Contact* are on hand at the Beinecke Library at Yale. I have also consulted Burke's correspondence with Williams, Tashjian's account of *Contact* in *Skyscraper Primitives* (chapter 4), Williams' own summary in chapter 30 of his *Autobiography*, and Munson's summary in *Destinations* (112–16). See also Hoffman, Allen, and Ulrich.

35. McAlmon was a colorful man who made his living for a time posing nude for the art students at Cooper Union. Rather on the spur of the moment he married H.D.'s wealthy friend Bryher. When the marriage soured, McAlmon accepted a settlement (he was henceforth known as "McAlimony") and joined the expatriates in Paris. He is described in Williams' *Autobiography*, chapter 30.

36. See Williams to Burke, February ?, 1921; April 27, 1921; April ?, 1921 ["Sunday"]; May 12, 1921; July 6, 1921; and Cowley to Burke, May 10, 1921. Burke had submitted a story to the international issue, and Williams flattered him by admiring a story ("I find your David Wasserman brilliant, thrilling, interesting and the best thing you have yet accomplished," November 15, 1921) and by calling Burke "the only interesting character writing in America today" (November 19, 1921). There were also plans for a *Contact* collection to be published by Boni and Liveright as late as 1925 (Williams to Burke, October 8, 1925; December 13, 1925; December 31, 1925), but apparently the publisher reneged at the last minute; Burke had not submitted anything in any case. In a March 22, 1921 letter to Burke, Williams proposed a long correspondence with his friend "which might be published some day," and indeed their correspondence, nourished by frequent visits to each others' homes (and betraying on both sides the scatological references that became prominent in Burke's later prose), lasted over forty years. (For Williams' impressions of Andover, see the preface to his *Autobiography* and his poem "At Kenneth Burke's Place.") Portions of the correspondence have been published in Williams' *Selected Letters*, edited by John Thirlwall, including excerpts from Williams' letters of January 26, March 22, and November 19, 1921.

37. My account of *Seven Arts* is based on my own survey of its contents as well as on histories by Munson (*Awakening*, chapter 7), by Wertheim, (chapter 11), by Abrahams, by Aaron (45–48), and by Hoffman, Allen and Ulrich (85–92). Bourne is also the subject of a remarkable, if impressionistic description in Dos Passos's *1919*.

38. For a reliable short history of *The New Republic*, to which my summary is indebted, see Abrahams' *The Lyrical Left*, 11–20, and Wertheim's *Little Renaissance*, chapters 3 and, especially, 11.

39. A famous instance was the appearance in *The New Republic* of Edmund Wilson's defense of the publication of Joyce's *Ulysses*.

40. The words are from Oppenheim's editorial announcement in the first issue of *Seven Arts*.

41. Letter of Dreiser to Mencken, April 20, 1915, quoted in Wertheim, 197. My history of *Smart Set* draws on Wertheim, 192–97; on Rascoe; on Munson's *Awakening*, 119–24; and on my own inspection of its contents. (See also Dolmetsch.) Mencken and Dreiser finally split in 1926 over Mencken's review of *An American Tragedy* (see Fitzgerald, "*American Mercury*").

42. In a warm letter, May 22, 1928, Burke invited Rosenfeld to join him for a weekend at his Andover farm, but a letter from Sibley Watson to Burke in 1926 referred to "P. R." as Burke's "*bête noir.*"

43. Four substantial letters survive from Burke to Brooks, written between March 1921 and June 1923, and two of them make reference to Brooks's letters to Burke (none of which survive, to my knowledge). Burke refers to a letter from Brooks in a note to Cowley, May 5, 1922. Six lengthy letters from Burke to Frank in 1922 survive, as well as others from the 1930s, and Burke received at least seventeen letters from Frank between May 3, 1922, and September 20, 1925, many of them obviously responses to Burke's letters.

44. See Munson to Burke, October 17, 1923; Burke to Wheelwright, December 19, 1922; and note 64 below.

45. In September 1922, Frank and Burke even discussed publishing their correspondence about aesthetics. A year later, Burke was countering Frank in *Aesthete, 1925* (see excursus, "Aesthete, 1925").

46. On the rejections, see Cowley to Burke, March 26, 1917, and Burke's letter to Nicholas Joost, November 3, 1958.

47. Burke to Brooks, November 5, 1921.

48. Munson to Burke, February 2, 1924.

49. In another such moment, in a letter to Cowley on January 14, 1922 (erroneously dated January 14, 1921, by Jay, on account of Burke's own misdating), he called Rosenfeld "next to Waldo Frank the sloppiest critic in America." See also Burke to Cowley, May 5, 1922.

50. Burke's essay, "Art and the Hope Chest," *Vanity Fair* 19. 4 (1922): 59, 102, appears in Armin Paul Frank and Mechthild Frank's bibliography of Burke's writing as a review. The essay is of considerable interest in that it contrasts Brooks's "extrinsic" Freudian criticism (in his book *The Ordeal of Mark Twain*) with "intrinsic criticism" of "the work itself." Waldo Frank attempted to correct Burke's views in a letter of November 23, 1922.

Perhaps this is the place to describe *Vanity Fair* and Burke's connections to it. *Vanity Fair* was a mass-circulation monthly that discussed in regular features theatre, poetry, "the world of art," other literature, sports, and "the world of ideas," all amid gorgeous ads for expensive homes, jewelry, cars, fashions, private boarding schools, and vacation destinations that appealed to its well-to-do readers. (As such, it is an extremely interesting site for future study, particularly because modernism usually identified itself in opposition to mass-circulation enterprises.) During 1922, when Burke's essay appeared, *Vanity Fair* published works by Pound, Lippmann, Djuna Barnes, Dos Passos, Edna St. Vincent Millay, Sandburg, and Tzara, among others less remembered. Its regular contributors were Rosenfeld (on music), Kenneth MacGowan (theatre), John Peele Bishop (the editor), Aldous Huxley, and Edmund Wilson. Burke was acquainted personally with Wilson by September of 1922 (Burke to Wheelwright, September 25, 1922), and by December 1922 the two were on familiar terms: "Next time I see Wilson . . . I will call his attention to [your book]. . . . There is only a small Book Review section in Vanity Fair, lost among the automobiles and underwear" (Burke to Wheelwright, December 27, 1922). Early in 1923, Burke, on behalf of *The Dial*, induced Wilson to replace Gilbert Seldes as theatre critic while Seldes took a leave of absence (Burke to Thayer, January 5, 1923). In the winter of 1924–25, Burke belonged to an "informal talking and tippling club" with Wilson and Bishop. For a further description of *Vanity Fair*, see Munson, *Awakening*, 113–16.

51. Stearns, as I noted in chapter 1, was editor of the 1922 book *Civilization in the United States*, a collection of thirty essays that roasted genteel and puritan America—business, politics, music, poetry, the press, law, sports, the university. Mencken, Nathan, and Brooks were among the contributors.

52. In a letter to Harold Loeb in 1959 (November 23), Burke emphasized once more his distance from the literary nationalists during the 1920s. He should not, he says, have been numbered in Loeb's memoir of the era *The Way It Was* among those who (on the strength of Josephson's testimony) were in the book included among the "skyscraper primitives." On the other hand, I should also note that Burke's sentiments in the letter to Cowley cited here recall Mencken's own ridiculing of the American booboisee. Mencken's 1922 essay "On Being American," for instance, explains why he, for one, had no plans to expatriate: "Here . . . the daily panorama of human existence, of private and communal folly—the unending procession of . . . miscellaneous rogueries, villainies, imbecilities, grotesqueries and extravagances—is so inordinately gross and preposterous, so perfectly brought up to the highest conceivable amperage, . . . that only the man who was born with a petrified diaphragm can fail to laugh himself to sleep every night" (quoted in Douglas 347).

53. Incidentally, the article also reveals Burke's blindness (in 1921) to certain non-European possibilities in American culture: "Our republic is founded on political ideas developed in Europe; our whole tradition of expression is European; our people is composed almost entirely of European blood, for the two bloods which might have offered some rejuvenation—Indian and Negro—have had no opportunity to affect us in any deep seated manner because there has been no transfusion. Thus, the real possibilities which lay in the influx of a new blood have not been developed, and will not be developed."

54. Allen Tate, who befriended Burke while living in New York from November 1924 through September 1928 (except for a period in 1925–26 when he lived with Crane and near Brown in Patterson, New York), contributed to *The Fugitive* while it lasted (from April 1922 until December 1925) and was one of the "Twelve Southerners" who produced *I'll Take My Stand* in 1930. Tate's relationship to the New Humanism was complicated, however (see note 60).

55. Quoted in Hoeveler, 24. Eliot was also critical of New Humanism in some respects, as Burke points out himself in his "The Allies of Humanism."

56. On Mencken's attacks on the New Humanists, see Tanner. The most sympathetic and thorough account of the movement is Hoeveler's *The New Humanism*. See also Hoffman, *The Twenties*, 139–41; Wasserstrom, 46–50; and Dakin's *Paul Elmer More*. More's ideas are contained in his *Sherburne Essays* (named after his New Hampshire retreat), fourteen volumes of which appeared from 1904 to 1936.

57. But see also Burke to Cowley, February 6, 1922: "Do you know, Malcolm,

that criticism is a subdivision not of dialectics, but of rhetoric? . . . For there is no ultimate element on which a critical system can be based."

58. According to Munson, Burke "urged on us the criticism of Paul Elmer More . . . [and] had praise for More's dualism, which he defined as 'unity through a balance of conflicting parts.' " Munson's own sympathetic essay on More in his 1928 *Destinations* very well may have derived from Burke's earlier sponsorship of More. See also Burke to Cowley, February 5, 1924: "This advocacy of dualism over against the usual romantic tendency toward monism, I feel much drawn towards." As I will indicate in chapter 4, More's dualisms influenced the composition of Burke's short story "Prince Llan"; perhaps the presence of unresolved dualisms in *Counter-Statement*, which I consider in chapter 6, also derives in some way from More.

59. All quotations in this paragraph, except the one by McKeon, are from Burke's letter to Josephson in Paris, December 27, 1921. Josephson, immersed at the time in "skyscraper primitivism" and Dada, "through with the old leper" of Old Europe and saturated in the new possibilities suggested by the "cinema, the aeroplane, the phonograph, and the saxophone," was horrified to learn that Burke was consorting with McKeon: "It cannot be! No! You do not listen to McKeon by the hour!" (Josephson to Burke, February 4, 1922).

60. See Grattan to Burke, January 27, 1930. Burke's essay was a critique of Humanist allies Charles Maurras, Jacques Maritain, and T. S. Eliot. Other contributors to Grattan's volume were Tate, Cowley, Edmund Wilson, Winters, and Blackmur. The *Critique of Humanism* was one of a series of responses to More's popularity published at the close of the decade. See also Cowley's "Angry Professors," *New Republic*, April 9, 1930, and Tate's "The Fallacy of Humanism" in *The Criterion*, July, 1929, both cited in Hoffman's *The Twenties*, 143.

61. Burke admitted privately that his essay on New Humanism was "gentle" and would "disappoint some of my more man-eating colleagues," but said that in the essay he also "got off several things which I had wanted to say for years" (Burke to Josephson, February 22, 1930). Grattan himself seems to have been somewhat disappointed by Burke's ambivalence, for "with some reluctance" he attacked Burke as an aesthete "attempting to make a last stand for leisure class dilettantism" in the November 1932 issue of *New Voices* (cited in Burke to Leach, October 22, 1932). This passage from Warren, incidentally, should be read against the fact that Warren himself was drawn to the New Humanists at the time (see his letters to Burke of August, 1932).

62. Bourne's essay appeared in a 1920 posthumous collection of his essays edited by Van Wyck Brooks. No doubt it also appeared elsewhere, but I have been unable to learn where. The notion of a "youngest generation" may well have originated with Burke, not Cowley. As early as August 1920 Burke had a plan for "an ideological commerce with the younger generation" (Josephson to Burke, August 25, 1920).

63. William Slater Brown was a writer friendly with Cowley, Burke, and Cummings. He was a prisoner with Cummings in France in the Great War episode that generated Cummings' memoir *The Enormous Room* (1922) and later in

the decade worked at *The New Republic*. Married to Sue Jenkins after her split with Jim Light, Brown belonged to the group of literary and artistic friends of Burke who congregated about Woodstock and Patterson, New York, in the early 1920s and who included Gorham Munson, Allen Tate, Caroline Gordon, Jean Toomer, Hart Crane, Edward Nagle, and Edwin Seaver, editor of *1924*. (Later Cowley, Peter Blume, and some others joined them in the general vicinity of Sherman, Connecticut.) Foster Damon (1893–1971) was a critic, poet, Provincetown Player, scholar, and, after 1927, a college professor at Brown; he also taught at Harvard from 1921 to 1927. Before World War I he befriended Cummings as a student at Harvard, met Cowley there as well, wrote poetry, organized the Harvard Poetry Society in 1915, and edited the Harvard *Monthly*, where he wrote enthusiastically about free verse. Later he published in *The Dial* and became a friendly correspondent of Burke's after they spent a few weeks together, with Cowley and Berenice Abbott, at Candor, New York, in June of 1918 (Cowley to Burke, May 11, May 25, June 7, 1919). Damon's biography of Amy Lowell appeared in 1935. A good memory of Damon is included in Cowley's *And I Worked at the Writer's Trade*, 35–50.

   I should also mention to the reader another "generational analysis" of the moderns generally instructive to students of Burke. While never mentioning Burke and only generally glancing at the modernist scene in America, Robert Wohl nevertheless delineates the general characteristics of four generations of early moderns: the Precursers (the generation of 1875, including artists such as Cezanne and Mallarmé), the Founders (the 1890 generation, including Freud, Kandinsky, Pirandello, and Matisse), the Realizers (the 1905 group, including Mann, Joyce, Picasso, Pound, Stravinky, and Proust), and the Generation of 1914 (including Duchamp, Eliot, Tzara, Faulkner, and Chaplin). Wohl catalogs some of the unifying characteristics of the Generation of 1914, characteristics that complement Cowley's sense of the traits held in common by his "Youngest Generation": the war as a central, disillusioning experience; a common sense of revolt against the old world and a commitment to the avant-garde; a common set of intellectual and spiritual guides (Nietzsche, Freud, Bergson, Pound, Apollinaire); and a developed sense of themselves as moderns that permitted them to defend modernist doctrine and spread it, most notably to the western hemisphere.

64. *The Freeman*, edited by Albert Jay Nock and positioned as a successor to *Seven Arts*, was produced in the same building as *The Dial* from March 17, 1920, to March 5, 1924, so Burke no doubt encountered Brooks—an associate editor of *The Freeman* and its intellectual standardbearer—there frequently (see Burke to Cowley, January 18, 1923). Both Burke and Cowley submitted work to *The Freeman* (see Burke to Cowley, January 14, 1922, erroneously published as January 14, 1921, in Jay; Burke to Cowley, May 5, 1922; and Cowley to Burke, March 30, 1922). Burke reports reading *The Freeman* in a January 12, 1923, letter to Wheelwright. *The Freeman* rejected Burke's "Some Aspects of the Word" (which may never have been published), but printed "André Gide, Bookman" in April 1922, and several book reviews in May 1921, January 1922, and May 1922. For a history of *The Freeman*, see

Turner. Munson also offers a short overview of *The Freeman* in *Awakening*, 93–101; see also *The Freeman Book*.

65. See also Joel Spingarn's dismissal of "the younger generation" in his patronizing essay in the June 1922 *Freeman* entitled "The Younger Generation: A New Manifesto": "And now the day for Revolt is over. . . . Destructivism, or Revolt for Revolt's Sake, is the excess that grows out of the need of destruction, as licence out of liberty. . . . The 'disease' of this small body of young men, this narrow group of *les jeunes*, is not an isolated thing. It is part of a long period of suffering through which the world has been going for a century or more." The essay is reprinted in (and quoted here from) Spingarn's 1931 version of *Creative Criticism*, 115–16.

66. That Munson was a friend of Burke's does not mean that he was unsympathetic to the literary nationalists. Indeed, Munson was a friend and admirer of Frank. Rather like Burke, Munson was at first sympathetic to the nationalists' project but later came to define himself against them.

67. Josephson met Munson in late October or very early November 1921 (see Josephson to Burke, November 4, 1921).

68. On the naming of *Secession*, see Munson, "Fledgling Years" and "Mechanics," and Josephson's *Life*, chapter 9. Neither of them mentions Stieglitz or the Secessionist Club.

69. On the rejections of Tate and Toomer, see Munson to Burke, September 1, 1922; October 19, 1922.

70. My descriptions of *Secession* and *Broom* derive from my own inspection and from my reading of correspondence by and between Burke, Munson, Josephson, Cowley, Loeb, and Wheelwright—all of them principals. On *Secession*, see also Munson, "Fledgling" and *Awakening*, chapter 11; Hoffman, Allen, and Ulrich, 93–101; Josephson, *Life*, chapter 9; and Tashjian, *Skyscraper*, chapter 6. On *Broom*, see also Munson, "Fledgling" and *Awakening*, chapter 11; Josephson, *Life*, chapter 9; Tashjian, *Skyscraper*, chapter 6; Hoffman, Allen, and Ulrich, 101–7; Nelson, *Repression*; and especially Loeb, *Way*.

71. Munson to Burke, December 27, 1921. The letter specifically mentions Cowley's essay "This Youngest Generation" and names the members of that group that Munson hoped to interest as contributors: Josephson, Cowley, Cummings, Burke, Brown, Crane, Damon, Stevens, Williams, Marianne Moore, T. S. Eliot, Aragon, Tzara, "and perhaps others."

72. For a good example of the extent of Burke's involvement, see his letter to Cowley of September 2, 1922.

73. Munson sent "Post Mortem" to *Secession* subscribers, including Burke (a copy is in the Burke files at Penn State). A near version is in Munson's "Fledgling" (52–53).

74. The title may also echo the language of Dadaism. Its founder Tristan Tzara proclaimed that "Dada is the abolition of all logic. . . . We must sweep everything away and sweep clean." See the discussion of Dada in chapter 5, below.

75. Of course, Cowley also called *The Dial* "the best magazine of the arts that we have had in this country" (Wasserstrom 75).

76. Actually, the meeting at the Broadway Central Hotel may well have occurred on Sunday, November 30, 1924: "Tomorrow morning we go to work in the Broadway Central Hotel to write as much of the issue as we can" (Cowley to Burke, November 29, 1924). Or perhaps there were two such meetings. (Tate was married on November 2, 1924, and then moved to Greenwich Village; he may or may not have arrived too late in New York to participate in the November planning.) Readers interested in *Aesthete, 1925* should probably also consult Bak, 323–28 and 294–95.

77. Burke's contribution to "New York: 1928" is not noted in any bibliography. He wrote three short, satiric items after the fashion of the mock ads that he had composed for *Aesthete, 1925*: "Cheat the Censor, Take Doctor Rubbm's Confidential Massage," "Important Communication to the Editor" (another satire of Mencken), and "She Brought the Wrong Book" (a satire of the Book-of-the-Month Club that touted a purported "Book of the Year Association"). Other contributors to "New York: 1928" were Brown, Coates, Josephson, Cowley, and "Hankel," who all convened once more in the Broadway Central Hotel in January 1928 to write together in the tradition of *Aesthete, 1925*. The seventeen-page collection of poems, essays, and witticisms appeared in Eugene Jolas's "International Quarterly for Creative Experiment," *transition*, in the summer of 1928. See Selzer, "Amusing."

78. In a letter written as early as June 17, 1921, before *Broom* had even appeared, Cowley told Burke that he "should contribute to Kreymborg's magazine, *The Broom*." (See also a postcard that Cowley sent to Burke on June 24, which asks Burke, who was in Monson, Maine, for the summer, to "send . . . 2 or 3 brief ms." for Cowley to submit to Kreymborg and *Broom*.) In his next letter to Cowley, Burke said that "he shall be damned glad to take up your offer [especially since *Broom* paid its contributors well], and I shall look through my opera for something to submit. . . . Unless Kreymborg has changed a good deal from the time of *Others*, my 'Rhapsody Under the Harvest Moon' (pinx 1916–17) looks like the most promising thing." As near as I can determine, Burke's correspondence with Josephson concerning *Broom* began June 18, 1922.

79. See Spanier, 10–11. Spanier mentions that the *Broom* social events were frequented by Moore, Williams, Dos Passos, Loving, E. A. Robinson, Frank, and other writers and artists. In a November 27, 1922, letter to Ridge, Marianne Moore mentioned one of the parties and stated, "I like Kenneth Burke" (Moore Archive). Munson ("Fledgling" 38) recalls "the Thursday afternoon teas Lola Ridge gave in the basement of 3 East Ninth Street. We sat around a huge table, so irregular in shape that no geometrical shape can describe it, and the conversation was very good. Burke and I went often to fraternize with *Broom*'s New York staff [Ridge and Boyle]" and with Konrad Bercovici, John Cournos, Glenway Wescott, Moore, Laura Benet, Elinor Wylie, Basil Thompson, Horace Brodsky, Loving, Edgar Lee Masters, and other members of the literary set.

80. Munson's description, in his letter to Burke of September 11, 1924.

81. References to *The Little Review* abound in Burke's correspondence. As early

as December 31, 1915, Wilkinson wrote to Burke that he had heard from Margaret Anderson that she was "considering printing 'Rhapsody Under the Autumn Moon' by Kenneth Burke in the February 1916 number of The Little Review." See also Cowley to Burke, August 25, 1920, and Burke to Cowley, September 6, 1920, in which the two discuss submitting material for an entire issue of *The Little Review* (Anderson to Burke, undated [1921?]; Heap to Burke, October 10, 1922; Anderson to Burke, 1928; Josephson to Burke, April 17 and May 1, 1926; Munson to Burke, May 13, 1926; and the excursus on *Aesthete, 1925*, which discusses Burke's plan to continue the *Aesthete* group in the pages of *The Little Review* (Burke to Josephson, March 16, 1925). See also Cowley's poem "Kenneth Burke" in *The Little Review* of spring/summer 1926 (later retitled "The Narrow House"). For lengthier accounts of *The Little Review*, consult Anderson's *My Thirty Years' War*; Munson, *Awakening*, 107–13; and Hoffman, Allen, and Ulrich, 52–64.

82. The reference in Moore's poem to "raccoon-like Burke" does not refer to Kenneth Burke. It appeared in the April 1920 *Dial*, so Moore probably hadn't even met Burke when she wrote it (see chapter 3, note 23, below).

83. *The Dial* did permit itself to editorialize against the suppression of *Ulysses*; Thayer also testified at the trial of Anderson and Heap. But it also printed a May 1921 essay by one Harold Cox that warned about "The Problem of Population"—the problem being the multiplication of the "lower races." *The Dial* avoided political issues almost entirely, however; in April 1920 Thayer wrote in his editorial comment that *The Dial* "is non-political and has no message for the million." This summary of *The Dial*'s history, incidentally, derives from my own study of the periodical and my examination of *Dial* papers archived at Penn State, at the Rosenbach Museum in Philadelphia, and at Yale. For secondary accounts, see Wasserstrom, Joost, and Sutton. Chapter 7 of Joost's *Transition* outlines ties between *The Dial* and *The Little Review*.

84. There is no shortage of descriptions of Greenwich Village of the period 1910–30. For detailed historical sociological data, see Ware and, to a lesser extent, McDarrah and Delaney. For descriptions of the artistic and intellectual scene, see Hoffman, *The Twenties*, chapter 1; Abrahams, chapter 1; Churchill; Fishbein, chapter 4; Aaron, 10–18; and Wertheim, chapters 5 and 6. For personal reminiscences especially relevant to Burke, see Josephson's *Life*, chapter 4; Munson, *Awakening*, chapters 8 and 9; and Cowley's *Exile*, 59–62. For fictional treatments that indicate the flavor of Village life, see Dell's *Love in Greenwich Village*, Edmund Wilson's *I Thought of Daisy*, and Reed's long poem *A Day in Greenwich Village*. On New York City in general in the 1920s, see Douglas.

85. The latter group is immortalized in Cowley's poem "The Flower and the Leaf," included in the introductory material in this book.

86. Fishbein, 76–79, outlines the phenomenon of the flight to the country that animated many Villagers, including Cook, Eastman, Dell, Cowley, Sherwood Anderson, Sinclair Lewis, Art Young, Allen Tate, Hart Crane, Gorham Munson, and any number of others. "City living produces in me a sense of

degradation, of self-nausea," Burke wrote to John Brooks Wheelwright on January 12, 1923. "But when I am installed in the country that whole process [is gone]."

87. Burke's correspondence brims with invitations for people to visit Andover. Usually people were invited to stay overnight or for the weekend. Besides the people mentioned here, who visited frequently, Burke also invited Marianne Moore, Carl Sprinchorn, Paul Rosenfeld, Berenice Abbott, Jean Toomer, and Alyce Gregory to Andover.

CHAPTER 3. BURKE AMONG OTHERS: THE EARLY POETRY

1. Burke later explained that he grew impatient with his studies at Columbia because he wished to take advanced courses but was not permitted to skip the prerequisites. In particular, he wanted to take a course in Greek mythology, but was denied admission despite his knowledge of Greek and Latin. "I couldn't play it that way, that I had to take a lot of prerequisites," he said. He also worried that at college he was "being programmed into a scholar, not a writer" (Skinner). Elsewhere Burke reports that he was denied admission to a course in medieval Latin (Skodnick 5; Rountree, "Richard Kostelanetz" 3). The episode was one that Burke commented on frequently in interviews; besides Skinner, Skodnick, and Rountree, see Woodcock (704).

2. See the letters to Burke written in 1915, 1916, and 1917 by Wilkinson, Jenkins, Light, and Cowley. I don't want to give the impression that Burke was reading only the moderns. He also studied all sorts of English, French, and Russian fiction of the previous half century (e.g., by Wilde, Hardy, Maupassant, Dostoevsky, Turgenev, and Chekhov), English Romantic poetry, and American writing by Dreiser, Masters, and any number of others. And he immersed himself in classics by Shakespeare, Marlowe, Moliere, Swift, and so on.

3. Wilkinson to Burke, September 22, 1915; October 5, 1915; December 6, 1915; December 19, 1915; Jenkins to Burke, January 29, 1916.

4. The meeting may not have been wholly amicable, for on March 13, 1916, Wilkinson wrote (possibly in response to a letter from Burke to Wilkinson, now lost, reporting the visit), "I have no doubt that you have offended Kreymborg for all time." The context of Wilkinson's remark suggests that it may have been a jocular exaggeration, but at the same time it is tempting to tie the suppression of Burke's "Revolt" (which in its later published version, at least, does not seem especially outrageous) from the *Others* anthology (where it was scheduled to appear) not to Knopf's objection but to Burke's meeting with Kreymborg. After all, the suppression occurred right after that meeting (Wilkinson to Burke, March 22, 1916), and it is not difficult to imagine that the literary nationalist Kreymborg, several years Burke's elder, might not have approved of the eighteen-year-old Burke's appreciation of Continental writers. On the other hand, Burke's "Adam's Song" did appear in *Others* so the session with Kreymborg could not have been too confrontational. And Burke and Kreymborg seem to have coexisted peaceably thereafter.

5. For placements of Burke among the Others, see Kreymborg (*Troubadour*), Williams (*Autobiography* and *Selected Letters*) and Munson (*Awakening*).

6. A fine detailed account of these events is in Crunden, 195–273. See also Pondron, 1–49.

7. Quoted in Nelson, *Repression*, 76. "Use no superfluous word," wrote Pound, no adjective that does not reveal something."

8. Crunden 105–9.

9. Chapters 12 through 22 of Williams' *Autobiography* record his struggle to get out from underneath the powerful influence of Pound to find his own voice. Chapter 40 concerns the passing of imagism. This very brief overview of Anglo-American experimental poetry from 1912–16 draws in part and in general from Schwartz, Crunden (195–273), Nelson (*Repression*, 75–85), Hoffman, Kenner (*Homemade*, chapter 1; *The Pound Era*, particularly the chapter on "Imagism," 173–91), Dasenbrock, and Wertheim (chapter 7).

10. Quoted in Bak 53.

11. The spelling of the title of "Hokku" is not meant to be experimental. Until the form grew more conventional, several spellings of the word were in competition.

12. Apollinaire and the Dadas experimented with radical typographical arrangements that influenced Burke's later poems, but it seems that Burke first read Apollinaire seriously in the summer of 1919, when his passion had turned to fiction. Perloff has reported on the radically free-verse poetry of the Futurists in *The Futurist Moment*.

13. See Cowley's *Exile*, 35, and *And I Worked*, 67–75, as well as Bak, 49–53.

14. As Wilson notes in the final chapter of *Axel's Castle*.

15. I have especially relied in this summary on older studies of the Symbolists by Burke's contemporaries Lewisohn, Wilson, and Symons, since the literature on Symbolism is so vast. For a starting point on that literature, see David L. Anderson's bibliography. In addition, in choosing passages to quote from Burke in this chapter, I've chosen mainly (though not entirely) poetry not readily available because it was not included in either Burke's *Collected Poems* or *Book of Moments*. Burke's own later definition of Symbolism, in relation to imagism and Williams' Objectivism, appears in *A Grammar of Motives* (486):

   Symbolism, imagism, and objectivism would obviously merge into one another, since they are recipes all having the same ingredients but in different proportions. In symbolism, the subject is much stronger than the object as an organizing motive. That is, it is what the images are symbolic of that shapes their treatment. In imagism, there would ideally be an equality of the two motives, the subjective and the objective. In objectivism, though an object may be chosen for treatment because of its symbolic or subjective reference, once it has been chosen it is to be studied in its own right.

16. Damon, Cowley, Berenice Abbott, and Burke in June 1918 cooperated in a literary spoof. While spending a few weeks together at a cabin in Candor, New York (joined for a time by Sue Jenkins: Cowley to Burke, June 11, 1918; May 11, 1918; June 7, 1918), they invented an imaginary rustic poet,

Earl Roppel, "the plowboy poet of Tioga County," and succeeded in getting older-generation moderns Amy Lowell, Witter Bynner, and Conrad Aiken to take him seriously (Bak 115–20).

17. The isolated, "morbid self" recurs in many of Burke's later poems, too, as Crucius has noted. "Rhapsody under the Autumn Moon" was not published until it was collected in *Book of Moments*. Composed in 1915, it was nearly accepted for *The Little Review* (Wilkinson to Burke, December 31, 1915; March 13, 1916; May 10, 1916), but something intervened. Burke later thought of sending it to *Broom*, but that possibility never developed either (Burke to Cowley, June 25, 1921).

18. Few of Burke's working manuscripts seem to have survived, but several drafts of "From Outside" exist in the *Dial* archives at Yale. Sensing that the poem was "awkward," Burke revised it thoroughly on the advice of his editor Marianne Moore (Burke to Moore, December 9, 1928), who encouraged greater metrical variety and paid him eighty dollars for it. Readers were not terribly impressed, however. As soon as Allen Tate read it, for instance, he wrote that "your lines were formal without decorative value, and the emotion was so dissipated by the time you got through, that there was no single value left to the poem. . . . the conclusion, as it stands, is an intellectual oversimplification, and its intensity is not emotional, but rhetorical. Your prose never commits to this kind of over-simplification. . . . [Your imagery] didn't come as the spontaneous illumination of the theme" (Tate to Burke, March 27, 1929). Burke answered his critics in a sonnet that was rejected by Moore and that has, to my knowledge, unfortunately not survived (Burke to Moore, December 20, 1928).

19. The part-by-part arrangement recalls the five-part arrangement of "The Waste Land," which Burke helped to set into print as an editorial assistant at *The Dial* in the summer of 1922. J. S. Watson, writing as W. C. Blum, called "From Outside" "a fascinating succession of recitatives and muted aria-episodes" (362).

20. Williams in 1926 recorded that "an imagistic style . . . can never be satisfactory to you, I know" (Williams to Burke, March 15, 1926).

21. "You fairly illustrate what Bob [McAlmon] and I mean by contact. Why the last paragraph . . . is a perfect exemplar of our attitude. Laforgue takes what he has and makes it THE THING. That is what we must do" (Williams to Burke, January 26, 1921).

22. See Munson, *Awakening*, chapter 12; Burke's letters from Crane (November 16, 1923; November 20, 1923; December 29, 1924); Susan Jenkins Brown's *Robber Rocks*; Unterecker's biography of Crane; Weber; and Libby Burke's letter to Bob Zachary, November 19, 1965.

23. The first mention of the relationship between Moore and Burke that I turned up was Moore's comment to Lola Ridge that "I like Kenneth Burke" (Moore to Ridge, November 27, 1922). Correspondence between the two began in late January 1923. I have found no hard evidence that Burke met Wallace Stevens during this period, Stevens having married and moved to Hartford in the spring of 1916. Moore and Stevens are the subject of Schultze's *The*

Web of Friendship; see chapters two and three for their relationship before 1930.

24. Burke first mentions Tate in a comment about *Secession* to Malcolm Cowley:
"A man named Allan Tate . . . has been sending us stuff" (Burke to Cowley,
September 2, 1922; Burke was an editor of *Secession* at the time, and Tate
was probably turned to *Secession* by Crane, with whom Tate was already
corresponding). For an illuminating account of Tate, Crane, and their inter-
relationship, see Hammer.

25. Before concluding this chapter, I should also say a few words about E. E.
Cummings. Cummings lived sporadically in Greenwich Village during the
1920s, was affiliated with Sibley Watson and Scofield Thayer from his undergraduate days at Harvard (and also with Elaine Orr, Thayer's wife, later
Cummings' wife), and placed his poetry and artwork in *The Dial* so frequently
that he won the Dial Award for 1925 and was considered one of *The Dial*'s
biggest discoveries. From his Harvard days, Cummings also knew very well
both Foster Damon and Malcolm Cowley (recall the notorious bookburning
incident in Giverny, and recall that Cowley considered both Cummings and
Burke members of "This Youngest Generation"); and he served in The Great
War with William Slater Brown, the "B" of Cummings' war memoir *The
Enormous Room*. Given Burke's intimacy with Cowley, Damon, Brown,
Watson, and Thayer, and given Cummings' loose affiliation with the Others
group and his association with *The Dial*, it would seem that Cummings and
Burke would naturally have struck up a relationship.

However, it does not seem that Burke ran very much with Cummings, if at
all. I don't recall any references to Cummings in Burke's correspondence of
the era, with the exception of this comment about possible contributions by
Cummings to *Secession* in a letter to Cowley of September 2, 1922: "Cummings is verbosity plus sentimentality, tears behind laughter; his poetry is a
continual stepping around banalities; occasionally the stepping is very neat,
neat to the point of genius, but if one translates him . . . , one discovers many
a distressing flatness. Cummings reminds me of a very skillful boxer doing his
steps before a babe in arms." The only letters that survive between the two
were written March 6 and 11, 1956; Burke wrote a letter of introduction on
behalf of a student, and Cummings responded. That Burke also took steps in
the letter to remind Cummings of who he was (i.e., a fellow *Dial* insider from
the old days) indicates to me that the two were never very close, though Burke
did memorialize Cummings with a poem on the occasion of Cummings' death
in 1964. In sum, Burke surely met Cummings in the 1920s and was aware
of Cummings' contributions to modernist prose and poetry and art, but, for
whatever reason, the two affiliated themselves socially with separate groups.
On Cummings' early career, see Cohen.

CHAPTER 4. THOMAS MANN, THE LITTLE
MAGAZINES, AND BURKE'S SHORT FICTION

1. "Idylls" probably shouldn't be considered fiction at all: the idylls were four
parable-like mock aphorisms, all of them fitting onto one page and all of them

designed to be clever for the sake of cleverness, in keeping with the manner of *Smart Set*. A story entitled "The Buried Titan" was completed in 1918 but never published (Wilkinson to Burke, August 16, 1918). Two other short stories from before 1919, "When the Gods Laugh" and "The Laying Down of Lives," now lost, sound from their titles like they may have been responses to the carnage of the Great War; *Fallow Ground* might have been in that same spirit.

2. A portrait of Butler is contained in Robert Coates's *The View from Here* (169–82); see also Susan Jenkins Brown's *Robber Rocks*, 10–12. Brown notes that it was Butler who helped establish Coates, the Cowleys, and the Josephsons at Giverny in 1922–23 (confirmed by an undated card from Cowley to Burke, ca. 1923). The son of an American artist who had come to France in his own youth and then settled in Giverny, Butler spent most of his life in France.

3. Letters from Lily to Kenneth Burke (April 25, 1919; July 9, 1919) confirm that members of the Batterham family were none too fond of Lily's husband. Burke did return for a six-week visit early in 1924.

4. Burke to Cowley, June 12, 1920. When *The Dial* rejected "David Wasserman," it also rejected "Bernice and Florio," which was probably another Burke story now lost (Mitchell to Burke, August 2, 1920).

5. Cowley to Burke, July 12, 1921, makes it clear that "Odyssey" became "A Progression."

6. At the publication of *Ulysses*, Burke found it "the last word in romanticism. . . . *Ulysses* is the book Matthew Arnold was talking about all his life. . . . *Ulysses* is a boring book; it is not an organism but a compendium. It is amazing and formidable by reason of its sheer bulk. . . . When I think of it, I think of Virgil's monstrum horrendum informe ingens cui lumen ademptem. Surely the book was made to order for Djuna Barnes" (letter to Cowley, September 2, 1922).

7. *Smart Set* was subtitled "A Magazine of Cleverness." As I indicated in chapter 2 and as I'll be indicating again in this one, Burke was in the process of rejecting "smartsetism" a year or two after the publication of "Idylls" and "A Man of Forethought." Looking back on the story many years later, Burke felt that it was "smart in a way that makes me smart [now]" (preface to *The Complete White Oxen*, xi).

8. Austin Warren saw Burke himself in the story: "As Burke is himself both artist and critic, he has, I think, split himself up, divided his sympathies, and succeeded in treating both artist of the Bohemian sort and critic with a relish for the civilized to equal satire" (232). If Warren saw Burke in the story, Cowley saw himself. Burke, however, assured Cowley—who was ever sensitive to veiled portraits (as in the case of *Aesthete, 1925* or Cowley's own story "Young Mr. Elkins," which offered a fictionalized portrait of Harold Stearns)—that he was "not the prototype of the Arrived Critic. Not you but Floyd Dell. In spots, that is, and in other places it is no one at all" (Burke to Cowley, February 1, 1920, in response to Cowley to Burke, January 26, 1920). "Portrait of an Arrived Critic" was especially suitable for a magazine of criticism, literature, and the arts like *The Dial*, where it was published in April of 1922, two years after its acceptance.

9. "The Olympians" seems to me one of Burke's better early stories, but he had trouble getting it into print. It was rejected by *The Little Review* (Margaret Anderson to Burke, undated, 1920), by *Broom* (Cowley to Burke, September 28, 1921), and by *The Dial* (Stuart Mitchell to Burke, March 27, 1920). Finally Burke offered it to *Manuscripts* (a.k.a. *MSS*), where it appeared in the first issue, in February 1922. *Manuscripts*, according to Lowe and Hoffman, Allen, and Ulrich (I have not seen a copy), appeared six times through March 1923, in short issues of two thousand copies. Financed, edited, and published by its contributors, it offered poetry by Williams, criticism by Waldo Frank, Burke's stories "The Olympians" and "Scherzando," and photography by Stieglitz. Although Lowe contends that *Manuscripts* was Stieglitz's idea (243–44), I get the impression from his correspondence that *Manuscripts* might instead (or also) have been Burke's brainchild: see Burke to Williams, January 27, 1921, which broaches the idea of a magazine financed and produced by about a dozen contributors. It appears that contributors to *Manuscripts* retained the right to publish their material elsewhere, for Burke in October 1922 resubmitted "The Olympians" to *Broom* again without success (*Broom* files, Princeton).

10. One example is in Brooks's "A Usable Past": "The professorial mind . . . puts a gloss on the past that renders it sterile for the living mind. Instead of reflecting the creative impulse in American history, it reaffirms the values established by the commercial tradition; it crowns everything that has passed the censorship of the commercial and moralistic mind" (338). The university is also ridiculed as staid and commercial, genteel and conventional, in Stearns's *Civilization in the United States* as well as in other modernist tomes, including *The Dial* (where George Santayana satirized "Dons" in August 1921) and *Sansculotte*: "[University professors are] the good and faithful servants of a state which conserves the interest of a capitalistic class; they have given themselves up to the manufacture of an uninquiring, listless, Philistine student body, 'moulded' to react to that series of stimuli termed 'good citizenship' " (April 1917: 8). As for other sources of the story's details, Burke once said that Mrs. Maecenas was based on a high school teacher in Pittsburgh who took a liking to Burke and whom he occasionally visited (Parker and Herenden 87); and Hart Crane felt that Siegfried bore a resemblance to Matthew Josephson (Weber 36).

11. *Impassibilité* as a stance of the Flaubertian narrator is a subject of Booth's *A Rhetoric of Fiction* (81–83). Frank has noted its presence in Burke's "White Oxen" and "Olympians" (31–32). I would also tie Burke's commitment to the ironic narrator to his reading of Laforgue, who sanctions the use of cynical commentary by a narrator when it is played against the feelings of other characters.

12. On the tangent ending, which Burke adopted from the Symbolists, see chapter 3, above. Burke comments on its appropriateness to fiction in a letter to Cowley of August 20, 1921: "[When using] the long tangent, you should return to the theme from which it originated, while in the short tangent this is not necessary. I agree with you on that; but there is a difference between a tangent and a succession. A succession follows out some gradation of a

super-plot, and in this way can simply ignore the adjoining part without being a tangent to it at all. To continue geometrically, the difference is that between the tangent and the plane. One plane, that is, while having its position in the figure as a whole, need not come in contact with another plane. The tangent, on the other hand, has an immediate contact with something else, and grows out of it"—just as the tangent at the end of "Mrs. Maecenas" grows out of the rest of the story.

13. Dating the composition of "David Wasserman" is a tricky matter. Burke's correspondence indicates that he had begun the story in the early spring of 1920. Percy Winner, a friend of Burke's from Columbia and possibly from Pittsburgh (he was also associated with the fringes of The Provincetown Players), wrote Burke from his newspaper job in Paris on May 4, 1920, to congratulate him for placing "Wasserman" with *The Little Review*. Yet Burke submitted the story, unsuccessfully, to *The Dial* in July 1920 (Mitchell to Burke, August 2, 1920). The story did eventually appear in the fall 1921 issue of *The Little Review*, where it was read by Winner, Josephson, and Williams (Williams to Burke, November 15, 1921: "I find your David Wasserman brilliant, thrilling, interesting and the best you have yet accomplished"). Two undated letters from Margaret Anderson, one accepting the story for *The Little Review* (and rejecting "Olympians"), another asking Burke's permission to delete a few sentences in order to get it past the postal censors, could have been sent in either 1920 or 1921. My best guess is that "David Wasserman" was written in the spring of 1920, sent to *The Dial* and rejected, and then submitted to *The Little Review* in early 1921; but it is quite possible that Anderson accepted the story in 1920, but held it for fear of the censors all the way until the fall of 1921—while Burke resubmitted it in frustration at the delay to *The Dial*.

14. Winner to Burke, November 9, 1921: "I shall be proud of your bastard [David Wasserman] since it was I that shot the load responsible for it." Wasserman as a character anticipates another fictional bastard of Burke's, John Neal, the protagonist of *Towards a Better Life*.

15. The passage on Wasserman's rejection by the leftist political group is drawn from Burke's personal experiences with a secret group of socialist-pacifists, The Guillotine Club, whose meetings Burke and Josephson had sampled in July 1917. The club is described in Josephson's *Life* (54) and alluded to in Josephson's letter to Burke of July 25, 1917. Burke quit the group when it asked him for the same blind loyalty that Red Flag asks of Wasserman.

16. "The White Oxen" was not published before it appeared in *The White Oxen, and Other Stories*. Burke tried it out on *The Dial*, but without success (Gregory to Burke, June 19, 1924), and he also had Williams consider it for *Contact*: "[Enclosed is a story which was written] last summer, and is a bit too much Huysmans and Little Review to satisfy me completely now" (Burke to Williams, January 24, 1921). The story's length would have made it difficult to place. It appeared as the first story in *The White Oxen* because it was the longest story, because it was so far unpublished, because its genesis placed it among the earliest fictional things Burke wrote, and of course because of the title chosen for Burke's collection. Initially Burke imagined that the title of

The White Oxen would be *Here and Elsewhere*, but his publisher suggested *The White Oxen* in order to capitalize on the association with a hot-selling contemporary book named *The Black Oxen* (Burke to Josephson, May 9, 1931; Burke to Vitanza, September 12, 1986, reprinted in *Pre/Text* 6 [1986]: 1366–77). Sales figures suggest that the marketing ploy wasn't very successful.

17. In its own way, Burke's "After Hours" is something of another rendition of the "White Oxen," in that its protagonist, Howard, is a more mature version of Matthew. Howard is also portrayed as trying without success to find meaning in a banal urban world full of desperate, though not-quite-like-minded searchers. Without benefit of much of a plot—Howard gets off work, rides a bus to Greenwich Village, gets drunk at a party, and returns home to his family—Burke portrays satirically the superficiality of a Village party scene as well as the futility of his sad protagonist in finding some better alternative. After being rejected by *The Double Dealer*, a substantial New Orleans little magazine that was the first publisher of Hemingway, that also carried Faulkner, Crane, Cowley, Toomer, Ridge, Tate, and Sherwood Anderson (Hoffman, Allen, and Ulrich 6–11), and that had solicited Burke for a contribution (John McClure to Burke, undated), the story was published in Howard Fitts's *S4N* in November of 1922. Hoffman et al. associated *S4N* with the *Broom* and *Secession* group; the journal "was founded on the conviction that opposing points of view would by an alchemy of the spirit produce a cultural unity" (108).

Fitts, incidentally, not only encouraged Burke and his circle in his magazine—Crane, Munson, Cummings, and Tate also appeared in it in 1922 and 1923, when it was a friendly competitor to *Secession* and *Broom* for the title as the most avant-garde of the little magazines—but he also offered to publish the collection of stories that became *The White Oxen*. Fitts was impressed both by the things Burke sent to *S4N*—"After Hours" and "Metamorphoses of Venus" as well as the poem "Two Portraits"—and by Burke's other fiction. After reading "Prince Yul" late in 1923, he was so enthusiastic that he offered to help bankroll the private publication of Burke's stories (Fitts to Burke, December 18, 1923), and the two negotiated over the possibility during much of 1924. In one version, Fitts, Burke, and John Brooks Wheelwright would have shared the risk and the profits of the venture. Finally, however, Burke found a commercial publisher in Boni and Liveright. (Waldo Frank was also helping Burke publish his collection of stories, even as he was simultaneously helping Jean Toomer get *Cane* published by Liveright. Having been alerted to the stories by Wheelwright late in 1922 [Wheelwright to Burke, December 30, 1922], he later dissuaded Burke from Fitts's scheme for private publication, tried unsuccessfully to get Burke into Harcourt, Brace, and advised Burke to try Knopf [Frank to Burke, March 21, 1923].) Though Burke finally accepted Liveright's offer to publish *The White Oxen*, the respect that both men held for each other is apparent in letters from Fitts to Burke during 1922, 1923, and 1924; in the final letter (October 3, 1924) Fitts compliments Burke on the publication of *The White Oxen* and reports that he has contracted tuberculosis, a development that must have hastened the demise of The S4N Society, which came in 1925.

18. Mann's "German Letter" appeared in *The Dial* in December 1922; June 1923; October 1923; January 1924; November 1924; October 1925; July 1927; and July 1928.

19. Burke himself acknowledged that "Mrs. Maecenas" was written under Mann's influence ("Kenneth Burke and Malcolm Cowley: A Conversation," *Pre/Text* 6 [1985]: 186).

20. I place *Contact* on the list of the less experimental modernist magazines that Burke contributed to on the basis of its other contents as well as Williams' enthusiasm for "The White Oxen" and the first version of "Mrs. Wurtelbach"— not to mention Williams' expressed distaste for Burke's "damned theorizing" and more abstract fiction: "So far I feel these stories as cerebral brick a brack—to hell with them" (Williams to Burke, August 23, 1921; undated August, 1921). I have already cited in chapter 2 Burke's impatience with Williams' inability to appreciate Burke's "cerebralism" during the summer of 1921, when he was revising "Mrs. Wurtelbach." (On the other hand, Williams did later appreciate the difficult "David Wasserman," and, later, "A Progression" [Williams to Burke, April 14, 1924].) No doubt the fact that *Contact* was simply out of business also persuaded Burke to send the revised "Mrs. Wurtelbach" to *Broom* instead of back to *Contact*. That Burke considered his 1921 stories to be a move in a significant and experimental new direction is also indicated by the comment he made to Williams on January 24, 1921. In those lines, already cited above, he described "The White Oxen" as "done last summer, and [as] a bit too Huysmans and Little Review to satisfy me completely now."

21. Burke was happy to be recognized as having "anticipated several [modern] literary developments"—"God knows, I'm grateful to you for your kind words on 'My Dear Mrs. Wurtelbach.'" But he was also quick to distance his story from Dadaism. His response to Cowley (January 18, 1923) acknowledges that "Mrs. Wurtelbach" is built on associations rather than logic, but, in spite of the "nothing, nothing" line, he still resisted the identification with Dadaism that does seem to appear in the story. For a full discussion of Burke and Dada, see chapter 5 below.

22. Burke also claimed that "Mrs. Wurtelbach" exhibited "symphonic form" (preface to *The Complete White Oxen*, xii): "Here I was trying to work out a form that would proceed somewhat like the movements of a symphony, with qualitative breaks from one part to the next (as though each were on a different 'level'), rather than embodying the kind of continuity 'natural' to conventional narrative."

23. The business about "minor forms" would find its way into the "Lexicon Rhetoricae" of *Counter-Statement*: "When analyzing a work of any length, we may find it bristling with minor or incidental forms—such as metaphor, paradox, disclosure, reversal, contraction, expansion, bathos, apostrophe, series, chiasmus—which can be discussed as formal events in themselves," etc. (127–28).

24. From Loeb's "Broom: 1921–23," 55–58. (Loeb may have been quoting from a letter to him by Burke accompanying the submission of "Mrs. Wurtelbach," which was published in the previous issue.) See also Cowley's comment in his review of *The White Oxen* in the December 1924 issue of *The Dial*: "We seek those territories of the imagination which lie across the border of the last formula. We are driven forward by a quotidian fever which Kenneth Burke likes to call 'a perpetual grailism' " (520). Burke and Cowley even toyed with the idea of founding a formal "school" around one or another experimental technique. As early as the summer of 1920, for instance, they discussed a "Courve" school for works "exist[ing] in the fourth dimension" that would somehow integrate poetry, painting, and sculpture and incorporate elements of city life and the machine (Cowley to Burke, June 9, 1920; see also Burke to Cowley, June 12, 1920). And later they contemplated something they called "integralism"—"the vision of art as a succession of units, or integers. . . . By striving for essences, by attempting to fix one entire facet of approach in a few sentences, we thus attain a unit, so distinct that it almost gains complete independence of the form as a whole" (e.g., Burke to Cowley, September 6, 1920).

    Burke's story "Scherzando" "exemplifies the far reaches of Integralism," Burke said in the same letter. Completed in the summer of 1920, submitted first to *Contact* (for Integralism owed more than a bit to Williams' notion of creating moments of "contact"), published in *Manuscripts* in February 1922, and reprinted in *The White Oxen*, "Scherzando" is a brief, experimental, and confusing *jeu d'esprit* that seems to me to be very much in the spirit of Dada. To Williams Burke accurately enough described it as a "three-page Tone-Picture . . . [which] signifies . . . my excursional dips into a sort of artificial emotion" (January 24, 1921). Employing a genteel, unreflective first-person narrator who is juxtaposed with an older poet possessed of a modernist, critical attitude towards traditional poetry about stars and "the play of fresh morning on a lake," "Scherzando" offers no narrative events. There is only the juxtaposition of narrator and adversary, two columns of print placed next to each other, and a strange closing coda in some third voice that inveighs about constructing "a vast hippopotamus to the glorification of our century." The artificial, technological hippo somehow stands in as a symbol for an age at cross purposes, an age caught between old and new, natural and mechanical. Since a scherzo is literally a short, light, playful stretch of music that typically serves as the second or third movement of a sonata, and since a coda is attached to the end, here Burke is no doubt exploiting experimentally the principles of music to generate a highly artificial narrative form for the purpose of creating "a simulacrum of emotions" in the form of his artificial hippo (Burke to Wheelwright, January 12, 1923). Burke's codas also seem related to the Laforgean "tangent endings" that he included in many of his early poems.

25. The commitment to Dadaism on the part of Cowley and Josephson ultimately brought about the ruin of *Secession*. Not only did Cowley and Josephson in Munson's absence take *Secession* in a Dada direction that Munson frowned

on (after overseeing the first two issues, Munson was back in America securing Burke's editorial help while *Secession* was being published in Europe by Cowley and Josephson); but they also compromised the contents in other ways. Josephson's story "Peep Peep Parish," an account of a New York City peeping Tom, found its way into issue three over Munson's objection; Josephson deliberately mutilated a poem in issue four; and the fifth and sixth issues were badly sabotaged, most notably in the mangling of an essay by Cummings, particularly by John Brooks Wheelwright's apparently innocent but profound incompetence as a proofreader (see Munson, "Fledgling," 36–40, and the vivid 1922–23 correspondence between Munson and Burke, Munson and Wheelwright, Cowley and Wheelwright, and Burke and Wheelwright; the copies of *Secession* 5 and 6 that I reviewed at Yale reveal Munson's pen-and-ink efforts to correct each mangled issue by hand). The excursus "A Great Date in History?" in this chapter contains further details of the falling out between Josephson and Cowley (on the one side) and Munson.

26. Form through "associations" as opposed to "logic" was also being considered by other Burke contemporaries. The distinction is emphasized, for instance, in Hart Crane's 1925 "General Aims and Theories" (Crane 217–23).

27. In a letter written to Rueckert many years later, Burke noted that both "The Book of Yul" and "In Quest of Olympus" are rooted in "snow ecstasy" (Burke to Rueckert, November 15, 1967; reprinted in the *Kenneth Burke Society Newsletter* 9 [1994]: 23). Burke's contemporaries were much impressed by "Yul": Josephson regarded it as a "prose masterpiece" (Josephson to Burke, December 10, 1921); Waldo Frank admitted that "it has impressed me deeply" (letter to Burke of August 7, 1922); Munson said that he had "never encountered so complete and final a sense of blotting out as the final paragraph conveys" (Munson to Burke, undated, spring 1922); and Wheelwright told Cowley that "Yul" was "impressive. He [Burke] has worked out the proper shape for the development of fiction . . . [although he] has let his metaphysical nature grow at the expense of everything else. He fills his form with cubes, curves, triangles" (August 31, 1922). Only Cowley remained unconvinced. The story was submitted unsuccessfully to *Broom* (Cowley to Burke, August 17, 1921; September 28, 1921).

28. Burke commented in detail on the composition of "The Death in Tragedy" in a lengthy, impatient letter to Williams, March 21, 1921, in which Burke defends his fictional method in the face of the "semi-Whitmanite" Williams' accusation that he lacked spontaneity. Cowley sent a critique of the story to Burke on July 13, 1921. In *The Philosophy of Literary Form*, Burke recalled that the story was in its conclusion a satire of a kind of Christianity "which struck me as more concerned with worldly vituperation and holier-than-thou posturing than with the love and fear of God" (333).

29. In this sentence and in the earlier quotation about the "Nordic warrior's heaven," I'm making use of Burke's own later rather humorous summary of the story in *Language as Symbolic Action* (334–37), which discusses "In Quest of Olympus" as revealing Burke's own conscious and especially

subconscious motives, notably in imaging bodily functions in the story. A similar summary appears in the preface to *The Complete White Oxen,* xii–xiii.

30. Burke was acquainted with both Toomer and Dos Passos. Parts of *Cane* were appearing in *The Double Dealer, The Liberator, The Little Review, S4N,* and *Broom* in 1922 and 1923; *Cane* appeared as a book in the late summer of 1923 (I noticed a copy of the first edition at Burke's Andover home when I visited in 1993). Burke and Toomer may have met before the end of 1921 (Cowley to Burke, August 17, 1921). They certainly were acquainted by the end of 1922 (Burke to Wheelwright, December 26, 1922), just as Toomer was completing *Cane* and delivering it to his publisher. Burke was writing regularly to Waldo Frank and attending Frank's lectures during the last seven months of 1922 (Burke to Wheelwright, December 19, 1922; six letters from Burke to Frank survive at the University of Pennsylvania, and Penn State holds eleven from Frank to Burke from the same year), the period of Frank's close affiliation with Toomer. By the middle of 1923 Toomer was definitely traveling in Burke's Greenwich Village set, and the two kept up a friendly and familiar correspondence after Toomer left New York for France and elsewhere in March 1924. Toomer reviewed *The White Oxen,* emphasizing its aestheticism and experimentalism, in *The Little Review* in the winter of 1924–25. The Toomer Papers at Yale contain ten letters from Burke to Toomer from 1923 to 1928 (as well as others from after 1934), and Penn State holds eight letters from Toomer to Burke in 1924, 1928, and 1933.

Cowley knew Dos Passos from Harvard (hence his inclusion of Dos Passos in "This Youngest Generation"), and there are references to Dos Passos in the Burke-Cowley correspondence. Dos Passos lived in Brooklyn in the same house as Hart Crane, and Burke and Dos Passos shared a great many other common acquaintances. But there is no indication that Burke knew Dos Passos very well, and Dos Passos was only sporadically present in Greenwich Village during the 1920s.

Incidentally, Burke later in the decade knew another fiction writer with ties to Greenwich Village: Katherine Anne Porter. Porter early in the 1920s spent time in Greenwich Village and grew close to Edmund Wilson and Allen Tate, so perhaps Burke met her between 1925 and 1928. She also carried on an affair with Josephson in 1928. In any case, by the summer of 1930, while *Flowering Judas* was being published, Porter was asking Burke in a friendly letter from Mexico to recommend her for a Guggenheim there (Porter to Burke, July 20, 1930; October 6, 1930). In Mexico she lived close to Crane and Peggy Cowley just before Crane's suicide in 1932, and she continued to correspond with Burke from there (she did receive the Guggenheim) and from Germany, where she was editing a magazine with Josephson. In fact, Burke submitted a poem to the magazine, but it failed before the poem could be published (Porter to Burke, October 29, 1931).

31. Burke believed that More had not worked out a coherent aesthetic position (see Burke's review of More's *The Religion of Plato*), but Burke was nonetheless attracted to More's dualism, which, according to Munson, "he defined as

'unity through a balance of conflicting parts,' " and which he "later embedded in the story 'Prince Llan' " ("Fledgling Years" 41).

32. The programmes before each segment of "Prince Llan" in *The Complete White Oxen* do not appear in the story as it first appeared in *Broom*.

33. As such "Prince Llan" reflects Burke's immersion not only in More but in Remy de Gourmont. I will have much more to say about Gourmont in chapter 6, in connection with the critical principles of *Counter-Statement*, but here it is worth adding that the tension between sexuality and the ideal is a central one in Gourmont's fiction. In Gourmont, sexuality is associated with his decadent fascination with the perverse.

34. "In its highly fantastic way," wrote Munson in *Destinations*, "this story gives a series of variations on a theme of monism, a series of disruptions by warfare among the head, heart, and solar plexus" that are balanced and reconciled in the ending (157).

35. Burke certainly understood Mann as anything but a "realist": "Mann's treatment is that of a musician [in *Death in Venice*]. . . . [He] turns rather to orchestration, to harmonization, putting out elements not as 'plants' but as themes to be picked up and developed later" (review of Schnitzler's *Casanova's Homecoming*, in *The Dial* [December 1921]: 710).

36. Josephson to Loeb, October 20, 1923. This description of the event is a compendium of accounts included in the correspondence cited here as well as accounts given in Josephson's *Life*, Cowley's *Exile*, Loeb's *Way*, Shi (86–89), Bak (285–88), and Munson's "Fledgling." See also Unterecker, as well as Crane's letter to Munson of October 28, 1923, in Weber.

37. The offending passage in Part 4 of the *Broom* version, deleted from *The Complete White Oxen* version, reads as follows:

> Love in the male should be subordinated to mastery, in order that the fine edge be not taken too soon from the attack.
>
> The male strives to remain calculatory until he has reached a point whereat decision is irrevocable. Then, and only then, he must shift the direction of his emotions, and speed in arithmetical ratios of progression, like an object drawn by gravitation, towards catharsis.
>
> Let the female remember simply that she is a flower holding up its chalice, a vase to be filled.
>
> While that act is most efficient in which, the two phenomena having transpired simultaneously, the parts are left ticking irregularly from the repercussion.

Burke himself was never completely sure whether it was this passage or the Durboraw story that caused the suppression of *Broom*. But he later felt that it may have been his association with the suppression, and not his ties to the Left during the 1930s, that cost him a position at the University of Washington about 1950 (Rountree, *Conversations*).

CHAPTER 5: AT *THE DIAL*–AND UP AGAINST DADA

1. In the same letter he notes that "Mrs. Maecenas" had first been rejected by *Smart Set*. Cowley congratulated Burke with a "magnificent ODE, on the Occasion of My Being Printed in *The Dial*, by K*nn*th B*rk*," the last stanza of

which read, "Some day he too may leave the bench of scholars / And live with me; / Some day he too may earn a hundred dollars. / And I shall treat him with a father's kindness, when / He comes at last through the supremest trial / And gets his poems printed in The DIAL." (Cowley to Burke, January 26, 1920).

2. Letter from Stuart Mitchell, managing editor, to Burke on January 22, 1920.

3. For a discussion of *The Dial* before it was acquired by Thayer and Watson, see Joost, *Transition*. My personal survey of the magazine's contents during those years fills out Joost's account.

4. My suspicion, derived from listening to a comment by Cowley in the Burke-Cowley conversation at Penn State ("Burke-Cowley Conversations, April 1985"), is that Watson probably lent Burke some financial support over the years as well.

5. Wasserstrom, chapter 3, and Joost, *Transition*, chapters 4 and 6, both have portraits of Thayer and Watson; see also Sutton. Mitchell was the first managing editor of *The Dial*; he was succeeded late in 1921 by Seldes, who began as associate editor. *The Dial* has of course been the subject of substantial study over the years, and my overview has profited not only from my study of its contents and my review of the *Dial*/Scofield Thayer Papers at Yale but also in a general way from previous studies by Joost, Wasserstrom, and Hoffman, Allen, and Ulrich. None of those accounts discusses Burke's first stint with *The Dial* in 1922–23.

6. Pound's contribution to the contents of *The Dial* has been recently documented by Sutton, who examined correspondence among Pound and the editors of *The Dial* that was unavailable to Joost and Wasserstrom. "Pound served the *Dial* variously as a foreign agent, talent scout, and regular contributor from March 1920 until Scofield Thayer finally discharged him" (xxi), first (temporarily) in April 1921 and for good in late March of 1923; "the distinctive quality of the magazine from its beginnings was shaped by the perceptions, viewpoints, and temperaments of Thayer, Watson, and Pound" (xxvi). After Marianne Moore became editor of *The Dial* in 1925, she restored relations between *The Dial* and Pound, who received the Dial Award in 1927 and contributed to *The Dial* regularly thereafter, but Pound did not significantly affect the contents of *The Dial* after 1923.

7. "Neither publisher [i.e., Watson] nor editor [i.e., Thayer] completely shared aesthetic interests; rather, each complemented the other, and together they brought to the magazine the eclecticism that allowed the publication of literary and artistic works expressing various points of view" (Joost, *Scofield Thayer* 29).

8. A witness at the trial of *The Little Review* over *Ulysses*, Thayer permitted the censor general himself, John Sumner, to defend his views in the July 1921 *Dial*, in response to *The Dial*'s editorial objection to the suppression that was published in December 1920. *The Dial* again excoriated the censors of *Ulysses* in the editorial Comment of October 1922. Censorship remained a factor in the publication of modernist works throughout the decade, as is indicated by a remark by Gorham Munson, editor of *Secession*, to John Brooks Wheelwright, his European representative, in a letter of May 1, 1923.

Advising Wheelwright to be wary of accepting censorable material, Munson mentioned that "a Clean Books Bill has passed the Assembly and is now before the Senate in N. Y. State—a very stringent and disagreeable measure with terrific teeth in it." If censorship affected *Secession*, it was bound to affect *The Dial*, because the financial stakes were much higher. Hence Pound's agreement to use "common sense" in acting as *The Dial*'s agent in securing manuscripts, "i.e., my understanding that America is NOT a free country; that the Dial cannot afford to be suppressed; that the American Post Office is a remnant of the counter-reformation. Thus, that 'Ulysses' wd. be impossible" (Pound to Thayer, March 24, 1920; quoted in Sutton, 16). Pound, incidentally, was also quite aware of Thayer and Watson's desire to keep *The Dial* out of politics. In 1927, when Marianne Moore was reestablishing ties between Pound and *The Dial*, Pound wrote: "The Dial has maintained a policy of aloofness (very valuable when it started) from public events. It has attended to the business of literature (as by it conceived), excluding politics, civics, etc. That's all right. I don't suggest departure from that course, in the main. BUT it seems to me that there are points when the civic incapacity of the americans becomes a definite menace to writing. I think that perhaps the most 'ivory towerish' periodical might occasionally glance at villainies that affect writers in particular" (Pound to Gratia Sharp, an assistant of Moore's, November 30, 1927; quoted in Sutton, 329).

9. Joost emphasizes the aestheticism of *The Dial* in chapter 8 of *Years of Transition*. For instance, he notes that the Comment closing the July 1922 issue placed the magazine in sympathy with the decadent aestheticism of the 1890s and with the proto-New Criticism of Joel Spingarn.

10. The Cournos review is notable for being Burke's first published review and for carrying Burke's beliefs about radical experimentalism in fiction, which he felt lacking in Cournos: "The novel is too rigid a form to express an age like the present. We need something that admits easily of interruptions, digression, and the mounting of hippogriffs" (498–99). Without the benefit of having read Woolf's later masterpieces, which were yet unwritten, Burke recognized Woolf as a major literary voice. He wrote that *Night and Day* was "a distinct advance upon the representative English novel," though he (rightly) regretted *The Voyage Out* as "composed of the characteristic English-novel accessories." The third review is notable for its ridicule of Oppenheim's overt Freudianism; as in "Art and the Hope Chest," Burke then believed that an over-reliance on Freud placed a work too much within the realistic tradition: "The emphasis is placed on information rather than presentation, and as such belongs either to journalism or Wednesday prayer meetings, but not to art" (234–35; cf. "Psychology and Form" in *Counter-Statement*, 31–37). "Psychoanalytic teachings, centering as they do about a set of systematized inhibitions, chain the artist's attention almost exclusively to the shedding of these inhibitions. . . . Just how much farther the intrusion of psychology into art will go it is hard to say. There is at least one promising young poet and critic I know of, however, who will no longer allow psychoanalysis to be mentioned in his home" (235). The Schnitzler novel Burke compared rather unfavorably to *Death in Venice*. The Williams review, built around Burke's command of

the term "Contact," shows that Burke understood his friend's poetry and his achievement extremely well even though he did not share Williams' aesthetic notions. The rather abstruse review of More is significant on several counts. It reveals Burke's flirtation with More's New Humanism, his impatience with the Sophists (at least at that moment), and his familiarity with Plato, Nietzsche, scholastic philosophy, and Spinoza—the latter two, no doubt, the product of conferences with Richard McKeon. And it reveals Burke's aestheticism, for Burke reads More as an aesthete: "Though More may protest, I maintain that he is trembling on the verge of just such an attitude of aesthetic priority, as any one must be who chooses to make a study of Plato. In the last analysis, a demand for spiritual affirmation can be justified on no grounds except the one that life is made less beautiful without it. . . . For Plato is so patently the artist that his ideology had best be looked upon as subordinate to his love for beauty" (530).

11. Gregory had befriended Burke by December 1921 (Gregory to Burke, December 30, 1921). Stewart Mitchell's letters to Burke by September of 1921 indicate that the two had already developed a personal relationship with Burke. Burke later claimed that the leaders of *The Dial* at first wanted Cowley, a fellow Harvard man, for the job, but Cowley was away in France.

12. Burke recalled the details of that assignment in a letter to Moore, December 30, 1944. The letter recounts the many hours Burke spent with Gilbert Seldes, managing editor, to ensure felicitous line placements and page breaks.

13. Letter to Burke, September 20, 1922.

14. Seldes to Burke, May 16, 1922; Joost, *Scofield Thayer* 150; Burke to Joost, October 17, 1958. Two other Hofmannsthal "Letters" appeared in March and September of 1923. The Vienna Letter, like the Paris Letter, Berlin Letter, and London Letter, was an established *Dial* feature in which a prominent Continental modern reported from time to time on avant-garde artistic developments in those cities.

15. Burke did the translation, but apparently Thayer made a few revisions (Seldes to Burke, September 16, 1922). Thayer hadn't been pleased by Burke's translation of Hofmannsthal and therefore asked to oversee Burke's translation of "Tristan," though Seldes was more than satisfied (Seldes to Burke, September 16, 1922). Seldes' guess that Burke's translation of "Tristan" would "probably reverse S. T.'s judgment" about Burke's ability as a translator was apparently borne out when Burke was assigned to translate Mann's German Letters and, of course, *Death in Venice*.

16. Burke often told the story of how his *Death in Venice* translation came about. In December of 1922, Gilbert Seldes shared with Burke the news from Thayer (seeking manuscripts and psychiatric help overseas) that *The Dial* had obtained the rights to *Death of Venice*. When Seldes wondered aloud where they would get a translation, Burke replied that he could "bring you one in the morning" (Woodcock 707; Rountree, "Richard Kostelanetz" 7; Rountree, *Conversations*)—since he'd done a translation of Mann's classic while at Ohio State, as a way of practicing his German.

The translation wasn't quite as easy as all that, however. By December 26, Burke had already begun working on a revision of what he regarded excitedly as "one of the most beautiful pieces of technique in all literature" (Burke to Wheelwright, December 26, 1922), and he worked steadily on the project throughout 1923, using the time on the train commuting to and from Andover in order to work on it as well as on other projects for *Secession* and *The Dial*. The translation proved to be "slow work" for the meticulous Burke because Burke wanted to get it just right and because Thayer was equally anxious that the job be done very well, even to the extent that he conferred with Burke over difficult passages (Burke to Thayer, April 9, 1923; May 19, 1923; Thayer to Burke, October 12, 1923). By the fall the first chapters had been finished satisfactorily, and Thayer was ready to publish the whole in several installments the next spring. In January Burke submitted the final two installments of what he was now calling "the hardest job of my life," for all of which he was paid $240 (Burke to Gregory, January 23, 1924).

17. See various letters in the *Dial*/Thayer correspondence, e.g., Burke to Marianne Moore, May 31 and June 14, 1926; October 1 and October 27, 1927. "The Heretic of Soana" is not listed in the Franks' bibliography.

18. The *Dial*/Thayer Papers reveal that beginning with the first days of 1923, Burke was performing the functions of managing editor, and that he continued in that role until the end of July 1923. The tension between Pound and Thayer is the subject of chapter 2 of Sutton. Burke explained the rejection of Freud's contribution—it was too academic for *The Dial*'s readership—in a letter to Thayer of April 20, 1923.

19. Joost (*Scofield Thayer*) indicates that Burke wrote the June 1923 Comment, not the July 1923 one. But it is apparent to me on the grounds of style and sense that Burke actually did the one for July; that conclusion is also supported by Munson's letter to Burke of August 4, 1923, which critiques Burke's July Comment. It is not impossible that Burke also wrote the Comment for June, but its voice seems more like Thayer's—e.g., "it was precisely in Paris (where we had gone to see a man about a painting) that we read an editorial in The Literary Review . . ." (637). Its subject matters—the relation of *The Dial* to American literary nationalism and a defense of *The Dial*'s taste for Continental artists: "We feel that Americans are at work in the same *milieu* and in the same tradition of letters as the Europeans" (638)—was certainly something congenial to Burke's tastes, so perhaps Joost was right in claiming that Burke was Thayer's ghostwriter in this instance.

20. "Tonio Kroger" and "Tristan" were published in the Modern Library volume with *Death in Venice*, but "Tobias Mundernickel" and "Cemetery Road" ultimately were not.

21. Burke was decidedly unimpressed by the poetry, but he was continuing to develop critical pronouncements that would find their way into *Counter-Statement*—"Beginning with engrossment in his material, the artist hunts the means to his expression, and these means in turn become hypertrophied into an aim of themselves" (161).

22. Submitted November 3, 1924 (Burke to Emily Amelia McMillan, a *Dial* employee).

23. Burke to Gregory, November 6, 1924. Burke was paid $310 for the job

(Burke to Gregory, June 11, 1924; Gregory to Burke, July 27, 1924; Gregory to Burke, November 13, 1924). Contributors to *The Dial* usually received twenty dollars per page of poetry, two cents per word of prose, and in the case of a translation, one cent per word to both translator and author (Joost, *Scofield Thayer* 57).

While never accepting Spengler's word as gospel, Burke was a great admirer of Spengler's work, as I will indicate in the next chapter, which includes a discussion of his review of Spengler. Burke's respect for Spengler is demonstrated in his letter to Munson of February 17, 1924, in which Burke responded to Munson's critique of Eliot by defending Spengler's (and Eliot's) pessimistic repudiation of progress ("the pendulum is still marching towards sterility"); and by a comment from Tate, who called Burke Spengler's "first American expositor and disciple" (Tate to Burke, September 1, 1926). Tate had written an essay himself on Spengler in *The New Republic* that he said Burke had "anticipated."

24. Edmund Wilson wrote reviews and articles on the theatre that appeared in 1925. He had also written earlier pieces for *The Dial*, including a celebrated explication of "The Waste Land." As I indicated in chapter 2, Burke early in 1923 talked Wilson into replacing Seldes as *The Dial*'s theatre critic while Seldes went on leave.

25. Although he defines Dada rather more broadly than I would—at some points in his book Dada becomes synonymous with modernism itself—Tashjian has compiled a history of the movement that is very useful to students of Burke. Because Tashjian's emphasis is on Dada in its American manifestations, it has particular relevance to students of Burke and his friends Cowley, Josephson, Munson, Williams, Cummings, Crane, and Sheeler, all of whom reacted to Dada or were influenced by it or both. Tashjian also offers an overview of *Secession* and *Broom* that has been instructive to me. The literature on Dada is voluminous; in understanding it, I have also drawn from Josephson's *Life* (chapters 7–9) and Cowley's *Exile* (146–80), since their versions of Dada are particularly relevant to Burke, and from Burke's own works—as well as from the anthology/histories of Motherwell and Dachy and the collection of Dada manifestos edited by Lippard. See also Ades; Crunden, 367–73; and Hoffman, *The Twenties*, 206–9. After completing this chapter I encountered Naumann's *New York Dada 1915–23*, a wonderfully illustrated account of Dada and the visual arts in New York.

26. Burke's own later poetic "Flowerishes" participate in this same tradition of typographical experiment, as Richard Lanham has also noticed (36). Mallarmé and Apollinaire also experimented with the visual effects of typography on the page.

27. Marinelli claimed that Dadaism was a direct offshoot of Futurism (Loeb, *Way* 60), and indeed several Dadas claimed Marinelli as a precursor. Perloff and Nelson also note the relations between Futurism and Dada at various points in *The Futurist Moment* and *Repression and Recovery*.

28. "Apollinaire: Or Let Us Be Troubadours," *Secession* 1 (spring 1922): 9–13. Josephson's debt to Dada is discussed at some length by Tashjian (*Skyscraper*

Primitives 123–30) in a way that complements the account I am offering here.

29. Richard Ashton was the pen name of Donald B. Clark.
30. The extent of Cowley's commitment to Dada is articulated very clearly in letters to Burke that Cowley wrote on January 6, January 18, and February 8, 1923. In the last of these, he admits "I am now officially a Dada," and defines the movement as a

> negation of all motives for writing, such as the Desire for Expression, the Will to Create, the Wish to Aid. A Dada has only one legitimate excuse for writing: because he wants to, because it amuses him. Therefore the movement becomes a series of practical jokes. Dada c'est le seul etat d'esprit vraiment logique.
>
> But not entirely logical. A writer who was truly dada would disdain collective action as he would disdain any other attempt to influence the mind of the public. The actual Dadas, on the contrary, try to accomplish things which are sometimes serious.

Bak offers a full account of Cowley's rendezvous with Dada in his ninth, tenth, and eleventh chapters.
31. E.g., Pound had reported on Dada in his Paris Letter of October 1920. Marcel Duchamp and Francis Picabia were living in Greenwich Village, where they would publish the only issue of their review *New York Dada* in April 1921; Crane could report in a letter to Josephson of January 14, 1921, that "New York has gone mad about Dada" (Weber 52); and Williams was rejecting Dada in the second issue of *Contact* (published January 1921). See Tashjian, *Skyscraper*, 85–90. As I noted in chapter 4, in the summer of 1920 Cowley and Burke had discussed by mail the possibilities of founding a new "school" of art (named by Burke "Courve") that would integrate poetry, painting, and sculpture and incorporate elements of city life and the machine; it derived inspiration from Duchamp, Ray, and Futurism. See Cowley to Burke, June 9 and August 25, 1920; and Bak, chapter 7.
32. Frank had lately enmeshed himself amid the followers of the Armenian mystic G. I. Gurdjieff and his disciples P. D. Ouspensky and A. R. Orage, who were espousing methods to achieve a new level of consciousness; the followers included Munson, Toomer, and, for a time, Crane. Burke and Cowley, while friendly with several of these people, remained apart from the cult and privately ridiculed it (Bak 286–87; Burke to Munson, February 17, 1924).
33. The debate between Frank and Burke, which also involved Cowley's "Communication on Seriousness and Dada," is further described in Tashjian, *Skyscraper*, 137–41.
34. In that list of pranks, I include the rest of *Aesthete, 1925*; a satiric drama satirizing Floyd Dell that he pursued with Cowley but never completed; a later satire in the tradition of *Aesthete, 1925* entitled *New York: 1928* (see Selzer, "Amusing Addition"); and the literary hoax perpetuated with Cowley, Damon, and Berenice Abbott in 1918 mentioned in chapter 3 above, in which Cowley and Foster Damon, with Burke's assistance and Abbott's secretarial help, concocted a set of bogus poems under the name of Earl Roppel, "the plowboy poet of Tioga County."
35. On a similar note, see Burke's April 1923 review of Gertrude Stein's *Geography and Plays*: "Here [in Stein's experimental use of language] is the

absurdity of romanticism, or individualism; here we see carried to the extreme the tendency to take the personality of the individual as a virtue in itself; for the only unity of these associations is the unity of their having been written by one person—which is the absurdity of Dadaism" ("Engineering with Words," 411).

36. In his response to this letter, Loeb said that he disagreed with Gourmont (and Burke): "I was reacting against the blindness of high-brow American [critics]. . . . I have become tired of the critical attitude which sees *only* ugliness and monotony in our industrial civilization" (November 15, 1922).

37. But on February 22, 1922, Burke wrote to Cowley, "Art is not a substitute for life [as the most radical aesthetes would have it] but the crowning of a life."

38. Burke's ambivalence toward Dada later expressed itself in *Permanence and Change*. In the midst of defining Dada as a positive instance of "perspective by incongruity," he nevertheless also noted that while "it was pursued by a group of very ambitious and serious-minded writers, many of them extremely well equipped in the traditional lore and in criticism, they allowed their movement to remain on the basis of mere waywardness, irresponsibility, refusal, which left it with too pretentious a critical backing" (115–16).

39. In what follows, as well as in what I've already indicated, I am implicitly countering Wasserstrom's claim that Burke was "*The Dial*'s official critic" (126) or "representative critic" (115). While I agree that Burke's outlooks were congenial to the general outlook of the magazine, *The Dial* was too eclectic to have a consistent editorial position, and Burke was certainly too independent to toe a particular line. As Thayer—or was it Burke, or Burke and Thayer? (see note 19)—wrote in the June 1923 Comment, "It has been The Dial's habit to find intelligent reviewers and then to let them have as free a hand as any creative artist can have" (639). The next chapter will indicate that Burke's criticism wasn't even consistent with itself, let alone consistent with some sort of normative *Dial* position.

40. Officially, Moore took over on April 27, but letters from Burke to Moore and from Watson to Burke make it clear that she was on duty all of April. Moore's appointment was formally announced in the June 1925 *Dial*.

41. Calverton, the socialist editor of *Modern Quarterly* (he is profiled in Aaron 322–33), had devised what Burke called a "sociological criticism": "He believes that aesthetic values are the result of certain environmental situations" (165). That Burke was critical of Calverton's contentions reveals once again how Burke was emphasizing aesthetic values over social and political ones through the first half of the 1920s. The Calverton review also makes use of the distinction between genetic and aesthetic criticism that later helped generate "The Status of Art" in *Counter-Statement* (see chapter 6, below).

42. See also Burke to Wheelwright, September 27, 1925: "After many disturbances, I finally resigned my job with Thayer (I was to go to Europe with him this fall as his secretary). I am now in line for a part-time arrangement at The Dial, to begin after this week." The July 15 letter of refusal may well have further turned Thayer against Burke, though it is clear from the contents that

Burke was already the subject of Thayer's accusations. Thayer, incidentally, again asked Burke to come to Europe to help him in February 1926 (cable from Thayer to Burke, February 13, 1926). In a letter to Cowley of February 24, 1927, Burke speculated that Thayer might have become unbalanced because of a sexual attraction to Burke.

43. Burke had originally contracted to stay on only through mid-December. Burke, incidentally, did indeed retain a professional respect and personal regard for Thayer. Apparently he understood that Thayer's accusations were prompted by illness, for in the same July 15 letter (1925) in which he refused Thayer's offer to serve as his secretary, he concludes by thanking Thayer for his generosity: "The very house that I live in, and the very acres it sits upon, are after all a continual reminder to me of The Dial's generosity." Burke's letter thanking Thayer on the occasion of the Dial Award three years later contains Burke's same warm regards (Burke to Thayer, December 5, 1928).

44. These are discussed especially in Burke's letters to Josephson in 1927 and 1928. For *The Little Review* he translated two pieces in 1926, and for Harcourt, Brace he translated Emil Ludwig's *Genius and Character* and Emile Baumann's *St. Paul.*

45. He described his routine in a letter to Josephson, June 29, 1927. From 6:30 until 7:30, he attended to *The Dial.* From 8 until 5 he worked at the Rockefeller Trust. From 5 to 6 it was back to *The Dial,* then supper, and then more *Dial* work and translations until 10.

46. Burke's Musical Chronicles appeared in January, February, March, April, May, June, July, and December of 1928, and January, February, March, April, May, and June of 1929. See Joost, *Scofield Thayer,* 149–53, for an account of Burke's musical criticism, which he was a bit self-conscious about as "one who is not only deficient in metaphors of marble, patina, and salvation, but also lacks absolute pitch, and cannot even play the piano beyond the Snowy Dewdrop stage" (Burke to Josephson, October 11, 1927; see also the note of apology in his first Musical Chronicle, December 1927, p. 535).

47. Watson urged the publication of the excerpt from *Finnegans Wake,* but Moore resisted him in a letter of March 10, 1927.

48. Watson later offered Burke support to start a new magazine (Watson to Burke, February 28, 1931; Burke to Tate, April 6, 1931; Williams to Burke, April 27, 1931). The idea never got off the ground, however.

49. Burke did not use the money to build a lake at Andover, as is commonly held. He had already acquired the land and begun construction before he ever learned of the award. A letter to Josephson, August 8, 1928, contains his plans to acquire additional land for the lake, and Burke told Moore on August 29 that he had acquired the land and the brook that he planned to dam up to form a four- to five-acre lake. Burke's letter to Cowley of October 15, 1928, indicates that "the main dam and the arm are finished," and that the spillway would be done in a few days. The Dial Award was given only in December (Watson to Burke, December 1, 1928). Of course the $2000 award might have been used to pay bills that Burke ran up during construction. On the other hand, Burke also wrote to Tate (December 19, 1929) that he had

invested the *Dial* money in the stock market just before it blew; I can't tell if he was being serious or not.

CHAPTER 6. *COUNTER-STATEMENT* AS COUNTER STATEMENT

1. In a letter to Tate, November 16, 1931, Burke described the contents of *Counter-Statement*. It contains, he said, an apology for art; a defense of art; a "rhetoric, or analysis of the relation between reader and writer, an account of the processes of artistic effectiveness"; a program, discussing the kind of art that might be appropriately fostered at that time; and "the whole backed by illustration from the study of writers that bear some aspect or another on my doctrines." Thirty years later Burke underscored his belief that the central issue in *Counter-Statement* is "relations between artist and society. . . . In fact, I think that every article in that book ends on that theme" (Burke to Cowley, October 4, 1961).

2. As later notes to this chapter will document, the chapters that ultimately constituted *Counter-Statement* were composed between 1920 and early 1931. Burke probably began thinking of the possibilities of such a collection of essays as early as the fall of 1926, when Alyse Gregory, his former colleague at *The Dial*, "wish[ed] very much that your essays on aesthetics could be brought out in book form" (Gregory to Burke, September 1926). A year later he was telling Josephson about a "Manifesto" he was then working on (Burke to Josephson, August 18, 1927; November 6, 1927). By August 7, 1930, Burke had decided on the book to become *Counter-Statement* (Burke to Josephson) and was beginning to seek a contract from Harcourt, Brace. Undated letters from C. A. Pearce, his Harcourt, Brace editor, from the first months of 1931 disclose that the specific contents of *Counter-Statement* remained unsettled until rather late. In one, Pearce proposed a list of contents that would have omitted "Psychology and Form" and "The Poetic Process" and included "Manifesto" (i.e., "Program"), "Three Adepts," "The Status of Art," "Mann and Gide," a chapter on Dewey and another on *A Decade of American Fiction* (both of which were recently published Burke reviews), and "Lexicon." *Counter-Statement* was nearly ready for the press by May 1, 1931 (Munson to Burke, May 11, 1931) and was in production June 15, 1931 (Pearce to Burke, June 15, 1931).

3. Come to think of it, American writers are conspicuously absent from consideration in *Counter-Statement*, unless you want to count Eliot as an American and unless you count vague allusions to Twain (in "Program") and to American theatre (156). In this way Burke distances himself and his book from the literary nationalists, still active late in the 1920s (as attested by Burke's reviews of the American Caravan books for *The New York Herald* in 1927 and 1928). Incidentally, throughout this chapter, *Counter-Statement* is quoted from the second edition (Berkeley: University of California Press, 1968).

4. "Three Adepts" is an amalgamation of three separate early essays by Burke. "The Correspondence of Flaubert" first appeared in *The Dial* early in 1922. "Notes on Walter Pater" Burke contributed to the short-lived avant-garde periodical *1924* in the year the journal was named for. (The *Counter-Statement*

version of that essay is very close to the one in *1924*, which was a product of the Woodstock community that supported some of Burke's friends. Burke excised his original introduction and made other small updates.) And "Approaches to Remy de Gourmont" appeared in *The Dial* in February 1921; it was Burke's first published essay.

5. This is the first use of the term "ideology" in *Counter-Statement*; it's a key term in the book, for, as Paul Jay has noted ("Kenneth Burke" 71), the relationship between ideology and form is a major issue in Burke's book. Indeed the two words *ideology* and *form* are ones that are central to the major tension in the book, the conflict between an artist's strivings for aesthetic achievement and his or her drive for social impact, between the artist as esthetician and the artist as rhetor, between the artist as segregated from society into a domain of art and the artist as emerging from and contributing to a localized social circumstance.

6. See Paul Elmer More, *The Drift of Romanticism* (1909; New York, 1967), 114; and Burke's former associate Gorham Munson, writing as a New Humanist in his essay "Our Critical Spokesman," in *Humanism in America*, ed. Norman Foerster (New York, 1930), 350. Burke responded (temperately) to the Foerster volume in his essay "The Allies of Humanism Abroad" in Grattan's *Critique of Humanism*. See also Hoeveler's account of the New Humanists' attitude toward Pater, 56–59.

7. Croce's *Aesthetic* (1902) posits both art and criticism as the expression of an individual's intuitions, rather than as the product of historical or social forces. A handbook on aestheticism, the book describes art as autotelic, as uninvolved with morality or practicality. Burke knew Croce's work well enough to work on an essay on Croce's views (never published; see Burke to Frank, June 13, 1922) and to recommend Croce's *Aesthetic* to Cowley in a letter of March 18, 1923. Spingarn's famous essay "The New Criticism," first delivered as a lecture in 1910, frequently reprinted, and later of course influential to the New Critics, defended Croce's positions on the autonomy of art. In centering critical attention on the work of art itself instead of on the critic's intuitions about the work, Spingarn (citing Croce) separated art from life, art from morality: "It is not the inherent function of poetry to further any moral or social cause, any more than it is the function of bridge-building to further the cause of Esperanto. . . . To say that poetry is moral or immoral is as meaningless as to say that an equilateral triangle is moral" ("The New Criticism," in *Creative Criticism*, 1931, 27–28).

8. The connection between Pound and Gourmont is the subject of Sieburth's *Instigations*. To learn more about Gourmont, the reader may also consult Schwartz (79–85); Burne; Pondrom; and Burke's longer, February 1921 *Dial* version of his *Counter-Statement* essay. Gourmont is also a leading figure in Wilson's *Axel's Castle*, the early analysis of the moderns that associates Joyce, Yeats, Eliot, Proust, and Stein with the Symbolist tradition. In his review, Pound felt that Aldington's lavish edition still failed to do adequate justice to "the inestimable value of Gourmont": "We cannot afford to lose sight of [Gourmont's] value, of his significance as a type, a man stand-

esty" (71).

9. Gourmont contracted a disfiguring form of lupus as a young man, a fact
    that contributed to his withdrawal into a cloistered world of letters. But
    Burke found out about the disease only late in the 1920s—he thought it was
    leprosy, as he notes in a section of *Counter-Statement* added just before its
    publication—and hence at first attributed Gourmont's asceticism to a desire
    to live the Symbolists' ideal existence, withdrawn from life into a world of art
    and ideas. "For years he lived alone with his books, seen by a few intimates,"
    Burke wrote in the version of the Gourmont essay published (February 1921)
    in *The Dial* (127), "For experience, he had his tomes, for vitality, the beating
    of his own veins. . . . He remained, until his death, a man closed in his study,
    living almost exclusively with books, yet one who never wrote a sentence that
    did not have in it the flux of a spontaneous emotion."

10. If Burke knew that Gourmont's nationality would bother Williams, he also
    anticipated that Gourmont's (and indeed Pater's) aestheticism would appeal
    to Williams' own views of art during this period. Witness Williams' defense of
    the autonomy of art in *Spring and All* and his promise there to seek, through
    the imagination and through art, "to refine, to clarify, to intensify that eternal
    moment in which we alone live."

11. Though Burke's essay on Gourmont appeared in *The Dial* in February 1921,
    it had been completed almost a year earlier. Originally the article was substan-
    tially longer, but Stuart Mitchell as managing editor cut one section which
    apparently had discussed Gourmont work by work. (See Mitchell to Burke,
    April 13, 1920; June 24, 1920; July 2, 1920.) I have been unable to find the
    excised passages in Burke's papers; the *Counter-Statement* version of the essay
    includes one major addition—the last four lines of page 16, all of pages 17–18,
    and the first six lines of page 19 (including the information about Gourmont's
    "leprosy" and testimony as to Gourmont's "experimentalism" and stylistic
    "opulence" and refinement)—but that addition doesn't fit Mitchell's descrip-
    tion of the material he planned to delete. When Burke composed *Counter-
    Statement*, he also deleted from the *Dial* version material on Gourmont's life
    that I have drawn on in my account of Gourmont above, as well as other
    assertions of Gourmont's rebelliousness, his drive for novelty, and Burke's
    final assessment of Gourmont as "one of the finest writers of his century."

12. The added section begins with the phrase "It is regrettable" at the bottom of
    page 23 and continues through the remainder of that paragraph.

13. Armin Frank contends that Burke himself made precisely this "development
    and schematization" of the ideas of Gourmont: "This concept of dissociation
    has had an enormous influence on Burke, and his basic approach to art
    and life, his method of 'perspective by incongruity' [in *Permanence and
    Change*], depends directly on de Gourmont's slightly different maneuvers.
    Another earlier and more direct sign of this influence is the essay, 'Thomas
    Mann and André Gide,' itself a delightful exercise in dissociation [in *Counter-
    Statement*]. . . . In *The Philosophy of Literary Form* Burke later does exactly
    that," i.e., he carries the dissociative method into literary criticism (52).

(For the record, in *Permanence and Change*, Burke links "perspective by incongruity" to Neitzsche. Cf. Burke's "On Stress," 98.) For a very complete description of "the dissociation of ideas," see Burke's own exposition in *A Rhetoric of Motives*, 149–54. "We need not try to persuade ourselves that dissociation is the ultimate in intellectual prowess," notes Burke there (153); "but we can make a strong case for it as a method for helping the initiate experimentally to break free from all topical assumptions, and thereby to cease being the victim of his own naive rhetoric."

14. In "Psychology and Form," Burke refers at some length to Eliot's "The Waste Land" (39). It is worth remembering that "Psychology and Form" originally appeared in the July 1925 issue of *The Dial*, less than three years after the spectacular first appearance of "The Waste Land," also in *The Dial*, in November 1922 (a major modernist event dramatically recalled in Williams' *Autobiography* 174).

15. For instance, see Harold Rosenberg's comment that Burke "advocates Form as the essence of art" (116) in an early review of *Counter-Statement* in *The Symposium* (January 1932; reprinted in Rueckert's *Critical Responses*). And see Munson in *Destinations*: "Burke endeavor[s] to make form the major element in art" (56).

16. Burke's distinction here between art and information, one that recurs in the preface to *Towards a Better Life*, repeats the terminology in Clive Bell's 1914 *Art*, which opposes art (a rarified concept associated with formal excellence) with information (a low-brow concept associated with politics): And "to associate art with politics [as in Italian Futurism] is always a mistake" (Bell 24).

17. As I noted in chapter 3, "One of the principal aims of Symbolism [was] to approximate the indefiniteness of music" (Wilson, *Axel's Castle* 13). Cf. Bell's association of form with music (31) and Burke's elaboration of this passage of "Psychology and Form" in "Lexicon Rhetoricae": "Painting, architecture, and music are probably more amenable to repetition without loss because the formal aspects are not obscured by subject matter in which they are embodied" (145).

18. *The Guardian* was a monthly magazine of modernist criticism and literature that came out of Philadelphia from November 1924 to October 1925. Burke's colleagues Frank, Tate, and Munson also placed work there, as did Robert McAlmon, John Gould Fletcher, and Max Bodenheim (Hoffman, Allen, and Ulrich 273).

19. Burke's recollection of the chronology and circumstances of the composition of "Psychology and Form" and "The Poetic Process" is also contained in his letter to Cowley of December 1, 1940. There Burke traces the germ of "Psychology and Form" to a review he wrote on J. Middleton Murry for the December 1922 issue of *The Dial* (a review that distinguishes "the psychology of form and the psychology of subject-matter"); recalls that the never-completed third essay would have been entitled "On the Sublime"; dates "Psychology and Form" to 1924 and "The Poetic Process" to the winter of 1924–25; and protests Cowley's claim that Burke's formula tying form

to audience expectations derived from I. A. Richards' *Principles of Literary Criticism* (published in 1924) or *Science and Poetry* (published in 1926) or Richards' and Ogden's *The Meaning of Meaning* (published in 1923). Burke says that he encountered *The Meaning of Meaning* only after completing "Psychology and Form" and "The Poetic Process" (and in fact Richards' book was reviewed in *The Dial* by Bertrand Russell as late as the August 1926 issue of *The Dial*), and that he "was so knocked over by it that I was unable to write the third essay. And it was not until the 'Philosophy of Literary Form' item . . . that I was able to treat of the material for the third essay, though it is there in a much altered state, affected by all that has intervened."

I am persuaded to take Burke as his word that he encountered Richards only after completing "Psychology and Form" and "The Poetic Process," but it is easy to see how Cowley made the connection. (Isidor Schneider also noted a link between Richards and Burke in his 1932 review of *Counter-Statement*, though on strictly chronological grounds Schneider is surely wrong in attributing a debt to Richards' *Practical Criticism* [1929], which offers a demonstration of the reading behaviors of actual readers in the act of encountering poetry.) *The Principles of Literary Criticism*, like "Psychology and Form," ties interpretation to the psychology of the audience; like the later essays in *Counter-Statement*, it also counters the art-for-art's sake community and conceives of poetry as "in no qualitative way different from actual experience." That phrase comes from Burke's brief review of *Principles of Literary Criticism* as "A New Poetics" in the September 1925 *Saturday Review*: Burke commended Richards for distancing himself from a too-strictly-aesthetic position and for understanding art as "incipient action" and as influencing the attitudes of an audience. ("Attitude," of course, would become an important term for Burke.) *The Meaning of Meaning*, meanwhile, argues from the work of C. S. Peirce that the interpretation of signs depends on context and that meaning is ultimately rhetorical and contextual in nature, notions that are certainly generally in line with Burke's views in the later-written essays of *Counter-Statement*. My own conclusion, based on a study of Burke's correspondence through the 1930s as well as his and Richards' writings, is that Richards' impact on Burke's thinking is found mostly in later works, such as *Permanence and Change* and *Philosophy of Literary Form*, and I plan to develop more completely the relationships among Richards' and Burke's works in a subsequent study of Burke in the 1930s. Incidentally, good introductions to Richards are John Paul Russo's *I. A. Richards*, Ann Berthoff's "I. A. Richards," Daniel Fogarty's essay on Richards in *Roots for a New Rhetoric*, Stanley Edgar Hyman's essay on Richards in *The Armed Vision*, and Marie Hochmuth Nichols' "I. A. Richards and the 'New Rhetoric.' "

20. As indicated in note 1 of chapter 1, above, the idea that art derives from the artist's need to express emotion is a Romantic notion that was fundamental to the Symbolists and many of their modernist successors. Clive Bell's emphasis on emotion in his 1914 *Art* is representative: e.g., "The starting point for all systems of aesthetics must be the personal experience of a particular emotion" (17); and artists "need a problem that will become the focus of their

vast emotions" (52). Richards in *Principles of Literary Criticism* (1924) thus called poetry "the supreme form of *emotive* language" (273). Even T. S. Eliot, who in " Tradition and the Individual Talent" (1919; reprinted in *The Sacred Wood*, 1928) advocated "depersonalization" and "the continual extinction of personality" such that "art may be said to approach the condition of science," nevertheless avowed in the same essay that "the passions [are] the material" for art, that poetry is "an expression of significant emotion." On the conflict between objectivity and subjectivity, impersonality and personality, in the work of Eliot, Pound, and other moderns, see Schwartz, especially 66–77.

21. As Armin Frank has noted, Gourmont also tied aesthetic sensitivity to physiology (52). Gourmont, however, favored a highly impressionistic criticism according to which the only reliable grounds for literary judgment was the individually cultivated sensibility.

22. In the first part of "Lexicon Rhetoricae," sections 1–10, Burke completes this catalogue of the kinds of form. Not only does Burke there embellish the famous definition of form offered in "Psychology and Form"—"Form in literature is an arousing and fulfillment of desires. A work has form in so far as one part of it leads a reader to anticipate another part, to be gratified by the sequence" (124)—but he contends that he has completed an exhaustive tabulation of the kinds of form that are observable in art ("no other terms should be required in an analysis of formal functionings" [129]): There is Progressive Form, including syllogistic form ("given certain things, certain things must follow, the premises forcing the conclusion" [124]) and qualitative form (according to which "the presence of one quality prepares us for the introduction of another" [125]). There is Repetitive Form, "the consistent maintaining of a principle under new guises" (125), which includes rhythm and rhyme, as well as other such manifestations. There is Conventional Form, which is akin to genre (139). And there are minor, "incidental" forms—tropes such as metaphor and paradox, disclosure and apostrophe, expansion and contraction, series and chiasmus, etc. All these kinds of form can be related and interconnected in a given work; sometimes they might even conflict with each other in arousing and fulfilling expectations.

23. Burke also articulated his position on the issue quite clearly in his introduction to another essay written in 1924, "Notes on Walter Pater," an introduction that was excised from the version of the Pater essay that reappeared in *Counter-Statement*. Because it was excised, let me quote it here:

> It seems that man, once he became man, has remained a constant, "progress" being a mere change of emphasis, a stressing of some new phase of this constant. The artist, therefore, who is deeply contemporaneous, will touch intimately one element of this constant, but in a way that will never be touched thereafter, when the stress or emphasis of society has undergone further readjustments. Each new condition, each new combination of forces, each new economic-intellectual situation, produces some new possibility of artistic excellence. The artist who portrays his age becomes truly inimitable, and at the same time assumes a certain lasting value in that he has touched the constant of humanity.

Compare Richards in *Principles of Literary Criticism* and *Practical Criticism*, which both contend that the psychological basis of artistic appeal makes it inevitably relative and encultured rather than "constant."

24. On pages 53–54, Burke distinguishes his position particularly from the Freudian approach of Van Wyck Brooks. Brooks in his *The Ordeal of Mark Twain* (1920) had explained Twain's fiction as an externalization of Twain's innermost drives, conflicts, and emotions, but stopped short of explaining how those emotions were then "formalized" in Twain's fiction. Burke had also criticized Brooks's brand of Freudian criticism in his essay on Brooks's book, "Art and the Hope Chest" (*Vanity Fair*, December 1922), because it emphasized Freudian explanations of the author to the exclusion of considerations of "the work as it is" (59). That article, as well as the emphasis in *Counter-Statement* on a work's formal properties, helps to explain why the early Burke has at times been identified with the New Criticism. (Of course Burke's use of the terms "desire" and "appetite" in "Psychology and Form" are not without their own Freudian resonances.)

25. I've been able to find no real indication of Burke's direct involvement with Marx before the publication of *Counter-Statement* (though of course the "vulgar Marxism" of Spengler is a major subject of Burke's critique in "The Status of Art"). Paul Jay agrees ("Kenneth Burke" 73). See also note 34 below.

26. An artistic elitism in keeping with the aesthetes does occasionally surface in the first half of *Counter-Statement*, not only in the chapter on Flaubert, Pater, and Gourmont but also in the general position that the artist "is, of all men, equipped to confront an issue" (75) by virtue of his special knowledge of form and psychological universals. "Because of his greater receptivity, the poet is able to become an expert, a specialist, in certain patterns of experience" (Rueckert, *Drama* 14). Cf. Burke's views in a letter to Harold Loeb, October 20, 1922, commenting on Loeb's essay "The Mysticism of Money" just published in *Broom*: "The question still remains as to whether the artist must build his excellence upon the foundation of this democratic manure, or whether he is entitled to pass up the matter entirely, accepting de Gourmont's rather enticing idea of the two currents of art, one for the populace and one for the elect. Latent in your article is the complete acceptance of democracy, the acceptance of the *vulgus* as the *vox domini*; why should artists start with this handicap?" Loeb, incidentally, responded from Berlin on November 15 by claiming that he was not an advocate for a democratic art: "I was reacting against the blindness of high-brow Americans. . . . I have become tired of the critical attitude which sees *only* ugliness and monotony in our industrial civilization. . . . What really matters is perfection of technique."

27. The discussion of the relation between literature and rhetoric continued throughout Burke's career. As late as 1976 Burke was involved in his celebrated exchange with Wilbur Samuel Howells in the pages of *Quarterly Journal of Speech* over the matter. Howells had objected in *Poetics, Rhetoric, and Logic* that Burke had insufficiently distinguished rhetoric and poetics, and Burke defended his position in terms that repeated his discussion in "Rhetoric and Poetics" (reprinted in *Language as Symbolic Action*): "There is a large area which [rhetoric and poetics] share in common" (302). "I began [my career] in the aesthete tradition, with the stress on self-expression. Things started moving for me in earnest when, as attested in *Counter-Statement*, I

made the shift from 'self-expression' to 'communication' " (305). In a later interview at the University of Iowa (Rountree, *Conversations*), Burke cheerfully agreed that Howells was right in noting in his *QJS* response a confusion in *Counter-Statement*: Burke in *Counter-Statement* began by finding literary form based in *self-expression* (with the lyric as the prototype of literature) but ended up finding that literary form was based in *communication* (with drama as the prototype). Burke again noted "the shift [in *Counter-Statement*] from self-expression to communication" in his 1978 "Questions and Answers about the Pentad" (331). (Cf. Richards' position on poetry as "a mode of communication" in *Practical Criticism* [77] and in *The Principles of Literary Criticism*.)

28. E.g., as I've indicated in earlier chapters, Burke had translated *Death in Venice* and other stories and essays by Mann, reviewed his *Buddenbrooks*, and modeled his own fiction in many ways after Mann; and he wrote "André Gide, Bookman" for *The Freeman* in April 1922.

29. In turning away from Gourmont late in the decade, Burke was in keeping with the attitudes of Cowley, who also was finding as the 1920s continued that Gourmont, though a great individualist, was nevertheless too specialized, too bookish, too committed to the past (Bak 416–17). See Cowley's review of Aldington's edition of Gourmont's writings, "A Messiah of the Skeptics," *New York Herald Tribune Books*, October 21, 1928, 7.

30. Burke's 1923 critique of Stein and Bell appeared in "Engineering with Words." The reference to "The Waste Land" which closes section 10 of "Lexicon" is lifted directly from the conclusion of that review, which Burke published in *The Dial*. Incidentally, it should be clear from what I have already said that I both agree and disagree with Gabin's assessment that Burke in *Counter-Statement* counters the intuitionism and aestheticism of Croce in its American (i.e., Spingarnian) form. Not one to set art above life, Burke *both* counters *and* reasserts the aestheticism of Croce and Spingarn.

31. Note that the word *distinguished* here is meant in two senses—as "different from" and as "extraordinary in quality."

32. *Counter-Statement* in general is a repository for concepts that would coalesce and develop much later under the general rubric of "reader-response criticism." On page 179, Burke even invents an "ideal reader" in a way that anticipated by fifty years Jonathan Culler's recoinage of the term in his *Structuralist Poetics* (24).

33. Of course now, from a late twentieth-century perspective that has had the benefit of observing some of the moderns' notorious compacts with fascism, it's easier to be more tolerant of the liberal pieties espoused in much of the civic verse of the Gilded Age.

34. As late as April 6, 1931, Burke was telling Tate that publication of *Counter-Statement* was being delayed "by a chapter of first principles, a Manifesto or Program." On May 9, 1931, he wrote to Josephson that he was still revising "Lexicon Rhetoricae," but those revisions were very late (e.g., see Munson to Burke, May 11, 1931). "Program" can also be read profitably against Burke's essay "Boring from Within" (*New Republic*, February 4,

1931), which is frankly socialist and evangelical in calling for radical changes in the American economy, including the dole. "Boring"—an essay that Hicks should have remembered as he reviewed *Counter-Statement*, incidentally—also anticipates the recommendations about rhetorical tactics that Burke would offer in his famous 1935 speech to the American Writers' Congress.

35. Burke was so incensed by Hicks's review (December 2, 1931) that he offered a "Counter-Blast on *Counter-Statement*" in the next issue (December 9), citing "Program" to refute Hicks. Hicks's counter-response, published on the same page, didn't budge from his original position, so Burke launched yet another blast, "A Modest Plea to be Allowed to be a Colleague of Mr. Hicks." When Hicks's short response still did not amend things, Burke penned yet another riposte, "A Bottle Put to Sea, being objections to Granville Hicks's objections to my objections to his objections to *Counter-Statement*," in which Burke acknowledged his emphasis on technique even as he stressed once more that *Counter-Statement* certainly does offer a social agenda to the artist. The last three installments of this exchange, perhaps fortunately, were never published; they are included under "Hicks" in Burke's file of 1931 correspondence at Pattee Library at Penn State. Burke also took the opportunity for one last chance to clarify his position with respect to Hicks and the necessity for a "proletarian" art when in 1936 he reviewed (for *Southern Review*) *Proletarian Literature in the United States: An Anthology*, edited by Hicks and others.

In fairness to Hicks and in support of my own view that *Counter-Statement* exhibits an unresolved tension between aesthete and social perspectives on art, I also should add two other notes. First, Burke's friend Cowley came to the same general conclusion about *Counter-Statement* as had Hicks. According to Cowley, Burke's "standards . . . tend to be Crocean by virtue of [his] emphasis on technique"—an emphasis that Cowley saw as at odds with his own new Marxist criticism, which by contrast "does consider art as organically related with its social background" (Cowley to Burke, October 20, 1931). It is likely that Cowley's views had been colored by Hicks's review, which he as a *New Republic* employee had read in manuscript. Burke therefore answered Cowley's letter by trying to set him straight about Burke's own late understanding of literature as a species of rhetoric (Burke to Cowley, October 22, 1931). In a letter to Cowley of June 2, 1932, Burke said that "Program" was "based specifically, explicitly, on the doctrine that the confiscation of wealth is an economic necessity."

Second, a year or so after *Counter-Statement* other people were still in agreement that Burke remained in the aesthete camp as opposed to a political one. For example, Austin Warren remarked in *The Sewanee Review* in 1933 that "more consistently than any of his generation, perhaps, Burke has persisted steadfastly at the practice of pure literature and at the creation of an aesthetic theory which shall be adequate to the interpretation of it" (229). And Hartley Grattan (for whom in *A Critique of Humanism* Burke had written an essay critical of the New Humanists—though apparently not critical enough to suit Grattan) in the November 1932 *New Voices* placed Burke not with the left but in "the Fastidious Movement, which is attempting to make a last stand for leisure class dilettantism." In a letter to Henry Goddard Leach, an editor at *New Voices* (Burke Papers, October 22, 1932), Burke offered to contribute a rejoinder, "The Rout of the Esthetes," that would demonstrate a compatibility between Marxist and aestheticist critiques of industrialism. ("Rout of the Esthetes" eventually grew into *Auscultation, Creation, and Revision*.) That the left responded in a rather hostile way to *Counter-Statement* is also the position of Daniel Aaron, 288–90.

For a contrary interpretation of *Counter-Statement*, one that both answers Hicks implicitly and shares Burke's own contention (in the letter to Leach) that *Counter-Statement* is essentially compatible throughout with Marxist principles, see Lentricchia's considered argument in Part 3 of *Criticism and Social Change* that Burke in *Counter-Statement* consistently "works against the grain of the modernist aesthetic" by criticizing theories of aesthetic autonomy (85). Lentricchia implicitly counters Aaron's assertion that "implicit in all of Burke's social and aesthetic theorizing was his belief in the autonomy of the artist and the priority of art over politics" (290).

36. "The artist has no responsibility to the public whatever. . . . Only certain kinds of people are capable of art emotion (aesthetic emotion). They are the artist himself and the critic whose capacity for appreciation proves itself by an equal capacity to create" (Anderson, "Obvious," 12; for pointing out this quotation to me, I am grateful to Rosa Eberly).

37. Conceptually Burke hit upon dramatism not simply from his immersion in modern drama but also from his exposure to "the schoolmen's subdivisions of a topic: quis, quid, ubi, quibus auxiliis, cur, quo modo, quando" (*Counter-Statement* 141). Aristotle's exposition of the Four Causes also contributed to the formulation of dramatism. Burke understood Aristotle's theories, like his own, as based "upon *action*. His whole system is a *dramatistic* mode of analysis. His formula for God was 'pure act,' which of course, Aquinas could take over" (Skodnick 22).

38. "The Status of Art" was written for the occasion of *Counter-Statement*, with the exception of the section on Spengler, which appeared in large part in Burke's brilliant long review of *The Decline of the West* (*The Dial*, September 1926; Burke, as I've indicated, also translated the long excerpts from *Decline of the West*—about sixty pages in all—that appeared in *The Dial* from November 1924 to January 1925). No doubt other portions of "The Status of Art" were composed before 1931. The analogy to dental work on page 90, for instance, appears almost verbatim in a letter to Josephson written October 11, 1927, and Paul Jay in *American Literary History* has rightly tied the origin of "Status" to Burke's August 1925 review of V. F. Calverton's *The Newer Spirit: A Sociological Criticism of Literature*. Since "The Status of Art" was written well into the 1930s, no wonder "its true subject . . . is the relation of aesthetics to politics" (Lentricchia, *Criticism* 95); Lentricchia's discussion of "The Status of Art," 96–102, is by far the best one that I know of. "Applications of the Terminology" is a slight revision of an essay called "Redefinitions," which appeared in three installments in *The New*

Republic from July to September 1931, even as *Counter-Statement* was being published. *Counter-Statement* includes everything in "Redefinitions" (albeit not always in the same order), but Burke also added to "Applications" the passages on Racine and Hamlet, as well as the final segments on "conventional form" and "rhetoric."

39. Burke to Gregory, April 15, 1925 (a letter accompanying the Calverton review), mentions the "tempest." Burke would return to the same conflict in his recent response to Jameson in *Critical Inquiry*.

40. Ironically, it was also in a way that some of the leftists among the moderns approved when they needed to: on page 65, Burke is probably recalling not only Flaubert's prosecution but also the famous *Masses* trials of the World War I era, when Eastman, Dell, Reed, and Young did indeed invoke a defense of art as "amoral" or "unmoral."

41. The version of this chapter that appeared in *The New Republic* began by stating explicitly that it "traces a few of the implications of the definition" of form that Burke had offered in "Psychology and Form" (286). Thus, this chapter too can be read as "codification, amplification, and correction" of earlier chapters in *Counter-Statement*.

42. Warren indicated that Burke's sections on "Hierarchy" and "Applications of the Terminology" were acceptable to a New Humanist point of view (Warren to Burke, October 12, 1932).

43. I am certainly not the first to note the internally contradictory character of *Counter-Statement*. In 1933, Austin Warren noted that *Counter-Statement* is "not a systematic treatise." In merging "essays of . . . quite different sorts . . . , it damages if not destroys any impression of unity" (354–55). I have also quoted Rueckert's opinion in *Kenneth Burke and the Drama of Human Relations* (32) that *Counter-Statement* expresses a tension in Burke between "two seemingly contradictory areas of investigation: the purely aesthetic and the sociological. In fact, Burke actually seems to contradict himself in the book." Jay has also said that "there is something of a split in the book . . . as he moves . . . away from conceptualizing art in aesthetic terms as self-expression and toward viewing it as a socially symbolic act" ("Kenneth Burke" 70). Henderson concludes that "the conflict between the aesthetic and the practical remains unresolved in *Counter-Statement*" (179). And Burke himself noted in "*Permanence and Change*: In Retrospective Prospect" that in *Counter-Statement*, under the tutelage of Flaubert, who on the one hand proclaimed aestheticism while on the other tweaked social norms, he "developed a theory of literary form designed to discuss the work of art *in itself*, as a set of *internal relationships* to be analyzed and appreciated in their own right. But in the course of considering how such pure principles of form and style become 'individuated' in terms of the details proper to each individual case, this line of thought ended with the recognition that the artist ultimately appeals to an audience's attitudes, which are ultimately grounded in natural susceptibilities quite outside their role in any one specific artistic tradition" (302).

CHAPTER 7. CONCLUSION: CONVERSING WITH
MODERNISM IN *TOWARDS A BETTER LIFE*

1. I never actually have seen the original book jacket of *Towards a Better Life*. In these paragraphs (and later in this chapter) I am quoting from a typescript entitled "Towards a Better Life" that has Burke's signature and a handwritten note entitled "book jacket" (Kenneth Burke Papers, Penn State). My assumption is that these were Burke's directions for the actual book jacket as it appeared.

2. "On Stress, Its Seeking" mentions several additional incidents from Burke's personal life that found their way into *Towards a Better Life*: Neal's notion that actors reenact offstage their roles onstage (Part 1, chapter 3) stemmed from Burke's "early years of loitering about the fringes of the Provincetown Playhouse"; a mystic vision of the narrator's derived from an incident in Burke's childhood; and certain observations about artists derived from his experience with *The Dial* (93–96).

3. See, for instance, Rountree, *Conversations*, where Burke says that "nothing in that book is literally" about him; and elsewhere in "On Stress," where he emphasizes again and again that "this story is fiction from start to finish" (93), that "the actual story is a fiction from beginning to end" (91), that "in real life there was no such love triangle as the plot [of *Towards*] is built around" (93).

4. The "steady march toward zero" sounds grimly foreboding, but it appears to me to refer to Burke's cash reserves rather than to any contemplation of death. Cf. Burke to Tate, October 16, 1931: "I am becoming a lily of the field—and the more my funds sink, the more I find myself inclining to write things which could earn me a little. This is a ghastly state of affairs for a papa of three children." The phrase "toward zero" recurs in the same economic sense in Burke to Wheelwright, February 11, 1933.

5. Judging from Burke's correspondence, it seems to me that if there is any sign of truly serious emotional or intellectual depression in Burke while he was composing his novel, it is earlier, in 1927. On February 24, 1927, for example, Burke, frustrated for once by a writer's block that was "making any statement, even a self-annihilating one, abhorrent," confessed to Cowley that he was "battling like a fiend, battling for nothing less than my mind itself. . . . I have some vague conflict—not with others but within myself." The letter, which alludes sympathetically to Thayer's bout with mental illness, is quoted in part in "On Stress," 92. Even that letter, however, speaks of Burke's "trembling with expectations" at the prospect that he might have solved a problem in composing a story that he was working on, a story that may have grown into *Towards a Better Life*. The story referred to in the letter at first seems unlike *Towards*: "I have laid out four parts of a four-part story, have written most of parts two and three. . . ." But then again, no short story written at this time by Burke was ever published, and he pretty much had given up short fiction with the publication of *The White Oxen, and Other Stories*, so Burke could have been referring to the germ of *Towards*.

6. Robert Adams agrees: The novel "is not really affiliated [with the 1930s].

Despite its title, it has no connections with the Depression" (32). Of course, Burke in the early and middle 1930s would resist the opposition between the personal and aesthetic, on the one hand, and the explicitly political on the other. Since "the esthetes were simply the imaginative or poetic side of Marx" (Burke to Josephson, March 24, 1933; cf. *Auscultation, Creation, and Revision*), an emphasis on the esthetic is not at the expense of the political.

On the title of *Towards a Better Life*, I should also report on Burke's own gloss on the term "towards." In a letter of January 12, 1923, he told John Wheelwright that he understood "towards" to mean an "attitude towards" something, while "toward" meant to him motion toward some destination. (On the other hand, consider the title of Burke's 1937 book *Attitudes toward History*.) Is *Towards* to be taken as a spiritual biography, i.e., as motion towards a better condition, or as a critical attitude toward the concept of "a better life"—or both?

7. Other early references to the novel also appear in letters to Josephson on July 28, 1927, and October 11, 1927. The very first possible reference to Burke's novel that I have come across is in Alyse Gregory's letter to Burke of November 14, 1926; but that letter leaves unclear whether Burke's plans had materialized in a significant way. In "On Stress," Burke says that *Towards* was "in utero" when he wrote the letter to Cowley of February 24, 1927 (92).

8. Allan Tate, Yvor Winters, and Blackmur were frequent contributors to *Hound and Horn*, which ran from 1927 to 1934, which was an imitator of *The Dial* and already an incubator of the New Criticism, and which in turn inspired its own imitators, *Kenyon Review*, *Southern Review*, and *Sewanee Review* (Hoffman, Allen, and Ulrich 207–13). The magazine began as a Harvard publication, but it moved to New York in 1929–30 and began carrying many of the writers and literary values associated with *The Dial*.

9. The Tenth Declamation was finished in March 1930 (Burke to Josephson, March 1930). That summer Burke complained to Cowley about the progress of his novel, but he had developed extensive notes for what remained unfinished (Burke to Cowley, September 14, 1930).

10. *Counter-Statement* was nearly complete by June 1, shortly after which Burke turned to *Towards* in earnest (Burke to Cowley, June 1, 1931). Much of the last half of *Towards* was written in early 1931, and during the summer it was completed. Burke later reported that he quit his job with Colonel Woods to finish his books ("On Stress" 95–96). In August Burke claimed still to have three chapters to go (Burke to Cowley, August 9, 1931), chapters that he wrote between then and Labor Day.

11. Certainly *Towards* addresses very obliquely if at all the conflicts that Burke in "Program" had identified as the likely artistic concerns of artists in the 1930s. If the book had been in tune with the 1930s, it might have had a greater impact. I don't know how well the book did in 1932, but according to a Harcourt, Brace statement in the Burke files at Penn State, in 1933 Burke sold fewer than a dozen copies of *Towards a Better Life*.

12. Josephson defined Unanimism by the example of Jules Romains' "plotless" novel *La Mort de quelqu'un*, translated in 1914 into English as *Death of a*

Nobody. Margaret Davies discusses Unanimism as one of the many kinds of experimental writing being tried in Paris just before The Great War. She defines it as an attempt to achieve *simultaneité*, to bring the multiple and random into some kind of oneness (150–54), and she ties it to Faulkner's efforts to link historical moments of time together—an effort also apparent in *Towards a Better Life*. Among other literary works that are formally intertextual with *Towards a Better Life* are also the texts cited by Burke in the preface to the second edition: Goethe's "The Sorrows of Young Werther," "pamphleteering" works by Leon Bloy, and Richard Huch's *Erinnerungen von Ludolf Ursleu dem Jungeren* (viii–ix), none of which I am really familiar with.

13. In a similar vein, note the exchange between Burke and Cowley of September 30–October 3, 1929. When Cowley complained mildly about the unrealistic quality of the dialogue in the Ninth Declamation, mentioning ever-so-indirectly Hemingway as an antidote, Burke hit the ceiling: "I do not have so strongly as you the test of naturalness in writing—for it leads too inexorably to Hemingway, whom I hate as though sent upon earth to hate him."

14. The analogy to the sonnet sequence also appears in Burke's letter to Tate of April 6, 1931: "Their interrelations are precisely those of the sonnets in a sonnet sequence, or individual garments on a clothes line—each hangs down by itself, but each carries things along a little farther than the one preceding."

15. Anthony plays the part of a young Greek and Florence the part of a Jewish girl that he seduces and makes the mother of Jesus. John Brooks Wheelwright offered that the play was after "the manner of Anatole France" (letter to Burke, February 9, 1932). Wheelwright knew the novel well, having advised Burke about the developing manuscript while they were at Yaddo together in May 1931. Worried about the obscurity of the still-incomplete book, Wheelwright gave Burke advice for clarifying things, including the idea of chapter summaries that Burke subsequently added to later editions of the book (Burke to Wheelwright, February 11, 1933).

16. Just how satiric Neal's writings are here is underscored by the fact that the "pamphlets" are no doubt in the tradition of "the 'pamphleteering' style of Leon Bloy" that Burke was recalling as he wrote (preface to the second edition ix). "[Bloy] was pleased to pose for a photograph of himself among his pigs, and wrote, as early as 1897: 'Que Dieu vous garde du feu, du couteau, de la litterature contemporaine et de la rancune des mauvais morts!' "

17. Was this formulation suggested to Burke by something Gorham Munson once said about Burke's cerebral fiction? In *Destinations* (136), Munson wrote: "With Kenneth Burke we enter the workshop of fiction, and he shows us the structural elements of good stories without concealment. There are certain mathematical propositions, psychological concepts, and problems in mechanics which can best be explained by a blackboard demonstration."

18. Burke offered something approaching the same reading as early as August 7, 1930, when he promised in a letter to Josephson a book about a protagonist's isolation and need for communion. But it was only much later, during the 1960s, that Burke actually began seeing the close of his book as more hopeful. First, in *Language as Symbolic Action*, in a passage published first in 1963, he

claimed that he "had ended [*Towards*] on a symbol of rebirth" (339), namely water. Upon the reissuance of *Towards a Better Life* in 1966, he offered that Neal's final lapse into silence "is interwoven with his cry: '*Resurgam! Resurgam!* I shall rise again' [217]. . . . Thus I personally look back upon the book as a kind of grotesque tragedy serving as a *rite de passage* into a cult of comedy" ("On Stress" 85). The Preface to the Second Edition consequently avers that Burke regarded *Towards* as a book about purgation and purification: "This book is to be classed among the many rituals of rebirth which mark our fiction. And though I did not think of this possibility at the time, I noticed later how the theme of resurgence is explicitly proclaimed, even at the moments of my plaintive narrator's gravest extremity" (vi–vii).

19. Further, Rueckert notes, "John Neal is a hopeful character because he represents the possibility of individual change and amelioration by means of self-knowledge" (136). Rueckert's discussion of *Towards a Better Life* in *Encounters* depends more than I would like on autobiographical elements, particularly on his sense "that if we but knew how to read the secret code of the novel we would realize that it was all about [Burke's] relationship with Libbie" in the guise of Genevieve (157), but it nevertheless remains the fullest and sharpest analysis of the novel yet published, with the possible exception of Burke's own commentary in "On Stress."

20. "The development may be inexorably back, back, back into silence . . . or things may be directed towards resurgence, as some of the final jottings explicitly promise" ("On Stress" 82). Rueckert's review ("Burke's Other Life" 649) also allows that the ending could be taken both ways, though he still favors the comic reading.

21. The comment appears on a draft of the Eighth Declamation, dated September 17, 1931, in Burke's Penn State file entitled "Notes, Typescripts, Galleys, Offprints."

22. In his letter to Cowley of July 19, 1972, he wrote, "My TBL is to my critical books as Nietzsche's *Zarathustra* is to his others. That is, it's the ritualized essence out of which comes the existence of my detailed analysis." In personal conversations with me, Richard Gregg and Gregory Clark have both said that Burke recommended *Towards* to them as a good place to begin a study of his work.

Works Cited and Consulted

MANUSCRIPT COLLECTIONS

Van Wyck Brooks Collection, Van Pelt Library, University of Pennsylvania.
Broom Collection, Princeton University Library.
Kenneth Burke Papers, Pattee Library, Pennsylvania State University.
Burke-Pound Correspondence, Manuscripts Department, Lilly Library, Indiana University.
Seward Collins Papers, Beinecke Rare Book and Manuscript Library, Yale University.
Malcolm Cowley Papers, Newberry Library, Chicago.
Hart Crane Collection (John Baker Papers), Beinecke Rare Book and Manuscript Library, Yale University.
Dial/Thayer Papers, Beinecke Rare Book and Manuscript Library, Yale University.
Waldo Frank Collection, Van Pelt Library, University of Pennsylvania.
Matthew Josephson Papers, Beinecke Rare Book and Manuscript Library, Yale University.
Harold Loeb Papers, Princeton University Library.
Marianne Moore Archive, Rosenbach Museum, Philadelphia.
Allen Tate Papers, Princeton University Library.
Jean Toomer Papers, Beinecke Rare Book and Manuscript Library, Yale University.
John Brooks Wheelwright Papers, John Hay Library, Brown University.

WORKS BY KENNETH BURKE
Books

Book of Moments: Poems, 1915–1954. Los Altos, CA: Hermes Publications, 1955.
Collected Poems, 1915–1967. Berkeley: U of California P, 1968.
The Complete White Oxen: Collected Short Fiction of Kenneth Burke. Berkeley: U of California P, 1968.
Counter-Statement. New York: Harcourt, Brace and Company, 1931; Berkeley: U of California P, 1968.
A Grammar of Motives. 1945. Berkeley: U of California P, 1962.

256

Language as Symbolic Action: Studies in Symbolic Action. Berkeley: U of California P, 1966.

The Philosophy of Literary Form. 1941. Berkeley: U of California P, 1967.

Towards a Better Life: Being a Series of Epistles, or Declamations. New York: Harcourt, Brace, 1932. Berkeley: U of California P, 1966.

The White Oxen, and Other Stories. New York: Albert and Charles Boni, 1924. Berkeley: U of California P, 1968.

Translations (roughly in chronological order of publication)

Mombert, Alfred. "Lullaby." *Sansculotte* 1 (January 1917): 4.

Mann, Thomas. "Loulou." *The Dial* 70 (April 1921): 428–42.

Purrmann, Hans. "From the Workshop of Matisse." *The Dial* 73 (July 1922): 32–40.

Hofmannsthal, Hugo von. "Lucidor: Characters for an Unwritten Comedy." *The Dial* 73 (August 1922): 121–32.

Specht, Richard. "Arthur Schnitzler." *The Dial* 73 (December 1922): 241–45.

Mann, Thomas. "German Letter." *The Dial* 73 (December 1922): 645–54; 74 (June 1923): 609–14; 75 (October 1923): 369–75; 76 (January 1924): 58–65; 77 (November 1924): 414–19; 79 (October 1925): 333–38; 83 (July 1927): 53–59; 85 (July 1928): 56–58.

Mann, Thomas. "Tristan." *The Dial* 73 (December 1922): 593–610; 74 (January 1923): 57–76. (with Scofield Thayer)

Zweig, Stefan. "Charles Dickens." *The Dial* 74 (January 1923): 1–24.

Hauptmann, Gerhart. "The Heretic of Soana." *The Dial* 74 (April 1923): 329–50; (May 1923): 475–93; (June 1923): 563–580. (assisted by Bayard Quincy Morgan)

Maier-Graefe, Julius. "German Art after the War." *The Dial* 75 (July 1923): 1–12.

Morand, Paul. "Paris Letter." *The Dial* 74 (August 1923): 174–78; 74 (November 1923): 474–79; 74 (December 1923): 583–87; 76 (March 1924): 265–73; 76 (May 1924): 449–51; 77 (July 1924): 64–68; 77 (September 1924): 239–43; 77 (December 1924): 505–08; 78 (February 1925): 139–41; 78 (March 1925): 221–24; 78 (June 1925): 499–502; 79 (July 1925): 55–59; 79 (September 1925): 231–34; 79 (October 1925): 329–32; 80 (April 1926): 312–16; 80 (June 1926): 503–09; 81 (September 1926): 237–41; 81 (November 1926): 427–30; 82 (January 1927): 53–58; 82 (March 1927): 233–38; 82 (June 1927): 497–501; 83 (October 1927): 333–38; 83 (December 1927): 502–07; 84 (February 1928): 141–45; 84 (June 1928): 505–510; 85 (December 1928): 507–12; 86 (February 1929): 132–36; 86 (April 1929): 325–28.

Hofmannsthal, Hugo von. "Vienna Letter." *The Dial* 75 (September 1923): 281–88; 76 (June 1924): 529–34; 84 (August 1928): 147–57.

Schnitzler, Arthur. "The Fate of Baron von Leisenbohg." *The Dial* 75 (December 1923): 565–82.

Mann, Heinrich. "Virgins." *The Dial* 76 (February 1924): 123–32.

Mann, Thomas. *Death in Venice*. *The Dial* 76 (March 1924): 213–35; 76 (April 1924): 311–33; 76 (May 1924): 423–43.

Spengler, Oswald. Introduction to *The Downfall of Western Civilization*. *The Dial*

77 (November 1924): 361–78; 77 (December 1924): 482–504; 78 (January 1925): 9–26.

Mann, Thomas. *Death in Venice* [with "Tristan and Tonio Kroger"]. New York: Knopf, 1925.

Hofmannsthal, Hugo von. "Honore de Balzac." *The Dial* 78 (May 1925): 357–68.

Schnitzler, Arthur. "Lieutenant Gustl." *The Dial* 79 (August 1925): 89–117.

Schnitzler, Arthur. "The New Song." *The Dial* 79 (November 1925): 355–69.

de Mare, Rolf. "The Swedish Ballet and the Modern Aesthetic." *The Little Review* 12 (spring–summer 1926): 24–28.

Loebe, Marx. "Georges Papazoff." *The Little Review* 12 (spring–summer 1926): 24.

Ludwig, Emil. *Genius and Character*. New York: Harcourt, Brace, 1927.

Mann, Thomas. "Pariser Rechenschaft." *The Dial* 82 (July 1927): 501–10.

Baumann, Emil. *Saint Paul*. New York: Harcourt, Brace, 1929.

Fiction (in addition to stories in *The White Oxen, and Other Stories*)

"Parabolic Tale, with Invocation." *Sansculotte* 1 (January 1917): 8.

"Idylls." *Smart Set* 57 (November 1918): 34.

"A Declamation." *The Dial* 85 (August 1928): 121–25.

"Second Declamation." *The Dial* 85 (October 1928): 328–32.

"Third Declamation." *The Dial* 85 (November 1928): 375–79.

"Fourth Declamation." *The Dial* 86 (January 1929): 1–5.

"Fifth Declamation." *The Dial* 86 (March 1929): 219–23.

"Sixth Declamation." *The Dial* 86 (May 1929): 389–93.

"Seventh Declamation." *Hound and Horn* 3 (fall 1929): 71–77.

"Eighth Declamation." *Hound and Horn* 3 (winter 1929–30) 204–11.

"Ninth Declamation." *Hound and Horn* 3 (spring 1930): 376–82.

"Tenth Declamation." *Pagany* 1 (fall 1930): 19–23.

Poems (in chronological order of publication)

"Adam's Song, and Mine" [free verse version]. *Others* 2 (March 1916): 184.

"Revolt." *Sansculotte* 1 (January 1917): 3.

"Hokku." *Sansculotte* 1 (January 1917): 4.

"La Baudelairienne." *Sansculotte* 1 (January 1917): 9.

"Invocations." *Sansculotte* 1 (January 1917): 11.

"Spring Song." *Slate* 1 (January 1917): 11.

"The Oftener Trinity." *Sansculotte* 1 (February 1917): 7.

"Bathos, Youth, and the Antithetical 'Rather'." *Sansculotte* 1 (February 1917): 7.

"Nocturne." *Sansculotte* 1 (April 1917): 9.

"Adam's Song, and Mine" [revised version]. *Sansculotte* 1 (April 1917): 10.

"Hymn of Hope." *Slate* 1 (April 1917): 80.

"Ver Renatus Orbis Est." *Contact* 4 (1921): 9.

"Eroticon: As from the Greek Anthology." *Secession* 3 (August 1922): 27.

"Two Portraits." *S4N* 23 (December 1922): n.p.

"Psalm." *S4N* 26–29 (May–June 1923), n.p.

"From Outside." *The Dial* 86 (February 1929): 91–94.

"Rhapsody under the Autumn Moon." Unpublished until *Book of Moments: Poems, 1915–1954.*

"Ambulando Solvitur." Unpublished until *Collected Poems, 1915–1967.*

"The Monster." Unpublished until *Collected Poems, 1915–1967.*

Essays (in chronological order of publication)

"The Armour of Jules Laforg[u]e." *Contact* 3 (1921): 9–10.

"Approaches to Remy de Gourmont." *The Dial* 70 (February 1921): 125–38.

"The Art of Carl Sprinchorn." *The Arts* 2 (December 1921): 158–59.

"The Correspondence of Flaubert." *The Dial* 72 (February 1922): 147–55.

"André Gide, Bookman." *The Freeman* 5 (April 1922): 155–57.

"Last Words on the Ephebe." *The Literary Review* [of the *New York Evening Post*] 2 (August 1922): 897–98.

"Art and the Hope Chest." *Vanity Fair* 19 (December 1922): 59, 102.

"Chicago and Our National Gesture." *The Bookman* 57 (July 1923): 497–501.

"Notes on Walter Pater." *1924* 2 (1924): 53–58.

"Dada, Dead or Alive." *Aesthete, 1925*: 23–26.

"The Poetic Process." *The Guardian* 2 (May–June 1925): 281–94.

"Psychology and Form." *The Dial* 79 (July 1925): 34–46.

"A 'Logic' of History" [review-essay of Spengler's *The Decline of the West*]. *The Dial* 81 (September 1926): 242–48.

"William Carlos Williams, the Method of." *The Dial* 82 (February 1927): 94–98.

"Cheat the Censor," "She Brought the Wrong Book," and "Important Communication to the Editor." In "New York: 1928." *transition* 13 (summer 1928): 88, 96, 99.

"A Decade of American Fiction." *The Bookman* 69 (August 1929): 561–67.

"The Allies of Humanism Abroad." *A Critique of Humanism*. Ed. Hartley Grattan. New York: Brewer and Warren, 1930. 169–92.

"Three Frenchmen's Churches." *The New Republic* 63 (May 1930): 10–14.

"Thomas Mann and André Gide." *The Bookman* 73 (June 1930): 257-64.

"Waste: The Future of Prosperity." *The New Republic* 63 (July 1930): 228–31.

"Boring from Within." *The New Republic* 65 (February 1931): 326–29.

"Redefinitions." *The New Republic* 68 (July 1931): 286–87; 69 (August, September 1931): 46–47; 74–75.

"Counter-Blast on *Counter-Statement*." *The New Republic* 69 (December 9, 1931): 101.

"On Stress, Its Seeking." *Why Man Takes Chances: Studies in Stress-Seeking*. Ed. Samuel Klausner. New York: Anchor Books, 1968. 75–103.

"Dancing with Tears in My Eyes." *Critical Inquiry* 1 (1974): 29–31.

"Methodological Repression and/or Strategies of Containment." *Critical Inquiry* 5 (1978): 401–16.

"Questions and Answers about the Pentad." *College Composition and Communication* 29 (1978): 330–35.

Works Cited and Consulted

"Afterword: *Permanence and Change* in Retrospective Prospect." *Permanence and Change.* 3rd ed. Berkeley: U of California P, 1984. 295–336.

Reviews (in chronological order of publication)

"Axiomatics" [review of John Cournos' *The Mask*]. *The Dial* 68 (April 1920): 496–99.

"Alcohol in the Eighties" [John Huneker's *Painted Veils*]. *The Literary Review* [of the *New York Evening Post*] 1 (October 1920): 3.

"A Transitional Novel" [Waldo Frank's *The Dark Mother*]. *The Literary Review* [of the *New York Evening Post*] 1 (November 1920): 6.

"Felix Kills His Author" [Floyd Dell's *Moon-Calf*]. *The Literary Review* [of the *New York Evening Post*] 1 (December 1920): 3.

"Puritans Defended" [J. S. Flynn's *The Influence of Puritanism*]. *The Literary Review* [of the *New York Evening Post*] 1 (February 1921): 2.

"The Bon Dieu of M. Jammes" [Francis Jammes's *The Romance of the Rabbitt*]. *The Freeman* 3 (May 1921): 211–12.

"The Modern English Novel Plus" [Virginia Woolf's *Night and Day* and *The Voyage Out*]. *The Dial* 70 (May 1921): 572–75.

Untitled review of Emanuel Morgan's *Pens for Wings. The Freeman* 3 (June 1921): 286.

"The Editing of Oneself" [James Oppenheim's *The Mystic Warrior*]. *The Dial* 71 (August 1921): 232–35.

"Modifying the Eighteenth Century" [Arthur Schnitzler's *Casanova's Homecoming*]. *The Dial* 71 (December 1921): 707–10.

"Chekhov and Three Others" [I. A. Bunin's *Reminiscences of A. Chekhov*]. *The New York Times Book Review* (January 1, 1922): 2.

"Heroism and Books" [Stefan Zweig's *Romain Roland*]. *The Dial* 72 (January 1922): 92–93.

Untitled review of Lewis Spence's *An Introduction to Mythology. The Freeman* 4 (January 1922): 478.

"Heaven's First Law" [William Carlos Williams' *Sour Grapes*]. *The Dial* 72 (February 1922): 197–200.

"Fides Quaerens Intellectum" [Paul Elmer More's *The Religion of Plato*]. *The Dial* 72 (May 1922): 527–30.

Untitled review of Ernst Buschor's *Greek Face Painting. The Freeman* 5 (May 1922): 238.

"Enlarging the Narrow House" [Evelyn Scott's *Narcissus*]. *The Dial* 73 (September 1922): 346–48.

"The Consequences of Idealism" [Waldo Frank's *Rahab* and *City Block*]. *The Dial* 73 (October 1922): 449–52.

"The Critic of Dostoevsky" [J. Middleton Murry's *Still Life* and *The Things We Are*]. *The Dial* 73 (December 1922): 671–74.

"Note on *Der Sturm*" [Herwarth Walden's "Kunstdämmerung" in *Der Sturm*]. *Secession* 4 (January 1923): 32–33.

"Realism and Idealism" [Giovanni Gentile's *The Reform of Education*]. *The Dial* 74 (January 1923): 97–99.

"Engineering with Words" [Gertrude Stein's *Geography and Plays*]. *The Dial* 74 (April 1923): 408–12.

"Immersion" [Djuna Barnes's *A Book*]. *The Dial* 76 (May 1924): 460–61.

"Deposing the Love of the Lord" [Solomon Ibn Gabirol's *Selected Religious Poems*]. *The Dial* 77 (August 1924): 161–62.

"Ethics of the Artist" [Thomas Mann's *Buddenbrooks*]. *The Dial* 77 (November 1924): 420–22.

"Delight and Tears" [Glenway Wescott's *The Apple of the Eye*]. *The Dial* 77 (December 1924): 513–15.

"After-Dinner Philosophy" [W. C. Brownell's *The Genius of Style*]. *The Dial* 78 (March 1925): 228–31.

"On Re and Dis" [V. F. Calverton's *The Newer Spirit: A Sociological Criticism of Literature*]. *The Dial* 79 (August 1925): 165–69.

"A New Poetics" [I. A. Richards' *Principles of Literary Criticism*]. *The Saturday Review of Literature* 2 (September 1925): 154–55.

"Codifying Milton" [Denis Saurat's *Milton: Man and Thinker*]. *The Dial* 79 (November 1925): 429–30.

"Idiom and Uniformity" [Robert Bridges' *The Society's Work*, and Logan Pearsall Smith's *Words and Idioms*]. *The Dial* 80 (January 1926): 57–60.

"American Pot-Pourri" [William Carlos Williams' *In the American Grain*]. *The New York Times Book Review* (February 7, 1926): 21.

"Idols of the Future" [T. V. Smith's *Notes on the American Doctrine of Equality*]. *The Dial* 81 (July 1926): 42–46.

"But They Have Settled" [*The American Caravan: A Yearbook of American Literature*]. *The New York Herald Tribune Books* 4 (September 18, 1927): 2.

"Righting an Ethnologic Wrong" [Paul Radin's *Primitive Man as Philosopher*]. *The Dial* 83 (November 1927): 439–40.

"Little Men" [Ferenc Molnaar's *The Paul Street Boys*]. *The New York Herald Tribune Books* 4 (December 4, 1927): 4.

"Van Wyck Brooks in Transition?" [Brooks's *Emerson and Others*]. *The Dial* 84 (January 1928): 56–59.

"Witchcraft in Our Day" [Jacob Wasserman's *World's End*]. *The New York Herald Tribune Books* 4 (January 15, 1928): 2.

"Werthers with a Future" [Frank Thiess's *The Gateway to Life*]. *The New York Herald Tribune Books* 4 (February 26, 1928): 7.

"Love among the Ruins" [Rene Schicke's *Maria Capponi*]. *The New York Herald Tribune Books* 4 (March 4, 1928): 7.

"Useful Distress" [Alfred Kreymborg et al.'s *The Second American Caravan*]. *The New York Herald Tribune Books* 5 (October 1928): 5.

"An Urn of Native Soil" [Malcolm Cowley's *Blue Juniata*]. *The New York Herald Tribune Books* 5 (August 1929): 2.

"The Eloquence of Barres" [Maurice Barres's *The Sacred Hill*]. *The New York Herald Tribune Books* 6 (November 1929): 4.

"Intelligence as a Good" [John Dewey's *The Quest for Certainty*]. *The New Republic* 64 (September 1930): 77–79.

"In Quest of the Way" [P. D. Ouspensky's *A New Model of the Universe*]. *The New Republic* 68 (September 1931): 104–6.

BIBLIOGRAPHIES

Frank, Armin Paul, and Mechthild Frank. "The Writings of Kenneth Burke."
Critical Responses to Kenneth Burke. Ed. William Rueckert. Minneapolis:
U of Minnesota P, 1969. 495–523.
Thames, Richard. "The Writings of Kenneth Burke, 1968–1986" and "A Se-
lected Bibliography of Critical Responses to Kenneth Burke, 1968–1986."
The Legacy of Kenneth Burke. Ed. Herbert W. Simons and Trevor Melia.
Madison: U of Wisconsin P, 1989. 297–315.

SECONDARY STUDIES

Aaron, Daniel. *Writers on the Left: Episodes in American Literary Communism.*
New York: Harcourt, Brace and World, 1961.
Abrahams, Edward. "Alfred Stieglitz's Faith and Vision." *1915: The Cultural
Moment.* Ed. Adele Heller and Lois Rudnick. New Brunswick: Rutgers U P,
1991. 185–95.
Abrahams, Edward. *The Lyrical Left: Randolph Bourne, Alfred Stieglitz, and the
Origins of Cultural Radicalism in America.* Charlottesville: U of Virginia P,
1986.
Adams, Robert M. "Restorations" [review of *Towards a Better Life*]. *New York
Review of Books* 7 (October 20, 1966): 31–33.
Ades, Dawn. "Dada and Surrealism." *Concepts of Modern Art: From Fauvism to
Postmodernism.* Ed. Nikos Stangos. New York: Harper and Row, 1981.
Ades, Dawn. *Dada and Surrealism Reviewed.* London: Arts Council of Great
Britain, 1978.
Anderson, David L. *Symbolism: A Bibliography of Symbolism as an International
and Multi-Disciplinary Movement.* New York: New York U P, 1975.
Anderson, Margaret. *My Thirty Years' War: An Autobiography.* London: Knopf,
1930.
Anderson, Margaret. "An Obvious Statement (for the millionth time)." *The Little
Review* 7.3 (September–December 1920): 8–16.
Arensberg, Walter. *Idols.* New York: Houghton Mifflin, 1916.
Arensberg, Walter. *Poems.* Boston: Houghton Mifflin, 1914.
Ashton, Dore. *The New York School: A Cultural Reckoning.* New York: Viking,
1973.
Auden, W. H. "A Grammar of Assent." *The New Republic* 105 (July 14, 1941): 59.
Babbitt, Irving. *Rousseau and Romanticism.* Boston: Houghton-Mifflin, 1919.
Bak, Hans. *Malcolm Cowley: The Formative Years.* Athens: U of Georgia P, 1990.
Baker, Houston A., Jr. *Modernism and the Harlem Renaissance.* Chicago: U of
Chicago P, 1987.
Beebe, Maurice. *Ivory Towers and Sacred Fonts: The Artist as Hero in Fiction
from Goethe to Joyce.* New York: New York U P, 1964.
Bell, Clive. *Art.* London: Chatto and Windus, 1913; rpt. New York: Capricorn
Books, 1958.
Bell, Daniel. "Modernism Mummified." *Modernist Culture in America.* Ed. Dan-
iel J. Singal. Belmont, CA: Wadsworth, 1991. 158–73.

Benstock, Shari. *Women of the Left Bank*. Austin: U of Texas P, 1986.

Berthoff, Ann. "I. A. Richards." *Traditions of Inquiry*. Ed. John Brereton. New York: Oxford U P, 1985. 50–80.

Bizzell, Patricia, and Bruce Herzberg. "Kenneth Burke." *The Rhetorical Tradition: Readings from Classical Times to the Present*. Boston: Bedford Books, 1990. 989–1041.

Blum, W. C. [Sibley Watson]. "A Poetry of Perspectives" [review of *Book of Moments*]. *Poetry* 87 (1956): 362–66.

Bode, Carl. *Mencken*. Southern Illinois U P, 1969.

Bodenheim, Maxwell. "Modern Poetry." *The Dial* 68 (January 1920): 97.

Booth, Wayne. *Critical Understanding: The Powers and Limits of Pluralism*. Chicago: U of Chicago P, 1979.

Booth, Wayne. "Kenneth Burke's Way of Knowing." *Critical Inquiry* 1 (1974): 1–22.

Booth, Wayne. *A Rhetoric of Fiction*. Chicago: U of Chicago P, 1961.

Bostdorff, Denise, and Phillip K. Tompkins. "Musical Form and Rhetorical Form: Kenneth Burke's *Dial* Reviews as Counterpart to *Counter-Statement*." *Pre/ Text* 6 (1985): 235–54.

Bourne, Randolph. "This Older Generation." *History of a Literary Radical and Other Essays*. Ed. with intro. by Van Wyck Brooks. New York: B. W. Huebsch, 1920. 107–27.

Bradbury, Malcolm. *The Modern World: Ten Great Writers*. New York: Viking, 1989.

Bradbury, Malcolm. "The Nonhomemade World: European and American Modernism." *Modernist Culture in America*. Ed. Daniel J. Singal. Belmont, CA: Wadsworth, 1991. 28–41.

Breon-Guerry, Liliane. *L'annee 1913*. Paris: Klincksieck, 1971.

Breslin, James E. B. *William Carlos Williams: An American Artist*. Chicago: U of Chicago P, 1985.

Brock, Bernard, ed. *Kenneth Burke and Contemporary European Thought*. Tuscaloosa: U of Alabama P, 1995.

Brooks, Van Wyck. *America's Coming of Age*. New York: B. W. Huebsch, 1914.

Brooks, Van Wyck. *An Autobiography*. New York: E. P. Dutton, 1965.

Brooks, Van Wyck. "On Creating a Usable Past." *The Dial* 66 (April 11, 1918): 337–41.

Brooks, Van Wyck. "A Reviewer's Notebook [on 'This Youngest Generation']." *The Freeman* 3 (November 9, 1921): 214–15.

Brown, Merle. *Kenneth Burke*. University of Minnesota Pamphlets on American Writers 75. Minneapolis: U of Minnesota P, 1969.

Brown, Milton W. *American Painting from the Armory Show to the Depression*. Princeton: Princeton U P, 1955.

Brown, Milton W. "The Armory Show and Its Aftermath." *1915: The Cultural Moment*. Ed. Adele Heller and Lois Rudnick. New Brunswick: Rutgers U P, 1991. 164–84.

Brown, Milton W. *The Story of the Armory Show*. Greenwich, CN: Joseph H. Hirschhorn Foundation, 1963. New York, Abbeville Press, 1988.

Brown, Susan Jenkins. *Robber Rocks: Letters and Memories of Hart Crane, 1923–1932*. Middletown, CN: Wesleyan U P, 1968.

Brown, William Slater, Kenneth Burke, Malcolm Cowley, Matthew Josephson, and Robert Coates. "New York: 1928." *transition* 13 (summer 1928): 83–102.

Burke, Carolyn. 'Getting Spliced: Modernism and Sexual Difference." *Modernist Culture in America*. Ed. Daniel J. Singal. Belmont, CA: Wadsworth, 1991. 126–57.

Burke, Kenneth, and Malcolm Cowley. "Kenneth Burke and Malcolm Cowley: A Conversation." *Pre/Text* 6 (1985): 186–93.

Burke, Kenneth. "Likings of an Observationist." *Marianne Moore: A Collection of Critical Essays*. Ed. Charles Tomlinson. Englewood Cliffs: Prentice-Hall, 1969. 125–33.

Burke, Kenneth. "The Party Line." *Quarterly Journal of Speech* 62 (1976): 62–68.

"Burke-Cowley Conversations, April 1985." Videotapes. Penn State Room, Pattee Library, Pennsylvania State University.

Burne, Glenn S. *Remy de Gourmont: His Ideas and Influence in England and America*. Carbondale: Southern Illinois U P, 1963.

Byard, Vicki. "Kenneth Burke and Cultural Studies." Paper given at the Rhetoric Society of America Conference, Norfolk, VA, May 1994.

Calinescu, Matei. *Five Faces of Modernity*. Durham: Duke U P, 1987.

Calinescu, Matei. "Modernism and Ideology." *Modernism: Challenges and Perspectives*. Ed. Monique Chefdor, Ricardo Quinones, and Albert Wachtel. Urbana: U of Illinois P, 1986. 79–93.

Calverton, V. F. *The Newer Spirit: A Sociological Criticism of Literature*. New York: Boni and Liveright, 1925.

Cantwell, Robert. Review of *Towards a Better Life. The Nation* 134 (March 9, 1932): 289–90.

Chefdor, Monique. "Modernism: Babel Revisited?" *Modernism: Challenges and Perspectives*. Ed. Monique Chefdor, Ricardo Quinones, and Albert Wachtel. Urbana: U of Illinois P, 1986. 1–4.

Chefdor, Monique, Ricardo Quinones, and Albert Wachtel, eds. *Modernism: Challenges and Perspectives*. Urbana: U of Illinois P, 1986.

Chesebro, James W., ed. *Extensions of the Burkeian System*. Tuscaloosa: U of Alabama P, 1993.

Chielens, Edward E., ed. *American Literary Magazines: The Twentieth Century*. Westport, CN: Greenwood Press, 1992.

Churchill, Allen. *The Improper Bohemians: A Re-Creation of Greenwich Village in Its Heyday*. New York: Dutton, 1959.

Clayton, Jan. *The Pleasures of Babel*. New York: Oxford U P, 1993.

Coates, Robert. *The View from Here*. New York: Harcourt, Brace, 1960.

Cohen, Milton A. *Poet and Painter: The Aesthetics of E. E. Cummings' Early Work*. Detroit: Wayne State U P, 1987.

Coles, Robert. *Dorothy Day: A Radical Devotion*. Reading, MA: Addison-Wesley, 1990.

Cowley, Malcolm. *After the Genteel Tradition*. New York: W. W. Norton, 1936.

Cowley, Malcolm. *And I Worked at the Writer's Trade.* New York: Viking, 1978.

Cowley, Malcolm. *Blue Juniata: Collected Poems.* New York: Viking, 1968.

Cowley, Malcolm. *Exile's Return.* New York: W. W. Norton, 1934.

Cowley, Malcolm. "A Messiah of the Skeptics." *The New York Herald Tribune Books* 5 (October 21, 1928): 7.

Cowley, Malcolm. Review of *Towards a Better Life. The New Republic* 70 (February 17, 1932): 23–24.

Cowley, Malcolm. "This Youngest Generation." *The Literary Review* [of *The New York Evening Post*] 2 (October 15, 1921): 1–2.

Cowley, Malcolm. "A Young Man with Spectacles." *Broom* 3 (October 1922); rpt. in *The Visionary Company* 2 and 3 (double issue, summer 1987): 81–86.

Cowley, Malcolm, and Waldo Frank. "Communications on Seriousness and Dada." *1924* 4 (November 1924): 140–42.

Crane, Hart. *The Complete Poems and Selected Letters and Prose of Hart Crane.* Ed. Brom Weber. New York: Doubleday, 1966.

Criticism in America: Its Function and Status. New York: Harcourt, Brace and Company, 1924.

Crowley, Alice Lewisohn. *The Neighborhood Playhouse: Leaves from a Theatre Scrapbook.* New York: Theatre Art Books, 1959.

Crucius, Timothy. "Kenneth Burke on His 'Morbid Selph': The *Collected Poems* as Comedy." *CEA Critic* 43 (1981): 18–32.

Crunden, Robert. *American Salons: Encounters with European Modernism 1885–1917.* New York: Oxford U P, 1993.

Culler, Jonathan. *Structuralist Poetics.* Ithaca: Cornell U P, 1975.

Dachy, Marc. *The Dada Movement 1915–1923.* New York: Rizzoli International Publications, 1990.

Dakin, Arthur H. *Paul Elmer More.* Princeton: Princeton U P, 1960.

Dasenbrock, Reed Way. *The Literary Vorticism of Ezra Pound and Wyndham Lewis.* Baltimore: Johns Hopkins U P, 1985.

Davidson, Abraham A. *Early American Modernist Painting 1910–1935.* New York: Harper and Row, 1981.

Davies, Margaret. "Modernité and Its Techniques." *Modernism: Challenges and Perspectives.* Ed. Monique Chefdor, Ricardo Quinones, and Albert Wachtel. Urbana: U of Illinois P, 1986. 146–58.

Day, Dorothy. *From Union Square to Rome.* Silver Spring, MD: Preservation of the Faith Press, 1940.

Day, Dorothy. *The Long Loneliness: An Autobiography.* New York: Harper and Row, 1952.

Delaney, Edmund T. *New York's Greenwich Village.* Barre, MA: Barre Publishers, 1968.

Dell, Floyd. *Love in Greenwich Village.* New York: George H. Doran, 1926.

Deutsch, Helen, and Stella Hanau. *The Provincetown: A Story of the Theatre.* New York: Farrar and Rinehart, 1931.

Dolmetsch, Carl. *Smart Set: A History and Anthology.* New York: Dial Press, 1966.

Donoghue, Denis. *Ferocious Alphabets.* Boston: Little, Brown, 1981.

Donoghue, Denis. "When in Rome, Do As the Greeks." *Critical Responses to Kenneth Burke.* Ed. William H. Rueckert. Minneapolis: U of Minnesota P, 1969. 479–91.

Dos Passos, John. *Manhattan Transfer.* New York: Grosset and Dunlap, 1925.

Dos Passos, John. *1919.* New York: Harcourt, Brace, 1932.

Douglas, Ann. *Terrible Honesty: Mongrel Manhattan in the 1920s.* New York: Farrar, Straus and Giroux, 1995.

Eberly, Rosa. "Proving Opposites: Kenneth Burke and the Dilemma of Cultural Criticism." Conference on College Composition and Communication, San Diego, 1993.

Eliot, T. S. *The Sacred Wood.* London: Methuen, 1928.

Ellman, Richard, and Charles Fiedelson, eds. *The Modern Tradition: Backgrounds of Modern Literature.* New York: Oxford U P, 1965.

Eysteinsson, Astradur. *The Concept of Modernism.* Ithaca: Cornell U P, 1990.

Fish, Stanley. *Doing What Comes Naturally.* Durham, NC: Duke U P, 1989.

Fishbein, Leslie. *Rebels in Bohemia: The Radicals of The Masses 1911–1917.* Chapel Hill: U of North Carolina P, 1982.

Fitzgerald, Vincent. "The *American Mercury.*" *Menckeniana* 123 (fall 1992): 1–6.

Fitzgerald, Vincent. "Dreiser, Mencken, and the *American Mercury* Years." *Dreiser Newsletter* 10 (fall 1979): 13–16.

Flint, F. S. "Contemporary French Poetry." *Poetry Review* 1 (August 1912): 355–414.

Foerster, Norman, ed. *Humanism in America.* New York: Brewer and Warren, 1930.

Fogarty, Daniel, S. J. "Kenneth Burke's Theory." *Roots for a New Rhetoric.* New York: Columbia U P, 1959. 56–87.

Foss, Sonja K., Karen Foss, and Robert Trapp. "Kenneth Burke." *Contemporary Perspectives on Rhetoric.* Prospect Heights, IL: Waveland Press, 1955. 153–88.

Frank, Armin Paul. *Kenneth Burke.* New York: Twayne, 1969.

Frank, Waldo. *Our America.* New York: Boni and Liveright, 1919.

Frank, Waldo. "Sigmund Freud." *Virginia Quarterly Review* 10 (1934): 529–34.

Frank, Waldo, et al., eds. *America and Alfred Stieglitz: A Collective Portrait.* New York: The Literary Guild, 1934.

The Freeman Book. New York: B. W. Huebsch, 1924.

Gabin, Rosalind. "Entitling Kenneth Burke." *Rhetoric Review* 5 (1987): 196–210.

Gelb, Arthur, and Barbara Gelb. *O'Neill.* New York: Harper and Row, 1960.

George, Ann. "*Permanence and Change*: Translating English into English." Paper given at the Rhetoric Society of America conference, Norfolk, VA, May 1994.

Gillis, Adolph. *Ludwig Lewisohn: The Artist and His Message.* New York: Duffield and Green, 1933.

Glicksberg, Charles. "Kenneth Burke: The Critic's Critic." *South Atlantic Quarterly* 36 (1937): 74–84.

Grattan, Hartley, ed. *A Critique of Humanism.* New York: Brewer and Warren, 1930.

"Greenwich Village." *The Dial* 62 (October 1, 1914): 239–41.

Gregory, Alyse. *The Day Is Gone.* New York: Dutton, 1948.

Grossberg, Lawrence, Cary Nelson, and Paula Treichler, eds. *Cultural Studies.* New York: Routledge, 1992.

Gunn, Giles. *The Culture of Criticism and the Criticism of Culture.* Chicago: U of Chicago P, 1987.

Gunn, Giles. *Thinking across the American Grain.* Chicago: U of Chicago P, 1992.

Hall, Donald. *Marianne Moore: The Cage and the Animal.* New York: Pegasus, 1970.

Hammer, Langdon. *Hart Crane and Allen Tate: Janus-Faced Modernism.* Princeton: Princeton U P, 1993.

Hankel, Walter S. [pseud.], ed. *Whither, Whither, or After Sex, What? A Symposium to End Symposiums.* New York: Macauley, 1930.

Hapgood, Hutchins. *A Victorian in the Modern World.* New York: Harcourt, Brace, 1939.

Harris, Wendell. "Critics Who Made Us: Kenneth Burke." *Sewanee Review* 96 (1988): 452–63.

Hartman, Geoffrey. *Criticism in the Wilderness.* New Haven: Yale U P, 1980.

Hassett, Michael. "Sophisticated Burke: Kenneth Burke as a Neosophistic Rhetorician." *Rhetoric Review* 13 (1995): 371–90.

Heath, Robert. "Kenneth Burke on Form." *Quarterly Journal of Speech* 65 (1979): 392–404.

Heath, Robert. "Kenneth Burke's Break with Formalism." *Quarterly Journal of Speech* 70 (1984): 132–43.

Heath, Robert. *Realism and Relativism: A Perspective on Kenneth Burke.* Macon, GA: Mercer U P, 1986.

Heller, Adele. "The New Theatre." *1915: The Cultural Moment.* Ed. Adele Heller and Lois Rudnick. New Brunswick: Rutgers U P, 1991. 217–32.

Heller, Adele, and Lois Rudnick, eds. *1915: The Cultural Moment.* New Brunswick: Rutgers U P, 1991.

Hemingway, Ernest. *A Moveable Feast.* New York: Charles Scribner's Sons, 1964.

Henderson, Greig. "Aesthetic and Practical Frames of Reference." *Extensions of the Burkeian System.* Ed. James W. Chesebro. Tuscaloosa: U of Alabama P, 1993. 173–85.

Hicks, Granville. "In Defense of Eloquence" [review of *Counter-Statement*]. *New Republic* 69 (December 2, 1931): 75–76.

Hicks, Granville. *John Reed: The Making of a Revolutionary.* New York: Benjamin Boom, 1968.

Hicks, Granville. "Response" [to Kenneth Burke's "Counter-Blasts on *Counter-Statement*"]. *New Republic* 69 (December 9, 1931): 101.

Hicks, Granville, Michael Gold, Joseph North, and Alan Calmer, eds. *Proletarian Literature in the United States, An Anthology.* New York: International, 1936.

Hoeveler, J. David, Jr. *The New Humanism: A Critique of Modern America, 1900–1940.* Charlottesville: U of Virginia P, 1977.

Hoffman, Frederick J. *Freudianism and the Literary Mind.* Baton Rouge: Louisiana State U P, 1945.

Hoffman, Frederick J. *The Twenties: American Writing in the Post-War Decade.* New York: Viking, 1955.

Hoffman, Frederick J., Charles Allen, and Carolyn Ulrich. *The Little Magazine: A History and a Bibliography*. Princeton: Princeton U P, 1946.

Holland, Virginia. *Counterpoint: Kenneth Burke and Aristotle's Theories of Rhetoric*. New York: Philosophical Library, 1959.

Homer, William Innes. *Alfred Stieglitz and the American Avant-Garde*. Boston: New York Graphic Society, 1977.

Howe, Irving. *The Idea of the Modern in Literature and the Arts*. New York: Horizon Press, 1967.

Howells, Wilbur Samuel. *Poetics, Rhetoric, and Logic: Studies in the Basic Disciplines of Criticism*. Ithaca: Cornell U P, 1975.

Howells, Wilbur Samuel. "The Two-Party Line: A Reply to Kenneth Burke." *Quarterly Journal of Speech* 62 (1976): 69–77.

Humphrey, Robert G. *Children of Fantasy: The First Rebels of Greenwich Village*. New York: Wiley, 1978.

Hyman, Stanley Edgar. *The Armed Vision: A Study in the Methods of Modern Literary Criticism*. New York: Knopf, 1948.

Irmscher, William. "Kenneth Burke." *Traditions of Inquiry*. Ed. John Brereton. New York: Oxford U P, 1985. 105–35.

Jameson, Fredric. *Fables of Aggression: Wyndham Lewis, the Modernist as Fascist*. Berkeley: U of California P, 1979.

Jameson, Fredric. "Ideology and Symbolic Action." *Critical Inquiry* 5 (1978–79): 417–22.

Jameson, Fredric. "Postmodernism, or the Cultural Logic of Late Capitalism." *New Left Review* 146 (July–August 1984): 53–92.

Jameson, Fredric. "The Symbolic Inference; or, Kenneth Burke and Ideological Analysis." *Critical Inquiry* 4 (1977–78): 507–23.

Jammerman, Donald. "Kenneth Burke's Poetics of Catharsis." *Representing Kenneth Burke*. Ed. Hayden White and Margaret Brose. Baltimore: Johns Hopkins U P, 1982. 31–51.

Jay, Paul. *American Literary and Cultural Criticism and the Problem of Modernity*. Unpublished manuscript.

Jay, Paul. "Kenneth Burke." *Dictionary of Literary Biography*. Vol. 63 of *Modern American Critics, 1920–55*. Ed. Gregory S. Jay. Detroit: Gale Research, 1987. 67–86.

Jay, Paul. "Kenneth Burke and the Motives of Eloquence." *American Literary History* 1 (1989): 535–53.

Jay, Paul. "Modernism, Postmodernism, and Critical Style: The Case of Burke and Derrida." *Genre* 21 (1988): 339–58.

Jay, Paul, ed. *The Selected Correspondence of Kenneth Burke and Malcolm Cowley 1915–1981*. New York: Viking, 1988.

Josephson, Matthew. *Life among the Surrealists*. New York: Holt, Rinehart and Winston, 1962.

Joost, Nicholas. *The Dial, 1912–1920: Years of Transition*. Barre, MA: Barre Publishers, 1967.

Joost, Nicholas. *Scofield Thayer and "The Dial."* Carbondale: Southern Illinois U P, 1964.

Kalaidjian, Walter. *American Culture between the Wars: Revisionary Modernism and Postmodern Critique.* New York: Columbia U P, 1993.

Kempf, James M. *The Early Career of Malcolm Cowley.* Baton Rouge: Louisiana State U P, 1985.

Kennedy, Alan. "The Rhetoric of Cultural Studies." Paper given at the Rhetoric Society of America Conference, Norfolk, VA, May 1994.

Kenner, Hugh. *A Homemade World: The American Modernist Writers.* New York: Knopf, 1974.

Kenner, Hugh. *The Pound Era.* Berkeley: U of California P, 1971.

Knopf, Alfred A. "H. L. Mencken, George Jean Nathan, and the *American Mercury* Venture." *Menckeniana* 78 (summer 1981): 1–10.

Kreymborg, Alfred. *Mushrooms: A Book of Free Forms.* New York: John Marshall, 1916.

Kreymborg, Alfred. *Troubadour: An Autobiography.* New York: Boni and Liveright, 1924.

Kuenzli, Rudolph E., ed. *New York Dada.* New York: Willis Locker and Owens, 1986.

Lanham, Richard. *The Electronic Word.* Chicago: U of Chicago P, 1993.

Leach, Eugene E. "The Radicals of *The Masses.*" *1915: The Cultural Moment.* Ed. Adele Heller and Lois Rudnick. New Brunswick: Rutgers U P, 1991. 27–47.

Leitch, Vincent. *American Literary Criticism from the 1930s to the 1980s.* Columbia: Columbia U P, 1988.

Lentricchia, Frank. *Criticism and Social Change.* Chicago: U of Chicago P, 1983.

Lentricchia, Frank. "Reading History with Kenneth Burke." *Representing Kenneth Burke.* Ed. Hayden White and Margaret Brose. Baltimore: Johns Hopkins U P, 1982. 119–49.

Levinson, Michael H. *The Genealogy of Modernism: A Study of English Literary Doctrine, 1908–1922.* Cambridge: Cambridge U P, 1984.

Lewisohn, Ludwig. *The Poets of Modern France.* New York: B. W. Huebsch, 1918.

Lewisohn, Ludwig. *Up Stream.* New York: Boni and Liveright, 1922.

Lippard, Lucy R., ed. *Dadas on Art.* Englewood Cliffs, NJ: Prentice Hall, 1971.

Loeb, Harold. "*Broom:* 1921–23." *Broom* 5 (August 1923): 55–58.

Loeb, Harold. "The Mysticism of Money." *Broom* 3 (September 1922): 115–30.

Loeb, Harold. *The Way It Was.* New York: Criterion Books, 1959.

Lowe, Sue Davidson. *Stieglitz.* New York: Farrar, Straus and Giroux, 1983.

Lowell, Amy. *Six French Poets.* New York: Macmillan, 1915.

Luhan, Mabel Dodge. *Intimate Memories.* Vol. 3 of *Movers and Shakers.* New York: Harcourt, Brace, 1936.

Martin, Taffy. *Marianne Moore: Subversive Modernist.* Austin: U of Texas P, 1986.

Matthews, Fred. "The New Psychology and American Drama." *1915: The Cultural Moment.* Ed. Adele Heller and Lois Rudnick. New Brunswick: Rutgers U P, 1991. 146–56.

McDarrah, Fred W. *Greenwich Village.* New York: Corinth Books, 1963.

McKeon, Richard. "Spiritual Autobiography." *Freedom and History and Other Essays.* Ed. Zahava K. McKeon. Chicago: U of Chicago P, 1990. 1–23.

Mencken, H. L. "The New Poetry." *Prejudices: First Series*. New York: Knopf, 1919. 83–96.

Miller, William D. *Dorothy Day: A Biography*. New York: Harper and Row, 1982.

Molesworth, Charles. *Marianne Moore: A Literary Life*. New York: Atheneum, 1990.

More, Paul Elmer. *Shelbourne Essays*. New York: G. P. Putnam, 1904; 1909; 1910; 1911.

More, Paul Elmer. *The Drift of Romanticism: Shelbourne Essays*. New York: G. P. Putnam, 1909; New York, 1967.

Motherwell, Robert. *Dada Painters and Poets*. New York: Wittenborn and Schultz, 1951.

Munson, Gorham. *The Awakening Twenties*. Baton Rouge: Lousiana State U P, 1985.

Munson, Gorham. "A Comedy of Exiles." *The Literary Review* 12 (1968): 41–75.

Munson, Gorham. "The Fledgling Years, 1916–1924." *Sewanee Review* 40 (January–March 1932): 24–54.

Munson, Gorham. "In and about the Workshop of Kenneth Burke." *Destinations: A Canvass of American Literature since 1900*. New York: J. H. Sears, 1928.

Munson, Gorham. "Mechanics for a Literary 'Secession.'" *S4N* 22 (November 1922): n.p.

Munson, Gorham. "Our Critical Spokesman." *Humanism in America*. Ed. Norman Foerster. New York: Brewer and Warren, 1930. 342–69.

Munson, Gorham. *Waldo Frank: A Study*. New York: Boni and Liveright, 1923.

Naumann, Francis. *New York Dada 1915–1923*. New York: Harry N. Abrams, 1994.

Nelson, Cary. *Repression and Recovery: Modern American Poetry and the Politics of Cultural Memory 1910–1945*. Madison: U of Wisconsin P, 1989.

Nelson, Cary. "Writing As an Accomplice of Language: Kenneth Burke and Post-structuralism." *The Legacy of Kenneth Burke*. Ed. Herbert W. Simons and Trevor Melia. Madison: U of Wisconsin P, 1989. 156–73.

Newman, Dorothy. *Alfred Stieglitz: An American Seer*. New York: Random House, 1973.

[Nichols], Marie Hochmuth. "I. A. Richards and the 'New Rhetoric.'" *Quarterly Journal of Speech* 44 (1958): 1–16.

Olson, Gary A. "Rhetoric, Cultural Studies, and the Future of Critical Theory: A Conversation with J. Hillis Miller." *Journal of Advanced Composition* 14 (1994): 317–45.

Parisi, Joseph, ed. *Marianne Moore: The Art of a Modernist*. Ann Arbor: UMI Research P, 1990.

Parker, Donald G., and Warren Herenden. "Kenneth Burke and Malcolm Cowley: An Interview with Kenneth Burke." *The Visionary Company* 2 and 3 (double issue, summer 1987): 87–99.

Parkes, Henry Bamford. *The Pragmatic Test*. San Francisco: Colt Press, 1941.

Perloff, Marjorie. *The Dance of the Intellect*. Cambridge: Cambridge U P, 1985.

Perloff, Marjorie. *The Futurist Moment: Avant-Garde, Avant-Guerre, and the Language of Rupture*. Chicago: U of Chicago P, 1986.

Perloff, Marjorie. "Modernist Studies." *Redrawing the Boundaries: The Transformation of English and American Literary Studies.* Ed. Stephen Greenblatt and Giles Gunn. New York: MLA, 1992. 154–78.

Poggioli, Renato. *The Theory of the Avant-Garde.* Cambridge: Harvard U P, 1968.

Pondrom, Cyrena N. *The Road from Paris: French Influence on English Poetry 1900–1920.* Cambridge: Cambridge U P, 1974.

Pound, Ezra. *Gaudier-Brzeska.* London/New York: John Lane, 1916. New York: New Directions, 1960.

Pound, Ezra. "Mr Aldington's Views on Gourmont." *The Dial* 86 (January 1929): 68–71.

Pound, Ezra. *Pavannes and Divisions.* New York: Knopf, 1918.

Rascoe, Burton. "Ernest Boyd: Elegant Reading Machine." *The New York Tribune* December 30, 1923: IV, 3.

Rascoe, Burton. "*Smart Set* History." *The "Smart Set" Anthology.* Ed. Burton Rascoe and Groff Conklin. New York: Reynal and Hitchcock, 1934. xiii–xliv.

Raymond, Marcel. *De Baudelaire au surrealisme.* 1947; English language rpt. as *From Baudelaire to Surrealism.* New York: Wittenborn and Schultz, 1950.

Reed, John. "A Day in Greenwich Village." *Complete Poetry of John Reed.* Ed. Jack A. Robbins. Freeman, SD: Pine Hill Press, 1973.

Richards, I. A. *Practical Criticism.* London, 1929; New York: Harcourt and Brace, 1930.

Richards, I. A. *Principles of Literary Criticism.* London: Routledge and Kegan, 1926.

Richards, I. A. *Science and Poetry.* New York: W. W. Norton, 1926.

Richards, I. A., and C. K. Ogden. *The Meaning of Meaning.* London, 1927; New York: Harcourt, Brace, 1927.

Roeder, George H., Jr. "What Have the Moderns Looked at? Experiential Roots of Twentieth-Century Painting." *Modernist Culture in America.* Ed. Daniel J. Singal. Belmont, CA: Wadsworth, 1991. 70–106.

Rosen, Daniel. "Mencken and Malcolm Cowley." *Menckeniana* 119 (fall 1991): 10–14.

Rosenberg, Harold. Review of *Counter-Statement. The Symposium* 3 (January 1932): 116–20.

Rountree, J. Clarke, III. *The 'Literary' Period: Early Life through "Towards a Better Life."* Vol. 1 of *Conversations with Kenneth Burke.* Videorecording. Iowa City: Department of Communication Studies, 1987.

Rountree, J. Clarke, III. "Kenneth Burke: A Personal Retrospective." *Iowa Review* 17 (fall 1987): 14–23.

Rountree, J. Clarke, III. "Richard Kostelanetz Interviews Kenneth Burke." *Iowa Review* 17 (fall 1987): 1–14.

Rueckert, William H. "Burke's Other Life" [review of *Towards a Better Life*]. *The Nation* 203 (December 12, 1966): 648–49.

Rueckert, William H., ed. *Critical Responses to Kenneth Burke.* Minneapolis: U of Minnesota P, 1969.

Rueckert, William H. *Encounters with Kenneth Burke.* Urbana: U of Illinois P, 1994.

Rueckert, William H. "A Field Guide to Kenneth Burke—1990." *Extensions of the Burkeian System.* Ed. James W. Chesebro. Tuscaloosa: U of Alabama P, 1993. 3–34.

Rueckert, William H. *Kenneth Burke and the Drama of Human Relations.* Berkeley: U of California P, 1963.

Russo, John Paul. *I. A. Richards: His Life and Work.* Baltimore: Johns Hopkins U P, 1989.

Sarlos, Robert K. *Jig Cook and the Provincetown Players: Theatre in Ferment.* Amherst: U of Massachusetts P, 1982.

Schneider, Isidor. "A New View of Rhetoric" [review of *Counter-Statement*]. *The New York Herald Tribune Books* (December 13, 1931): 4.

Schneider, Isidor. Review of *Towards a Better Life. The Bookman* 75 (1932): 101–2.

Schultze, Robin G. *The Web of Friendship: Marianne Moore and Wallace Stevens.* Ann Arbor: U of Michigan P, 1995.

Schwartz, Sanford. *The Matrix of Modernism: Pound, Eliot, and Early Twentieth-Century Thought.* Princeton: Princeton U P, 1985.

Scott, Bonnie Kime, ed. *The Gender of Modernism: A Critical Anthology.* Bloomington: Indiana U P, 1990.

Selzer, Jack. "An Amusing Addition to the Kenneth Burke Bibliography." *Kenneth Burke Society Newsletter* 11 (May 1996): 20–22.

Selzer, Jack. "Burke's Permanence and Change and Contemporary Social Constructivism." Conference on College Composition and Communication, San Diego, CA, 1993.

Sheaffer, Louis. *O'Neill: Son and Playwright.* Boston: Little, Brown, 1968.

Sheard, Cynthia M. "*Kairos* and Kenneth Burke's Psychology of Political and Social Communication." *College English* 55 (1993): 291–310.

Shi, David E. *Matthew Josephson, Bourgeois Bohemian.* New Haven: Yale U P, 1981.

Sieburth, Richard. *Instigations: Ezra Pound and Remy de Gourmont.* Cambridge: Harvard U P, 1978.

Singal, Daniel J. "Towards a Definition of American Modernism." *Modernist Culture in America.* Ed. Daniel J. Singal. Belmont, CA: Wadsworth, 1991. 1–27.

Singal, Daniel J., ed. *Modernist Culture in America.* Belmont, CA: Wadsworth, 1991.

Singleton, M. K. *H. L. Mencken and the American Mercury Adventure.* Durham, NC: Duke U P, 1962.

Skinner, Olivia. "An Intellectual for All Seasons." *St. Louis Post-Dispatch* (November 2, 1970): 3D.

Skodnick, Roy. "Counter-Gridlock: An Interview with Kenneth Burke." *All-Area* 2 (spring 1983): 4–32.

Spanier, Sandra Whipple. *Kay Boyle: Artist and Activist.* Carbondale: Southern Illinois U P, 1986.

Spingarn, Joel. *Creative Criticism.* 1917; 1925; expanded ed. New York: Harcourt, Brace, 1931.

St. John, Bruce, ed. *John Sloan's New York Scene: From the Diaries, Notes, and Correspondence, 1905–1913*. New York: Harper and Row, 1965.

Stearnes, Harold, ed. *Civilization in the United States: An Inquiry by Thirty Americans*. New York: Harcourt, Brace, 1922.

Sutton, Walter, ed. *Pound, Thayer, Watson, and "The Dial."* Gainesville: U of Florida P, 1994.

Symons, Arthur. *The Symbolist Movement in Literature*. London: Heinemann, 1899. Revised and enlarged ed. New York: Dutton, 1919.

Tanner, Stephen L. "Sinclair Lewis and the New Humanism." *Modern Age* 33 (1990): 33–41.

Tashjian, Dickran. *Skyscraper Primitives: Dada and the American Avant-Garde 1910–1925*. Middletown, CT: Wesleyan University Press, 1975.

Tashjian, Dickran. *William Carlos Williams and the American Scene, 1920–1940*. Berkeley: U of California P, 1978.

Tompkins, Philip. "On Hegemony—'He Gave It No Name'—and Critical Structuralism in the Work of Kenneth Burke." *Quarterly Journal of Speech* 71 (1985): 119–31.

Toomer, Jean. "Oxen Cart and Warfare" [review of *The White Oxen, and Other Stories*]. *The Little Review* 10 (autumn–winter 1925): 44–48.

Turner, Susan J. *A History of "The Freeman."* New York: Columbia U P, 1963.

Tzara, Tristan. "Some Memoirs of Dadaism." *Vanity Fair* 19 (March 1922): 70, 92, 94.

Unterecker, John. *Voyager: A Life of Hart Crane*. New York: Farrar, Straus and Giroux, 1969.

Vendler, Helen. *Part of Nature, Part of Us: Modern American Poets*. Cambridge: Harvard U P, 1980.

Walker, Jeffrey. *Bardic Ethos and the American Epic Poem: Whitman, Pound, Crane, Williams, Olson*. Baton Rouge: Louisiaina State U P, 1989.

Ware, Carolyn. *Greenwich Village, 1920–1930*. Boston: Houghton Mifflin, 1935.

Warnock, Tilly. "Reading Kenneth Burke: Ways In, Ways Out, Ways Roundabout." *College English* 48 (1986): 62–75.

Warren, Austin. "Kenneth Burke: His Mind and Art." *Sewanee Review* 41 (1933): 225–36; 344–64.

Wasserstrom, William. *The Time of the Dial*. Syracuse: Syracuse U P, 1963.

Weber, Brom, ed. *The Letters of Hart Crane*. New York: Hermitage House, 1952.

Wertheim, Arthur Frank. *The New York Little Renaissance: Iconoclasm, Modernism, and Nationalism in American Culture, 1908–1917*. New York: New York U P, 1976.

Wheaton, Mabel Wolfe. *Thomas Wolfe and His Family*. New York: Doubleday, 1961.

Whelan, Richard. *Alfred Stieglitz: A Biography*. New York: Little, Brown, 1995.

White, Hayden, and Margaret Brose, eds. *Representing Kenneth Burke*. Baltimore: Johns Hopkins U P, 1982.

Williams, Raymond. *The Politics of Modernism: Against the New Conformists*. New York: Verso, 1989.

Williams, William Carlos. *Al Que Quiere! A Book of Poems*. Boston: The Four Seas, 1917.

Williams, William Carlos. *The Autobiography of William Carlos Williams*. New York: Random House, 1948.

Williams, William Carlos. *In the American Grain*. New York: Albert and Charles Boni, 1925.

Williams, William Carlos. *Kora in Hell: Improvisations*. Boston: The Four Seas, 1920. San Francisco: City Lights, 1957.

Williams, William Carlos. *Selected Letters*. Ed. John C. Thirlwall. New York: McDowell, Obolensky, 1957.

Williams, William Carlos. *Spring and All*. N. p.: Contact Publishing, 1923.

Wilson, Edmund. *Axel's Castle: A Study in the Imaginative Literature of 1870–1930*. New York: Charles Scribner's Sons, 1931.

Wilson, Edmund. *I Thought of Daisy*. New York: Scribner's, 1929.

Winterowd, Ross W. "Kenneth Burke." *American Poets, 1880–1945*. Ed. Peter Quartermain. Dictionary of Literary Biography. 1st ser. 45. Detroit: Gale Research, 1986. 74–79.

Winters, Yvor. *In Defense of Reason*. Chicago: U of Chicago P, 1947.

Wohl, Robert. "The Generation of 1914 and Modernism." *Modernism: Challenges and Perspectives*. Ed. Monique Chefdor, Ricardo Quinones, and Albert Wachtel. Urbana: U of Illinois P, 1986. 66–78.

Woodcock, John. "An Interview with Kenneth Burke." *Sewanee Review* 85 (1977): 704–18.

Woods, Arthur. *Dangerous Drugs: The World Fight against Illicit Traffic in Narcotics*. New Haven: Yale U P, 1931.

Yagoda, Ben. "Kenneth Burke." *Horizon* 23 (June 1980): 66–69.

Zurier, Rebecca. "*The Masses* and Modernism." *1915: The Cultural Moment*. Ed. Adele Heller and Lois Rudnick. New Brunswick: Rutgers U P, 1991. 196–215.

Index

The Wisconsin Project on American Writers

Frank Lentricchia, General Editor

Gaiety Transfigured: Gay Self-Representation in American Literature
David Bergman

American Puritanism and the Defense of Mourning: Religion, Grief, and Ethnology in Mary White Rowlandson's Captivity Narrative
Mitchell Robert Breitwieser

F. O. Matthiessen and the Politics of Criticism
William E. Cain

In Defense of Writers: The Poetry and Prose of Yvor Winters
Terry Comito

Get the Guests: Psychoanalysis, Modern American Drama, and the Audience
Walter A. Davis

A Poetry of Presence: The Writing of William Carlos Williams
Bernard Duffey

Selves at Risk: Patterns of Quest in Contemporary American Letters
Ihab Hassan

Reading Faulkner
Wesley Morris with Barbara Alverson Morris

Repression and Recovery: Modern American Poetry and the Politics of Cultural Memory, 1910–1945
Cary Nelson

Lionel Trilling: The Work of Liberation
Daniel T. O'Hara

Visionary Compacts: American Renaissance Writings in Cultural Context
Donald E. Pease